Governance Quality, Fiscal Policy, and the Path to a Low-Carbon Future:

Perspectives From Developing Economies

Ibrahim Nandom Yakubu
University for Development Studies, Ghana

IGI Global
PUBLISHER of TIMELY KNOWLEDGE

A volume in the Advances in Public Policy and Administration (APPA) Book Series

Published in the United States of America by
IGI Global
Engineering Science Reference (an imprint of IGI Global)
701 E. Chocolate Avenue
Hershey PA, USA 17033
Tel: 717-533-8845
Fax: 717-533-8661
E-mail: cust@igi-global.com
Web site: http://www.igi-global.com

Library of Congress Cataloging-in-Publication Data

Names: Yakubu, Ibrahim Nandom, 1989- editor.
Title: Governance quality, fiscal policy, and the path to a low-carbon future : perspectives from developing economies / edited by Ibrahim Nandom Yakubu.
Description: Hershey, PA : Engineering Science Reference, [2024] | Includes bibliographical references and index. | Summary: "A successful energy transition requires considerable investments in renewable energy and low-carbon technologies. Recognizing the interplay between governance quality, fiscal policy, and the energy sector is crucial to driving these investments. From the perspective of developing economies, this book seeks to examine the role of institutional quality in the transition to a low-carbon economy. The book will also assess how the various fiscal policy tools, such as carbon taxes, subsidies for renewable energy, and green bonds, promote the energy transition. The proposed book will make a significant contribution to the literature on energy transition and sustainable development in developing economies. While there is a burgeoning literature on energy transition, the majority of it is centered on developed economies. This proposed book will fill a significant research gap in the literature by offering an in-depth examination of the challenges and opportunities that confront developing economies in transitioning to cleaner forms of energy and how good governance and sound fiscal policies can facilitate this transition. It will also offer insights and practical recommendations for policymakers and practitioners in developing economies"-- Provided by publisher.
Identifiers: LCCN 2023029632 (print) | LCCN 2023029633 (ebook) | ISBN 9781668492727 (hardcover) | ISBN 9781668492734 (paperback) | ISBN 9781668492741 (ebook)
Subjects: LCSH: Energy policy--Developing countries. | Energy development--Developing countries | Renewable energy sources--Developing countries.
Classification: LCC HD9502.D442 G69 2024 (print) | LCC HD9502.D442 (ebook) | DDC 333.7909172/4--dc23/eng/20230706
LC record available at https://lccn.loc.gov/2023029632
LC ebook record available at https://lccn.loc.gov/2023029633

This book is published in the IGI Global book series Advances in Public Policy and Administration (APPA) (ISSN: 2475-6644; eISSN: 2475-6652)

British Cataloguing in Publication Data
A Cataloguing in Publication record for this book is available from the British Library.

Advances in Public Policy and Administration (APPA) Book Series

ISSN:2475-6644
EISSN:2475-6652

Mission

Proper management of the public sphere is necessary in order to maintain order in modern society. Research developments in the field of public policy and administration can assist in uncovering the latest tools, practices, and methodologies for governing societies around the world.

The **Advances in Public Policy and Administration (APPA) Book Series** aims to publish scholarly publications focused on topics pertaining to the governance of the public domain. APPA's focus on timely topics relating to government, public funding, politics, public safety, policy, and law enforcement is particularly relevant to academicians, government officials, and upper-level students seeking the most up-to-date research in their field.

Coverage

- Government
- Law Enforcement
- Political Economy
- Politics
- Public Administration
- Public Funding
- Public Policy
- Resource Allocation
- Urban Planning

IGI Global is currently accepting manuscripts for publication within this series. To submit a proposal for a volume in this series, please contact our Acquisition Editors at Acquisitions@igi-global.com or visit: http://www.igi-global.com/publish/.

The Advances in Public Policy and Administration (APPA) Book Series (ISSN 2475-6644) is published by IGI Global, 701 E. Chocolate Avenue, Hershey, PA 17033-1240, USA, www.igi-global.com. This series is composed of titles available for purchase individually; each title is edited to be contextually exclusive from any other title within the series. For pricing and ordering information please visit http://www.igi-global.com/book-series/advances-public-policy-administration/97862. Postmaster: Send all address changes to above address.

Titles in this Series

For a list of additional titles in this series, please visit: http://www.igi-global.com/book-series/advances-public-policy-administration/97862

Legal and Economic Aspects of State Control Over Compliance With Labor Legislation
Galina Ognqnova Yolova (University of Economics – Varna, Bulgaria) Andriyana Andreeva (University of Economics – Varna, Bulgaria) Darina Nedelcheva Dimitrova (University of Economics – Varna, Bulgaria) Hristina Vilhelm Blagoycheva (University of Economics – Varna, Bulgaria) Plamena Nedyalkova (University of Economics – Varna, Bulgaria) and Hristosko Bogdanov (University of Economics – Varna, Bulgaria)
Information Science Reference • © 2023 • 221pp • H/C (ISBN: 9781668490679) • US $215.00

Global Perspectives on the Emerging Trends in Public Diplomacy
Samet Kavoğlu (Marmara University, Turkey) and Ergün Köksoy (Marmara University, Turkey)
Information Science Reference • © 2023 • 282pp • H/C (ISBN: 9781668491614) • US $240.00

Insights and Explorations in Democracy, Political Unrest, and Propaganda in Elections
Opeyemi Idowu Aluko (Ajayi Crowther University, Nigeria) and Lalekan Bolu Oluwadele (Walden University, USA)
Information Science Reference • © 2023 • 377pp • H/C (ISBN: 9781668486290) • US $215.00

Historical and Political Analysis on Power Balances and Deglobalization
Emily Brynn Stacey (Rose State College, USA)
Information Science Reference • © 2023 • 300pp • H/C (ISBN: 9781668456330) • US $205.00

Integrating Principles of Success in Planning Denial and Deception Missions
Eugenie de Silva (Booz Allen Hamilton, USA)
Information Science Reference • © 2024 • 330pp • H/C (ISBN: 9781668468401) • US $215.00

Governmental Power Market-Ing in the VU-CHAOS World
Kittisak Jermsittiparsert (University of City Island, Cyprus) Srirath Gohwong (Universitas Muhammadiyah Sidenreng Rappang, Indonesia) Shayut Pavapanunkul (Universitas Muhammadiyah Sidenreng Rappang, Indonesia) and Nasaran Mahittichatkul (Universitas Muhammadiyah Sidenreng Rappang, Indonesia)
Information Science Reference • © 2024 • 360pp • H/C (ISBN: 9781668472804) • US $205.00

Reimagining Systems Thinking in a Post-Pandemic World
M. Elizabeth Azukas (East Stroudsburg University of Pennsylvania, USA) and Minkyoung Kim (University of West Florida, USA)
Information Science Reference • © 2023 • 325pp • H/C (ISBN: 9781668472859) • US $215.00

IGI Global
PUBLISHER of TIMELY KNOWLEDGE

701 East Chocolate Avenue, Hershey, PA 17033, USA
Tel: 717-533-8845 x100 • Fax: 717-533-8661
E-Mail: cust@igi-global.com • www.igi-global.com

Table of Contents

Detailed Table of Contents

This study explores the impact of political stability on the United Arab Emirates' (UAE) sustainable energy transition. It highlights how political stability enables long-term planning, policy continuity, investment attraction, and public acceptance of renewable energy. The study employed quantitative methodology, using the Phillips-Perron (PP) unit root test for stationarity assessment, the Autoregressive Distributed Lag (ARDL) cointegration test to confirm long-term relationships, and the Fully Modified Ordinary Least Square (FMOLS) technique proposed by Phillips and Hansen to investigate the relationships between the variables in the empirical model. The findings emphasize a positive correlation between political stability and the UAE's progress in diversifying its energy mix and embracing renewable sources. The research underscores the significance of political stability as a catalyst for a sustainable energy transition.

The Caribbean region is particularly vulnerable to the impacts of climate change. Climate change pose a threat to the lives and livelihoods of the people living in the region. To mitigate these impacts, the Caribbean has joined with the international community, and pledged to implement their Nationally Determined Contributions (NDCs) to the Paris Agreement. The cost of implementing the NDCs measures in the Caribbean is high, and the region have not been receiving the required financial support. To address this limitation, a market-based mechanism such as an Emissions Trading System (ETS) could be implemented. This would create a financial incentive for emitters to reduce their GHG emissions, which in turn would help achieve the emissions reduction targets of the NDCs. An ETS is a policy tool that allows companies to trade emission allowances, which are permits that represent the right to emit a certain amount of GHGs. This study explores the mechanics of a potential regional ETS for the Caribbean.

Climate change has been perceived as a security issue too crucial to be left solely in the hands of politicians. The chapter will examine the securitization of climate change in the UN Security Council during 2017-2018. By analyzing the framing of the issue by Council members and the resonance of these frames with the audience, the research determines which frames are accepted and which are disregarded, shedding light on the securitization process. The findings indicate that the Security Council has unanimously securitized climate change as a regional issue but not a global one. While some members have attempted to push for further securitization, even the limited securitization of climate change on a smaller scale is a novel development for the Council.

The industrial revolution, which started with the invention of coal-fired steam engines, led to the intensive consumption of fossil fuels and environmental pollution all over the world. In the 1960s, the first international steps were taken to prevent environmental pollution. The main ones are the United Nations Framework Convention on Climate Change, the Kyoto Protocol, and the Paris Agreement. Building on the Paris Agreement, the European Union announced the Green Deal and prepared the carbon border adjustment mechanism in line with the objectives of the Deal. The peculiarity of this mechanism is that it will price carbon not only for European producers, but also for the countries with which Europe trades. Large economies that do not want to lose the European Market are updating their own emissions trading systems in line with the European Union emissions trading system. The aim of this study is to propose a model for a carbon market to be established in Türkiye based on the carbon markets implemented in selected large countries.

This study explores the factors influencing energy transition in Africa, specifically focusing on the impact of institutional quality and remittances on renewable energy consumption. Using a comprehensive dataset covering 45 African countries from 2000 to 2020 and employing the generalized method of moments (GMM) technique, the analysis controls for industrialization, financial development, and population growth. The results demonstrate a significant negative effect of institutional quality and remittances on renewable energy consumption. However, the finding reveals a positive and significant interactive effect

This study examines the impact of government expenditure and government effectiveness on renewable energy consumption in Africa from 1990 to 2021. Utilizing the fixed effects technique, the findings indicate a positive significant relationship between government expenditure and renewable energy consumption, while government effectiveness demonstrates a significant negative influence. Additionally, trade openness and urbanization exhibit a negative impact on renewable energy usage. The effect of foreign direct investment (FDI) on renewable energy consumption is found to be mixed. To facilitate the transition towards a greener energy future in Africa, the study recommends several measures including increasing government expenditure on renewable energy, enhancing government effectiveness, promoting sustainable trade practices, and prioritizing sustainable urban planning.

Climate change significantly affects climate-induced migration, particularly on low-lying atoll islands in the Pacific. This impact is particularly relevant for Kiribati, a country highly affected by climate change and expected to experience climate-induced migration. A study conducted a comparative analysis of the problem representations of climate-induced migration in Kiribati and New Zealand's national policies. The study, grounded in post-structuralism and post-colonialism, examined how the issue is portrayed in policy and how migrants are constructed as subjects. The analytical framework used was 'What's the problem represented to be?' (WPR). The findings revealed that climate-induced migration is depicted as both a challenge and an adaptation strategy. Transnational climate-induced migration is portrayed as a strategy for increased resilience, while internal migration is seen as challenging.

The development of renewable energies and technological progress offer new possibilities for project operators. In particular, the gradual interconnection of off-grid systems and mini-grids could prove to be more suited to economic constraints and local socio-demographic specificities, leading to long-term energy systems that differ from the current centralized systems of industrialized countries. The objective of universal access to energy poses the challenge of disseminating large-scale competitive, sustainable, and

Preface

In the face of escalating climate change and its consequences, the need for immediate action is more pressing than ever before. The global community has come together under initiatives like the Paris Agreement and the Sustainable Development Goals (SDGs) to tackle the urgent challenges posed by greenhouse gas emissions. Developing economies, in particular, have a pivotal role to play in shaping a low-carbon future due to their growing energy needs and potential for renewable energy adoption.

In this edited reference book, titled *Governance Quality, Fiscal Policy, and the Path to a Low-Carbon Future: Perspectives From Developing Economies*, we delve into the complexities of energy transition in developing countries. It is my privilege to serve as the editor, Ibrahim Nandom Yakubu, and to present this comprehensive collection of insights and analyses from esteemed scholars and experts in the field.

As we explore the transition towards cleaner energy systems, we recognize that developing economies often confront unique challenges, such as limited access to financing, infrastructure deficiencies, and technical know-how. These challenges demand a multidimensional approach that encompasses robust regulatory policies, efficient institutional frameworks, and seamless integration of renewable technologies.

Key to achieving a successful energy transition is the understanding of the interplay between governance quality, fiscal policy, and the energy sector. This book sets out to scrutinize the role of institutional quality in facilitating the transition to a low-carbon economy. Additionally, we assess the impact of fiscal policy in promoting sustainable energy adoption in developing countries.

While there is a wealth of literature on energy transition in developed economies, this book bridges a crucial research gap by focusing on the challenges and opportunities specific to developing economies. Our goal is to provide policymakers, academics, practitioners, and students with valuable insights, practical recommendations, and a deeper understanding of the energy transition landscape in these regions.

The book is structured around several key themes, including the relationship between institutional quality and renewable energy adoption, the role of fiscal policies, emission trading systems, green finance, climate resilience and climate-induced migration, among others. By exploring these themes, we aim to foster informed decision-making and guide policy formulation towards achieving sustainable development goals.

Chapter Overview

Chapter 1 investigates the impact of political stability on the United Arab Emirates' (UAE) sustainable energy transition. It emphasizes how political stability facilitates long-term planning, policy continuity, investment attraction, and public acceptance of renewable energy. The study employs quantitative methodologies to analyze the correlation between political stability and the UAE's progress in diversifying its energy mix and embracing renewable sources.

Chapter 2 focuses on the vulnerability of the Caribbean region to climate change and explores the potential of an Emissions Trading System (ETS) as a market-based mechanism to mitigate its impacts. The ETS would create financial incentives for emitters to reduce greenhouse gas emissions, aligning with the region's Nationally Determined Contributions (NDCs) to the Paris Agreement.

Chapter 3 examines the securitization of climate change in the UN Security Council during 2017-2018. It analyzes how Council members frame the issue and the resonance of these frames with the audience, shedding light on the securitization process. The research indicates that the Security Council has securitized climate change as a regional issue but not on a global scale, representing a novel development for the Council.

Chapter 4 proposes a model for a carbon market to be established in Turkey, building on the European Union's Carbon Border Adjustment Mechanism and carbon markets implemented in selected large countries. The chapter explores Turkey's efforts to align with the EU Emissions Trading System, a vital step towards sustainable carbon pricing in the country.

Chapter 5 explores the factors influencing energy transition in Africa, with a focus on the impact of institutional quality and remittances on renewable energy consumption. Using a comprehensive dataset and advanced statistical techniques, the study provides valuable insights for policymakers in formulating effective strategies for sustainable energy transition in the continent.

Chapter 6 delves into the environmental challenges posed by globalization and climate change, emphasizing the need for collaboration between education, government, society, and industry. The proposed triad approach aims to develop quality educational policies and integrate them with economic support and R&D projects to address climate change on an international scale.

Chapter 7 examines the impact of inclusive finance and control of corruption on environmental pollution in Ghana. The research underscores the significance of promoting financial inclusion and combating corruption to reduce CO2 emissions. The chapter also explores the influence of remittances and renewable energy consumption on pollution.

Chapter 8 investigates the relationship between government expenditure, government effectiveness, and renewable energy consumption in Africa. It reveals a positive significant relationship between government expenditure and renewable energy consumption, while government effectiveness shows a significant negative influence. The chapter also explores the impacts of foreign direct investment, trade openness, and urbanization on renewable energy usage.

Chapter 9 conducts a comparative analysis of the problem representations of climate-induced Migration in Kiribati and New Zealand's national policies. Grounded in post-structuralism and post-colonialism, the research examines how the issue is portrayed in policy and how migrants are constructed as subjects. The chapter sheds light on the challenges and adaptation strategies for climate-induced Migration in the Pacific region.

Chapter 10 explores the development of renewable energies and technological progress in Benin, focusing on the interconnection of off-grid systems and mini-grids. The chapter aims to guide legislators in crafting robust and relevant energy acts for the future, aligning with the Paris Agreement and sustainable development goals.

Chapter 11 investigates the relationship between financial development and the issuance of green sukuk (Islamic financial instruments). Initial results indicate that countries that are already financially developed are more inclined to issue green sukuk, but a detailed examination is needed to understand the nature of this relationship.

Chapter 12 examines the relationship between institutional efficiency and energy outcomes in the MINT economies (Mexico, Indonesia, Nigeria, and Turkey). The study analyzes various energy indicators and their correlation with institutional efficiency, industrialization, trade openness, and other factors. The findings reveal both positive and negative impacts, shedding light on the complexities of achieving sustainable energy outcomes in these economies.

The intended audience for this book is diverse and wide-ranging. Policymakers will gain valuable insights to inform their energy strategies and climate policies. Academics and researchers will find in-depth analyses that contribute to the growing body of knowledge on energy transition in developing economies. Additionally, students will benefit from the book's comprehensive coverage of topics related to environmental economics, making it an invaluable resource for educational purposes.

As the editor, I express my gratitude to the contributors who have shared their expertise and passion for sustainable development in developing economies. Their collective efforts have resulted in a book that we believe will pave the way for a greener, more equitable future.

I sincerely hope that *Governance Quality, Fiscal Policy, and the Path to a Low-Carbon Future: Perspectives From Developing Economies* will inspire and empower readers to join the journey towards a cleaner, more sustainable energy landscape. Together, we can make a significant difference in shaping the path to a low-carbon future for the well-being of our planet and generations to come.

Ibrahim Nandom Yakubu
University for Development Studies, Ghana

Chapter 1
Renewable Energy Resilience:
Probing the Role of Political Stability in UAE's Sustainable Energy Transition

Abdul Jalil Mahama
https://orcid.org/0000-0002-8622-1714
Westford University College, UAE

Mubarik Abdul Mumin
https://orcid.org/0000-0003-1855-5883
University for Development Studies, Ghana

ABSTRACT

This study explores the impact of political stability on the United Arab Emirates' (UAE) sustainable energy transition. It highlights how political stability enables long-term planning, policy continuity, investment attraction, and public acceptance of renewable energy. The study employed quantitative methodology, using the Phillips-Perron (PP) unit root test for stationarity assessment, the Autoregressive Distributed Lag (ARDL) cointegration test to confirm long-term relationships, and the Fully Modified Ordinary Least Square (FMOLS) technique proposed by Phillips and Hansen to investigate the relationships between the variables in the empirical model. The findings emphasize a positive correlation between political stability and the UAE's progress in diversifying its energy mix and embracing renewable sources. The research underscores the significance of political stability as a catalyst for a sustainable energy transition.

INTRODUCTION

In response to the anticipated impact of global warming and the accelerated depletion of fossil fuels, governments worldwide have been driven to pursue the development of robust and sustainable energy infrastructures. This imperative has led to a widespread shift away from reliance on traditional energy resources, prompting governments to diversify their economies (Mezher, Dawelbait, & Abbas, 2012).

The United Arab Emirates (UAE) has embarked on an extraordinary path towards achieving a sustainable energy future. Recognizing the need to decrease dependence on fossil fuels, the UAE has made

DOI: 10.4018/978-1-6684-9272-7.ch001

significant efforts to embrace renewable energy sources (Murooshid, 2018). The successful transition towards a sustainable energy system relies not only on technological advancements and economic considerations but also on the crucial factor of political stability.

Political stability plays a pivotal role in providing a conducive environment for long-term planning, policy implementation, and investment in renewable energy infrastructure. The strategy aims to position the economy at the forefront of global competitiveness. By prioritizing the development of renewable energy and sustainable practices, the UAE seeks to enhance its economic standing in the global economy. This strategy not only addresses environmental concerns but also recognizes the potential economic benefits and opportunities that arise from being a leader in the renewable energy sector (Al-Maamary, Kazem, & Chaichan, 2017).

The ambitious sustainable energy goals of the UAE necessitate a supportive environment that fosters long-term investments, policy continuity, and firm commitment from the government. It is crucial for the UAE to provide a stable and predictable framework that encourages both domestic and foreign investments in renewable energy projects. By ensuring policy consistency and demonstrating a steadfast dedication to sustainable energy initiatives, this could further assist the UAE to attract the necessary resources and expertise to achieve RE goals effectively (Poudineh, Sen, & Fattouh, 2018).

Studies have indicated that the UAE is among the countries with the highest carbon emissions and fossil fuel burning rates (Hassan Jamil Al Farra, 2012). These emissions and burning rates are primarily attributed to the significant reliance on fossil fuels for energy production, transportation, and industrial sectors. However, it's important to note that the UAE has recognized this challenge and has been taking proactive measures to address it. Through initiatives such as diversifying its energy mix, investing in renewable energy projects, and implementing energy efficiency measures, the UAE aims to reduce its carbon footprint and transition towards a more sustainable and low-carbon future (Murooshid, 2018). As a consequence of this circumstance, the UAE has acquired membership in both OPEC and OPEC+. Consequently, there arises a necessity to focus on the development of renewable energy infrastructure.

In recent years, the UAE government has demonstrated its commitment to environmental sustainability by establishing an ambitious Net-Zero initiative to be achieved by 2050, aligning with the goals of the Paris Agreement. To drive the transition towards a greener economy, the government has leveraged its resources, including sovereign wealth funds like Mubadala, as well as entities like Abu Dhabi National Oil Company and Abu Dhabi National Energy Company, PJSC (TAQA). Notably, the creation of Masdar, an innovative company dedicated to renewable energy development, has played a crucial role in advancing the government's efforts to achieve the target of 50GW of renewable energy capacity by 2030 (United Arab Emirates Embassy Wadhington DC, 2023).

The RE system can only be implemented through the cohesive support of both unified political and economic forces from the federal government. Findings from previous research proposes effective legislative amendments, provision of adequate inducements to finance renewable energy projects, development of green energy generation quotas and policy framework for energy management (Saidur, Islam, Rahim, & Solangi, 2010). The successful adoption of renewable energy (RE) infrastructure goes beyond the sole reliance on political stability and regulation. It encompasses various factors, including tariffs, price mechanisms, Behavioral intentions, and the acceptance of users and adopters of Renewable Energy. These elements play pivotal roles in ensuring the widespread implementation and acceptance of Renewable Energy (Sovacool, 2016).

Previous studies have identified various factors that hinder the adoption of Renewable Energy (RE). These factors encompass technological limitations, financing constraints, market barriers, environmental considerations, government policies, and societal factors. These findings highlight the multifaceted challenges that can impede the process of adopting RE (Bhattarai, Maraseni, & Apan, 2022). However, existing investigations have not yet determined the correlation between the aforementioned factors and their alignment with the motivations of renewable energy (RE) adoption specifically in the UAE. Further research is needed to explore and understand how these factors interact and influence the drivers and motivations behind RE adoption in the UAE context. By examining these relationships, a clearer picture can be obtained regarding the specific challenges and opportunities related to RE implementation in the UAE.

However, research conducted by the Organization for Security and Co-operation in Europe has shown a positive correlation between political stability and economic development. The success of economic growth is heavily reliant on the stability of a country's energy resource infrastructure. This relationship is exemplified by the case of Serbia and Montenegro, which experienced external political seclusion, wars, and mismanagement of energy resources. These factors of political instability had detrimental effects on the state of energy management in the country. The case serves as evidence highlighting the significant impact that political instability can have on the energy sector and overall economic development (OSCE, 2003).

A study conducted by Adebayo (2022) explored the impact of political stability in Canada on the country's renewable energy consumption regime. The research highlighted the role of numerous foreign direct investments in the renewable energy sector, which were facilitated by the political stability of the country. These investments have played a positive role in mitigating and reducing environmental pollution.

In another study focused on energy transition, the findings revealed that the price and volume of renewable energy, along with the experience curves in technology, act as mediating factors in determining the adoption of sustainable energy regimes. This analysis was conducted within the political geographies of North America and Europe (Breetz, Mildenberger, & Stokes, 2018). However, it is worth noting that the aforementioned research studies did not specifically address the factors that impact the transition of renewable energy (RE). This creates a gap in the existing research, particularly in the context of sustainable energy adoption in the UAE, given the turbulent and volatile nature of the region's political climate. Further research is necessary to investigate and identify the specific factors that influence the transition towards Renewable Energy in the UAE, considering the unique political dynamics of the region. By addressing this research gap, a more comprehensive understanding of the challenges and opportunities associated with Renewable Energy adoption in the UAE can be attained.

In this study, our objective is to explore the complex relationship between political stability and the sustainable energy transition in the United Arab Emirates (UAE). We aim to investigate the impact of political stability on the development and adoption of renewable energy within the UAE. By examining this relationship, we seek to gain insights into how political stability influences the progress and implementation of sustainable energy initiatives in the country. Through our research, we aim to contribute to a better understanding of the interplay between political stability and the UAE's transition towards a more sustainable energy future.

Recognizing the significance of the relationship between political stability and sustainable energy transition, our study aims to provide valuable insights for policymakers, investors, and stakeholders engaged in the renewable energy sector in the UAE. By uncovering the underlying dynamics, we seek to identify the factors that either facilitate or impede progress towards achieving a sustainable energy landscape in the country.

To accomplish the study objective, we will utilize secondary data from various sources, ensuring the reliability and relevance of the information collected. Additionally, we will employ appropriate econometric techniques to analyze the data and derive meaningful conclusions. This rigorous approach will enable us to draw robust insights and contribute to the existing knowledge on the interplay between political stability and sustainable energy transition in the UAE.

LITERATURE REVIEW

Political Stability and Renewable Energy Transitions

In the 21st century, there has been extensive research conducted on the field of stable energy production and its implications on the overall economic climate. The significance of energy stability is well recognized, as it holds substantial influence over the economy, politics, and social aspects of a society. As part of efforts to diversify energy sources and meet evolving energy needs, studies have been undertaken to explore the spectrum of energy transitions. These studies aim to understand the processes, challenges, and opportunities associated with transitioning from conventional energy sources to more sustainable and renewable alternatives (Araújo, 2014).

Initial research efforts in this field primarily focused on Socio-Technical Analysis, leaving a gap in our understanding of the political landscape's influence. This knowledge gap can be attributed, in part, to the challenges faced in acquiring appropriate technology and the associated costs during the early stages of the renewable energy transition. However, in recent times, there has been a growing recognition of the significant role that politics plays in shaping and determining the success of energy prospects in any given state. As a result, political factors have gained increased attention and are now seen as crucial in understanding the realization of energy goals and objectives.

Political stability refers to the condition of a country or region that is marked by a consistent, peaceful, and orderly political environment. It signifies the absence of significant political disturbances, civil unrest, or frequent governmental transitions, thereby providing a predictable and stable governance system within a country. This stability is essential for fostering an environment conducive to sustainable development, attracting investments, and enabling effective policymaking and implementation. (Feng, 1997;Leonardo R. Arriola,2009).

Political stability is commonly assessed through various indicators that gauge the continuity of government, adherence to the rule of law, absence of violence or conflicts, and the effectiveness of governance institutions. These indicators provide insights into the overall strength and resilience of a country's political system and its ability to function cohesively towards the achievement of long-term government agendas. By evaluating these factors, analysts can assess the level of political stability and its impact on economic development, social cohesion, and policy implementation within a given country or region. (Langbein & Knack, 2010).

Energy production stability is an essential requirement for fostering economic growth and development. However, it is crucial to acknowledge the detrimental impacts of fossil fuel usage, which significantly contribute to climate change and global warming. Renewable energy, on the other hand, encompasses carbon-free energy sources that can mitigate the adverse effects of environmental degradation and contribute to the attainment of global sustainability objectives (Adebayo, 2022). The conducive environment created by the UAE's supportive policies and long-term commitment to sustainable energy could attract significant investments from private entities. Such investments can have substantial benefits for the economy. Private sector involvement in renewable energy projects can lead to job creation, technology transfer, and the development of local industries (Olawuyi, 2021). Public-private partnerships can leverage the expertise, innovation, and financial capabilities of the private sector, while benefiting from the regulatory framework, infrastructure, and public support provided by the government (Dulaimi, Alhashemi, Ling, & Kumaraswamy, 2010). This collaborative approach fosters efficiency, accelerates the deployment of renewable energy technologies, and promotes the overall transition to a sustainable energy future.

While it is true that some countries in the Middle East have experienced civil unrest and political upheavals, resulting in instability, the UAE has managed to maintain a relatively stable political environment. This stability has been attributed to various factors such as effective governance, social cohesion, and a focus on economic diversification. Economic hardship can indeed be a contributing factor to political unrest, as it can lead to dissatisfaction among the population and a desire for change. However, the UAE has taken proactive measures to address economic challenges by implementing robust economic policies, investing in infrastructure development, and diversifying its economy beyond oil and gas (Salem & Jagadeesan, 2022;Stewart M. Godwin,2017).

Significance of Political stability in the furtherance of RE regime include,

Policy Continuity: Political stability has ensured the continuity of government policies and long-term planning. It allows for the development and implementation of consistent renewable energy policies, targets, and regulations. This continuity provides a clear roadmap for businesses, investors, and stakeholders in the renewable energy sector, promoting confidence and reducing uncertainty (Elwereflli & Benhin, 2018).

Long-Term Planning: Political stability allows governments to engage in long-term planning for sustainable energy transitions. Stable political environments support the development of ambitious and achievable renewable energy targets, such as those outlined in the UAE's Energy Strategy 2050. Long-term planning helps the country align its economic diversification goals with renewable energy objectives, ensuring a smooth transition from fossil fuel dependence to a sustainable energy future.

Political stability in the UAE, driven by competent leadership, has fostered the establishment of supportive and consistent renewable energy policies and regulations. The absence of political opposition has enabled the implementation of comprehensive government initiatives like the UAE Energy Strategy 2050, the National Renewable Energy Program, and the Abu Dhabi Vision 2030. These initiatives provide a clear policy framework with specific targets, incentives, and regulatory measures to attract investments, encourage innovation, and facilitate the integration of renewable energy sources into the national energy grid.

The UAE's political stability has been instrumental in driving the development and implementation of renewable energy policies. It has served as a strong basis for long-term strategic planning, attracting investments in the renewable energy sector, fostering international partnerships, ensuring effective governance, and aligning with the country's energy diversification objectives. As the UAE progresses towards a sustainable future, the continued political stability will play a crucial role in further advancing renewable energy adoption and fostering innovation in the field.

Moreover, the political stability in the UAE has played a significant role in the successful execution of major renewable energy initiatives. Prominent examples include the Mohammed bin Rashid Al Maktoum Solar Park in Dubai and the Shams Solar Power Station in Abu Dhabi. These projects have been made possible thanks to the stable political climate in the country. The active participation of government entities and collaborations with international renewable energy companies have been vital in ensuring the effective planning, construction, and operation of these large-scale renewable energy facilities.

As a result of the political stability, the UAE has been able to push towards creating.

A. **Consistent Policy Framework:** UAE's political stability has provided a conducive environment for long-term planning and consistent policy formulation. Stable governance unified under a single visionary leadership championed by Abu Dhabi has allowed for the development of comprehensive strategies, targets, and regulations for renewable energy, ensuring a clear roadmap for implementation. This can be attributed to the first RE policy which had seek to increase the UAE clean energy power production to 7% by the end 2020 (Choucri, Goldsmith, & Mezher, 2010).
B. **Attraction of Foreign Investment:** Political stability instils confidence in investors, as it signals a lower risk of policy reversals or political disruptions that could impact project viability. Increased investments can lead to economies of scale, technological advancements, and cost reductions, which can ultimately benefit consumers by reducing the overall costs of renewable energy generation. Investors seek stable environments that minimize risks and uncertainties, making the UAE an attractive destination for renewable energy investments (Mosteanu, 2019).
C. **International Collaboration:** UAE's political stability has facilitated international collaboration and partnerships around the globe. The country has actively engaged in global initiatives, such as the International Renewable Energy Agency (IRENA), to share best practices, access expertise, and collaborate on research and development with governments and corporations that share same energy agenda. Political stability has therefore strengthened the UAE's credibility as a reliable partner in renewable energy endeavours (Jeong, 2020).
D. **Effective Governance and Regulatory Framework:** Political stability has enabled the UAE to establish and enforce effective governance and regulatory frameworks for renewable energy. Thus, enabling the government to create and enforce legislation, standards, and incentives that promote renewable energy adoption, ensuring a stable and supportive regulatory environment for businesses and consumers. Research has shown that, part of this regulation is developed to offer subsidies to their citizens (Poudineha, Senb, & Fattouh, 2018).
E. **Energy Diversification Goals:** UAE's political stability aligns with its long-term energy diversification goals. Recognizing the finite nature of fossil fuel reserves, the government has prioritized renewable energy as a strategic sector for economic diversification (Bachellerie, 2012). Political stability allows for the implementation of ambitious renewable energy targets and initiatives.

Notwithstanding the above, political stability promotes stakeholder engagement and collaboration within the renewable energy sector. Stable political environments allow for meaningful involvement of various stakeholders, including government entities, industry players, academia, local communities, and civil society organizations (Sisodia, Awad, Alkhoja, & Sergi, 2020). This collaboration enables knowledge sharing, consensus building, and the alignment of interests, which are critical for the sector's resilience and long-term sustainability. However, in recent years, various scholars discovered how most interest groups opposed the RE ideology in power generation especially from Wind and Biomass sources (Toke, 2010). Other findings have pointed out to the non-existence of prior information and knowledge concerning the effectiveness and potentials of RE and its impacts in reducing the climate change or environmental degradation. Studies conducted in Greece and other parts of the world asserts that, wrong perceptions of the populace on general issues relating to traditional form of power generation contributes to higher emission levels with a small number of people believing that, the innovative Clean Energy technology could help mitigate against the effects of climate change (Savvanidou, Zervas, & Tsagarakis, 2010).

Further investigation by UAE based research revealed the extent to which domestic subsidies initiated by the federal government given to Emiratis influenced their judgements towards the issues relating to emerging clean energy technologies. Findings on their recent studies on the interest groups and political institutions recommended the need for decision makers to integrate various stakeholders' opinions in the fossil fuel sectors on a wide range of potential information that pertains to the effectiveness of RE technology on both economy and the environment (Aswad, Al-Saleh, & HananTaleb, 2013). The above information when use to create awareness could help increase the acceptance of the CE innovative systems. Additionally, increased private sector investment can contribute to economic growth, enhance competitiveness, and foster innovation in the renewable energy sector, further strengthening the overall economy of the UAE (Kelly, 2021). Indeed, public-private partnerships play a significant role in realizing a sustainable energy future. Collaborations between the public and private sectors combine the strengths and resources of both entities, facilitating the implementation of sustainable energy projects on a larger scale.

UAE's RE Initiatives and Policies

UAE Energy Strategy 2050: In 2017, the UAE launched the Energy Strategy 2050, which outlines the country's long-term vision for the energy sector. The strategy aims to increase the share of clean energy in the UAE's total energy mix to 50%, reduce carbon footprint of power generation by 70%, increase energy efficiency by 40%, and achieve savings of AED 700 billion by 2050. The UAE also seeks to reduce its carbon emissions through the continuous introduction of structural innovative business frameworks. Further studies into the impacts of massive investments in RE has shown positive correlation between the latter and substantial increase in job creation (DEWA, 2020). The Waste to Energy project under construction has projected capacity to power more than 20,000 residential buildings when completed. Other initiatives towards the achieving the 2050 strategy include the carbon capture through the increase of mangroves, which has a potential of reducing the carbon emissions through absorption. ADNOC carbon capture installation plant is yet another significant initiative.

Figure 1. RE strategy 2050

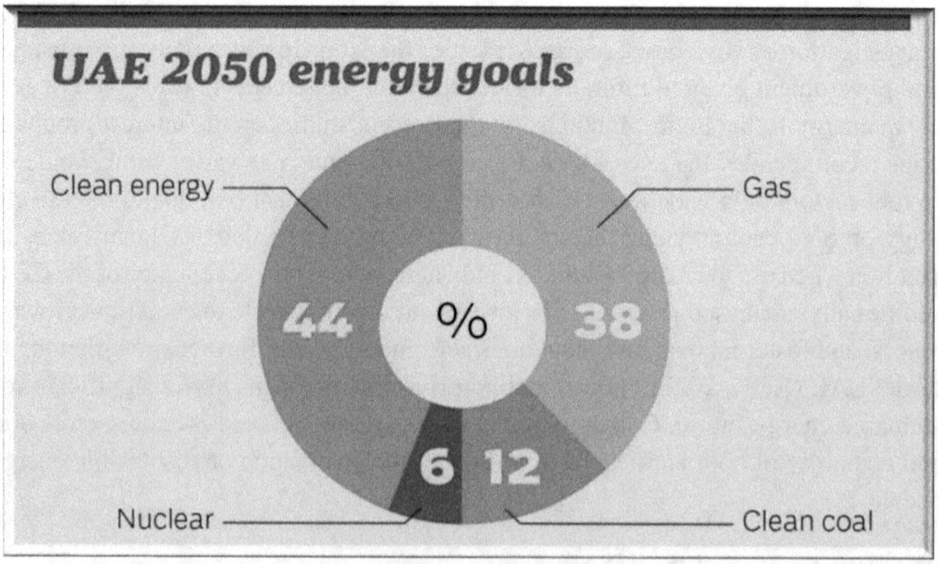

Renewable Energy Targets: As part of the Energy Strategy 2050, the UAE has set specific targets for renewable energy generation. The goal is to achieve 44% clean energy contribution to the total energy mix by 2050, with 27% coming from renewables and 6% from nuclear energy, while increasing clean energy resource by 30% by the end of 2030. These targets demonstrate the UAE's commitment to transitioning to a more sustainable energy future. As part of the government's strategy of increasing the RE sector, the Dubai governments aside its previous massive development of Mohammad bin Rashid Al Maktoum Solar Park, intends to expand the Solar system generation capacity by extending investments to create additional floating solar park in the Arabian gulf.

Masdar Initiative: Masdar, a subsidiary of the Mubadala Investment Company, is a key driver of renewable energy development in the UAE. As a flagship project of the UAE to be specific Abu Dhabi Masdar has been instrumental in implementing various renewable energy projects and initiatives, including the development of Masdar City, a sustainable urban development that aims to be a global centre for renewable energy and clean technologies (Sankaran & Chopra, 2020; Petch, Neil,2016). The government of Abu Dhabi has invested over $20 Billion in RE projects through Masdar, an innovative institution that has championed the investments within the UAE and other developing economies. The political stability of the UAE has enabled the government to provide the necessary support and resources for the development and ongoing operation of Masdar City, showcasing the country's commitment to renewable energy (Griffiths & Sovacool, 2020).

Feed-in Tariffs: The UAE introduced a Feed-in Tariff (FiT) program to incentivize the development of renewable energy projects. The program guarantees long-term contracts and fixed electricity prices for renewable energy producers, providing stability and attracting private investments in the sector (Mezher, Dawelbait, & Abbas, 2012). Further investigations have shown the benefits of reducing taxes on private firms that invest in the UAE RE sector (Samour, Shahzad, & Mentel, 2022). According to IRENA, the need to support the deployment policies by governments is significant to increasing the level of investment in the RE sector (Yuliani, 2017). Hence the support of the government in this direction could help increase the number of both local and private firms in further expanding the production of clean energy in the UAE.

Auctions and Competitive Bidding: The UAE has adopted a competitive bidding mechanism for procuring renewable energy projects. Through a series of auctions, developers compete to secure contracts for the development of utility-scale renewable energy projects. The UAE government usually considers the efficient bidding based on the RE technology type and the location of RE access (Lucas, Ferroukhi, & Hawila, 2013). This approach has led to cost reductions and increased efficiency in the deployment of renewable energy infrastructure (Atalaya, Kalfagianni, & Pattberg, 2017).

International Renewable Energy Agency (IRENA): The UAE actively participates in the International Renewable Energy Agency (IRENA), an intergovernmental organization that promotes renewable energy globally. The UAE hosts IRENA's headquarters in Abu Dhabi and collaborates with other member countries to share knowledge, best practices, and support the growth of renewable energy (Mengi-Dinçer, Ediger, & Yesevi, 2021). Recently the UAE has collaborated with several institutions in Italy, France, China, and South Korea in common shared areas of interest under RE through energy diplomacy (Griffiths S., 2019).

Research and Development: The UAE has invested in research and development (R&D) initiatives to advance renewable energy technologies. Institutions like the Masdar Institute of Science and Technology and the Khalifa University of Science and Technology are at the forefront of R&D efforts, focusing on areas such as solar energy, energy storage, and smart grid technologies (Atalay, Biermann, & Kalfagianni, 2016). The UAE has spent the past decade investing in sustainable solar energy. The advent of the above has led to a significant reduction in carbon emissions level in the UAE. Studies by UAE agencies responsible for RE policies estimated how the country would expel the rising emissions when ongoing large solar plants are commission, which according to industry experts, stated that, over 1 million Mt/year (United Arab Emirates Embassy Wadhington DC, 2023).

These policies and initiatives highlight the UAE's commitment to renewable energy and sustainable development. By setting ambitious targets, implementing supportive regulations, and promoting innovation, the UAE is positioning itself as a global leader in the transition to a clean energy future.

Facilitators and Hindrances to Progress Toward a Sustainable Energy Landscape in the UAE

The apparent and projected effects of climate change and the inevitable prospects of fossil fuel has therefore convinced policy makers to device an alternative strategy towards developing an effective and sustainable renewable energy regime.

Facilitators

Political Will and Vision: The UAEs has a strong political will and vision to diversify its energy mix and transition to a sustainable energy landscape have been instrumental in driving progress (Jamil, Ahmad, & Jeon, 2016). The government's commitment to renewable energy policies, as demonstrated through initiatives like the Energy Strategy 2050, provides a foundation for sustainable energy development. The above is evident in the actions of their past and present leadership. The ruler of Dubai, Abu Dhabi and other emirates have all championed the success of RE projects. The unveiling of the new Jebel Ali

Island and the subsequent initiation of RE policies to power its infrastructure is an example of the Dubai Rulers commitment towards meeting the sustainable energy targets (The National, 2023).

Abundance of Renewable Resources: The geographical location of the UAE has an influence on its resources such as sunlight and wind, aiding opportunities for the development of solar and wind energy projects. The abundance of these renewable resources facilitates the generation of clean and sustainable energy in the country (Kazim, 2010). The abundance of the above resources extends across the middle east due to similar climatic conditions therefore making the adoption of the RE imminent (Nathaniel, Adeleye, & Adedoyin, 2021).

Financial Resources and Investments: the UAE has been endowed with natural resources through which the country has generated significant wealth, from both domestic and foreign investments to support the development of renewable energy projects. Investments generated from public and private entities from international and domestic market have helped in financing the necessary infrastructure and technologies required for sustainable energy generation. Recently, investors have emerged from China and South Korean firm (Kepco). The Barakah Nuclear project is a perfect example of knowledge investments in clean energy infrastructure from south Korean firms (Staff Writer, 2022). Another significant investment has been the joint United States and UAE in RE (Abdallah & Eltahir, 2023).

Technological Innovation and Expertise: Lately, the UAE has focused on fostering technological innovation and building expertise in the renewable energy sector. This commitment to research and development has resulted in advancements in areas such as solar power, energy storage, and smart grid technologies, enabling more efficient and cost-effective deployment of sustainable energy solutions (Jamil, Ahmad, & Jeon, 2016). The inclusion of these technological systems will further enhance the RE usage and its impact in reducing the environmental degradation.

International Collaborations and Partnerships: The UAE actively participates in international collaborations and partnerships, such as its involvement with IRENA, to share knowledge, best practices, and collaborate on research and development. These partnerships facilitate access to expertise, technology transfer, and global support, accelerating progress toward a sustainable energy landscape.

Hindrances

Reliance on Fossil Fuel Economy: The UAE's economy has historically been reliant on fossil fuel exports, which poses challenges in transitioning to a sustainable energy landscape. The shift away from fossil fuels requires careful management of economic and social factors, including the need to diversify the economy and mitigate potential impacts on the existing energy sector. However, the recent strategic RE initiatives implemented by visionary leadership of UAE is evidence toward the sustainable energy transition (Mezher, Dawelbait, & Abbas, 2012).

Water Scarcity and Desalination: Water scarcity is a significant challenge in the UAE, studies have shown how the desalination process consumes a substantial amount of energy which causes environmental degradation through substantial emission levels (Assad, AlMallahi, Abdelsalam, AlShabi, & AlMallahi, 2022). Similar research revealed how the desalination process has resulted in higher energy consumption patterns in China, this further solidifies the cost effectiveness of the process (Jia, Klemeš, Varbanov, & Alwi, 2019). Balancing the need for water security with sustainable energy goals presents a complex challenge that requires innovative solutions and efficient resource management.

Infrastructural Requirements: Building the necessary infrastructure for renewable energy generation and distribution can be a challenge to many governments. Developing grid systems capable of integrating renewable energy sources and ensuring transmission and distribution infrastructure is in place requires substantial investments and coordinated planning to include the emerging renewable energy technological systems, institutional overhaul as well as new regulations and reforms in the energy industry (Naqbi, Tsai, & Mezher, 2019).

Energy Storage and Grid Integration: The intermittent nature of renewable energy sources necessitates effective energy storage solutions and grid integration. Hence, overcoming the technical challenges and implementing energy storage technologies, such as batteries or pumped hydro storage, is critical for balancing energy supply and demand and ensuring grid stability. Studies has asserted that, in recent years, UAE has invested in new technologies related to energy storage, notably among which includes, the Battery Energy Storage System (BESS). Investment in this power storage system has therefore helped in enhancing the effectiveness of the grid resilience (Dupont & Baltus, 2009).

Cost Competitiveness: While the cost of renewable energy technologies has significantly reduced in recent years, achieving cost competitiveness with conventional energy sources remains a challenge. Further advancements in technology, economies of scale, and supportive policies are required to enhance cost-effectiveness and make renewable energy more competitive. According to some studies deregulation of the sector would enhance competition among private players (Mezher, Dawelbait, & Abbas, 2012).

Public Awareness and Behavioral Change: Promoting public awareness and encouraging Behavioral change toward sustainable energy practices is crucial. Educating and engaging the public in the benefits and importance of renewable energy is essential for driving demand and wider adoption of sustainable energy solutions.

Furthermore, political stability creates an environment conducive to public support and awareness of renewable energy. Stable political environments allow for consistent communication, education, and awareness campaigns that promote the benefits of renewable energy among the public. Building public support and awareness are crucial for the long-term sustainability of the renewable energy sector and can facilitate the social acceptance of renewable energy projects.

Figure 2. Renewable energy generation percentage (1990–2020) and energy production type (2020)
Source: (EnerData, 2022)

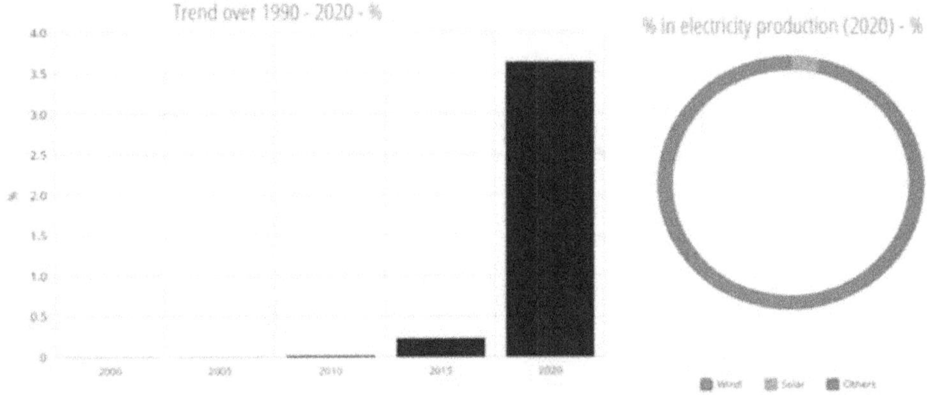

Changed in the Renewable Energy Mix (Solar Power Generation)

Pertaining to the results of the above data, production of electricity was even/insignificant in the early 2000s (Salimi, Husseinpour, & Borhani, 2022). Partly due to the lack / low Research and Development coupled with the higher cost of RE technologies during that period. However, it is pertinent to note that, the traditional forms of energy production still lead over the new RE innovative technological systems, hence creating a big gap between the RE and the fossil fuels led power generation. Recent developments in the RE space has shown massive support for sustainable power generation by the government. The data between 2015 -2020 is an evident to this claim. In relation to the current expansion of the UAEs economy especially on massive infrastructural developments, greater emphasis could be placed on increasing RE investments in Solar and Wind due to the opportunities in climatic induced conditions in the middle east.

Figure 3. Solar energy generation installed capacity (2011–2021)
Source: *(IRENA, 2022).*

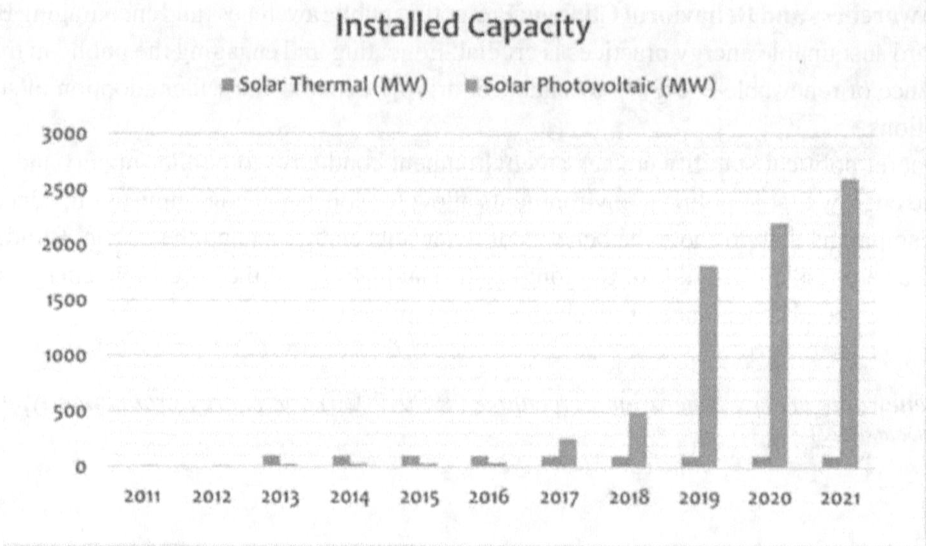

Figure 4. Biogas generation

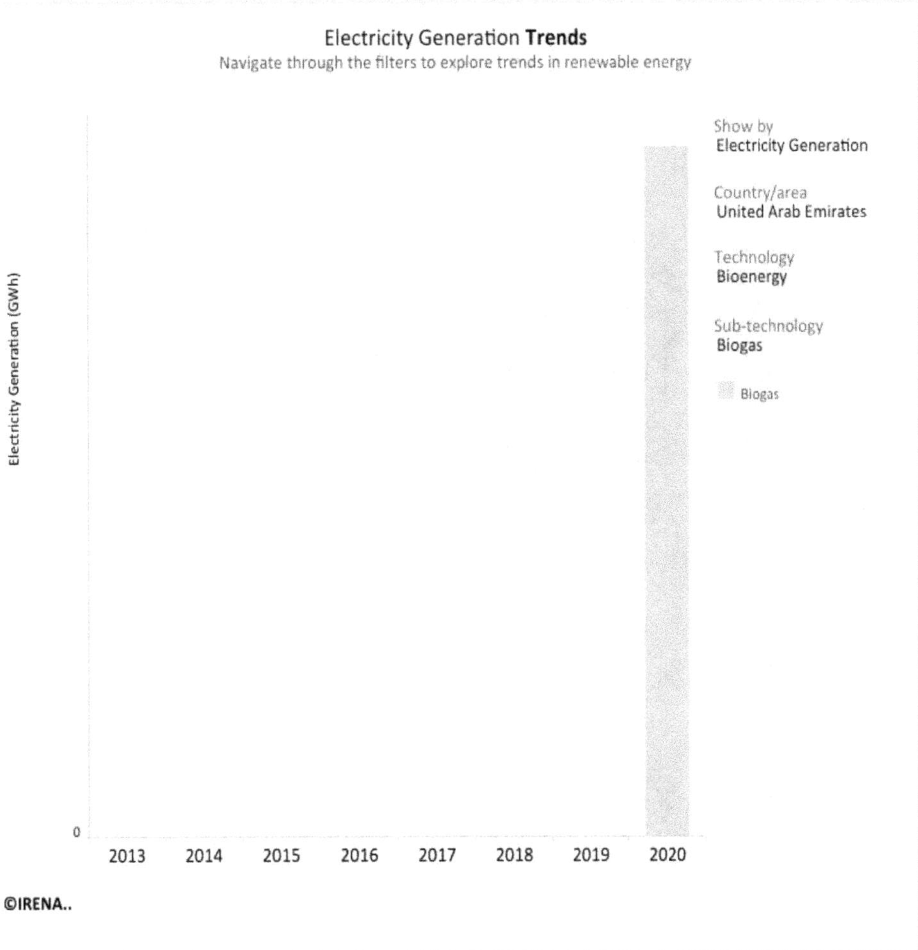

Biogas Generation Capacity of 0.8700 GWh

Figure 5. Wind generation trends

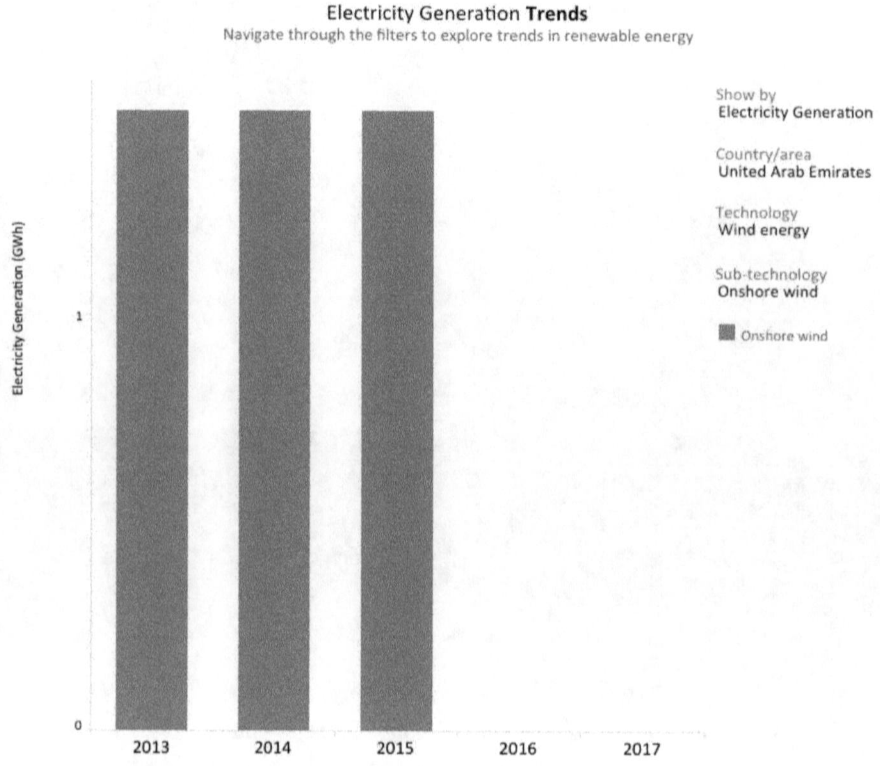

©IRENA..

Wind energy generation capacity of 1.489GWh, Its production capacity was uniform between 2013-2015, this sector has not received enough investments in recent years. Hence providing opportunities for further development.

Figure 6. Energy production in the UAE by type
Source: *(EIA, 2021).*

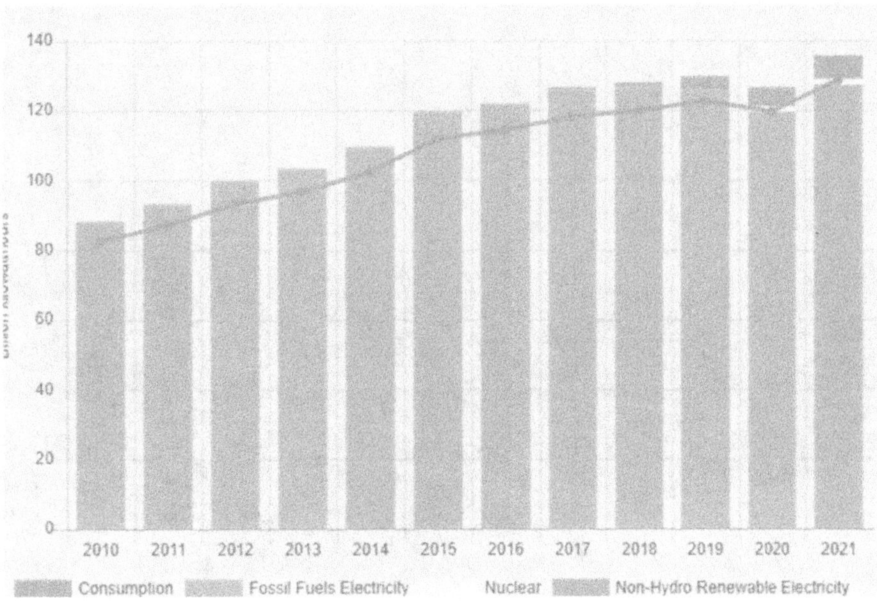

According to the BP Statistical Review of World Energy 2022, total primary energy consumption in the United Arab Emirates in 2021 was 4.53 exajoules, about 55.2% constituted natural gas, Oil had 39.7% share, nuclear energy constituted 2.2%, Coal constituted 1.5% with renewables of 1.1%.

Consumption has increased in recent years and the introduction of RE sources has received significant investments leading to an energy production mix.

Figure 7. Mohammad bin Rashid Al Maktoum solar park
Source: *Masdar (2023)*

Observations made in Figure 9. Illustrates the difference between energy consumption by sector, transformation and losses and supply by RE technology type. The data shows a gap in the RE technology used. Solar PV and thermal are widely utilized than all other clean energy sources hence creating an opportunity for more investments in Wind and Solid Biofuels.

Investments in the new RE areas could be used to supplement the sectors with higher energy consumption from non-renewables.

Figure 8. Renewable energy balances
Source: *(IRENA, 2022)*

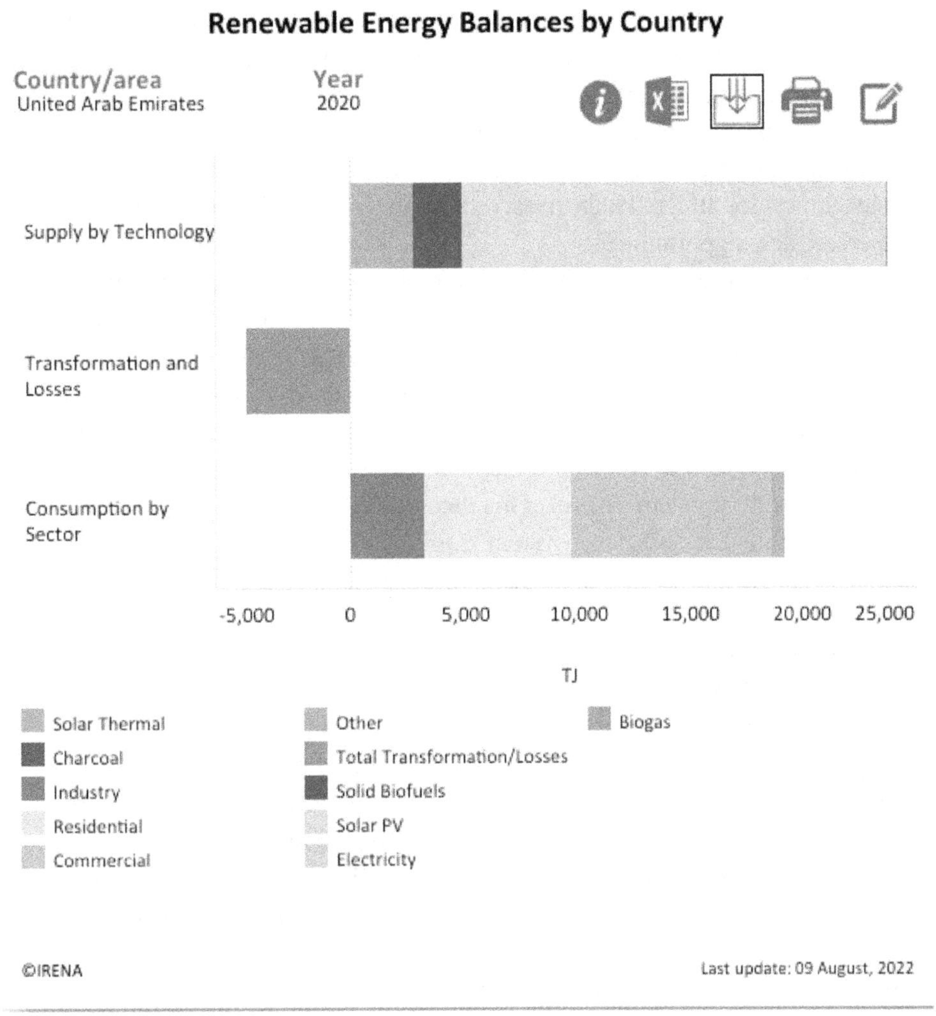

EMPIRICAL REVIEWS

Historical Institutional Theory Perspective

Indeed, it is crucial to acknowledge that the relationship between political stability and renewable energy in the UAE is not without challenges. The framework of historical institutionalism emphasizes that existing institutions and vested interests can significantly influence policy outcomes. In the case of the UAE, the historical dominance of the oil and gas sector, which has served as the backbone of revenue generation, creates obstacles for a complete transition to renewable energy sources (Choucri, Goldsmith, & Mezher, 2010).

Balancing the interests of various stakeholders, ensuring policy consistency over time, and managing potential disruptions to existing economic structures are vital considerations in this context. The transition to renewable energy requires navigating complex dynamics, including the need to address the concerns and priorities of stakeholders involved in the traditional energy sector. It is necessary to find ways to align and reconcile these interests with the objectives of sustainable energy development (Aswad, Al-Saleh, & HananTaleb, 2013).

Furthermore, managing the potential disruptions to existing economic structures requires careful planning and implementation of strategies that minimize adverse impacts. This may involve measures such as providing support for affected industries, retraining, and transitioning workers, and diversifying the economy to create new opportunities.

Considering these challenges and complexities, it is essential for policymakers and stakeholders in the UAE to develop a comprehensive and inclusive approach that takes into account the interests of various actors, ensures policy coherence and stability, and addresses the potential disruptions and implications of transitioning to renewable energy sources (Mezher, Dawelbait, & Abbas, 2012).

Politics plays a vital role in every economic context, particularly concerning the development of policy frameworks. To fully understand the impact of institutions on energy transitions, it is essential to incorporate the Historical Institutionalism Theory. This theory focuses on the interactions and relationships among various actors within the energy ecosystem, aiming to analyze how they influence and shape the transition process. By incorporating the Historical Institutionalism Theory, researchers can gain valuable insights into the dynamics of energy transitions. This approach considers not only the formal institutions such as government bodies and regulatory agencies but also the informal institutions and social norms that influence decision-making in the energy sector. It emphasizes the interplay between these actors and institutions, highlighting their roles, interests, and power dynamics (Lowndes & Roberts, 2013).

By employing the Historical Institutionalism Theory, a more comprehensive understanding of the complex interrelationships within the energy ecosystem can be achieved. It sheds light on how institutions and actors interact, adapt, and shape the development and implementation of renewable energy policies and initiatives. Recognizing the influence of politics, institutions, and the interactions between actors is crucial for effective policymaking in the energy sector. Incorporating the Historical Institutionalism Theory provides a framework to analyze and evaluate the role of institutions and actors in energy transitions, facilitating the development of more robust and inclusive policies.

Historical institutionalism places emphasis on the significance of historical legacies, institutional arrangements, and path dependencies in shaping policy outcomes. This perspective recognizes that past events and decisions, along with existing institutional structures, have a profound influence on the formulation and implementation of policies. (Lockwood, Kuzemko, Mitchell, & Hoggett, 2016). Hence, considering the role of politics as an institutional force and the impact of past governmental decisions, the energy industry in the UAE has been modelled and its future vision is centred around reducing carbon emissions through the adoption of renewable energy (RE).

As an example, the identification of substantial oil and gas reserves in the UAE during the 1960s resulted in the establishment and commercialization of these resources. The Abu Dhabi Government, being the sole owner, has played a significant role in driving the operations of ADNOC (Abu Dhabi National Oil Company) and implementing strategies to diversify its activities for enhanced value creation. The government takes a visionary approach in overseeing the management of ADNOC, primarily through its primary sovereign wealth fund, Abu Dhabi Development Holding (ADQ).

The UAE's strong leadership in promoting sustainable development is evident through the ongoing reorganization of ministries and their progressive expansion of roles to align with current priorities. Over the years, the ministries have undergone structural changes and increased responsibilities, demonstrating the country's visionary approach. For instance, committees representing ministries were established in the 1970s as an initial step towards integrating sustainable policies. Subsequently, in the 1990s and 2000s, further structural changes and an expansion of duties took place.

A recent significant development in this regard is the transformation of the Ministry of Environment and Water into the Climate Change and Environment Ministry. This change solidifies the UAE's commitment to maintaining a consistent and enduring focus on sustainable policies. Through continuous restructuring, the UAE demonstrates its proactive approach to sustainable development, ensuring that ministries are well-equipped to address contemporary challenges. This adaptive approach aligns with global trends and underlines the country's dedication to a sustainable future (UAE Ministry of Climate Change and Environment, 2023).

The effective collaboration and close cooperation between the oil and gas sector and the climate change and environment ministry serve as a testament to the positive impact of political stability on institutional frameworks.

The aforementioned theory reveals the historical decision-making patterns of political institutions regarding the implementation of energy projects, taking into account factors such as diversity and change (Steinmo S, K, & F, 1992). Therefore, examining whether the current or past political institutions in the UAE have supported the clean energy ecosystem reveals that the political stability provided by its institutional framework has been instrumental in facilitating the country's transition towards renewable energy. The UAE has demonstrated a steadfast commitment to diversifying its energy mix and reducing reliance on fossil fuels. (Atalay, Biermann, & Kalfagianni, 2016). The UAE's dedication to renewable energy transition has been bolstered by its long-standing political stability, which has fostered a consistent and conducive environment for sustainable development. Scholars such as Parag and Derby (2009) and Hughes et al. (2012) have conducted comprehensive investigations, shedding light on the interplay of power actors within the energy system and reaffirming the significance of this relationship.

Figure 9. Actors and relationships in the energy system
Source: (Lockwood, Kuzemko, Mitchell, & Hoggett, 2016).

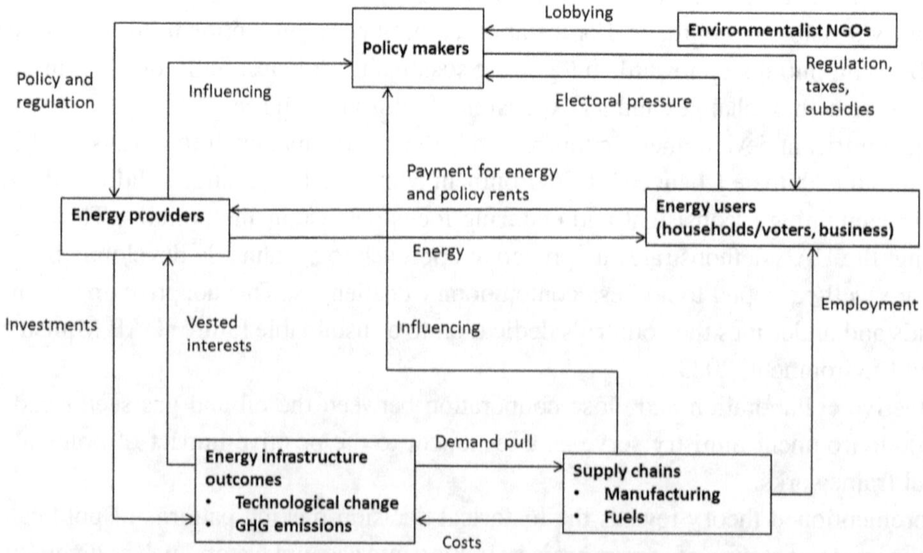

Political Economic Theory Perspective

The government's control and dominance of the energy sector in the UAE can be interpreted as a strategic measure to minimize competition and allocate generated revenue towards the advancement of clean energy initiatives. This deliberate approach is intended to foster the expansion of the renewable energy sector and facilitate the attainment of sustainable development objectives. Similar strategies have been observed among other Gulf Cooperation Council (GCC) governments, suggesting a shared tendency in the region to prioritize investments and progress in clean energy endeavours (Al-Sarihi & Cherni, 2022).

The involvement of major investors or private firms in the utility production sectors has the potential to introduce competition into the energy market. However, if regulatory measures are not adequately enforced, this competition can lead to price competition and the formation of unions within the power sector. Such a scenario could result in the government losing revenue to rival firms. Therefore, it emphasizes the significance of establishing strong regulatory frameworks to ensure fair competition and to strike a balance between the interests of various stakeholders, including the government, private firms, and consumers. Effective implementation of regulations is crucial in addressing these challenges and fostering a sustainable and efficient energy market (Mezher, Dawelbait, & Abbas, 2012).

Political stability plays a crucial role in ensuring equitable distribution of costs and benefits in the context of energy affordability and access. A stable political environment enables the design and implementation of targeted policies to address energy poverty, ensuring that the costs associated with renewable energy transition do not disproportionately impact vulnerable or low-income populations. This can involve the introduction of energy subsidies, financial assistance programs, or innovative pricing mechanisms that promote equitable access to affordable renewable energy. By prioritizing the needs of disadvantaged communities, political stability facilitates a just and inclusive transition to renewable energy sources (Al-Sarihi & Cherni, 2022).

The UAE has made significant strides in the renewable energy sector, and its political stability is a key contributing factor to this progress. The country's political leadership structure has played a pivotal role in shaping and advancing renewable energy policies. Additionally, the UAE's serene political environment and recent modifications to labor laws have attracted a surge in population, enhancing its competitive business climate within the Gulf Cooperation Council (GCC) region. However, the rise in population also increases the demand for energy resources and puts pressure on existing energy infrastructure. This necessitates the development and expansion of sustainable energy infrastructure to meet the growing energy demands of the population (Arman, 2015).

Therefore, it becomes necessary to implement effective renewable energy sources to complement the existing production limits. Renewable energy (RE) strategies are specifically designed to reduce environmental degradation and emissions associated with traditional energy sources. By transitioning to renewable energy, the UAE can mitigate its carbon footprint, minimize environmental pollution, and contribute to global efforts in combating climate change. The adoption of RE technologies and practices will not only help diversify the energy mix but also promote sustainable development and ensure a greener and more sustainable future for the UAE (Jamil, Ahmad, & Jeon, 2016).

Figure 10. Conceptual model
Source: Developed by the Authors (2023)

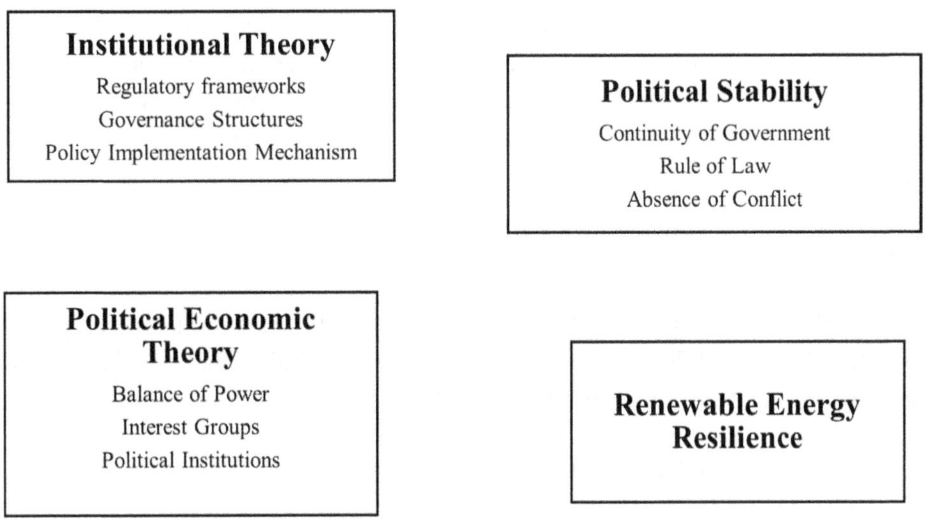

METHODOLOGY

Data and Description of Variables

The purpose of this study is to investigate the relationship between political stability and the adoption of renewable energy in the United Arab Emirates (UAE). To accomplish this research objective, the study utilizes data provided by the World Bank, covering the period from 1996 to 2021. The data for the dependent variable, which is renewable energy consumption, is obtained from the World Development Indicators maintained by the World Bank. As for the main independent variable, political stability, the data is extracted from the World Governance Indicators. Additionally, the study considers the potential influence of gross fixed capital formation, financial development, and economic growth, and the corresponding data for these variables are also sourced from the World Development Indicators.

In measuring the variables, the study employs renewable energy consumption (% of total final energy consumption) as a measure of the adoption of renewable energy. This metric provides insights into the extent to which renewable energy sources are being utilized in the overall energy consumption. As per the definition provided by the World Bank, political stability and absence of violence encompass the perceptions regarding the probability of the government being destabilized or overthrown through unconstitutional or violent means, including politically motivated violence and terrorism. This variable is evaluated on a scale ranging from -2.5 to +2.5, where a higher score indicates a higher level of political stability. Gross fixed capital formation (annual % growth) serves as an indicator of domestic investment. It measures the growth rate of domestic investments in tangible assets such as buildings, machinery, and infrastructure. Financial development is approximated by the percentage of domestic credit provided by banks to the private sector in relation to the country's GDP. This metric reflects the extent to which financial institutions are supporting economic activities through credit provision. Furthermore, GDP (constant 2015 US$) is utilized as an indicator of economic growth. It represents the inflation-adjusted value of the country's goods and services produced over a specified period, providing insights into the overall economic performance.

Empirical Model

The empirical model for examining the relationship between political stability (POLS) and renewable energy consumption (REN), while controlling for gross fixed capital formation (GFCF), financial development (FIND), and economic growth (ECG), can be specified as follows:

$$\ln REN_t = \alpha_0 + \beta_1 \ln POLS_t + \beta_2 \ln GFCF_t + \beta_3 \ln FIND_t + \beta_4 \ln ECG_t + \varepsilon_t \quad (1)$$

From equation 1, α represents the intercept while ε is the error term, accounting for unobserved factors in the model. β_1 to β_4 are the regression coefficients.

Estimation Approach

This study employs rigorous statistical procedures to ensure the validity of the regression analysis. These include the use of the Phillips-Perron (PP) unit root test for stationarity assessment, the Autoregressive Distributed Lag (ARDL) cointegration test to confirm long-term relationships, and the Fully Modified

Ordinary Least Square (FMOLS) technique proposed by Phillips and Hansen (1990). The FMOLS technique addresses issues of serial correlation and endogeneity, ensuring reliable and accurate estimation (Bashiru, Yakubu, Bunyaminu, & Faryan, 2022).

RESULTS AND DISCUSSIONS

Descriptive Statistics

The descriptive statistics presented in Table 1 provide a summary of the key characteristics of the variables being analyzed. The mean values indicate that, on average, renewable energy consumption accounts for around 13.5% of total final energy consumption. Political stability is relatively high, with a mean score of 0.815. Gross fixed capital formation shows moderate levels of domestic investment, while financial development, measured by domestic credit to the private sector by banks, appears relatively substantial. Economic growth, represented by GDP, shows a considerable magnitude. Measures of dispersion, such as standard deviations, reveal the variability within the dataset. Renewable energy consumption exhibits a relatively low level of variation, while gross fixed capital formation and financial development demonstrate wider ranges. Skewness values suggest the shape of the distributions, with renewable energy consumption showing positive skewness, indicating a longer tail on the right side. Kurtosis measures the peakedness of the distributions, with renewable energy consumption exhibiting a significantly higher value than the others, indicating a more peaked distribution. The Jarque-Bera test reveals departures from normality, with renewable energy consumption showing a significant deviation.

Table 1. Descriptive statistics

	REN	POLS	GFCF	FIND	ECG
Mean	0.135	0.815	5.291	56.651	2.85E+11
Median	0.110	0.863	4.316	58.725	2.84E+11
Maximum	0.670	0.995	43.290	87.919	4.03E+11
Std. Dev.	0.126	0.132	12.142	19.513	8.34E+10
Skewness	3.537	-0.344	1.289	-0.002	-0.021
Kurtosis	15.218	1.817	6.549	1.496	1.678
Jarque-Bera	199.328	1.795	15.234	2.451	1.897
Probability	0.000	0.408	0.000	0.294	0.387
Observations	24	23	19	26	26

Stationary Test Results

The Phillips Perron (PP) unit root test results, as presented in Table 2, provide insights into the stationarity properties of the variables under examination. In the level form, the variables renewable energy consumption, political stability, financial development, and economic growth show adjusted t-statistics that are insignificant, suggesting insufficient evidence to reject the null hypothesis of a unit root, indicating non-stationarity. However, when considering the first difference, the adjusted t-statistics for all variables range from -9.434 to -1.633 and are highly significant, indicating strong evidence of stationarity after differencing.

Table 2. Phillips Perron (PP) unit root test results

Variables	Level	First Difference
	Adj. t-Stat	Adj. t-Stat
lnREN	-1.247	-1.633*
lnPOLS	-0.737	-7.949***
lnGFCF	-2.395**	-9.434***
lnFIND	1.336	-3.108***
lnECG	4.697	-2.738***

Note: *, **, *** indicate stationarity at 10%, 5%, and 1% respectively

Cointegration Test Results

Following the research conducted by Musah and Yakubu (2022), this study utilizes the ARDL bound test approach to examine the presence of cointegration, and the results are presented in Table 3. The table displays the F-statistic values at different significance levels, as well as the corresponding critical values for the I(0) and I(1) cases. The F-statistic of 4.498 is highly significant at the 1% level, indicating strong evidence of cointegration between the variables. This suggests the existence of a long-run relationship among the variables under investigation.

Table 3. Cointegration test

F-statistic	Significance	I(0)	I(1)
4.498***	10%	1.9	3.01
	5%	2.26	3.48
	1%	3.07	4.44

*** indicates 1% significance

Regression Results on the Impact of Political Stability on Renewable Energy Consumption

The regression results presented in Table 4 provide insights into the impact of political stability on renewable energy consumption in the UAE, as estimated using the Fully Modified Ordinary Least Square (FMOLS) technique. The coefficient estimates for the variables are reported, along with their corresponding standard errors in parentheses.

Table 4. Regression results

Variables	FMOLS Estimates
lnPOLS	1.864**
	(0.558)
lnGFCF	-0.191***
	(0.035)
lnFIND	-0.697
	(0.366)
lnECG	3.280***
	(0.709)
C	-36.985***
	(7.625)
R-squared	0.868
Adjusted R-squared	0.762
S.E. of regression	0.128
Long-run variance	0.007

Note: ** and *** indicate significance at 5% and 1% respectively

The coefficient estimates for lnPOLS, representing the impact of political stability on renewable energy consumption, is 1.864 and statistically significant at 5%. This finding suggests that as political stability increases, there is a corresponding increase in the adoption of renewable energy sources in the UAE. The result aligns with expectations and implies that a stable political environment fosters a favourable climate for renewable energy development and implementation. Similar studies have been widely explored by (Adebayo, Akadiri, Uhunamure, Altuntaş, & Shale, 2022).

In addition, domestic investment has a negative impact on renewable energy consumption in the UAE, given the negative coefficient of gross fixed capital formation. The negative sign suggests that higher levels of domestic investment may divert resources away from renewable energy projects, potentially hindering their development and adoption. This finding raises concerns about the need to align investment strategies with renewable energy goals to ensure sustainable and environmentally friendly energy systems in the country.

The results reveal that financial development does not have a significant impact on renewable energy consumption in the UAE. This finding suggests that financial factors may not be the primary drivers influencing the adoption and utilization of renewable energy sources in the country.

Furthermore, a positive and statistically significant relationship between economic growth and renewable energy consumption is documented, indicating that as the UAE experiences economic growth, there is a simultaneous increase in the adoption and consumption of renewable energy sources. This finding suggests that economic prosperity can facilitate the transition to cleaner and more sustainable energy systems.

The R-squared value of 0.868 indicates that the regression model explains approximately 86.8% of the variation in renewable energy consumption, suggesting a good fit.

CONCLUSION AND POLICY IMPLICATIONS

This study examines the influence of political stability on renewable energy adoption in the UAE by utilizing annual data from 1996 to 2021. The research relies on data from the World Bank and applies the Fully Modified Ordinary Least Squares (FMOLS) technique to analyze the relationship. The results indicate that political stability has a statistically significant and positive impact on renewable energy consumption. In contrast, domestic investment exhibits a negative association with renewable energy adoption. Additionally, the study reveals a positive and significant relationship between economic growth and renewable energy consumption. Interestingly, the findings suggest that financial development does not have a significant effect on the adoption of renewable energy sources.

The findings of this study have important policy implications for promoting renewable energy adoption in the UAE. Firstly, the positive and significant impact of political stability on renewable energy consumption highlights the need for policymakers to prioritize stable governance and create a supportive policy environment. Strengthening political stability through transparent regulations, long-term energy strategies, and incentives for renewable energy investments can encourage businesses and investors to embrace clean energy technologies. Secondly, the negative relationship between domestic investment and renewable energy adoption calls for targeted policy interventions. Policymakers should redirect investments towards renewable energy infrastructure and technologies, promoting sustainable development and reducing dependence on non-renewable energy sources (OECD, 2013). Implementing financial mechanisms, such as subsidies, tax incentives, and favourable financing options specifically designed for renewable energy projects, can help overcome the current negative impact of domestic investment. In addition, recognizing the positive and significant effect of economic growth on renewable energy consumption, policymakers should integrate renewable energy into their economic development plans. Aligning renewable energy strategies with economic growth objectives can create synergies, promote job creation in the renewable energy sector, and enhance energy security while reducing greenhouse gas emissions, an investigation further emphasized by (Jamil, Ahmad, & Jeon, 2016). Encouraging collaboration between the government, private sector, and research institutions can drive innovation and technological advancements in the renewable energy sector, further supporting sustainable economic growth (Kelly, 2021). Furthermore, although financial development does not currently show a significant effect on renewable energy adoption, policymakers should explore alternative mechanisms to finance renewable energy projects. This could involve fostering partnerships with international financial institutions, promoting green bonds and investment funds, and developing innovative financial instruments specifically tailored for the renewable energy sector.

While this study provides valuable insights into the impact of political stability on renewable energy adoption in the UAE, some limitations should be acknowledged. For instance, this study focuses solely on the UAE, and the findings may not be directly applicable to other countries or regions. Cross-country comparative analyses or case studies could be conducted to understand how different contextual factors influence renewable energy adoption in various settings. Likewise, while this study analyzes the impact of political stability on renewable energy consumption, it does not delve into the specific mechanisms or pathways through which political stability influences renewable energy adoption. Future research could explore these mechanisms, such as the role of policy frameworks and macroeconomic conditions to provide a deeper understanding of how political stability affects renewable energy adoption.

REFERENCES

Abdallah, N., & Eltahir, N. (2023). *20 billion investment fun in clean energy.* Reuters. https://www.reuters.com/business/sustainable-business/us-uae-say-20-billion-investment-fund-15-gw-new-clean-energy-2023-01-15/

Adebayo, T. S., Akadiri, S. S., Uhunamure, S. E., Altuntaş, M., & Shale, K. (2022). *Does political stability contribute to environmental sustainability? Evidence from the most politically stable economies.* National Library of Medicine. https://www.ncbi.nlm.nih.gov/pmc/articles/PMC9800197/

Al-Maamary, H. M., Kazem, H. A., & Chaichan, M. T. (2017). Renewable energy and GCC States energy challenges in the 21st century: A review. *International Journal of Computation and Applied Sciences, 02*(01). https://www.researchgate.net/profile/Hussein-A-Kazem/publication/312534224_Renewable_energy_and_GCC_States_energy_challenges_in_the_21st_century_A_review/links/5880ff344585150dde3f3c83/Renewable-energy-and-GCC-States-energy-challenges-in-the-21st-century-. doi:10.24842/1611/0018

Al-Sarihi, A., & Cherni, J. A. (2022). *Political economy of renewable energy transition in rentier states: The case of Oman.* Wiley. https://onlinelibrary.wiley.com/doi/full/10.1002/eet.2041

Arman, H. (2015). Uncertainties, risks and challenges relating to CO2 emissions and its possible impact on climate change in the United Arab Emirates. *International Journal of Global Warming, 08*(01), 1–17. https://www.inderscienceonline.com/doi/abs/10.1504/IJGW.2015.071575. doi:10.1504/IJGW.2015.071575

Assad, M. E., AlMallahi, M. N., Abdelsalam, M. A., AlShabi, M., & AlMallahi, W. N. (2022). *Advances in Science and Engineering Technology International Conferences (ASET)* (pp. 1-4). Dubai: IEEE.

Aswad, N. G., Al-Saleh, Y., & HananTaleb. (2013). Clean energy awareness campaigns in the UAE: An awareness promoters perspective. *International Journal of Innovation and Knowledge Management in the Middle East and North Africa, 02*(02). https://www.researchgate.net/profile/Yasser-Alsaleh/publication/275299871_Clean_Energy_Awareness_Campaigns_in_the_UAE_An_Awareness_Promoters_Perspective/links/553744500cf268fd001892da/Clean-Energy-Awareness-Campaigns-in-the-UAE-An-Awareness-Promoters-Pers

Atalay, Y., Biermann, F., & Kalfagianni, A. (2016). Adoption of renewable energy technologies in oil-rich countries. *Renewable Energy, 85*, 206–214. https://www.sciencedirect.com/science/article/abs/pii/S0960148115300689?via%3Dihub. doi:10.1016/j.renene.2015.06.045

Atalaya, Y., Kalfagianni, A., & Pattberg, P. (2017). Renewable energy support mechanisms in the Gulf Cooperation Council. *Renewable & Sustainable Energy Reviews, 72*, 723–733. doi:10.1016/j.rser.2017.01.103

Bachellerie, I. J. (2012). *Renewable Energy in the GCC Countries- Resources, Potential and Prospects.* Gulf Research Centre.

Bashiru, S., Yakubu, I. N., Bunyaminu, A., & Faryan, M. A. (2022). Drivers of Financial Inclusion: Insights from Sub-Saharan Africa. *Journal of Money and Business.* http://www.mdpi.com

Bhattarai, U., Maraseni, T., & Apan, A. (2022). Assay of renewable energy transition: A systematic literature review. Science of The Total Environment. *The Science of the Total Environment, 833*, 155–159. https://www.sciencedirect.com/science/article/abs/pii/S0048969722022525. doi:10.1016/j.scitotenv.2022.155159

Choucri, N., Goldsmith, D., & Mezher, T. (2010). Renewable energy policy in an oil exporting country: The case of the United Arab Emirates. *Renewable Energy Law and Policy Review, 1*(1), 77–86.

DEWA. (2020, November 01). *DEWA invests 86 billion in energy sector over the next five years.*. Government of Dubai. https://www.dewa.gov.ae/en/about-us/media-publications/latest-news/2020/11/dewa-invests-aed-86-billion-in-energy-sector-over-the-next-5-years

Dulaimi, M., Alhashemi, M., Ling, F. Y., & Kumaraswamy, M. (2010). The execution of public-private partnership projects in the UAE. *Construction Management and Economics, 28*(04), 393–402. doi:10.1080/01446191003702492

Dupont, G., & Baltus, P. (2009). *Dimensioning and Grid Integration of Mega Battery Energy Storage System for System Load Leveling. IEEE Bucharest PowerTech*. IEEE., https://www.ieeexplore.ieee.org

EIA. (2021). *U.S Energy Information Administration.* EIA. https://www.eia.gov/

Elwereflli, A., & Benhin, J. (2018). Oil a blessing or curse: A comparative assessment of Nigeria, Norway and the United Arab Emirates. *Theoretical Economics Letters, 08*(05), 1136–1160. http://hdl.handle.net/10026.1/11272. doi:10.4236/tel.2018.85076

EnerData. (2022). *Electricity Domestic Consumption.* EnerData. https://yearbook.enerdata.net/electricity/electricity-domestic-consumption-data.html

Feng, Y. (1997). Leonardo R. Arriola,2009). Democracy, Political Stability and Economic Growth. *British Journal of Political Science, 27*(03), 391–418. https://www.cambridge.org/core/journals/british-journal-of-political-science/article/abs/democracy-political-stability-and-economic-growth/1630FBD0E7690CAF595EE9C612E405AE. doi:10.1017/S0007123497000197

Griffiths, S. (2019). Energy diplomacy in a time of energy transition. *Energy Strategy Reviews, 26*, 100-386. https://www.sciencedirect.com/science/article/pii/S2211467X19300793

Griffiths, S., & Sovacool, B. K. (2020). Rethinking the future low-carbon city: Carbon neutrality, green design, and sustainability tensions in the making of Masdar City. *Energy Research & Social Science, 62*, 101–368. https://www.sciencedirect.com/science/article/pii/S2214629619308904. doi:10.1016/j.erss.2019.101368

Hassan Jamil Al Farra, B. A.-H. (2012). The potential role of nuclear energy in mitigating CO2 emissions in the United Arab Emirates. *Energy Policy*, 272–285. http://www.sciencedirect.com

Jamil, M., Ahmad, F., & Jeon, Y. (2016). Renewable energy technologies adopted by the UAE: Prospects and challenges – A comprehensive overview. *Renewable & Sustainable Energy Reviews, 55*, 1181–1194. https://www.sciencedirect.com/science/article/abs/pii/S1364032115006000. doi:10.1016/j.rser.2015.05.087

Jeong, H. W. (2020). Between Economic Diversification and Nation-Branding: The UAE's Pivot to Asia and Innovation Strategies in the Post-Zayed Era. *Journal of Global South Studies*, 181-208. doi:10.1353/gss.2020.0025

Jia, X., Klemeš, J. J., Varbanov, P. S., & Alwi, S. R. (2019). Analyzing the Energy Consumption, GHG Emission,and Cost of Seawater Desalination in China. *Energies*. doi:10.3390/en12030463

Kazim, A. (2010). Strategy for a sustainable development in the UAE through hydrogen energy. *Renewable Energy*, *35*(10), 2257–2269. https://www.sciencedirect.com/science/article/abs/pii/S0960148110001308. doi:10.1016/j.renene.2010.03.013

Kelly, C. (2021). Leveraging renewable energy technologies for climate change mitigation and adaptation in the Middle East:The role of public-private partnerships. In C. Kelly (Ed.), *The Climate Change Policy and Law in the Middle East and Noth Africa Region*. Roudledge.

Langbein, L., & Knack, S. (2010). The Worldwide Governance Indicators: Six, One, or None. *The Journal of Development Studies*, *46*(02), 350–370. https://www.tandfonline.com/doi/abs/10.1080/00220380902952399?role=button&needAccess=true&journalCode=fjds20. doi:10.1080/00220380902952399

Lockwood, M., Kuzemko, C., Mitchell, C., & Hoggett, R. (2016). Historical institutionalism and the politics of sustainable energy transitions: A research agenda. *Environment and Planning C: Government and Policy*.

Lowndes, V., & Roberts, M. (2013). *Why Institutions Matter: The new institutionalism in political science*. Palgrave Macmillan. doi:10.1007/978-1-137-32913-4

Lucas, H., Ferroukhi, R., & Hawila, D. (2013). Renewable Energy Auctions in Developing. ⟨https://www.irena.org/DocumentDownloads/Publications/IRENA_Renewable_energy_auctions_in_developing_countries.pdf

Mengi-Dinçer, H., Ediger, V., & Yesevi, Ç. (2021). Evaluating the International Renewable Energy Agency through the lens of social constructivism. *Renewable & Sustainable Energy Reviews*, *152*, 111–705. https://www.sciencedirect.com/science/article/abs/pii/S1364032121009795. doi:10.1016/j.rser.2021.111705

Mezher, T., Dawelbait, G., & Abbas, Z. (2012). Renewable energy policy options for Abu Dhabi: Drivers and barriers. *Energy Policy*, *42*, 315–328. https://www.sciencedirect.com/science/article/abs/pii/S0301421511009876. doi:10.1016/j.enpol.2011.11.089

Mezher, T., Dawelbait, G., & Abbas, Z. (2012). Renewable energy policy options for Abu Dhabi: Drivers and barriers. *Energy Policy*, *42*, 315–328. https://www.sciencedirect.com/science/article/abs/pii/S0301421511009876. doi:10.1016/j.enpol.2011.11.089

Mosteanu, N. R. (2019). Intelligent foreign direct investments to boost economic development – UAE case study. *Conference proceedings of the Academy of Business and Retail Management (ABRM). 10*, (pp. 1-9). The Business and Management Review.

Murooshid, H. (2018). The Adoption of Renewable Energy Policies in a Rentier State: A Case Study of the United Arab Emirates. *Arab World Geographer*, *21*(1), 43–57. doi:10.5555/1480-6800.21.1.43

Naqbi, S. A., Tsai, I., & Mezher, T. (2019). Market design for successful implementation of UAE 2050 energy strategy. *Renewable and Sustainable Energy Reviews*. Elsevier. https://sci-hub.se/10.1016/j.rser.2019.109429

Nathaniel, S., Adeleye, N., & Adedoyin, F. F. (2021). Natural resource abundance, renewable energy, and ecological footprint linkage in MENA countries. *Estudios de Economía Aplicada*, *39*(02). doi:10.25115/eea.v39i2.3927

OECD. (2013). *Expanding access to clean energy for green growth and development*. OECD. https://www.oecd.org/daf/inv/investment-policy/CleanEnergyInfrastructure.pdf

Olawuyi, D. S. (2021). *Climate Change Law and Policy in the Middle East and North Africa Region*. Routledge. doi:10.4324/9781003044109

Phillips, P., & Hansen, B. (1990). Statistical Inference in Instrumental Variables Regression with I(1) Processes. *The Review of Economic Studies*, *57*(1), 99–125. doi:10.2307/2297545

Poudineh, R., Sen, A., & Fattouh, B. (2018). Advancing renewable energy in resource-rich economies of the MENA. *Renewable Energy*, *123*, 135–149. https://www.sciencedirect.com/science/article/abs/pii/S0960148118301587. doi:10.1016/j.renene.2018.02.015

SalemS. B.JagadeesanP. (2022;Stewart M. Godwin,2017). Food supply chain in pandemic, geopolitical, and climate change era - efforts of United Arab Emirates (UAE). AgriRxiv. https://www.cabidigitallibrary.org/doi/abs/10.31220/agriRxiv.2022.00142

Salimi, M., Husseinpour, M., & Borhani, T. N. (2022). Analysis of Solar Energy Development Strategies for a Successful Energy Transition in the UAE. *Processes*. https://www.mdpi.com/2227-9717/10/7/1338

Samour, A., Shahzad, U., & Mentel, G. (2022). Moving toward sustainable development: Assessing the impacts of taxation and banking development on renewable energy in the UAE. *Renewable Energy*, *200*, 706–713. doi:10.1016/j.renene.2022.10.020

Sankaran, V., & Chopra, A. (2020; Petch, Neil,2016, October 12). Creating Global Sustainable Smart Cities (A Case Study of Masdar City). *First International Conference on Advances in Physical Sciences. 1706*. IOP Publishing Ltd. Entrepreneur Middle East. https://iopscience.iop.org/article/10.1088/1742-6596/1706/1/012141/meta

Savvanidou, E., Zervas, E., & Tsagarakis, K. P. (2010). Public acceptance of biofuels. *Energy Policy*, *38*(07), 3482–3488. https://www.sciencedirect.com/science/article/abs/pii/S0301421510001023. doi:10.1016/j.enpol.2010.02.021

Sisodia, G. S., Awad, E., Alkhoja, H., & Sergi, B. S. (2020). Strategic business risk evaluation for sustainable energy investment and stakeholder engagement: A proposal for energy policy development in the Middle East through Khalifa funding and land subsidies. *Business Strategy and Environment*. https://onlinelibrary.wiley.com/doi/abs/10.1002/bse.2543

Sovacool, B. (2016). *The History and Politics of Energy Transitions: Comparing Contested Views and Finding Common Ground*. Oxford University Press. doi:10.35188/UNU-WIDER/2016/124-6

Staff Writer. (2022). UAE strengthens ties with South Kora across energy value chains. *Arabian Business*. https://www.arabianbusiness.com/industries/energy/uae-strengthens-ties-with-south-korea-across-energy-value-chains

Steinmo, S. K, T., & F, L. (1992). Historical institutionalism in comparative politics. Cambridge: Cambridge University Press.

The National. (2023). Shikh Mohammed approces master plan for palm jebel ali. *The National*. https://www.thenationalnews.com/uae/2023/05/31/sheikh-mohammed-approves-master-plan-for-palm-jebel-ali/

Toke, D. (2010). Wind Power in UK and Denmark: Can Rational Choice Help Explain Different Outcomes? *Environmental Politics*, *11*(04), 83–100. doi:10.1080/714000647

UAE Ministry of Climate Change and Environment. (2023). *About*. UAE Ministry of Climate Change and Environment. https://www.moccae.gov.ae/en/about-ministry/about-the-ministry.aspx

United Arab Emirates Embassy. (2023). *Climate and Energy*. United Arab Emirates Embassy Wadhington DC: https://www.uae-embassy.org/discover-uae/climate-and-energy/uae-energy-diversification

Yakubu, I. N., & Musah, A. (2022). The Nexus between financial Inclusion and bank profitability: a dynamic panel approach. *Journal of Sustainable Finance and Investment*. doi:10.1080/20430795.2022.2105792

Yuliani, D. (2017). *Is Feed-In-Tariff Policy Efffective for Increasing Deployment of Renewable Energy in Indonesia*. Oxford University Press.

Chapter 2
Emissions Trading and Climate Resilience in the Caribbean:
Building Bridges Towards a Low-Carbon Future

Don Charles
University of the West Indies, Trinidad and Tobago

ABSTRACT

The Caribbean region is particularly vulnerable to the impacts of climate change. Climate change pose a threat to the lives and livelihoods of the people living in the region. To mitigate these impacts, the Caribbean has joined with the international community, and pledged to implement their Nationally Determined Contributions (NDCs) to the Paris Agreement. The cost of implementing the NDCs measures in the Caribbean is high, and the region have not been receiving the required financial support. To address this limitation, a market-based mechanism such as an Emissions Trading System (ETS) could be implemented. This would create a financial incentive for emitters to reduce their GHG emissions, which in turn would help achieve the emissions reduction targets of the NDCs. An ETS is a policy tool that allows companies to trade emission allowances, which are permits that represent the right to emit a certain amount of GHGs. This study explores the mechanics of a potential regional ETS for the Caribbean.

1.0 INTRODUCTION

In recent years, the international community has recognized the urgent need to address climate change and has taken significant steps to reduce greenhouse gas (GHG) emissions and mitigate the impacts of climate change. The Paris Agreement, which was adopted in 2015, aims to limit global warming to well below 2°C above pre-industrial levels and to pursue efforts to limit the temperature increase to 1.5°C (Rogelj et al., 2016). The agreement also includes provisions for countries to report on their GHG emissions and to develop and implement national climate action plans, referred to as Nationally Determined Contributions (NDCs) (Hsu et al., 2020).

DOI: 10.4018/978-1-6684-9272-7.ch002

The Caribbean region is particularly vulnerable to the impacts of climate change, including more frequent and severe hurricanes, flooding, and sea-level rise. The region is home to over 40 million people, many of whom live in low-lying areas that are vulnerable to climate change impacts (Lewsey et al., 2004; Patil et al., 2016).

Caribbean countries face significant challenges in financing their climate change mitigation and adaptation efforts, as they have limited financial resources and a high debt burden. The cost of implementing climate action measures is also high, and the necessary investments often require significant external financing. Mohan (2022) notes that the financing gap in the Caribbean region is significant, and it is projected to increase in the coming years. However, the region currently only receives a fraction of this amount in international climate finance. To address this gap, Caribbean countries must pursue more innovative and diversified options for climate finance.

One of the key financing mechanisms of the Paris Agreement is the use of market-based approaches, such as an emissions trading scheme (ETS), to incentivize the reduction of GHG emissions (Bayer & Aklin, 2020). This is achieved by the state setting a limit on the amount of emissions that specific emitting stakeholders can produce and allowing the trading of emissions allowances to facilitate compliance. By setting a limit on emissions, the ETS creates a financial incentive for emitters to reduce their GHG emissions.

However, the implementation of a potential ETS in the Caribbean requires careful consideration of several factors. These include the emissions of different stakeholders in countries and the profitability and competitiveness of sectors. These are significant issues as several emitting stakeholders compete in international trade, and earners of foreign exchange for countries. Therefore, any ETS implementation must be developed through a participatory process involving all stakeholders and be tailored to the specific circumstances of the Caribbean region.

The objective of this study is to examine the mechanics of a regional ETS for the Caribbean.

The rest of this study is structured as follows. Section 2 explores some ETS in other countries. Section 3 examines the mechanics of a potential ETS for the Caribbean. Section 4 assesses the challenges in implementing a regional ETS in the Caribbean. Section 5 compares an alternative mechanism to reduce GHG emissions. Section 6 discusses the social and economic impact of the ETS. Section 7 concludes this study. Section 8 provides additional practical considerations.

2.0 ETS IN OTHER COUNTRIES

An ETS is a policy tool used to reduce GHG emissions by putting a price on them. It works by the authorities setting a limit on the total amount of emissions that can be produced by participating companies, then allowing these entities to buy and sell permits or allowances to emit a certain amount of GHGs (Ellerman et al., 2010).

2.1 European Union ETS

In 2005, the European Union (EU) launched the first international ETS, known as the EU ETS (Skjærseth & Wettestad, 2010). It was launched to help facilitate the achievement of the EU's Kyoto target of a 20% reduction of GHG emissions by 2020 relative to 1990 levels. The EU ETS works by capping the total amount of GHG emissions that can be produced by regulated entities.[1] The regulated entities include over 11,000 industrial facilities and power plants across the EU, which are responsible for around 40% of the region's total GHG emissions. These entities are allocated a certain number of emissions allowances, which represent the right to emit a certain amount of GHG, usually measured in metric tons of carbon dioxide equivalents (CO_2e).[2] Regulated entities that emit more GHGs than their allowances can either reduce their emissions or purchase additional allowances on the market. Similarly, entities that emit less than their allowances can sell their unused allowances on the market. This creates a market for GHG emissions allowances, where the price is determined by supply and demand (Ellerman et al., 2016).

The EU ETS has both a primary market and a secondary market. In the primary market, the EU issues allowances to covered entities through auctions or free allocation. Under the auctioning process, the EU sells a limited number of allowances to covered entities through bidding. The revenue generated from the auctioning process is used to fund climate-related projects in the EU. On the other hand, the free allocation process involved the distribution of the allowances with a fee. It is allocated to regulated entities based on their historical emissions, a process known as grandfathering (Stenqvist & Åhman, 2016).

In the secondary market, regulated entities can trade allowances with each other. This market operates similarly to the stock market, where the market demand and supply determine the price of the asset traded on the exchange. The EU ETS secondary market is highly liquid, with a high volume of transactions taking place daily. The price of the emissions allowances is marked-to market-daily and can fluctuate. Subsequently, emissions allowances prices can be subjected to volatility, speculation, jumps, and other financial market dynamics.

The EU ETS was implemented in several phases. Phase I covered the 2005 to 2007 period. It was a pilot that allowed for the establishment of a market for emissions allowances. There was also some success as it allowed for a reduction of approximately 200 million tons of CO_2 in the EU by 2006. Unfortunately, too many EU Emissions Allowances (EUAs) were available in the market, subsequently sabotaging the carbon credits' prices (Engels, 2009).

Phase II covered the 2008 to 2012 period. It involved the EU cutting the EUA supply by 6.5% relative to 2005. This phase also saw the introduction of auctions, and up to 10% of the initial public offerings of EUAs were allocated through auctions. The EU also increased the penalty for non-compliance to €100 per ton of CO_2e. Although the EU sought to trigger a rebound in prices when it cut the EUA supply, it undermined its efforts as it allowed regulated entities to offset their emissions with Certified Emission Reductions (CERs)[3] and Emission Reduction Units (ERUs)[4]. These alternate forms of carbon credits effectively increase the supply of carbon credits on the market. The deflationary pressure on the EUAs was also compounded by the weak macroeconomic demand in the 2008/2009 global economic recession (Bayer & Aklin, 2020).

Phase III covered the 2013 to 2020 period. The EU sought to correct the oversupply problem and increase the EUA's market prices. This was achieved through the introduction of the market stability reserve (MSR) in 2015, which removed some of the EUAs from the market. This was complemented by the EU auctioning up to 40% of the new EUAs on the primary market (Wildgrube, 2022).

Phase IV covers the 2021 to 2028 period. The EU intends to decrease the emissions cap to a target of 43% below the 2005 level by 2030. This will require a significant increase in the price of carbon credits to incentivize companies to reduce their emissions (Wildgrube, 2022).

The EU ETS has faced criticism and challenges over the years. One of the main criticisms is that the allocation of free EUAs to certain industries has resulted in windfall profits for some companies, as they have been able to sell their excess credits for a profit. There have also been concerns about the lack of enforcement and monitoring, which has led to instances of fraud and market manipulation.

Despite these challenges, the EU ETS remains one of the most established and significant carbon markets in the world. It has served as a model for other countries and regions looking to implement their own carbon pricing mechanisms.

2.2 ETS in China

In October 2011, the National Development and Reform Commission (NDRC) issued the Notice on the Implementation of Carbon Emission Trading Pilots, which approved the pilot projects of ETS in seven regions including Beijing, Shanghai, Tianjin, Chongqing, Hubei, Guangdong, and Shenzhen (Zhang et al. 2019a). Later in 2016, the eighth ETS was piloted in the Fujian province (Jiang et al. 2022). These pilots aimed to test the feasibility and effectiveness of carbon trading in different regions and industries and provide a basis for the future development of the national ETS (Zhang et al., 2019b).

The pilot projects aimed to integrate several companies collectively producing approximately 3000 key emission units. The schemes' ultimate goal was to help reduce China's GHG emissions and meet the country's mid-term quantitative GHG mitigation targets for 2020 and 2030, as announced at the Copenhagen and Paris climate conferences (Zhang et al., 2019b).

The main elements of pilot ETS include the emissions cap, the scope, the emissions allocations, the monitoring reporting and verification (MRV) system, and compliance.

2.3 ETS in the United States

The United States (US) has also explored the option of ETS to help facilitate the reduction of its GHG emissions. In fact, in 2005 it introduced a program called the Regional Greenhouse Gas Initiative (RGGI).[5] The RGGI involved cooperative effort among ten states namely, Connecticut, Delaware, Maine, Maryland, Massachusetts, New Hampshire, New Jersey, New York, Rhode Island, and Vermont (Wang et al., 2023).

The program is an ETS that applies to power plants with a capacity of 25 MW or greater. The program sets a cap on the emissions of power plants in the participating states. This covers 19% of all GHG emissions in the RGGI states. The RGGI program is set up in three-year compliance periods. Therefore, at the end of each period, covered entities must submit one allowance for each ton of CO_2 emitted. When the RGGI was operationalized in 2009, the emissions cap exceeded the actual emissions. There was a review of the program's effectiveness in 2012. Subsequently, the excess supply was eventually addressed by decreasing the cap by 45% to match emissions (CRS, 2020). Additionally, over the 2015 to 2022 period, the cap was decreased by 2.5% per annum. For 2022, the RGGI cap for the participating states was 156,828,784 CO_2 allowances (RGGI, 2023).

Under the RGGI, emissions allowances are administered through a regional auction platform. The covered entities are required to submit bids for the allowances. The price of allowances in the primary market is determined by the highest accepted bid. The revenue generated from such proceeds is used to fund green projects in the respective states. The emissions allowances in the RGGI are linked through allowance reciprocity. This allows an allowance issued by any participating state to be recognized by all participating states. Subsequently, the RGGI is a regional ETS among the participating states (C2ES, 2019).

2.4 ETS in Brazil

On May 19, 2022, the Brazilian Federal Government issued Decree No. 11,075/2022, introducing the National Greenhouse Gas Emissions Reduction System ("Sinare"). This system's primary purpose is to serve as a central repository for recording greenhouse gas (GHG) emissions, removals, reductions, and offsets, as well as facilitating the trade, transfers, and transactions of certified emission reduction credits. While Sinare is not an ETS itself, it functions as a registry system for carbon credits' recording and trading, representing a significant step towards operationalizing the carbon market in Brazil (Bezerra et al., 2022).

The Sinare registry will enable various sectors, including electric energy, urban public and cargo transport, manufacturing, and agriculture, to record their carbon footprints and participate in the voluntary carbon market. This development positions Brazil to become a major player in the carbon market, especially given its potential for surplus Emissions Reductions (ERs) through participation in the Amazon Jurisdictional Reducing Emissions from Deforestation and Forest Degradation (J-REDD+) programs (Riva et al., 2022).

The J-REDD+ program falls under Article 5 of the Paris Agreement and aims to reduce emissions from deforestation and forest degradation in developing countries. By preserving its vast tropical forests, with the Amazon region covering approximately 60% of the country's territory, Brazil has the opportunity to generate significant carbon credits that can be traded in the voluntary carbon market (Riva et al., 2022).

Moreover, Brazil's participation in the Article 6 mechanism under the Paris Agreement, which fosters cooperation between countries striving to achieve their NDCs, could further benefit the nation. The success of Brazil's efforts to reduce emissions from Amazon forest loss and degradation will be crucial in leveraging the revenue potential of the carbon market for the country.

2.5 ETS in Chile

Chile passed its Climate Change Framework Law on 13 June 2022. This law establishes a comprehensive framework encompassing various policies, including sector-specific mitigation and adaptation plans, intending to reduce the country's greenhouse gas emissions and enhance its resilience to climate change impacts (ICAP, 2022).

Article 14 of the law outlines the Ministry of Environment's responsibilities in specifying greenhouse gas emission limits for various sources. These limits will be based on a system of emission standards categorized by technology, sector, or activity. Additionally, there is a potential for creating an emission trading market, with aggregate emission limits or caps, allowing regulated entities to trade emissions allowances among themselves and potentially setting the stage for a future Emissions Trading System (ETS) (ICAP, 2022).

Article 15 introduces the framework for tradable emissions standards. This is done by allowing the entities that outperform their emission standards can have their surplus emission reductions certified. These certified reductions can then be sold to other regulated entities that may be struggling to meet their respective emission standards. This system encourages a cooperative approach among entities, with high-performing entities incentivized to support others in their emission reduction efforts while creating a dynamic market for emission certificates (ICAP, 2022).

Article 37 of the law serves as a foundation for the development of market, fiscal, and financial-based instruments to achieve Chile's NDCs. While specific details of these instruments are yet to be defined, this provision suggests a potential future tradable performance standard system. This system would likely incorporate innovative market-based mechanisms to support the attainment of Chile's climate objectives (ICAP, 2022).

2.6 ETS in Mexico

Mexico's pilot ETS was launched in January 2020, as a climate change policy mitigation instrument aimed at facilitating the country's NDCs (ICAP, 2023). The pilot ETS covers direct carbon dioxide emissions from fixed sources in the energy and industry sectors emitting at least 100,000 tCO_2 per year, which accounts for approximately 40% of Mexico's GHG emissions (ICAP, 2023).

During the pilot phase (2020-2022), companies participating in the ETS received free allowances based on their historical emissions, while new entrants received allowances based on their verified emissions when they first crossed the 100,000 tCO2 threshold. The secondary trading of emissions allowances in the pilot ETS occurs through negotiations between participants on an over-the-counter market. The sectors covered by the scheme include heavy industry and power (ICAP, 2023).

The ETS incorporates three reserves to supplement the cap: the auction's reserve (equivalent to 5% of the cap), intended for regular auctions that have not yet occurred; the new entrants' reserve (equivalent to 10% of the cap), allocated for new entrants and increases in production among existing regulated entities; and the general reserve (equivalent to 5% of the cap), designated for ex-post adjustment allocation for entities with higher emissions relative to their baselines. These reserves serve as safeguards to mitigate potential economic impacts on regulated entities (ICAP, 2023).

Importantly, the pilot ETS in Mexico imposes no direct economic impact on regulated entities. Instead, entities that do not comply with their emissions targets during the pilot phase risk losing the ability to carry forward unused allowances into subsequent compliance periods within the Pilot. This restriction on banking unused allowances could limit entities' flexibility in meeting future emissions targets. For each allowance not delivered during the pilot phase, non-compliant entities will receive two fewer allowances in the initial allocation of the operational phase (ICAP, 2023).

Overall, Mexico's pilot ETS represents a proactive approach to addressing climate change by targeting a significant portion of the country's emissions and aligning with its NDC goals. By incentivizing emission reductions and providing allowances based on verified emissions, the ETS aims to improve emissions data quality, build capacity in emissions trading, and enhance the system's design for the operational phase beginning in 2023 (ICAP, 2023).

The next section explores the mechanics of an ETS for the Caribbean.

3.0 MECHANICS OF A POTENTIAL CARIBBEAN EMISSIONS TRADING SCHEME

The success of a regional ETS is dependent on several elements that work together to create an effective and efficient system for reducing emissions. Key factors that must be considered in a potential regional emissions trading scheme for the Caribbean include 1) the emissions cap, 2) sectors covered, 3) the emissions allocation, 4) compliance and penalty fees, 5) emissions trading, 6) currency for the emissions trading, 7) price controls and market stability reserve, 8) monitoring and reporting.

3.1 Emissions Cap

The emissions cap is the cornerstone of the regional ETS. It sets a limit on the total amount of greenhouse gas emissions that are allowed within the region. The cap should be based on scientific assessments of what is necessary for various stakeholders to achieve emissions reduction targets. Therefore, an assessment of the GHG emissions of the stakeholders should be performed to determine what is feasible rather than making ad hoc targets. A successful ETS must set a cap that is ambitious enough to achieve emissions reduction targets, but not so strict that it creates an economic burden on entities subject to the scheme.

3.2 Sectors Covered

Ideally, the ETS should cover all sectors that emit GHGs. However, several practical factors should be considered such as the emissions intensity of each sector, the technical feasibility of adopting low-carbon alternatives, as well as the cost of implementing GHG emission reduction initiatives.

Furthermore, for the Caribbean region, the appropriate sectors for inclusion in the ETS should align with the sectors identified in the countries' NDCs. This approach ensures that the ETS effectively targets sectors in which the countries have deemed the most urgent for climate change mitigation action.

3.2.1 Energy Generation

Many CARICOM Member States have identified the electricity sector as a sector for GHG emission reduction action in their NDCs (Mohan, 2022).

GHG emissions in the electricity sector can be reduced by adopting energy-efficient technologies, or by fuel switching to cleaner fuels. In the case of the first option, upgrading power plants from a single cycle to a combined cycle can result in reduced GHG emissions.[6] In the second option, plant upgrading to fuel switch from diesel-based electricity generation to natural gas-based electricity generation can result in significantly less GHG emissions. However, both technology options carry huge sunk costs which goes into the millions. The exact cost will be determined by the plant design, capacity, as well as local cost factors.

3.2.2 Transport

Transport is another sector that contributes significantly to GHG emissions in the Caribbean region. Cars, buses, and trucks fueled by diesel and gasoline are the main source of emissions from this sector. While governments can announce a cap for the transportation sector, in practice it would be difficult to implement an emissions cap on individual persons. The most practical option would be to implement a cap on public bus companies.

However, Huber et al. (2019) notes, state-owned organizations in the Caribbean are often inefficient, loss-making, and dependent on government subsidies to survive. Therefore, care must be taken not to increase the burden on an essential but fragile sector.

In this regard, the government can include the transportation sector in the ETS by the following measures.

- Step 1 – set a cap for the public transportation company based on historical emissions.

- Step 2 – create a plan for reducing emissions by either fuel switching to CNG, or using hybrid (electric) buses.
- Step 3 – import the required hybrid buses for the fleet.
- Step 4 – allocate emissions allowances to the public transportation company to cover their emissions.
- Step 5 – allow the public transportation company to trade any surplus emissions allowances.
- Step 6 – monitor compliance and monitor the emissions of the public transportation company.
- Step 7 – gradually reduce the cap of the transportation company to allow the achievement of the NDC target for the transportation sector over time
- Step 8 – implement soft penalties for the transportation sector if there is non-compliance. This is an important consideration since the government will be the owner of the public transportation company, and indirectly would be penalizing itself for non-compliance.

Notably, the public transportation company should be encouraged to meet its targets, as the surplus emissions allowances can be sold, and the additional revenue can be used to help cover operational costs.

3.2.3 Heavy Industry

Heavy industrial manufacturing such as cement manufacturing, and petrochemical production are also significant sources of GHG emissions (Yoro & Daramola, 2020).

The techniques required to reduce the GHG emissions from the manufacturing of cement, petrochemicals, and other heavy industry products all carry a cost. Placing a cap on the emissions in the heavy industry sector would invariably mean that the companies i) adopt some expensive techniques into their manufacturing process, ii) purchase additional emissions allowances, or iii) pay fines for non-compliance.

Notably, the heavy industry sector is very important to a small economy such as Trinidad and Tobago (T&T) for export revenue, foreign exchange, tax revenue, and employment generation. The Government of the Republic of Trinidad and Tobago (GORTT) is likely to be reluctant to introduce any measure that would chase away foreign investment from this sector. Therefore, a balance needs to be found between promoting GHG reduction action and maintaining an attractive business and investment environment.

3.2.4 Agriculture, Forestry, and Other Land Use (AFOLU)

Trees absorb carbon dioxide from the atmosphere and store it in their biomass through the process of photosynthesis (Shukla et al., 2022). Therefore, reforestation can help reduce GHG emissions. Assuming a typical steam cracker petrochemical plant produces 1 metric ton of CO_2 per metric ton of product, and a mature tree can absorb 48 pounds (or about 0.022 metric tons) of CO_2 per year, it would require about 45,455 mature trees to absorb the emissions produced by one metric ton of product annually. Assuming an average spacing of 3 meters between trees, it would require about 136,365 square meters or about 13.6 hectares (33.6 acres) of land to grow 45,455 mature trees.

However, this is a simplistic calculation, and the actual number of trees required to absorb the emissions would depend on various factors such as the species of trees planted, their age and growth rate, and the local environmental conditions such as temperature, precipitation, and soil quality. Additionally, the actual land area required to grow the trees could vary widely depending on various factors such as the topography of the land, the availability of water resources, and the soil quality.

Nevertheless, reforestation and the conservation of forested areas can assist with the reduction of GHG emissions. For this reason, the the agriculture, forestry, and other land use (AFOLU) sector should also be considered as part of a potential Caribbean regional ETS.

Notably, the forestry sector is different from the power, heavy industry, and transportation sectors as it is a carbon sink. In fact, the inclusion of the AFOLU can be done to help countries and the region achieve their GHG emission reduction targets.

By including the forestry sector, landowners and the government can earn revenue from the sale of their surplus emissions allowances. This incentivizes forestry conservation activities and discourages deforestation.

3.3 Emissions Allocation

In the implementation of an ETS, emissions allowances are allocated to covered entities. These allowances can be distributed for free or sold through auctions. The emissions are allocated through an initial public offering on the primary market.[7] The allocation of allowances is a critical element of the ETS, since if some covered entities receive more allowances than they need, then they can easily cover all of their emissions without any need for mitigation action. Furthermore, they can sell their excess emissions allowances and earn a profit. Alternatively, if some covered entities receive significantly less allowance than they need, this will place them under a burden to reduce their emissions. If they cannot reduce their emissions they will face two options, either purchase extra emissions allocations or pay non-compliance penalty fees. This can increase the companies' cost, which is a crucial factor to determine the success of a business, especially those involved in international trade.

3.4 Compliance and Penalty Fees

Compliance is a crucial aspect of any ETS as it ensures that covered entities meet their emission reduction targets (Zhang et al., 2014). The compliance mechanism in an ETS typically involves the surrender of emissions allowances by covered entities to account for their emissions. If a covered entity emits more than its allocated allowances, it must purchase additional allowances or face penalties for non-compliance.

Penalties for non-compliance can take various forms, such as fines, deduction of allowances, or loss of access to government subsidies or loans. The severity of these penalties can vary depending on the objectives of the policy makers while designing the ETS.

3.5 Emissions Trading

Emissions trading is the process of buying and selling emissions allowances. Regulated entities that emit less GHG than their cap will have surplus emissions allowances. These emissions allowances can be sold to regulated entities that have produced more GHG emissions than their cap.

Emissions allowances are traded in two types of secondary markets: the over-the-counter (OTC) market and exchanges. The OTC market is decentralized, allowing direct negotiations between buyers and sellers with flexible and customized contracts. In contrast, exchanges are centralized markets with specific terms, conditions, and daily marking to market. Exchanges offer more transparency and liquidity, making them accessible to smaller market participants (Campos & Paz, 2014).

The secondary market for emissions allowances is subject to strict regulations to ensure that trading is fair, transparent, and efficient. In most cases, the relevant authorities will oversee the operation of the market and ensure that it operates following established rules and guidelines. These rules and guidelines will typically cover issues such as the eligibility of market participants, the types of transactions that can be conducted, the reporting and disclosure requirements, and the enforcement of penalties for non-compliance.

3.6 Price of the Emissions Allocations

The price of emissions allowances is determined by their demand and supply on the secondary market (Benz & Trück, 2009). When buyers are more eager to buy the emissions allowances than sellers are to sell them, this increases the bid price, which in turn increases the settlement price and the overall market price. Likewise, when there is weak demand and stronger supply, the ask price declines, pushing down the overall market price.

The price of emissions allowances is a crucial element of an ETS and is important for several reasons. First, it provides an economic incentive for covered entities to reduce their GHG emissions. If the price of the emissions allowances is too low, then the covered entities can easily take no steps to reduce their emissions. Rather, they would just purchase the emissions allowances while the GHG emissions rise. In contrast, if the price of the emissions allowances is too high, it increases the marginal cost of companies, thus affecting their profitability and competitiveness in international trade. Moreover, as the cost becomes very high, covered entities that are multinational corporations may shift their operations to countries with less stringent climate change regulations. This can result in the loss of foreign direct investment, which is highly undesirable for the Caribbean.

Given the importance of price, this study utilizes an econometric model to forecast the price of the emissions allowances. The EUAs are used as a proxy for this forecasting analysis as presently no price for emissions allowances exist in the Caribbean. An Artificial Neural Network (ANN) is used for forecasting. More specifically, a Non-Linear Autoregressive (NAR) model is used for the forecasting. Further details on the data and methodology are in the Appendix. However, the model performs relatively good and has high predictive accuracy.

The importance of a stable price for emissions allowances in an ETS cannot be overstated. Given such importance, it would be logical for the regulators at the ETS to include a market stability reserve.

The MSR works by automatically adjusting the supply of emissions allowances in the market based on changes in demand, which helps to prevent large fluctuations in the price of emissions allowances. The MSR is also designed to provide a safety valve for the ETS in the event of unforeseen events or shocks to the system.

3.7 Currency for the Emissions Trading

The currency used to facilitate trading on the regional emissions exchange can have a significant impact on the efficiency and effectiveness of the trading system. There are two possible options for the currency on an ETS. They are i) a common currency approach, and ii) a multiple currency approach.

A common currency approach involves using a single currency for all transactions on the exchange. This is advantageous as it simplifies the trading process by providing a standardized unit of exchange. It is possible to use multiple currencies on the ETS. When regulatedentities are located in different countries the emissions allowances will be quoted in different currencies. Therefore, every time a cross-border transaction occurs, a currency conversion must also occur. This exposes the covered entities to exchange rate risks as slides can occur if there is not instant settlement.

Notably, fluctuations in exchange rates can affect the profitability of trades, making it more difficult for participants to manage their risk exposure. Using a single currency can reduce these risks and provide a more stable trading environment.

While the Caribbean region presently does not have a single common currency for all countries, it can be noted that the Eastern Caribbean Central Bank recently piloted a digital currency called DCash in 2020 (IMF, 2022). It would be rational if a similar single common currency is used as the legal tender on the ETS.

3.8 Monitoring, Reporting, and Verification

A monitoring, reporting, and verification (MRV) system is a critical component of an ETS (Wang et al., 2016). It ensures that the emissions reduction targets set by the scheme are achieved and the emissions are accurately measured, reported, and verified. This will help the participating countries when they report to the UNFCCC at the Global Stocktake. By following these three steps, regulators can ensure that the ETS is effective in achieving its GHG emission reduction goals.

The first step in the MRV process is monitoring. Accurate monitoring of emissions is critical to the success of the ETS, as it provides a baseline against which emissions reductions can be measured. To achieve this, monitoring systems must be capable of measuring emissions in real-time or through indirect methods such as statistical sampling or estimations based on production or consumption data. The monitoring process can be done through direct measurements, such as continuous emissions monitoring systems (CEMS), or through indirect methods, such as statistical sampling.

The second step in the MRV process is reporting. After monitoring emissions, covered entities must report their emissions to the regulatory body overseeing the ETS. This reporting must be transparent, accurate, and timely to ensure the effectiveness of the ETS. To achieve this, reporting requirements and templates are usually specified in the ETS regulation, and it is the responsibility of the covered entities to comply with these requirements.

The third in the MRV process is verification. Verification involves checking the reported emissions data against the monitoring data to ensure accuracy and completeness. Verification is important because it provides an independent check on the reported data, thus increasing the confidence and reliability of the data. Third-party verification by independent verifiers is desirable as it provides assurance that emissions are being accurately reported.

It is worth noting that the MRV process is not a one-time event, but an ongoing process that needs to be repeated regularly to ensure that emissions are being accurately measured, reported, and verified over the entire ETS cycle.

The next section considers the challenges in implementing a potential ETS in the Caribbean.

4.0 CHALLENGES IN IMPLEMENTING A POTENTIAL ETS IN THE CARIBBEAN

Implementing an ETS in the Caribbean region comes with its fair share of challenges.

One key challenge is the availability and accuracy of emissions data, as many Caribbean countries lack comprehensive GHG inventories. Conducting GHG inventory audits before the ETS operational phase and conducting regular annual audits are crucial steps to ensure data accuracy and monitor the scheme's performance over time. Balancing ambitious emission reduction targets with economic growth poses another challenge. Caribbean countries must strike the right balance to ensure that environmental goals align with economic realities. The countries must not impose stringent requirements that will chase away the much-desired foreign investments, or make the existing business operators significantly less price competitive in international trade.

Due to the need to strike a balance between mitigation action and facilitating investment, one must consider what actions are required in various sectors to reduce GHG emissions. Common sectors identified for emission reduction action in the Caribbean's NDCs include electricity generation, transportation, heavy industry, agriculture, and waste management (UNFCCC, 2018); Charles, 2019).

The electricity generation sector, except in T&T, primarily relies on diesel combustion (Hosein, 2021). Diesel-based electricity production is inherently carbon-intensive, contributing to higher GHG emissions (EIA, 2022b). As previously mentioned, GHG emissions from the power sector can be reduced by several projects such as upgrading power stations to combine-cycle, installing fuel switching infrastructure. This results in a high sunk cost which will be a burden for some power producers/

Moreover, the cost of electricity generation in the Caribbean is high and averages around US$0.25 per kWh. In some countries, the average cost is higher than US$0.40 per kWh (World Bank, 2022). For cross-comparison, the average price of electricity generation in the United States ranges from US$0.07 per kWh for industrial customers to US$0.13 per kWh for residential customers (EIA, 2022a). Imposing a cap on the emissions of the electricity sector is likely to increase the cost of electricity generation for all independent power producers in the sector. This can be problematic as the electricity utilities in several Caribbean countries are state-owned, loss-making, and reliant on government subventions to continue operation (Huber et al., 2019).

In the transportation sector, several measures can be implemented to effectively reduce GHG emissions in the Caribbean. Endorsing fuel economy policies, such as setting fuel efficiency standards and promoting the use of more fuel-efficient vehicles, encouraging carpooling and adopting mass transit systems can lead to significant emissions reductions. These initiatives focus on changing behavior and promoting sustainable travel options, which can have positive impacts on emissions without requiring major infrastructure investments.

Fuel switching to compressed natural gas (CNG) is another potential strategy for emissions reduction in the transportation sector. However, this transition requires considerable investment in refueling station infrastructure and, in some cases, import infrastructure if natural gas is not readily available locally. Additionally, retrofitting existing vehicles to run on CNG can be costly, deterring some individual commuters from making the switch. In fact, the initial costs associated with infrastructure upgrades and vehicle retrofits may deter widespread implementation. As such, promoting the import and use of hybrid electric vehicles offers a more economically feasible option for reducing emissions in the transport sector.

The heavy industry sector in the Caribbean is diverse, with different countries having unique industrial profiles (Garone et al., 2020). However, one common heavy industry present in several Caribbean countries is the cement industry, with production ocurring in T&T, Barbados, Jamaica, and Guyana. The cement manufacturing process is inherently energy-intensive and emits substantial amounts of carbon dioxide.

Adopting energy-efficient technologies, optimizing production methods, and improving waste heat recovery can enhance the overall efficiency of cement manufacturing, leading to reduced energy consumption and lower emissions. However, it is crucial to acknowledge that the implementation of these emission reduction initiatives in the cement industry comes with high sunk costs.

As previously mentioned, deforestation also contributes significantly to GHG emissions in the Caribbean. To combat this issue, sustainable land-use practices and forest protection policies should be implemented. However, this would require action by forest NGOs, and national forestry divisions, both of which are often underfunded. Mobilizing sufficient donor funding would be crucial to support forestry conservation activities.

Inadequate waste management practices, such as open burning of municipal solid waste, contribute to GHG emissions in the Caribbean. To reduce GHG emissions from waste disposal, the implementation of integrated solid waste management (ISWM) is essential. ISWM involves a holistic approach that encompasses various stages of waste management, including waste generation, transfer, sorting, recycling, and treatment.

However, infrastructural developments required for ISWM can be costly, especially for the Caribbean countries that have limited financial resources. Additionally, implementing ISWM requires a shift in waste management practices and public behavior, which may encounter resistance from stakeholders and communities accustomed to traditional waste disposal methods.

Stakeholder engagement is a critical challenge in ETS implementation. Involving industries, policymakers, and civil society is crucial for success, but overcoming resistance or lack of awareness may prove challenging. Achieving sustained government support and political will over the long term is essential for creating a regional ETS in the Caribbean, as stable policy frameworks are necessary for effective emission reductions.

The next section considers an alternate strategy for the reduction of GHG emissions. This provides additional justification for the development of an ETS in the Caribbean.

5.0 COMPARATIVE ANALYSIS OF AN ALTERNATE STRATEGY

As an alternate strategy to an ETS, policy makers may consider a carbon tax. A carbon tax is a market-based policy instrument that aims to internalize the external costs associated with GHG emissions by imposing a financial penalty on companies based on the amount of carbon dioxide and other GHGs they emit. The tax provides a clear economic incentive for businesses to reduce their emissions, as higher emissions result in higher tax liabilities (Metcalf & Weisbach, 2009).

The essence of the carbon tax lies in its economic principle of "polluter pays" as companies are made responsible for their GHG emissions, which in turn has climate change effects. By forcing producers to internalize the negative cost of the externality from their GHG emissions, a carbon tax seeks to shift the cost burden of environmental damage back to the polluters themselves.

Introducing a carbon tax system presents manufacturers with a challenging dilemma. While the intention behind the carbon tax is to incentivize emission reductions, the costs associated with implementing such projects can be prohibitively high for some industries, especially in sectors like power generation and heavy industry. In these cases, some manufacturers may find themselves with limited options, as they may be in a situation where they cannot afford to incur sunk costs to implement GHG emission reduction projects.

For manufacturers unable to invest in emission reduction initiatives, paying the carbon tax becomes their only available choice. This can place them in a situation where they are forced to bear the additional cost of the tax without the ability to offset it.

Consequently, this may hinder their competitiveness in the international market, as the higher production costs resulting from the carbon tax may make their products less price-competitive compared to those produced in regions without such a tax.

The issue of international competitiveness is a significant concern, especially for export-oriented industries. If manufacturers attempt to pass on the increased costs to consumers through higher prices, it may result in reduced demand for their products, further impacting their market position. Additionally, businesses that are price-takers in global markets might struggle to recover the increased production costs imposed by the carbon tax, potentially leading to reduced profit margins which can challenge the business viability.

The Caribbean region heavily relies on foreign investment as a critical driver of economic growth and development. due to the region's relatively small economies and limited domestic markets, attracting and retaining foreign investments is vital for sustaining economic prosperity. Therefore, policymakers in the Caribbean are likely to be reluctant to introduce new taxes that can case away foreign investment.

For this reason, a carbon tax is not the best option to stimulate GHG emission reduction action in the Caribbean. The better approach would be the ETS as it allows the most efficient producers to reduce their emissions, then sell their surplus emissions allocations to the least efficient producers. Thus an ETS incentivizes GHG emission reduction action, encourages efficiency, and allows the most efficient producers to be rewarded for reducing their emissions.

The next section considers the potential social and economic impact of an ETS on the Caribbean.

6.0 SOCIAL AND ECONOMIC IMPACT OF AN ETS

While the primary goal of an ETS is to reduce GHG emissions and combat climate change, the way it is designed and implemented can influence various aspects of society and the economy.

One of the key social concerns with an ETS is its potential impact on employment. If the ETS is not properly designed and many regulated entities are unable to reduce their emissions, they may face penalties. If high fines are charged as penalties, this may significantly increase the cost for the business. The increase costs from the penalties can reduce the business' profitability, which may prompt them to retrench part of their labor force in an attempt to cut costs. Job losses can lead to a significant loss of income for affected workers and their families, making them more vulnerable to economic hardships and poverty. Secondly, governments are generally concerned about job losses, as it affects public perception and voter support. Therefore, and government will be reluctant to impose any measure that can result in unemployment.

Apart from the potential social impact on labor, an ETS economically impacts business. Due to the need to have a strong economy, commerce, and the earning of foreign exchange, policy makers need to ensure that an ETS does not negatively impact the competitiveness of local businesses. Policymakers need to be mindful that some competitors in international trade do not have similar carbon pricing mechanisms, and thus they should avoid putting their domestic industries at a significant disadvantage.

The next section concludes this study.

7.0 CONCLUSION

Climate change poses significant challenges for the Caribbean region. While the governments in the region have pledged to reduce their GHG emissions in their NDCs, the NDCs are conditional upon the receipt of technical and financial support from the international community. Thus, there is a need for a market-based mechanism to stimulate GHG emission reduction action in the Caribbean.

One such mechanism is an ETS. An ETS can be an appropriate mechanism to stimulate action in the Caribbean region to mitigate climate change. It can provide an economic incentive for companies to reduce their greenhouse gas emissions and encourage the development of clean energy solutions.

However, the implementation of an ETS in the Caribbean would require a comprehensive approach that considers the specific circumstances of the region.

The emissions cap is the most critical aspect of any ETS, as it determines the level of emissions reduction achieved. The emissions cap must be set at a level that is ambitious enough to drive down emissions while also being realistic and achievable for covered entities. It is essential to ensure that the cap takes into account the region's economic and social circumstances while seeking to achieve the GHG emission reduction goals.

The sectors included in the ETS should be from the countries NDCs. Sectors such as power generation, transportation, and heavy industry are likely to covered by the ETS. While forestry is a carbon sink sector, it should also be included as it presents an opportunity to address deforestation. Moreover, the ETS can present an avenue for the generation of revenue that can encourage forestry conservation.

The allocation of emissions allowances is also an important aspect of the ETS. It determines the initial distribution of allowances to covered entities, which in turn affects the costs of acquiring them on the primary market, and the supply that will be available on the secondary market.

Compliance is critical to the success of any ETS. A robust compliance and penalty framework must be established to ensure that covered entities comply with the ETS regulations. Penalties for non-compliance should be set at a level that is sufficient to deter covered entities from violating the ETS regulations, but also not too high that it becomes a significant financial burden.

Emissions trading is the core mechanism of an ETS. It enables regulated entities to buy and sell allowances with one another, providing a market-based incentive to reduce emissions. It is crucial to establish a fair and transparent market where covered entities can easily buy and sell allowances.

The MSR helps prevent significant price fluctuations caused by changes in supply and demand. It provides a buffer that stabilizes the market and ensures that the price of allowances remains within a reasonable range.

To ensure the integrity of the emissions trading scheme, robust monitoring, and reporting mechanisms must be established. This includes regular emissions reporting by regulated entities, independent verification of emissions data, and a system for tracking the ownership and transfer of emissions allowances.

The Caribbean is a small emitter of GHGs. However, the region's vulnerability to climate change highlights the need for regional cooperation to address climate change collectively. The implementation of an ETS in the Caribbean sends the market signal to provide flexibility and help covered entities find a cost-effective way to reduce GHGs in the region. This can be an important step towards achieving the Paris Agreement goals and contribute to the global effort to limit global warming to well below 2°C above pre-industrial levels and pursue efforts to limit it to 1.5°C.

The next section considers some practical issues in moving forward.

8.0 PRACTICAL CONSIDERATIONS

Implementing an ETS in the Caribbean region presents practical considerations that need to be carefully addressed. Firstly, the issue of technical support becomes crucial, as the region needs assistance to properly monitor its GHG emissions. Moreover, there is a need for technical assistance to help potentially regulated entities reduce their emissions and help the region achieve its NDC goals. To successfully implement an ETS, the international community must provide technical support to bridge this gap.

Secondly, ensuring strong stakeholder engagement and buy-in is essential. Governments, industries, and civil society must collaborate in the design and implementation of the ETS to build support and consensus. Raising awareness about the benefits of an ETS and its role in mitigating climate change can help address potential resistance and foster a cooperative approach. Engaging all stakeholders in decision-making processes will also help tailor the ETS to the unique circumstances and needs of the Caribbean region, enhancing its effectiveness and ensuring that it aligns with regional economic and social objectives.

Thirdly, capacity building and institutional strengthening are necessary to establish and sustain an effective ETS. Building local expertise, especially in monitoring, reporting, and verifying emissions data is crucial to ensure the integrity of the trading scheme and prevent potential loopholes or non-compliance. Governments need to invest in the necessary infrastructure and human resources to establish robust monitoring and enforcement mechanisms. Additionally, regional cooperation and knowledge sharing can play a significant role in enhancing technical capabilities and creating a supportive environment for ETS implementation across Caribbean nations.

REFERENCES

C2ES (Center for Climate and Energy Solutions). (2019). *Regional Greenhouse Gas Initiative*. C2ES. https://www.c2es.org/content/regional-greenhouse-gas-initiative-rggi/

Al-Saati, N. H., Omran, I. I., Salman, A. A., Al-Saati, Z., & Hashim, K. S. (2021). Statistical Modeling of Monthly Streamflow Using Time Series and Artificial Neural Network Models: Hindiya Barrage as A Case Study. *Water Practice & Technology*, *16*(2), 681–691. doi:10.2166/wpt.2021.012

Babu, M. N., Pavan, P., Mohan, K. R., Rao, G. R., Rao, K. S., & Tejaswi, G. (2023). Energy Management for Renewable Hybrid System Based On Artificial Neural Networks (ANN). *International Journal for Research in Applied Science and Engineering Technology*, *2*(4), 1–14. doi:10.22214/ijraset.2021.33423

Bayer, P., & Aklin, M. (2020). The European Union Emissions Trading System Reduced CO2 Emissions Despite Low Prices. *Proceedings of the National Academy of Sciences of the United States of America*, *117*(16), 8804–8812. doi:10.1073/pnas.1918128117 PMID:32253304

Benz, E., & Trück, S. (2009). Modeling the Price Dynamics of CO2 Emissions Allowances. *Energy Economics*, *31*(1), 4–15. doi:10.1016/j.eneco.2008.07.003

Bezerra, L. G., Gomes, G., & Rodrigues, V. (2022). *Brazil's Federal Government Publishes Decree Establishing National Greenhouse Gas Emissions Reduction System.* Mayer Brown. https://www.mayerbrown.com/en/perspectives-events/publications/2022/05/brazils-federal-government-publishes-decree-establishing-national-greenhouse-gas-emissions-reduction-system

Campos, R. C., & Paz, M. Q. (2014). Secondary Markets. In *Research Handbook on Securities Regulation in the United States* (pp. 185–200). Edward Elgar Publishing. doi:10.4337/9781782540076.00011

CRS. (2020). *The Regional Greenhouse Gas Initiative: Background, Impacts, and Selected Issues.* Every CRS Report. https://www.everycrsreport.com/reports/R41836.html

EIA (Energy Information Administration). (2022a, April 20). *Electricity Explained: Factors Affecting Electricity Prices.* EIA. https://www.eia.gov/energyexplained/electricity/prices-and-factors-affecting-prices.php

EIA (Energy Information Administration). (2022b). *Carbon Dioxide Emissions Coefficients.* EIA.https://www.eia.gov/environment/emissions/co2_vol_mass.php

Ellerman, A. D., Convery, F. J., & De Perthuis, C. (2010). *Pricing Carbon: The European Union Emissions Trading Scheme.* Cambridge University Press.

Ellerman, A. D., Marcantonini, C., & Zaklan, A. (2016). The European Union Emissions Trading System: Ten Years and Counting. Review of Environmental Economics and Policy. *Review of Environmental Economics and Policy, 10*(1), 89–107. doi:10.1093/reep/rev014

Engels, A. (2009). The European Emissions Trading Scheme: An Exploratory Study of How Companies Learn to Account for Carbon. *Accounting, Organizations and Society, 34*(3-4), 488–498. doi:10.1016/j.aos.2008.08.005

Garone, L. F., Villalba, P. A. L., Maffioli, A., & Ruzzier, C. A. (2020). Firm-level Productivity in Latin America and the Caribbean. *Research in Economics, 74*(2), 186–192. doi:10.1016/j.rie.2020.04.004

Greene, W. H. (2019). *Econometric Analysis.* Pearson.

Hosein, R. (2021). History of Oil Refining in T&T. In *Oil and Gas in Trinidad and Tobago: Managing the Resource Curse in a Small Petroleum-Exporting Economy* (pp. 49–730). Springer Link. doi:10.1007/978-3-030-77669-5_3

Hsu, A., Brandt, J., Widerberg, O., Chan, S., & Weinfurter, A. (2020). Exploring Links Between National Climate Strategies and Non-State and Subnational Climate Action in Nationally Determined Contributions (NDCs). *Climate Policy, 20*(4), 443–457. doi:10.1080/14693062.2019.1624252

Huber, J., Jara, M., Kim, H., Ter-Minassian, T., & Wagner, R. (2019). *Fixing State-Owned Enterprises: New Policy Solutions to Old Problems.* Inter-American Development Bank.

ICAP (International Carbon Action Partnership). (2022). *Chile publishes Climate Change Framework Law, Paving The Way for Market-Based Policy.* ICAP. https://icapcarbonaction.com/en/news/chile-publishes-climate-change-framework-law-paving-way-market-based-policy

ICAP (International Carbon Action Partnership). (2023). Mexico ETS Description. ICAP. https://icap-carbonaction.com/en/ets/mexico

IMF (International Monetary Fund). (2022). *2022 Article IV Consultation with Member Countries On Common Policies of the Eastern Caribbean Currency Union*. IMF. https://www.imf.org/-/media/Files/Publications/CR/2022/English/1ECCEA2022001.ashx

Jiang, T., Song, J., & Yu, Y. (2022). The Influencing Factors of Carbon Trading Companies Applying Blockchain Technology: Evidence from Eight Carbon Trading Pilots in China. *Environmental Science and Pollution Research International*, *29*(19), 1–13. doi:10.100711356-021-18425-y PMID:34988820

Lewsey, C., Cid, G., & Kruse, E. (2004). Assessing Climate Change Impacts On Coastal Infrastructure in the Eastern Caribbean. *Marine Policy*, *28*(5), 393–409. doi:10.1016/j.marpol.2003.10.016

Metcalf, G. E., & Weisbach, D. (2009). The Design of a Carbon Tax. *The Harvard Environmental Law Review*, *33*, 499.

Mohan, P. S. (2022). Implementing Nationally Determined Contributions Under the Paris Agreement: An Assessment of Climate Finance in Caribbean Small Island Developing States. *Climate Policy*, *22*(9-10), 1281–1289. doi:10.1080/14693062.2022.2101978

Patil, P. G., Virdin, J., Diez, S. M., Roberts, J., & Singh, A. (2016). *Toward a Blue Economy: A Promise for Sustainable Growth in the Caribbean*. World Bank., Retrieved from https://openknowledge.worldbank.org/handle/10986/25061 doi:10.1596/25061

RGGI (Regional Greenhouse Gas Initiative). (2023). *Regional Greenhouse Gas Initiative (RGGI): An Initiative of Eastern States of the US*. RGGI. https://www.rggi.org/program-overview-and-design/elements

Ritchie, H., Roser, M., & Rosado, P. (2020). CO_2 and Greenhouse Gas Emissions. Our World in Data. *Our World in Data*. https://ourworldindata.org/co2-emissions?utm_source=tri-city%20news&utm_campaign=tricity%20news%3A%20outbound&utm_medium=referral

Riva, F. R., Paes-De-Souza, M., & Talamini, E. (2022). REDD+: Analysis of Its Components Through a Systematic Review of Scientific Literature from Brazil and Indonesia. *International Forestry Review*, *24*(1), 72–84. doi:10.1505/146554822835224829

Rogelj, J., Den Elzen, M., Höhne, N., Fransen, T., Fekete, H., Winkler, H., Schaeffer, R., Sha, F., Riahi, K., & Meinshausen, M. (2016). Paris Agreement Climate Proposals Need a Boost to Keep Warming Well Below 2 C. *Nature*, *534*(7609), 631–639. doi:10.1038/nature18307 PMID:27357792

Shukla, P. R., Skea, J., & Reisinger, A. (2022). [*Mitigation of Climate Change: Working Group III Contribution to the Sixth Assessment Report of the Intergovernmental Panel on Climate Change*. Intergovernmental Panel on Climate Change.

Skjærseth, J. B., & Wettestad, J. (2010). Making the EU Emissions Trading System: The European Commission as an Entrepreneurial Epistemic Leader. *Global Environmental Change*, *20*(2), 314–321. doi:10.1016/j.gloenvcha.2009.12.005

Stenqvist, C., & Åhman, M. (2016). Free Allocation in the 3rd EU ETS period: Assessing Two Manufacturing Sectors. *Climate Policy*, *16*(2), 125–144. doi:10.1080/14693062.2014.979130

UNFCCC (United Nations Framework Convention on Climate Change). (2018). INDCs as Communicated by Parties. UNFCCC. https://www4.unfccc.int/sites/submissions/indc/Submission%20Pages/submissions.aspx

Wang, W., Luo, Y., Xie, P., Luo, Z., & Zhao, D. (2016). The Key Elements Analysis of Guangdong & Shenzhen ETS & Tips for China National ETS Construction. *Zhongguo Renkou Ziyuan Yu Huanjing, 14*(4), 282–291. doi:10.1080/10042857.2016.1258801

Wang, Y., Yao, G., Zuo, Y., & Wu, Q. (2023). Implications of Global Carbon Governance for Corporate Carbon Emissions Reduction. *Frontiers in Environmental Science, 11*, 3. doi:10.3389/fenvs.2023.1071658

Wildgrube, T. (2022). *Fit for 55? An Assessment of the Effectiveness of the EU COM's Reform Proposal for the EU ETS (No. 22/04).* (EWI Working Paper).

World Bank. (2022). *AskWBCaribbean: Talking Energy, Finding Solutions*. World Bank. https://www.worldbank.org/en/events/2022/10/11/caribbean-talking-energy-finding-solutions

Yoro, K. O., & Daramola, M. O. (2020). CO2 Emission Sources, Greenhouse Gases, and the Global Warming Effect. In *Advances in Carbon Capture* (pp. 3–28). Woodhead Publishing. doi:10.1016/B978-0-12-819657-1.00001-3

Zhang, D., Karplus, V. J., Cassisa, C., & Zhang, X. (2014). Emissions Trading in China: Progress and Prospects. *Energy Policy, 75*, 9–16. doi:10.1016/j.enpol.2014.01.022

Zhang, K., Xu, D., Li, S., Zhou, N., & Xiong, J. (2019b). Has China's Pilot Emissions Trading Scheme Influenced the Carbon Intensity of Output? *International Journal of Environmental Research and Public Health, 16*(10), 1854. doi:10.3390/ijerph16101854 PMID:31130641

Zhang, L., Zeng, Y., & Li, D. (2019a). China's Emissions Trading Scheme: First Evidence on Pilot Stage. *Polish Journal of Environmental Studies, 28*(2), 543–551. doi:10.15244/pjoes/84871

Zhongming, Z., Linong, L., Xiaona, Y., Wangqiang, Z., & Wei, L. (2021). *The Role of China's ETS in Power Sector Decarbonisation*. International Energy Agency.

ENDNOTES

1 Regulated entities, are companies or organizations that are required to reduce their GHG emissions in the ETS. These entities are allocated a certain number of emissions allowances, which represent the right to emit a certain amount of GHGs. If an entity emits less than its allocated allowances, it can sell the surplus allowances to other entities. Conversely, if an entity emits more than its allocated allowances, it must purchase additional allowances to cover the excess emissions.

2 One allowance allows a regulated entity to emit 1 ton of CO_2e.

3 CERs are carbon credits that project developers earn from implementing Clean Development Mechanism (CDM) projects in non-Annex I countries.

4 ERUs are carbon credits earned from the implementation of under the Joint Implementation projects in non-Annex I countries.

5 The RGGI agreement was signed in 2005. However, it took effect in 2009 (CRS, 2020).

6 The main reason why a combined cycle power plant has a higher efficiency and lower emissions is because it utilizes the waste heat from the gas turbine exhaust to generate additional electricity through the steam turbine. This means that less fuel is needed to produce the same amount of electricity, reducing GHG emissions.

7 A distinction can be made for two markets for emissions allowances. The first is the primary market, where the emissions allowances are distributed to traded entities for the first time. The handing out to these new emissions allowances is referred to an initial public offering. The second market is the secondary market. This is the market where existing emissions allowances are traded between regulated entities.

8 The data was available at https://www.investing.com/commodities/carbon-emissions-historical-data

APPENDIX

This study attempts to forecast the price of emissions allowances. The EUAs are used as a proxy for this forecasting analysis as presently no price for emissions allowances exist in the Caribbean.

A.1 Data

Data on the EUAs were available at the daily frequency from Investing.com[8] over January 2, 2019, to July 21, 2023 period. This produced 1174 observations.

A.2 Methodology

In the econometric literature, traditionally, linear models were used for forecasting. More specifically, the Autoregressive Integrated Moving Average (ARIMA) family of models was used for univariate forecasts. However, the aforementioned models suffered from problems of linearity and normality, as economic time series data is often non-linear and not normally distributed. The consequence of using a model based on the assumptions of linearity and normality when these assumptions are violated is the results of the model will be inaccurate (Greene, 2019).

Non-linear models have been developed for univariate forecasting. In fact, machine learning models such as the Artificial Neural Network (ANN) can be used for univariate forecasting.

An ANN model is a type of machine-learning algorithm designed to mimic the structure and functioning of the human brain. It consists of interconnected nodes, arranged in layers, and each node performs a simple mathematical function on its inputs. Over time, numerous ANN models have been proposed, and one commonly used type is the multi-layer perceptron (MLP). The MLP typically consists of several layers of nodes, starting with the input layer that receives data, followed by an intermediate hidden layer. Within this hidden layer, nodes perform calculations to discern patterns in the data. The nodes are interconnected by acyclic arcs, and as the data passes through these layers, it undergoes transformations based on learned weights. Finally, the output layer presents the model's solution or prediction (Babu et al., 2023).

In the training of artificial neural networks (ANNs), data is typically divided into three sets: the training set, the validation set, and the testing set. The training set is used to train the model by adjusting the weights and biases of the nodes in each layer. Through the process of forward propagation, data enters the input layer and is transferred to the hidden layer, where an activation function, often a sigmoid function, is applied to the weighted data to determine the output. This procedure is repeated for each input vector, and the nodes adjust their weights based on the accumulated derivatives of the error concerning each weight. The goal during training is to minimize a cost function that quantifies the difference between the predicted output and the actual output. To prevent overfitting, the validation set is employed to monitor the training process, ensuring that the model generalizes well to new data.

The backward propagation algorithm utilizes the partial derivatives obtained from the forward pass to update the weights during training. This iterative process continues until the error reaches a point where it no longer decreases substantially, and the output generated at this stage is considered the model's forecast (Babu et al., 2023).

For this study, a Non-Linear Autoregressive (NAR) ANN model is used for the forecasting. A NAR model is an ANN model used for univariate time series forecasting. Unlike traditional linear autoregressive models, NAR models are capable of capturing non-linear relationships. In a NAR model, the future value of a time series is predicted based on its past values, where the input data is fed into the model as a sequence. Each input neuron in the NAR model represents a past time step, and the hidden layers and activation functions introduce non-linearity to capture intricate dependencies within the data. The NAR model is trained using the backpropagation algorithm to minimize the error between the predicted and actual values, allowing it to learn and approximate non-linear relationships between past and future time series observations (Al-Saati et al., 2021).

A.3 Results

The diagnostic results of the NAR ANN are presented in the following diagrams. See Figure 1 for the performance and validation results.

Figure 1.

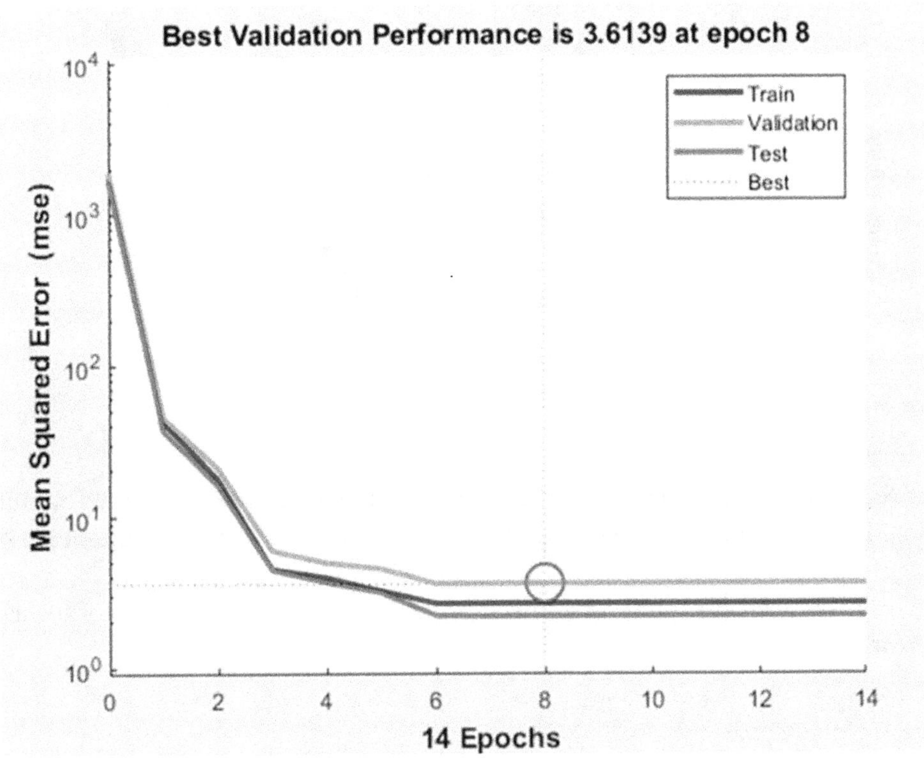

As can be seen from Figure 1, the results indicated that the NAR ANN achieved its best performance after 14 epochs, and the mean squared error stopped declining afterward.

Next, the time series response results are displayed. See Figure 2 for the time series response.

Figure 2.

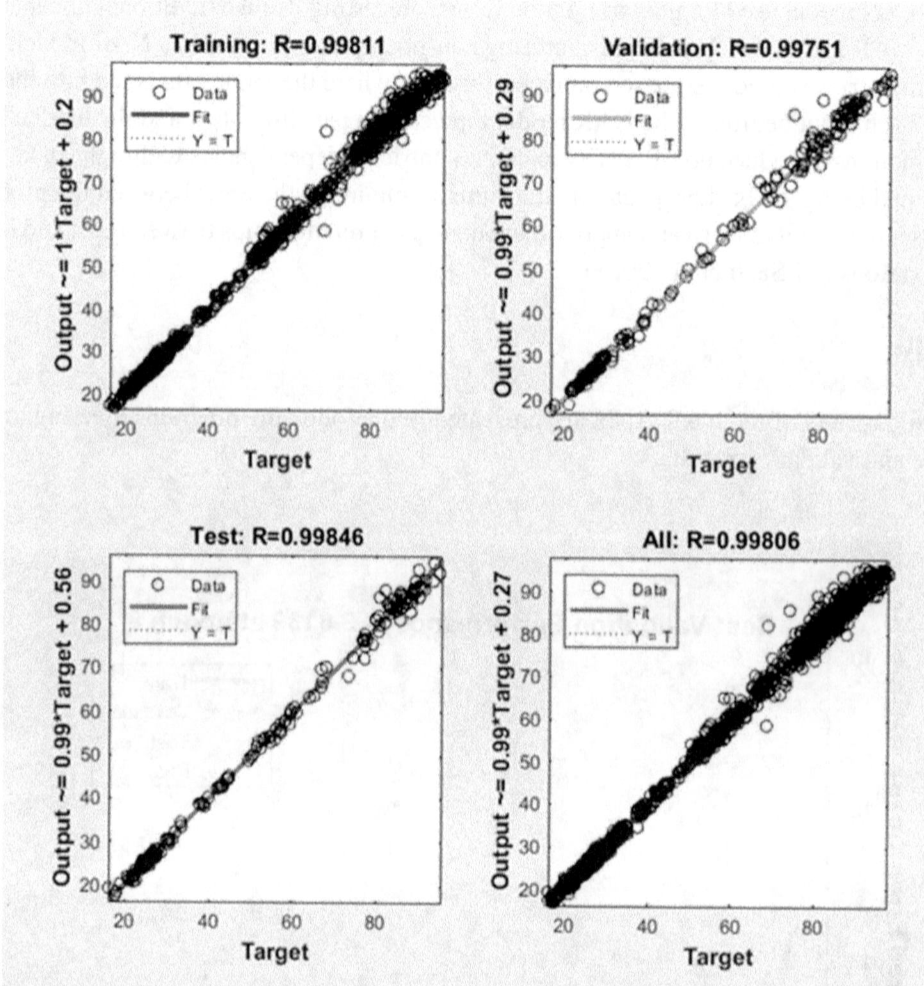

As can be seen from Figure 2, the results suggest a very strong regression fit for the training, testing, and validation data. Therefore, the model performed well in all stages of training to learn the pattern of the data.

Next, the results of the autocorrelation of the error are displayed. See Figure 3 for the autocorrelation of the error.

Figure 3.

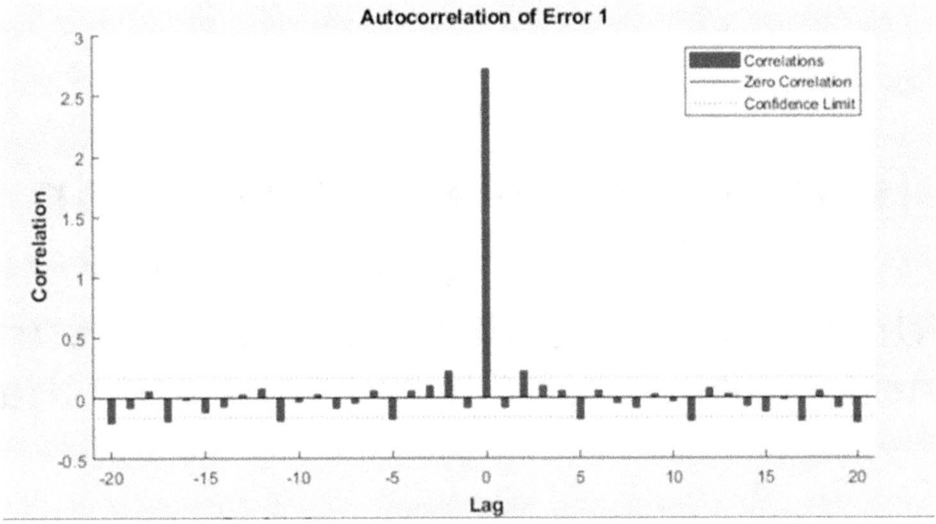

As can be seen from Figure 3, there was an initial large error from the early training, however, the error quickly died out. Thus, there is weak dependence in the error structure, and past errors are not affecting future errors. Additionally, the latter errors are very small suggesting the high predictive accuracy of the model.

The out-of-sample forecasts of the NAR ANN are presented in Table 1. Due to the good predictive accuracy of the model, the forecasts should be reliable. See Table 1.

Table 1. Forecasted Price for the EUAs

	Forecasted EUAs
1 step ahead	$91.28
2 step ahead	$90.82
3 step ahead	$90.43
4 step ahead	$90.10
5 step ahead	$89.81
6 step ahead	$89.56
7 step ahead	$89.34
8 step ahead	$89.15
9 step ahead	$88.97
10 step ahead	$88.81

Chapter 3
Is It a Policy Formulation or "Threat Multiplier"?
Addressing the United Nations Security Council Framing of Global Climate Change

Akash Bag
https://orcid.org/0000-0001-8820-171X
Amity University, India

Shashikant Saurav
Symbiosis International University (Deemed), India

Ashika Pradhan
https://orcid.org/0000-0002-4239-5608
Symbiosis International University (Deemed), India

Sujata Newton
O.P. Jindal Global University, India

ABSTRACT

Climate change has been perceived as a security issue too crucial to be left solely in the hands of politicians. The chapter will examine the securitization of climate change in the UN Security Council during 2017-2018. By analyzing the framing of the issue by Council members and the resonance of these frames with the audience, the research determines which frames are accepted and which are disregarded, shedding light on the securitization process. The findings indicate that the Security Council has unanimously securitized climate change as a regional issue but not a global one. While some members have attempted to push for further securitization, even the limited securitization of climate change on a smaller scale is a novel development for the Council.

DOI: 10.4018/978-1-6684-9272-7.ch003

INTRODUCTION

Agriculture, school results, and xenophobia have already been part of it – new topics are constantly being politicized, i.e., subject to political debate. For better or worse, this has become a natural part of society; issues that could have been left out of politics are considered important enough for politicians and voters to make decisions about them. But what happens when it goes even further? Can issues be too important to let politicians decide on them? It is precisely the idea behind the securitization theory (Baysal & Karakaş, 2017). Securitization means that an issue goes from "just" being political to being about security, making the issue more urgent to address and important enough not to go through the sometimes drawn-out democratic process (Buzan et al., 1998). One topic that has already undergone politicization and could be on the way to securitization is climate change –the focus of this paper. Climate change affects all countries and people, and the consequences become clearer daily. All UN member states signing the global goals for sustainable development in 2015 agree that urgent measures are needed to combat climate change. Is this enough to secure the climate issue? To examine it, the UN Security Council in 2017-2018 is chosen as a case; a justification for this choice comes in the chapter on design & boundaries.

Debates about bringing new issues onto the Security Council's agenda are hardly commonplace, but they do occur. In 2000, the Security Council determined that HIV/AIDS was a threat to peace and security (Fletcher, 2009, p. 807), and the following year, the debate was largely about terrorism after the 9/11 attacks (Rychnovská, 2014, p. 21). A few years later, attempts to securitize the climate issue began to gain more and more supporters in the USA as a backlash to Hurricane Katrina. The influential CNA Corporation released a report on the climate threat with securitizing ambitions, and in Congress, formerly skeptical senators began to frame the climate threat as a security issue (Fletcher, 2009, p. 808). In the Security Council, this process has primarily been led by Great Britain, writes Shirley Scott in the Cambridge Review of International Affairs (S. Scott, 2022). Great Britain has sometimes received support from, for example, Germany and the United States, as well as from states most threatened by the effects of climate change, Stephanie Cousins points out in Global Change, Peace and Security. However, there is still much resistance to the securitization of the climate issue: "*Emerging large economies such as China, Russia, and India are more skeptical of this approach*"(Cousins, 2013). A desire to securitize the climate issue can be identified in some member states, which Security Council has already discussed. Regarding authority, there is a consensus within political science research that the Security Council can have the climate issue on the agenda and make decisions about it, should they choose to do so (S. V. Scott & Andrade, 2012).

As demonstrated, some research on the securitization of the climate issue has been conducted, but there is a gap within science. Firstly, very little has been added after the autumn of 2015, when the agreement on the global goals was reached and the Paris Agreement was concluded; these two events raise questions about what the discourse in the Security Council looked like after that. Secondly, there is a lack of studies on how the climate issue has been framed in securitizing attempts, which would show more clearly why or why the issue has not been securitized and if certain aspects or framings have been securitized to a greater extent than others. Further research on this has been requested by, among others, Dagmar Rychnovská, whose analytical framework this study will use and will return to later.

PURPOSE AND QUESTIONS

This chapter aims to fill the scientific gap and investigate whether the climate issue has been secured. To investigate this, the study wants to see how the climate issue is framed in securitizing contexts and how these frameworks have been received. In addition to ascertaining whether the issue has been secured, the investigation will also see what specific frameworks have led to it. The main questions are thus:

- How is the climate issue framed in the Security Council?
- What frameworks, if any, have been accepted by the Security Council?

THEORETICAL UNDERPINNINGS

This chapter aims to provide a background to the theory and research from which the study is based. It aims to provide a basic understanding of what it means to securitize an issue and presents the analytical framework used for the investigation.

Securitization Theory

For an issue to be relevant to the Security Council, it must be secured by the members. Securitization theory is mainly associated with the so-called Copenhagen School, whose leading figures are Barry Buzan, Ole Wæver, and Jaap de Wilde. Together they have written the book Security: A New Framework For Analysis, which established securitization theory in political science (Munster, 2018). Buzan et al. believe that securitization is a more extreme version of politicization. "'*Security' is the move that takes politics beyond the established rules of the game and frames the issue either as a special kind of politics or as above politics*" (Buzan et al., 1998, p. 23). All problems or issues can be placed on a scale, from non-politicized to politicized to securitized. Securitization means that the issue gets the highest priority. It justifies emergency solutions. Any question can end up anywhere on the scale, depending on other circumstances (Buzan et al., 1998, p. 23-24). While securitization can be considered the most extreme level of politicization, it can also be the opposite of politicization. Indeed, securitizing an issue is always a political move. It has obvious tactical attractions - "*for example, as a way to obtain sufficient attention for environmental problems*" (Buzan et al., 1998, p. 29) and securitizing actions for climate threats. However, it is important to see that applying a security perspective to the issue can have problematic side effects. Politicization means an issue goes from not being governed by politics to being open to debate, free opinions, and choices. Securitization means considering that an issue is so urgent and existentially important that it should not be subject to the bureaucratic and often rigid approach of politics but should be left to decisive top leaders (Buzan et al., 1998, p. 29). Sometimes, it is necessary, but it is not always appropriate to bypass the democratic process.

The Copenhagen School advocates the de-security of issues precisely because issues that go from "just" being politics to security exceed some democratic rights. "*Thus the framework of securitization has perhaps most frequently been deployed as a way of critiquing securitization processes and highlighting the potential dangers of treating an issue as a security threat,*" writes Simon Rushton in The Concise Oxford Dictionary of Politics and International Relations (Wenham, 2019). This study will strive to take a more neutral stance toward the result, as there are both positive and negative sides to securitizing the climate issue. When it comes to the securitization process itself, Buzan et al. that securitization is what in the philosophy of language can be called a speech act. This means a statement is not primarily interesting because it refers to something real but is an act of interest (Buzan et al., 1998, p. 26). Securitization, however, does not mean that an issue must be explicitly named in terms of security; rather, the issue takes top priority, is presented as an existential threat, and justifies extraordinary solutions. It doesn't necessarily have to be an existential threat, but it is described as such (Buzan et al., 1998, p. 24).

"It is important to note that the security speech act is not defined by uttering the word security. What is essential is the designation of an existential threat requiring emergency action or special measures and the acceptance of that designation by a significant audience. There will be instances where the word security appears without this logic and other cases that operate according to that logic with only a symbolic security reference" (Buzan et al., 1998, p. 27).

Thus, qualitative interpretation is required to determine when an issue is secured. The way to study securitization is by studying discourse; presenting an issue as an existential threat is a securitizing act, but the issue becomes securitized only when the receiving audience accepts it. It must not go so far as to adopt an emergency solution or carry out extraordinary action, but a space must be created where it would be accepted and legitimized (Buzan et al., 1998, p. 25). Not everyone believes that certainty must be a matter of interpretation, dependent on context and speech acts; some try to define security instead (Bremberg et al., 2022). For example, the political scientist Arnold Wolfers distinguished between objective and subjective security, when there is or is not a real threat (objective) and when there is or is not a perceived threat (subjective) (Wolfers, 1952). Buzan et al. are critical of this; how will it be possible to objectively determine what a threat is, and how will it be possible to agree on defining security issues? According to the authors, it won't work, nor is it possible to see security as completely subjective since people do not always form their own opinion on all issues (Buzan et al., 1998, p. 31).

The securitization theory instead assumes that security is intersubjective; the view of what constitutes security is created between actors (Brown et al., 2007). There is no objective, inherent certainty in events or situations, just as the perception of what constitutes certainty does not only exist in the actors (subjects) themselves. Security is created and reinforced by constructions and relationships between actors (Buzan et al., 1998, p. 31). Thus, no single actor has the power to secure an issue on his own, as security always depends on context, power relations, and an accepting audience. The Copenhagen School, therefore, believes that securitization rather than actors should be at the center of the analysis (Buzan et al., 1998, p. 32-33). Furthermore, the authors point to several facilitating circumstances when securitizations are more likely to arise and take hold (Engelbrekt, 2016). A successful speech act combines so-called internal and external circumstances; internal are purely linguistic circumstances in that the actor expresses himself correctly according to the norms of the context. External circumstances can be divided into two parts: firstly, the actor has social capital and authority to express himself in the context, and secondly that the actor can demonstrate something that can be perceived as a real threat (Buzan et al., 1998, p. 32-33).

Criticism of the Copenhagen School

The Copenhagen School's securitization theory immediately impacted political science but has not been immune to criticism. In recent years, a more sociological perspective on securitization has emerged, mainly described by Thierry Balzacq in Securitization Theory: how security problems emerge and Dissolve. According to Balzacq, the focus on discourse is too great in what he calls the "philosophical" view of securitization, the theory of the Copenhagen School. He believes that discourse can be important in explaining how security issues arise, but it is primarily in relationships and given contexts that security occurs; actors do not necessarily need to talk about issues in a certain way to be considered secure (Balzacq, 2011). Furthermore, the sociological perspective examines the Copenhagen School's audience description. According to Balzacq, the philosophical perspective assumes that the audience is always given and obvious to the analyst; the sociological perspective doubts this and believes that the question of who constitutes the audience can be more fluid than that (Balzacq, 2011, p. 1-2)

Based on these two differences between the philosophical and the sociological perspective, this study can and should be based on the philosophical perspective of the Copenhagen School. Since the survey is about how the climate issue is framed in the Security Council, it would be impossible as well as unnecessary to analyze what unspoken perceptions exist among the member states about what is about security and what is not; for an issue to officially enter the Security Council's agenda, it is a necessity to discuss it, to debate and agree (Holland, 2014). In the Security Council, the audience is also always a given; when an actor, a member state, raises a question, the other 14 audience members. In principle, all of the criticism that Balzacq raises against the Copenhagen School, which is thus supposed to justify sociological securitization theory, deals in one way or another with how the field of use for the philosophical perspective is limited, that the sociological perspective is required to be able to apply securitization theory in more situations (Balzacq, 2011, p. 4-8). However, the criticism is irrelevant to this study, meaning further deepening the sociological perspective would only lead to complications.

Compatibility of Perspectives

This study will use an analytical framework that Dagmar Rychnovská has developed to analyze the construction of threat images in less discourse-oriented social contexts, such as the Security Council. Rychnovská believes the framework should be based on the "second generation" securitization theorists, including Balzacq, rather than the Copenhagen School - but it is not entirely clear why this must be the case. She highlights that both the Copenhagen School and the second generation adopt a radical constructivist perspective and that intersubjectivity is prioritized by the second generation(Rychnovská, 2014, p. 11-12), just like Buzan et al. previously mentioned. Despite the similarities, Rychnovská claims that the philosophical perspective is unsuitable for examining international organizations' securitization (Rychnovská, 2014, p. 11). I'm afraid we have to disagree with this; Buzan et al. used their theory to investigate securitization at several levels of analysis, from local to global (Buzan et al., 1998, p. 164-166). One difference that is, however, valid to mention is the audience's role in the Security Council. The audience does not necessarily have to be as passive as the Copenhagen school believes but can participate and influence the securitizing actor in the Council. Public members have power because securitization actors must receive their support and current power relations in the Security Council (Rychnovská, 2014, p. 13). We still think that the differences between the Copenhagen school and the second-generation theorists are exaggerated; after all, the second generation starts from the theory first developed by the Copenhagen School. Large parts of the second-generation literature are more a complement to Buzan et al. rather than a new theory. The two perspectives are relatively compatible and can often use the same analytical framework, which is exactly what this study will do (Hommel & Murphy, 2013).

The Analytical Framework

To successfully securitize an issue in the Security Council, in addition to using correct language, the securitizing actor must also meet the external circumstances by, according to Rychnovská, finding a way to insert the threat image into the existing institutional framework and then "negotiate" with the audience to convince them that the issue should be securitized (Rychnovská, 2014, p. 14). The securitizing actor will therefore strive to meet the audience's preferences and may therefore frame the issue in ways that appeal to it. Rychnovská, therefore, proposes framing analysis to examine the securitization process; it is not enough to only analyze speech acts in themselves. We must see these acts as part of a larger context (Rychnovská, 2014, p. 14-15). Frames are ways of highlighting particular aspects of events or issues and adapting their presentation to the context to make an impact as large as possible(Rychnovská, 2014, p. 15). Rychnovská refers to Snow and Benford's work on framing for a deeper understanding of this. In the chapter Ideology, Frame Resonance and Participant Mobilization, they have developed a categorization of frames – three tasks that frames have: diagnostic, prognostic, and motivational.

Diagnostic framing is about identifying a problem and either blaming someone for it or giving a possible explanation for why the situation looks the way it does (Snow & Benford, 1988, p. 200). Prognostic framing offers suggestions for solutions and, more specifically, what needs to be done immediately – they identify "*strategies, tactics, and goals*" (Snow & Benford, 1988, p. 201). Motivational framing aims to motivate the audience to do something about the problem; it is an attempt to mobilize and create active participation in the solution. Benford and Snow further discuss a concept they call frame resonance, on which Rychnovská bases a large part of the analytical framework (Snow & Benford, 1988, p. 202). Framing resonance explains why certain frames are more effective than others by examining how they resonate with the audience and the context in which the audience is (Rychnovská, 2014, p. 16-17). This means looking at how audience members respond to the framing—whether they agree, object, or ignore it altogether. It also means comparing the framing with previously accepted framings to see what sets them apart and possibly why they meet with different reactions. This is part of the external circumstances; the actor has social capital and successfully convinces the audience that there is a threat (Rychnovská, 2014, p. 17).

The main purpose of Rychnovská's framework is to investigate how new threat images can occur in a social context such as the Security Council, where a certain understanding of what a security threat means exists.39 How does the framing fit into the prevailing discourse, and how is the framing negotiated to fit better? The analysis takes place in two stages. First, the framing of the securitization discourse is analyzed; Snow and Benford's categorization of frames are applied, so the frames are sorted into diagnostic, prognostic, or motivational and analyzed individually (Rychnovská, 2014, p. 18). The second step directs the analysis toward the framing resonance; does the framing fit into the prevailing discourse? How does the specific framing relate to the larger, so-called overall framing, and how does the audience receive it?

(Rychnovská, 2014, p. 18)

DESIGN AND BOUNDARIES

This chapter aims to explain the survey design. It describes and justifies the choice of cases and materials and discusses limitations and problems with the investigation. It operationalizes relevant concepts to define the starting points of the investigation.

The Security Council As A Case In Point

According to the UN Charter, the Security Council is primarily responsible for maintaining international peace and security. They make decisions on a case-by-case basis and establish peace-building missions when necessary (Malone, 2013). The Council has a unique role in the UN system; while other UN bodies issue recommendations to member states, all UN members must accept and implement decisions made by the Security Council. What they decide on becomes international law and can thus have major consequences. After 9/11, the Security Council adopted a resolution that forced all UN member states to criminalize terrorism at the national level (Rychnovská, 2014, p. 21), and the year before, the Security Council's debates on HIV/AIDS created a new standard for how to look at epidemics, according to Alexandra Ossola:

"Because of HIV and those discussions that began in 2000, governments and international organizations have logistical protocols to address new epidemics. Emerging diseases are now discussed at the Security Council, as Aids was. [...] The rhetoric of national security has shaped the way activists and officials address epidemic diseases today, solidifying partnerships and funding streams" (Ossola, 2017)

If the climate issue were secured similarly, the Security Council could override political decisions at the national level, e.g., those that deal with climate goals. Therefore, Studying the Security Council seems to be the most appropriate forum to determine when a political issue has been securitized. The study is limited to only studying statements made within the framework of the Security Council and, of these, only the statements made by Security Council members. External guests are often invited to speak at the Council, such as knowledgeable people in a certain field or other UN member states who want their opinions heard. However, these are not considered in this study (McDonald, 2023). As the guests do not have the right to vote on the issues being debated and cannot participate in the Security Council's day-to-day work, only statements from members will be counted as potentially securitizing moves unless a member, for example, makes a point of quoting an outside source. Examining only statements within the Security Council, not statements in other contexts can also appear to be a problem. As previously mentioned, a question can only be secured when the audience, i.e., the other members, has accepted it (Murphy, 2019). For this to be evident, the issue must still be discussed within the framework of the Security Council, where the public can officially support possible securitization.

The Mandate Period 2017-2018 As A Case

The investigation is limited to the mandate period 2017-2018 in the Security Council. There are a couple of reasons for this. Firstly, the climate issue has probably never been as hotly debated as it is now; in the fall of 2015, UN member states agreed on both the global goals and the Paris Agreement, marking the first time that all UN member states agreed to take action against climate change (Ayaz, 2022).

World leaders now officially agree that climate change is a real problem and that something must be done about it. The Paris Agreement entered into force in November 2016 (United Nations, 2018), so the term of office, which began on January 1, 2017, is the first after that – this should influence the tone of the Security Council's debates. No one can deny anymore that something must be done about climate change, and the Paris Agreement can open the way to easier discussion of the problem, even in the Security Council. Half of the Security Council's ten temporary members are replaced annually, and the five permanent states (France, China, Russia, Great Britain, and the USA) make up the Council. In 2017, Sweden joined as a temporary member. Sweden is one of the world's most climate-conscious countries; they rank consistently high in the Environmental Performance Index (EPI), which measures countries' climate policies and how well they meet various goals. Every two years, an index update is released, produced by Yale and Colombia University and the World Economic Forum.

There are problems with only studying the 2017-2018 term. Firstly, the period is not over at the time of writing, so there is still time, e.g., Sweden, to have a greater influence on the Council's work. However, the study's main purpose is not to study what impact Sweden has had specifically, but the period has been chosen because the conditions are good for the issue to be addressed. Second, we cannot be sure that these conditions have improved after the Paris Agreement, although that is what we suspect (Pleuger, 2014). The idea behind this is that the Paris Agreement may have increased the desperation to take more drastic measures in the fight against climate change, but it could be that it has rather justified not tackling the issue on other levels. If the agreement is accepted as a good solution, the problem may not feel as pressing now; some countries could consider the climate issue to be resolved with the agreement entering into force, which would tone down the debate on the issue in the Security Council. To find out whether this is true, further research would be required - for example, comparing the discourse in the Security Council before and after the Paris Agreement would be interesting (Project, 2012). However, it would be far too large a task to take on in this candidate's chapter, which is why it is limited to 2017-2018.

MATERIAL

To examine framing in the Security Council, this study uses official protocols almost exclusively. The UN publishes minutes of all official Security Council meetings and resolutions on its website. The meeting minutes are complete transcriptions of the meetings held in the Security Council chambers. The resolutions published are unchanged from those adopted by the Security Council; the parties affected by the resolution must follow the text the members agreed upon. These documents provide unfiltered insight into the official meetings and the Council's work, making them the most appropriate material to study to perform as impartial an analysis as possible.

For this study, we have reviewed all meetings and resolutions from January 1, 2017, to April 30, 2018. During this period, the Security Council has held 391 meetings and adopted 78 resolutions. This large number makes it impossible to read through every meeting and resolution carefully; however, far from all meetings are relevant to this study. Therefore, we have read the agenda of each meeting and the subject of each resolution to determine which documents may be suitable for further analysis (S. V. Scott, 2015). Since the study deals with framing the climate issue, it is assumed that the climate must be mentioned relatively explicitly – if a framing only suggests that climate change is linked to security, it is difficult to draw any conclusions about securitization. To reduce the risk of having missed something, we have also done a keyword search in all meetings and resolutions on the terms' environment', 'environmental,' 'climate,' and 'global warming.'

In most documents, none of these concepts were mentioned; in some, they were mentioned in other contexts, e.g.,' political environment' or 'climate of impunity'; the documents where these concepts were linked to climate change have been analyzed more closely. To compare statements from 2017-18 with the overall context in which the Security Council finds itself regarding the securitization of the climate issue, two previous meetings, from 2007 and 2011, have been studied. We have carefully gone through 20 meetings, 2 resolutions, and 1 statement by the then President of the Security Council (this was adopted in one of the meetings, like a resolution). Many of the Security Council's work is unofficial and thus not published. This can, for example, involve informal meetings, negotiations, and lobbying between members. In these contexts, several framings and securitizing attempts would be relevant to this study; however, this material is not available. Dagmar Rychnovská, whose analytical framework the study uses, has discussed this problem.

"[G]iven the inaccessibility of this data type for the present research, the analysis has to draw only on the recorded debates and the secondary literature. It is assumed, though, that different positions would be voiced by the actors also in the official debates, and the framing struggles should still be identifiable, albeit documented by less extensive data"(Rychnovská, 2014, p. 20).

As Rychnovská believes, framing in unofficial contexts will probably still appear in formal meetings. Moreover, it is only in the official contexts that any securitizing framings matter; for a question to be fully secured by the Security Council, it must be stated and accepted by the audience, the other members. If the discourse looks different "outside the council's chambers," it does not matter - for the work of the Security Council to have practical effects, it must appear in formal meetings or resolutions.

RESULTS AND ANALYSIS

Background To The Climate Issue In The Security Council

According to Scott and Andrade (S. V. Scott & Andrade, 2012) and Conca, Thwaites, and Lee (Conca et al. (2017), only two pure debates on climate change have been held in the Security Council, one in 2007 at the initiative of Great Britain and one in 2011 at the initiative of Germany. These can be seen as the clearest securitization attempts of the climate issue in the Security Council. None of the debates led to a concrete decision or resolution, but they have possibly created more space for the issue to take place on the Security Council's agenda, despite some opposition (S. V. Scott & Nguyen, 2023).

During 2017 and the beginning of 2018, the climate issue arose several times during "regular" meetings of the Security Council, especially during discussions about particularly vulnerable areas such as Lake Chad and the Sahel region in Africa. A commonly used concept mentioned as a framework to solve the problem is Agenda 2030, the global goals for sustainable development that UN member states adopted in 2015 (Gera et al., 2018, p. 30).

Diagnostic Frameworks

Sweden began its mandate in the Security Council with one month as the country's President, a post that rotates among the members. António Guterres, who had just taken office as Secretary-General, is also present at the year's first meeting. In the opening speech, Guterres takes up a framework that occasionally recurs in the Security Council; that climate change indirectly increases the risk of conflict (UNSC, 2017a, p. 3). France's expected returns to this later in the meeting: "*Allow me also to stress the role of climate change. While it is not a direct cause of conflict, it exacerbates vulnerabilities, aggravates their immediate causes, and threatens progress*"(UNSC, 2017a, p. 14). He says explicitly that climate change is not a direct cause of conflicts but rather blocks the circumstances that, in its luck, can lead to conflicts. In other meetings, for example, Bolivia is on the same track; "*Several factors cause the famine [...] which also shows that the effects of climate change increase the potential for conflict*"(UNSC, 2017d, p. 17)– as well as Ethiopia; "*Moreover, we cannot overlook the impact of climate change, and the extent to which it fuels conflict*"(UNSC, 2017b, p. 11). Framing climate change indirectly increasing the risk of conflict is relatively cautious in this context. Other actors have consistently framed climate change as a root cause of conflict, mainly Sweden and Italy, in 2017.

Italy's representative was clear about this in the first meeting of the year through a statement in which he called climate change a growing root cause of conflicts (UNSC, 2017a, pp. 7–8). This way of framing climate change was given further life in meeting 7894, which dealt with the conflict at Lake Chad in central Africa. Swedish Carl Skau described the reasons behind the conflict as follows:

"The roots of the conflict run deeper than the Boko Haram insurgency. They include abject poverty, climate change, and underdevelopment. Indeed, the situation in the Lake Chad basin vividly illustrates the links between security, development, human rights, and climate-change-related risks. In Niamey, President Issoufou of the Niger cited the shrinking of Lake Chad as a direct and major reason for the rise of Boko Haram"(UNSC, 2017c, p. 11).

Skau does not attempt to distance himself from the statement by Niger's President but rather takes it as an example of how climate change is a direct security threat. This kind of framing can secure the issue and place it on the Security Council's agenda if more states follow suit and accept the framing. At the same time, this can be interpreted as a description of an indirect threat; climate change leads to the shrinking of Lake Chad, which in itself is the direct threat. Skau's link Instead, seeing climate change as one of many underlying factors behind specific regional security threats is all the more popular. In March 2017, the Security Council unanimously adopted resolution 2349, which dealt with the situation at Lake Chad. One of the seven points on the root causes of the conflict was as follows:

"[The Security Council] Recognises the adverse effects of climate change and ecological changes among other factors on the stability of the Region, including through water scarcity, drought, desertification, land degradation, and food insecurity, and emphasizes the need for adequate risk assessments and risk management strategies by governments and the United Nations relating to these factors"(UNSC, 2017k, p. 7).

The difference between this and the framing of climate change as a root cause may seem non-existent or insignificant, but wording matters in a context like the Security Council, where speech acts are central.

Citing climate change as a root cause of conflict gives the issue a top priority, while it may be perceived as less urgent if it is one of many causes (Sindico, 2007). The unanimous official statements and resolutions mentioning climate change are only three in number between January 2017 and April 2018, but the other two are worded exactly like the first.

In January 2018, the then-presidential country made the following statement on behalf of the entire Security Council regarding the situation in West Africa and the Sahel region:

"The Security Council recognizes the adverse effects of climate change and ecological changes, among other factors, on the stability of West Africa and the Sahel region, including through drought, desertification, land degradation, and food insecurity, and emphasizes the need for adequate risk assessments and risk management strategies by governments and the United Nations relating to these factors"(S. Scott, 2022).

In Resolution 2408 of March 2018, we find this passage regarding Somalia:

"[The Security Council is] recognizing the adverse effects of climate change, ecological changes, and natural disasters among other factors on the stability of Somalia, including through drought, desertification, land degradation, and food insecurity, and emphasizing the need for adequate risk assessments and risk management strategies by governments and the United Nations relating to these factors" (UNSC, 2018e, p. 3)All three statements are essentially verbatim identical; The members of the Security Council have found a formulation that they can all agree on when it comes to addressing the climate issue, and that is to see climate change as one of several causes behind regional security threats. However, member states may choose to interpret this common agreement in different ways (Smith, 2020). Some see it as a sign that the climate issue is established on the Security Council's agenda; in connection with resolution 2349 being voted through, Ethiopia's representative claimed that all members now agree on the link between security and climate change (UNSC, 2017e, p. 4). This was also what Ukraine meant when they were happy about the resolution at the last meeting of the year and stated that the Security Council's agenda had expanded to include the link between security threats and climate change (UNSC, 2017j, p. 5).

Not all members agree with the perception that the climate issue has established itself in the Security Council. Russia responded with this statement at the same meeting:

"We proceed from the Charter of the United Nations assigned to the General Assembly and the Economic and Social Council a mandate to consider socioeconomic and environmental issues, including combating climate change and ensuring sustainable water use, health care, and similar issues. The General Assembly, with its universal membership, makes recommendations on such issues, all of which have many different aspects. They are all considered in specialized committees and individual forums, such as the United Nations Framework Convention on Climate Change. Combining all these elements and preparing balanced decisions on them demands diverse expertise and time that the Security Council does not possess"(UNSC, 2017j, p. 20).

We interpret this as Russia not wanting to see the climate issue on the Security Council's agenda. The representative believes that other UN bodies are already dealing with the climate issue; if the Security Council is to try to pay attention to climate change as well, it will be too much to handle. China also adopts this position to some extent; they have no problem admitting that the current famine in South Sudan, Somalia, Yemen, and Nigeria is largely due to climate change, but then the famine is not named as a security problem (UNSC, 2017g, pp. 9–10). Both China and Russia seem to work actively to keep the climate and traditional security issues apart. However, it should be mentioned that the interpretations are not always obvious; sometimes, even the more securitizing countries can seem to keep climate change and security separate. It is possible to see patterns in the behavior of the Member States, but even if, e.g., Sweden generally emphasizes climate change more than many other members, there is sometimes skepticism about possible conclusions, for example, as a result of a statement like this by Swedish Olof Skoog:

"Remaining challenges, many common to the region's countries, can be overcome through stronger regional cooperation. They include security threats and radicalization, managing shared water and energy resources, and addressing the effects of climate change"(UNSC, 2018b, p. 16).

Is this a statement that actively distinguishes between security threats and the effects of climate change, or is it more about clarifying that climate change is part of larger security threats? It's not entirely easy to tell from that quote alone, but members' opinions are usually revealed when compared to more statements.

The diagnostic frameworks that have been identified are as follows:

- Climate change indirectly increases the risk of conflict
- Climate change is a fundamental cause of conflict
- Climate change is one of several underlying factors behind regional security threats
- The climate issue is established on the Security Council's agenda
- The climate issue does not belong on the Security Council's agenda

The framing that appears most often and seems to be accepted in the Security Council is that climate change is one of several underlying factors behind regional security threats. This framing has appeared in the majority of unanimous statements.

Prognostic Frameworks

Agenda 2030 was seen by many as a major advance, and the Security Council has also highlighted it as a way to solve climate problems. Sweden used this framework to arrive at a solution for the conflict at Lake Chad. "*Working within the framework of the 2030 Agenda, we must ensure a coordinated and better linked humanitarian, reconstruction, and development response*"(UNSC, 2017c, p. 11). The coordinated response could be that the entire UN system works together to tackle the problem holistically on several fronts. When solutions for the Sahel region were discussed in January 2018, Olof Skoog expressed this more explicitly; "*Only sustained and holistic approaches that take into account the root causes of conflict and instability in the region, and linkages between them can lead to long-term solutions*"(UNSC, 2018a, p. 6). The Netherlands, which replaced Italy in the Security Council for 2018, also pointed them to the multifaceted design of Agenda 2030 when a solution for the Sahel region was discussed. "*The multi-pronged approach of the Sustainable Development Goals (SDGs) constitutes the ultimate prevention tool*"(UNSC, 2018a, p. 8)

Regarding more specific proposals for solutions, it is common to advocate more regional approaches. Regarding Lake Chad, Japan's representative spoke about cooperation between the UN Peace-building Commission, subregional and regional organizations, local UN departments, and other support mechanisms. "*The issues facing the Lake Chad Basin, which range from terrorism and trafficking to food inse-*

curity and climate change, cannot be solved individually"(UNSC, 2017e, p. 3). Bolivia's representative believes cooperation between the local governments - Cameroon, Chad, Niger, and Nigeria - can find solutions, e.g., climate problems. "*We are confident that the leadership of these countries will allow us to establish a regional strategy that will address these root causes, as that is one of the main shortcomings we are currently facing*"(UNSC, 2017f, p. 18). Resolution 2349 also mentioned a regional solution to climate change at Lake Chad, the Lake Chad Development and Climate Resilience Action Plan (UNSC, 2017k, p. 6). While it is not necessarily the main goal, this framing still functions to place the problem on other actors. Admittedly, the Security Council and the UN system, in general, may still be involved in putting together regional collaborations, but through these statements, they still surrender part of the responsibility for arriving at solutions.

There are more regional solutions from the UN side, which Kazakhstan highlighted regarding the Sahel region.

"However, we realize that a military approach alone will not address the instability in the region, which is the result of an accumulation of problems of which violent extremism is only the most recent layer. [...] In that regard, the effective implementation of the United Nations Integrated Strategy for the Sahel, with increased investments in sustainable development, climate mitigation, and development, can help us to achieve the goals I have discussed"(UNSC, 2017h, p. 20).

The representative advocates an approach adapted to the Sahel region, not only about military interventions. To create security in the region, he believes that more is required. More investment is needed in, for example, combating the climate threat to achieve security. There is already a framework for this, the United Nations Integrated Strategy for the Sahel – it's just a matter of implementing it without getting distracted or abdicating responsibility. Not everyone agrees that it is enough to formulate such a framework on the part of the UN. One of the most common framings in the Security Council is that the UN is not doing enough - it is an internal criticism that the system must work better. Sweden has raised this several times; they believe that the resolution on Lake Chad showed that the Security Council had paid attention to the climate threat, but this does not mean that the issue has taken hold or that sufficient measures have been taken (UNSC, 2017i, p. 6). Furthermore, they believe that the UN should take the issue more seriously.

"As highlighted by numerous countries at the [informal] meeting on climate and security last Friday, there is a clear need for the United Nations to enhance its capabilities to foresee better, understand and respond to climate-related security risks. That includes identifying and responding to the risks of instability and insecurity arising from how climate change's effects interact with social, economic, and political factors"(UNSC, 2017j, p. 8).

There are no concrete proposals here on how the UN should proceed, but Sweden nevertheless points out that they would like to get more done if only more member states would agree. In February 2018, however, a debate about a minor reform of the Security Council came on the agenda. The purpose of meeting 8185 was to discuss how the Security Council should interpret the UN Charter and how they should best use their tools and power. The meeting begins with António Guterres, together with former Secretary-General Ban Ki-moon, stating that the Charter still stands today, but today's conflicts look different than when the UN was created (UNSC, 2018c, pp. 2–6). The Ivory Coast's representative follows it up with a statement that The current system, which originates from the UN Charter, must find a way to provide new answers to a contemporary challenge such as the climate threat (UNSC, 2018c, p. 11). Equatorial Guinea supports the statement, "*[I]t is up to us, the Member States, to be brave enough to modernize the Organization's structures and procedures; otherwise, the credibility, legitimacy and moral authority of the purposes and principles of the Charter will be increasingly questioned and undermined*"(UNSC, 2018c, p. 18). This can be interpreted as an appeal to other members to act now and take new threats, such as climate change, seriously - the trust in the system may soon run out. There were no strong objections at that meeting, but in a meeting the following month, Russia again opposed possible changes to the Security Council's mandate and position in the UN.

"We are not arguing with the fact that there is a whole range of diverse problems that are undoubtedly exacerbating the overall situation in the region. The climate and habitat naturally have a serious impact on people's lives. However, there are other, more suitable forums for discussing these issues — the Second Committee of the General Assembly and the Economic and Social Council. There is no need to disrupt the existing division of responsibilities and overload the Security Council's agenda. Any erosion of its mandate, and the consequent diminution of its effectiveness, must be guarded against"(UNSC, 2018d, p. 19).

Russia seems to have its views clear on the place of the climate issue in the Security Council as this statement is very reminiscent of the one from the last meeting of 2017, on the resolution on Lake Chad. The representative mentions that the Security Council's mandate risks being "*eroded*" - perhaps Russia feels that its strong position as a permanent member is threatened if they start to change how the Security Council works or that respect for the Council is weakened if they start dealing with less traditional security issues. Other members mention Lake Chad and resolution 2349 in a more positive sense; The Netherlands, for example, wants the resolution to be "*the rule rather than the exception*"(UNSC, 2018d, p. 23) for future work. Sweden believes that the Security Council has secured the climate issue through resolution 2349 and statement 2018/3 - and in the future, the Security Council must take greater account of research at the local and international levels before decision-making. "*Conflict prevention efforts would be more effective if the climate and environmental stress put on societies is properly understood and addressed*" (UNSC, 2018d, p. 12).

The prognostic frameworks that have been identified are as follows:

- Climate problems must be solved through Agenda 2030
- Regional solutions must be developed
- The UN system must work better to solve the climate issue

Solving the climate issue through Agenda 2030 or regionally can be seen as a simplified solution from the Security Council, as, in practice, you transfer the problem to other actors or bodies. However, It must be said that this is often how the Security Council works - they decide who should proceed with the problem. Often the debate in the Security Council is primarily about the fact that the UN system as a whole must work more effectively with the climate issue, but proposals for reforms have encountered resistance.

Motivational Framing

When securitizing actors try to convince others that action is required, they use motivational framing; there, it is possible to identify some different variants that have appeared in the Security Council. In meeting 8069, which dealt with the famine in South Sudan, Somalia, Yemen, and Nigeria, Sweden framed it as saying that entire conflicts can be stopped by stopping climate change.

"Yes, we need more funding; yes, we need more access; but that will not end those crises or stop new ones from emerging. There must be political solutions to the conflicts driving those entirely preventable humanitarian crises, exponentially increasing the needs and suffering that make a robust humanitarian and longer-term response much harder. Ending such conflicts also means tackling the root causes that are driving them, including underdevelopment, inequality, and exclusion, which are, in turn, exacerbated by the effects of climate change. We must make, build and sustain peace"(UNSC, 2017g, p. 5).

The representative here means that we already know how to stop something like the famine from happening, so now is the time to act. This is an obvious appeal to the rest of the Security Council, as confirmed by the last sentence. "Make, build and sustain peace" is completely consistent with what the UN itself states as the primary tasks of the Security Council. In other situations, climate change has been framed as threatening the survival of entire regions. In one of the first meetings about Lake Chad, Sweden's Olof Skoog recalled a story from Fatima Askira, who works in a women's rights organization in Nigeria and has seen how climate change has affected her neighborhood. "Her voice was powerful, but the line was slightly weak. She said, "*Picture a woman lying sick in the sand, covering herself with a tattered rug. Her children, four, six, and seven years old, sit beside her, with no idea what to eat that day*"(UNSC, 2017b, p. 21). This is how motivating frames can also look; sometimes, they are more about playing on emotions than anything else. Skoog wants to call for action by using Askira's story to make an emotional connection between the members and the situation at Lake Chad. In this way, France also spoke on another occasion about climate change's impact in practice; "*We can no longer ignore its profoundly destabilizing consequences. The most vulnerable populations, already exposed to other conflict factors, whether political, social or environmental, are the first victims. For small island developing States and coastal countries, their survival is at stake*"(UNSC, 2017j, p. 12). France's representative believes that the small developing states already have it worst on so many other levels and are also the hardest hit by climate change; it cannot continue.

Some have framed climate change from a broader perspective – as if the entire planet is at stake. An example of this is when Bolivia's representative spoke at the beginning of 2017 that the UN's most important and urgent role is to combat conflicts, which, according to him, includes combating climate change. "*There is only one world, and the threat of climate change is genuine, which means that we have common but differentiated responsibilities. The fight against climate change is the same fight for the rights of Mother Earth*"(UNSC, 2017a, p. 27). Finally, there have also been more encouraging framings, which want to motivate action by making it clear that it is not too late to save the planet. France pointed this out one occasion; "We now have the technological and financial means to build a clean and secure future and protect future generations. Climate change is not — or not yet — inevitable" (UNSC, 2017j, p. 12). I interpret adding "or not yet" as a clarification that action is still required. The conditions may be good for stopping climate change, but that does not mean nothing has happened. The representative believes that the situation is worsening, but if we manage to reach a solution, we can stop the negative trend.

The motivational frameworks that have been identified are the following:

- Entire conflicts can be stopped by stopping climate change
- The survival of entire regions is threatened by climate change
- The entire planet is at stake
- It is not too late to save the planet

To motivate the Security Council to act, the most common way is, above all, to point out that it is the regions that are already suffering in many ways that are hit hardest by climate change.

Resonance of Diagnostic Framings

The diagnostic frameworks in 2017 and the beginning of 2018 do not surprise the Security Council. When Britain chaired the meeting on climate change in 2007, they immediately pointed out that climate change indirectly increases the risk of conflict. "*An unstable climate will exacerbate some of the core drivers of conflict, such as migratory pressures and resource competition*" (UNSC, 2007, p. 7). This was relatively new at the time and pointed out that it is the Security Council's responsibility to ensure that climate change does not go too far because it is their responsibility to maintain global security. This type of framing has not directly changed since 2007 but can be considered established at this point. Framing climate change as a fundamental cause of the conflict was also done in 2007, when, for example, France said, "*All of the climate change threats are real threats. They will affect security among nations in the medium and the long term*"(UNSC, 2007, p. 11). A new framework was created Through the resolutions and official statements previously mentioned when the Security Council recognized climate change as one of many underlying factors behind security threats. It can be seen as a vaguer framework, but in doing so, it also allowed all members to agree on a formulation regarding climate change. Even though this framework has not been mentioned in previous debates (2007 and 2011), it had therefore taken hold and, by definition, resonates well with the context of the Security Council when the resolutions were adopted unanimously.

As the resolution on Lake Chad was the first time a unanimous statement by the Security Council drew attention to climate change as a threat, no one has previously, like Ethiopia and Ukraine, claimed that the climate issue had guaranteed its place on the Security Council's agenda. However, the criticism that it belongs there has been there from the beginning. Above all, China and Russia raised this in both 2007 and 2011. China has considered that the Security Council can hardly improve the situation – they would rather be in the way. "*The developing countries believe that the Security Council lacks expertise in handling climate change and is not the right place to take decisions with extensive participation leading to widely acceptable proposals*"(UNSC, 2007, p. 13). Russia has argued that there are more appropriate forums for discussing the climate issue, and it may not be so good to force solutions through the Security Council. "*Given this, Russia is skeptical about the repeated attempts that have been made to place on the agenda of the Security Council the issue of the threat posed by climate change to international peace and security*" (UNSC, 2011, p. 13). Based on these statements, it is no great surprise that China and Russia have continued to oppose the entry of the climate issue on the Security Council's agenda. When two such large international players, who are also permanent members and have veto rights in the Security Council, do not want to see the climate issue debated in the Security Council, it is difficult to say that the issue has taken hold. Proponents see the resolutions adopted as progress, but with relatively vague wording, opponents such as China and Russia may continue to try to move the issue to other parts of the UN system.

To summarize this section, we can state that the framing of climate change, as indirectly increasing the risk of or being a fundamental cause of conflict has occurred in the past and generally receives some support from the Security Council but not by all. As long as there have been proposals to bring the climate issue up on the Security Council's agenda, there has been criticism of it, above all by the two permanent members, China and Russia. With the resolution on Lake Chad, however, the Security Council seems to have found a framework that has taken hold - that climate change is one of several underlying factors behind security threats. This framing has appeared in three unanimous resolutions and statements and can thus be accepted by the Security Council. As it is a relatively vague formulation, it is subject to interpretation whether the climate issue has been secured or not. Worth noting is that the Security Council has not had a debate that is entirely about the climate issue since 2011; this could mean that the climate issue is not seen as relevant to the Council, but as it is often brought up in other contexts, it is more likely that the issue has been "sneaked in" on the agenda. That statements about climate change are now included in unanimous resolutions may be a sign that the issue has become a natural part of the Council's work.

Resonance of Prognostic Framings

Since the 2030 Agenda was only adopted in 2015, the specific framework that climate change is best combated through that framework is relatively new. However, most states mentioned at the meeting in 2007 that the fight against climate change should be seen as part of sustainable development, which is ultimately what Agenda 2030 is about (UNSC, 2007, p. 7). The agenda has given Security Council members a fully developed solution to point to; all UN member states accept it, and it contains goals such as including climate change. There is not much opposition to this framing - it can either be angled to mean that the Security Council must take the agenda into account or that the responsibility for fulfilling the agenda primarily lies with other UN bodies. The framework for combining climate change through regional solutions is also new. Neither in 2007 nor in 2011 did framing come up, while now it is one of the most common ways to frame potential solutions. Of course, this may be because the meetings in 2007 and 2011 dealt with climate change more generally rather than the more specific situations that have been debated in meetings in 2017 and 2018, but it still says something that the only time climate change has been mentioned in Security Council resolutions are when they have touched on its regional impact.

Furthermore, it is worth noting that there has long been internal criticism of how the UN system functions and deals with the climate issue. Sweden's criticism that the UN must become better at anticipating, identifying, and warning about security threats from climate change was not the first - the UN's so-called "*early warning systems*" were criticized by Belgium in 2007 (UNSC, 2007, p. 6) and the USA in 2011 (UNSC, 2011, p. 7). Also, the appeal that the Security Council must be modernized and include "*new threats*" has been there since 2007 when Belgium stated that "*we must abandon the idea that the future will look like the past*" (UNSC, 2007, pp. 5–6). Attempts at reform have, however, been stopped, even though the Security Council has, for example, determined that a non-traditional threat such as HIV/AIDS threatens peace and security, as previously mentioned. In 2011, the US criticized certain members of the Security Council precisely because climate change should not be more difficult to securitize than HIV/AIDS; "*Instead, because of the refusal of a few to accept our responsibility, by its silence the Council is saying in effect 'tough luck.' That is more than disappointing; it is pathetic, short-sighted, and, frankly, a dereliction of duty*"(UNSC, 2011, p. 7).

In retrospect, it is not entirely obvious that a statement was needed for the Security Council to take more responsibility for the climate issue. In 2007, Panama's representative said the following about how HIV/AIDS got on the agenda:

"On previous occasions, the Council has debated its role in competence shared among the other United Nations organs. For example, in 2000, we debated the impact of HIV/AIDS on peace and security on the African continent. We sought then to provide visibility to the problem. Although the debate led to no direct action, it demonstrated the international community's consensus on setting objectives. No one can deny the positive effect of actions undertaken because of that and other debates"(UNSC, 2007, p. 15).

Perhaps that is what has happened or is happening with the climate issue in the Security Council. The more debates that are held on the topic and the more statements that are made, no matter how vague, the issue can gain a stronger hold on the agenda. A resolution like the one on Lake Chad would have been hard to imagine in 2007, but with small steps, the Council has reached that statement. To summarize this section, we can continue to state that the new frameworks on Agenda 2030 and regional solutions resonate well with Security Council members - all UN members have adopted Agenda 2030, and the only time climate change has been mentioned in resolutions are when these resolutions have dealt with regional solutions for conflicts. On the other hand, criticism of the UN system is not new, but all council members do not accept reform proposals.

Resonance of Motivational Framings

The first motivating framing we identified, that entire conflicts could be stopped by stopping the climate threat, did not appear in the meetings in 2007 and 2011. This could be a sign that the climate issue has gained a stronger foothold in the Security Council - that the members are sufficiently used to framing climate change's (indirect) impact on security that it is then possible to test a more emphatic motivational framing. Not all members need to agree that climate change affects security, but as long as that kind of framing is relatively common, it is not shocking to use a stronger one.

Framing climate change as threatening the survival of entire regions is a kind of emotional argument that has worked well since 2007. Then Italy's representative drew attention to the fact that as many as 50 million people in developing countries, already suffering on many other levels, could be forced to flee from climate change, which no one could argue against (UNSC, 2007, p. 4). Even Russia, which is otherwise skeptical of discussing the impact of climate change in the Security Council, has expressed its concern about vulnerable regions; "*We share the concern of small island developing States, in particular those situated in the Pacific Ocean, about the continuing rise in sea levels*"(UNSC, 2011, p. 13). When the Security Council is also visited by people who experience the impact of climate change firsthand, such as Fatima Askira at Lake Chad, this framing is effective and meets no resistance.

Bolivia's framing that the entire planet is at stake also has historical backing. At the 2007 meeting, Qatar said, "*Since we all run the risk of being submerged, we must work collectively to save ourselves from drowning*"(UNSC, 2007, p. 10) - Panama's representative quoted a poem: "*The gradual accumulation of consequences is precisely its most dangerous quality, because, as the poet T.S. Eliot wrote, 'This is the way the world ends/ Not with a bang but a whimper*"(UNSC, 2007, p. 15). It is possibly the kind of statement that later, during the meeting, Russia's representative said, "*I would like to appeal to avoid panicking and overdramatizing the situation*"(UNSC, 2007, p. 17). The more encouraging framing that it is not too late to save the planet was possibly preceded by the UK's statement when they held the meeting in 2007; "*Climate change is a threat that can bring us together if we have the wisdom to prevent it from driving us apart*"(UNSC, 2007, p. 19).

Something common to the motivational framings is that neither in 2007 nor in 2017 did they meet much resistance from the audience. There is consensus within the Security Council that climate change is a real problem that must be dealt with in one way or another; the debate is not about convincing the members that an action must be taken but rather how it should be done. That said, motivational framing still has its role in the Security Council's climate discussions, as some members feel that too little is being done or that reforms need to be implemented. From that point of view, it seems rather that the frames bounce off and disappear - there are no counterarguments, but there are no actions either. In summary, it can be assumed that the climate issue is now a higher priority for the members of the Security Council than before, as certain motivating frameworks have become stronger and more urgent. The motivational frameworks generally fit well into the prevailing discourse in the field and do not meet much resistance. There is consensus that climate change must be combated somehow.

CONCLUSION

The Security Council is a forum whose composition is constantly changing with its temporary members, so it isn't easy to draw conclusions based on the statements of individual members. Members' opinions and framings often differ widely, but it is possible to identify certain recurring framings of the climate issue, as well as single framings that are accepted by all. A common diagnostic framework is that climate change is one of several underlying factors behind security threats. Other framings, such as that climate change is a fundamental cause of conflict or that the Security Council should address the climate issue, usually encounter resistance from states such as China and Russia, but climate change is one of several factors agreed upon by all. This has been demonstrated through three unanimous resolutions and statements from 2017-2018. Admittedly, this framing did not occur before this period, but it is telling that the first Security Council resolutions that have mentioned climate change use that framing. The Council has found a framework that all have accepted.

The Paris Agreement is not used as a predictive framework, but there are, on the other hand, many proposals to solve the climate issue through Agenda 2030 and the global goals. The framework can be used in several ways but doesn't meet much resistance in the Council. However, it is still difficult to state that this framing has been accepted as a solution to climate change as a security issue; there is no doubt that the members agree on Agenda 2030 as a solution to the climate problem, but it has not been mentioned in any resolutions or the like. Regional solutions are the prognostic framework that can be said to have been accepted by the Security Council. The Council has issued resolutions in these contexts where climate change is included.

Regarding motivational framing, painterly, emotional framing has been used and has been effective. They claim that solutions to the climate issue are solutions to conflicts or that the entire planet is at stake here and now has not fully caught on, as these framings are either foreign to the Council or can be seen as overly dramatic. The framework that has mainly been accepted is that climate change will hit the region's already worst off hardest. As the motivating frameworks can generally be seen as independent of the Security Council has responsibility, they have not encountered much resistance – members can link these motivations to what the UN system should do about the problem.

In conclusion, this study can state that the climate issue is generally in a sort of intermediate position between politicization and securitization. There is consensus in the Security Council that climate change is real and action must be taken, but members' opinions differ on how strong the link between climate and security is and whether it is the Council's responsibility to address the issue. During the period 2017-2018, however, a trend has emerged – the frameworks that deal with climate change having regional impacts must be solved regionally or are particularly devastating for individual regions are accepted by the Security Council. Climate change as a regional problem has been secured. That the issue has not been secured as a global problem may be because some members believe that the Council does not have the knowledge or time to deal with the issue, as China and Russia believe. It could also be because these large emitter states do not want to recognize the extent of the problem and are thus forced to take greater responsibility at the national level. Further research could investigate the potential reasons for this more deeply, compare the securitization of the climate issue in the Security Council with other forums, or see what consequences the securitization of climate change as a regional problem has in practice. In the Security Council, one question will remain, and the debate will surely spin on: is global climate change about politics or security?

REFERENCES

Ayaz, A. (2022). Unsustainable Systems: Externalization as a Nonviable Form of Migration Management in the Face of Climate Change. *Insight Turkey, 24*(1), 37–54. https://www.jstor.org/stable/48655650

Balzacq, T. (2011). *Securitization Theory: How Security Problems Emerge and Dissolve*. Routledge.

Baysal, B., & Karakaş, U. (2017). Climate Change and Security: Different Perceptions, Different Approaches. *Uluslararası İlişkiler. International Relations, 14*(54), 21–44. https://www.jstor.org/stable/26406850

Bremberg, N., Mobjörk, M., & Krampe, F. (2022). Global Responses to Climate Security: Discourses, Institutions and Actions. *Journal of Peacebuilding & Development, 17*(3), 341–356. doi:10.1177/15423166221128180

Brown, O., Hammill, A., & McLeman, R. (2007). Climate Change as the "New" Security Threat: Implications for Africa. *International Affairs (Royal Institute of International Affairs 1944-), 83*(6), 1141–1154. https://www.jstor.org/stable/4541915

Buzan, B., Wæver, O., & de Wilde, J. (1998). *Security: A New Framework for Analysis*. Lynne Rienner Publishers.

Conca, K., Thwaites, J., & Lee, G. (2017). Climate Change and the UN Security Council: Bully Pulpit or Bull in a China Shop? *Global Environmental Politics, 17*(2), 1–20. doi:10.1162/GLEP_a_00398

Cousins, S. (2013). UN Security Council: Playing a role in the international climate change regime? *Global Change, Peace & Security, 25*(2), 191–210. doi:10.1080/14781158.2013.787058

Engelbrekt, K. (2016). Climate Change Mitigation. In *High-Table Diplomacy* (pp. 157–196). Georgetown University Press., https://www.jstor.org/stable/j.ctt1c84cd2.11

Fletcher, A. L. (2009). Clearing the air: The contribution of frame analysis to understanding climate policy in the United States. *Environmental Politics*, *18*(5), 800–816. doi:10.1080/09644010903157123

Gera, R., Narwal, R., Jain, M., Taneja, G., & Gupta, S. (2018). Sustainable Development Goals: Leveraging the Global Agenda for Driving Health Policy Reforms and Achieving Universal Health Coverage in India. *Indian Journal of Community Medicine : Official Publication of Indian Association of Preventive & Social Medicine*, *43*(4), 255–259. doi:10.4103/ijcm.IJCM_41_18 PMID:30662175

Holland, A. (2014). *Climate Change and National Security: Briefing Note*. American Security Project. https://www.jstor.org/stable/resrep05973

Hommel, D., & Murphy, A. B. (2013). Rethinking geopolitics in an era of climate change. *GeoJournal*, *78*(3), 507–524. https://www.jstor.org/stable/42002526. doi:10.100710708-012-9448-8

Malone, E. L. (2013). Climate Change and National Security. *Weather, Climate, and Society*, *5*(1), 93–95. https://www.jstor.org/stable/24907507. doi:10.1175/WCAS-D-12-00016.1

McDonald, M. (2023). Immovable objects? Impediments to a UN Security Council resolution on climate change. *International Affairs*, *99*(4), 1635–1651. doi:10.1093/ia/iiad064

Murphy, A. (2019). The United Nations Security Council and Climate Change: Mapping a Pragmatic Pathway to Intervention. *Carbon & Climate Law Review*, *13*(1), 50–62. https://www.jstor.org/stable/26739643

Ossola, A. (2017, May 22). How HIV became a matter of international security. *The Independent*. https://www.independent.co.uk/news/long_reads/how-hiv-became-a-matter-of-international-security-a7732701.html

Pleuger, G. (2014). Climate Change as a Threat to International Peace – The Role of the UN Security Council. In S. von Schorlemer & S. Maus (Eds.), *Climate Change as a Threat to Peace* (pp. 33–36). Peter Lang AG. https://www.jstor.org/stable/j.ctv2t4cvp.6

Project, A. S. (2012). *Part Two: Climate Change & Global Security*. American Security Project. https://www.jstor.org/stable/resrep05971

Rychnovská, D. (2014). Securitization and the Power of Threat Framing. *Perspectives*, *22*(2), 9–31. https://www.jstor.org/stable/24625251

Scott, S. (2022). Great Power Responsibility for Climate Security in the United Nations Security Council. In R. Falkner & B. Buzan (Eds.), Great Powers, Climate Change, and Global Environmental Responsibilities (p. 0). Oxford University Press. doi:10.1093/oso/9780198866022.003.0009

Scott, S. V. (2015). Implications of climate change for the UN Security Council: Mapping the range of potential policy responses. *International Affairs (Royal Institute of International Affairs 1944-)*, *91*(6), 1317–1333. https://www.jstor.org/stable/24539058

Scott, S. V., & Andrade, R. C. D. (2012). The Global Response to Climate Change: Can the Security Council Assume a Lead Role? *The Brown Journal of World Affairs*, *18*(2), 215–226. https://www.jstor.org/stable/24590874

Scott, S. V., & Nguyen, N. (2023). The UN Security Council and Climate Security: Responding to a Multifaceted Threat. In A. Warren (Ed.), *Global Security in an Age of Crisis* (pp. 374–394). Edinburgh University Press. https://www.jstor.org/stable/10.3366/j.ctv32vqn3h.22

Sindico, F. (2007). Climate Change: A Security (Council) Issue? *Carbon & Climate Law Review, 1*(1), 29–34. https://www.jstor.org/stable/24323646

Smith, E. S. (2020). *Climate Change in Women, Peace and Security National Action Plans.* Stockholm International Peace Research Institute. https://www.jstor.org/stable/resrep25311

Snow, D., & Benford, R. (1988). Ideology, Frame Resonance and Participant Mobilization. *International Social Movement Research, 1*, 197–217.

United Nations. (2018). *7.d Paris Agreement.* United Nations.

UNSC. (2007). *5663rd meeting* (S/PV.5663). United Nations Security Council.

UNSC. (2011). *6587th meeting* (S/PV.6587). United Nations Security Council.

UNSC. (2017a). *7857th meeting* (S/PV.7857). United Nations Security Council.

UNSC. (2017b). *7861st meeting* (S/PV.7861). United Nations Security Council.

UNSC. (2017c). *7894th meeting* (S/PV.7894). United Nations Security Council.

UNSC. (2017d). *7906th meeting* (S/PV.7906). United Nations Security Council.

UNSC. (2017e). *7911th meeting* (S/PV.7911). United Nations Security Council.

UNSC. (2017f). *8047th meeting* (S/PV.8047). United Nations Security Council.

UNSC. (2017g). *8069th meeting* (S/PV.8069). United Nations Security Council.

UNSC. (2017h). *8080th meeting* (S/PV.8080). United Nations Security Council.

UNSC. (2017i). *8106th meeting* (S/PV.8106). United Nations Security Council.

UNSC. (2017j). *8144th meeting* (S/PV.8144). United Nations Security Council.

UNSC. (2017k). Resolution 2349 (Vol. S). United Nations Security Council., RES/2349.

UNSC. (2018a). *8156th meeting* (S/PV.8156). United Nations Security Council.

UNSC. (2018b). *8162nd meeting* (S/PV.8162). United Nations Security Council.

UNSC. (2018c). *8185th meeting* (S/PV.8185). United Nations Security Council.

UNSC. (2018d). *8212th meeting* (S/PV.8212). United Nations Security Council.

UNSC. (2018e). Resolution 2408 (Vol. S). United Nations Security Council., RES/2408.

van Munster, R. (2018). Securitization. *The Concise Oxford Dictionary of Politics and International Relations.* Oxford Press. https://www.oxfordbibliographies.com/display/document/obo-9780199743292/obo-9780199743292-0091.xml

Wenham, C. (2019). The oversecuritization of global health: Changing the terms of debate. *International Affairs*, *95*(5), 1093–1110. doi:10.1093/ia/iiz170

Wolfers, A. (1952). "National Security" as an Ambiguous Symbol. *Political Science Quarterly*, *67*(4), 481–502. doi:10.2307/2145138

ADDITIONAL READING

Ayaz, A. (2022). Unsustainable Systems: Externalization as a Nonviable Form of Migration Management in the Face of Climate Change. *Insight Turkey, 24*(1), 37–54. https://www.jstor.org/stable/48655650

Balzacq, T. (2011). *Securitization Theory: How Security Problems Emerge and Dissolve*. Routledge.

Baysal, B., & Karakaş, U. (2017). Climate Change and Security: Different Perceptions, Different Approaches. *Uluslararası İlişkiler. International Relations*, *14*(54), 21–44. https://www.jstor.org/stable/26406850

Bremberg, N., Mobjörk, M., & Krampe, F. (2022). Global Responses to Climate Security: Discourses, Institutions and Actions. *Journal of Peacebuilding & Development*, *17*(3), 341–356. doi:10.1177/15423166221128180

Brown, O., Hammill, A., & McLeman, R. (2007). Climate Change as the "New" Security Threat: Implications for Africa. *International Affairs (Royal Institute of International Affairs 1944-)*, *83*(6), 1141–1154. https://www.jstor.org/stable/4541915

Buzan, B., Wæver, O., & de Wilde, J. (1998). *Security: A New Framework for Analysis*. Lynne Rienner Publishers.

Conca, K., Thwaites, J., & Lee, G. (2017). Climate Change and the UN Security Council: Bully Pulpit or Bull in a China Shop? *Global Environmental Politics*, *17*(2), 1–20. doi:10.1162/GLEP_a_00398

Cousins, S. (2013). UN Security Council: Playing a role in the international climate change regime? *Global Change, Peace & Security*, *25*(2), 191–210. doi:10.1080/14781158.2013.787058

Engelbrekt, K. (2016). Climate Change Mitigation. In *High-Table Diplomacy* (pp. 157–196). Georgetown University Press., https://www.jstor.org/stable/j.ctt1c84cd2.11

Fletcher, A. L. (2009). Clearing the air: The contribution of frame analysis to understanding climate policy in the United States. *Environmental Politics*, *18*(5), 800–816. doi:10.1080/09644010903157123

Gera, R., Narwal, R., Jain, M., Taneja, G., & Gupta, S. (2018). Sustainable Development Goals: Leveraging the Global Agenda for Driving Health Policy Reforms and Achieving Universal Health Coverage in India. *Indian Journal of Community Medicine : Official Publication of Indian Association of Preventive & Social Medicine*, *43*(4), 255–259. doi:10.4103/ijcm.IJCM_41_18 PMID:30662175

Holland, A. (2014). *Climate Change and National Security: Briefing Note*. American Security Project. https://www.jstor.org/stable/resrep05973

Hommel, D., & Murphy, A. B. (2013). Rethinking geopolitics in an era of climate change. *GeoJournal, 78*(3), 507–524. https://www.jstor.org/stable/42002526. doi:10.100710708-012-9448-8

Malone, E. L. (2013). Climate Change and National Security. *Weather, Climate, and Society, 5*(1), 93–95. https://www.jstor.org/stable/24907507. doi:10.1175/WCAS-D-12-00016.1

McDonald, M. (2023). Immovable objects? Impediments to a UN Security Council resolution on climate change. *International Affairs, 99*(4), 1635–1651. doi:10.1093/ia/iiad064

Murphy, A. (2019). The United Nations Security Council and Climate Change: Mapping a Pragmatic Pathway to Intervention. *Carbon & Climate Law Review, 13*(1), 50–62. https://www.jstor.org/stable/26739643

Ossola, A. (2017, May 22). How HIV became a matter of international security. *The Independent*. https://www.independent.co.uk/news/long_reads/how-hiv-became-a-matter-of-international-security-a7732701.html

Pleuger, G. (2014). Climate Change as a Threat to International Peace – The Role of the UN Security Council. In S. von Schorlemer & S. Maus (Eds.), *Climate Change as a Threat to Peace* (pp. 33–36). Peter Lang AG., https://www.jstor.org/stable/j.ctv2t4cvp.6

Project, A. S. (2012). *Part Two: Climate Change & Global Security*. American Security Project. https://www.jstor.org/stable/resrep05971

Rychnovská, D. (2014). Securitization and the Power of Threat Framing. *Perspectives, 22*(2), 9–31. https://www.jstor.org/stable/24625251

Scott, S. (2022). Great Power Responsibility for Climate Security in the United Nations Security Council. In R. Falkner & B. Buzan (Eds.), Great Powers, Climate Change, and Global Environmental Responsibilities (p. 0). Oxford University Press. doi:10.1093/oso/9780198866022.003.0009

Scott, S. V. (2015). Implications of climate change for the UN Security Council: Mapping the range of potential policy responses. *International Affairs (Royal Institute of International Affairs 1944-), 91*(6), 1317–1333. https://www.jstor.org/stable/24539058

Scott, S. V., & Andrade, R. C. D. (2012). The Global Response to Climate Change: Can the Security Council Assume a Lead Role? *The Brown Journal of World Affairs, 18*(2), 215–226. https://www.jstor.org/stable/24590874

Scott, S. V., & Nguyen, N. (2023). The UN Security Council and Climate Security: Responding to a Multifaceted Threat. In A. Warren (Ed.), *Global Security in an Age of Crisis* (pp. 374–394). Edinburgh University Press. https://www.jstor.org/stable/10.3366/j.ctv32vqn3h.22

Sindico, F. (2007). Climate Change: A Security (Council) Issue? *Carbon & Climate Law Review, 1*(1), 29–34. https://www.jstor.org/stable/24323646

Smith, E. S. (2020). *Climate Change in Women, Peace and Security National Action Plans*. Stockholm International Peace Research Institute. https://www.jstor.org/stable/resrep25311

Snow, D., & Benford, R. (1988). Ideology, Frame Resonance and Participant Mobilization. *International Social Movement Research, 1*, 197–217.

United Nations. (2018). *7.d Paris Agreement*. United Nations.

UNSC. (2007). *5663rd meeting* (S/PV.5663). United Nations Security Council.

UNSC. (2011). *6587th meeting* (S/PV.6587). United Nations Security Council.

UNSC. (2017a). *7857th meeting* (S/PV.7857). United Nations Security Council.

UNSC. (2017b). *7861st meeting* (S/PV.7861). United Nations Security Council.

UNSC. (2017c). *7894th meeting* (S/PV.7894). United Nations Security Council.

UNSC. (2017d). *7906th meeting* (S/PV.7906). United Nations Security Council.

UNSC. (2017e). *7911th meeting* (S/PV.7911). United Nations Security Council.

UNSC. (2017f). *8047th meeting* (S/PV.8047). United Nations Security Council.

UNSC. (2017g). *8069th meeting* (S/PV.8069). United Nations Security Council.

UNSC. (2017h). *8080th meeting* (S/PV.8080). United Nations Security Council.

UNSC. (2017i). *8106th meeting* (S/PV.8106). United Nations Security Council.

UNSC. (2017j). *8144th meeting* (S/PV.8144). United Nations Security Council.

UNSC. (2017k). Resolution 2349 (Vol. S). United Nations Security Council., RES/2349.

UNSC. (2018a). *8156th meeting* (S/PV.8156). United Nations Security Council.

UNSC. (2018b). *8162nd meeting* (S/PV.8162). United Nations Security Council.

UNSC. (2018c). *8185th meeting* (S/PV.8185). United Nations Security Council.

UNSC. (2018d). *8212th meeting* (S/PV.8212). United Nations Security Council.

UNSC. (2018e). Resolution 2408 (Vol. S). United Nations Security Council., RES/2408.

van Munster, R. (2018). *Securitization*. The Concise Oxford Dictionary of Politics and International Relations. https://www.oxfordbibliographies.com/display/document/obo-9780199743292/obo-9780199743292-0091.xml

Wenham, C. (2019). The oversecuritization of global health: Changing the terms of debate. *International Affairs*, *95*(5), 1093–1110. doi:10.1093/ia/iiz170

Wolfers, A. (1952). "National Security" as an Ambiguous Symbol. *Political Science Quarterly*, *67*(4), 481–502. doi:10.2307/2145138

KEY TERMS AND DEFINITIONS

Climate Change: Refers to long-term shifts and alterations in weather patterns, including temperature, precipitation, wind patterns, and more, resulting from human activities, primarily the emission of greenhouse gases. Climate change is a global phenomenon with significant environmental, social, and economic impacts.

Global Goals for Sustainable Development: Also known as the Sustainable Development Goals (SDGs), they are a set of 17 interconnected goals adopted by all United Nations member states in 2015. The goals aim to address global challenges, including poverty, inequality, climate change, environmental degradation, and promote sustainable development.

Paris Agreement: An international treaty adopted in 2015 under the United Nations Framework Convention on Climate Change (UNFCCC). The agreement aims to limit global warming to well below 2 degrees Celsius above pre-industrial levels and pursue efforts to limit the temperature increase to 1.5 degrees Celsius. It sets out commitments for countries to reduce greenhouse gas emissions and provides a framework for climate change adaptation and finance.

Regional Solutions: Refers to approaches and strategies that focus on addressing climate change impacts and challenges within specific geographic regions. It recognizes that certain climate-related issues and vulnerabilities are region-specific and require tailored responses. Regional solutions often involve collaboration and cooperation among neighboring countries or within specific regional frameworks to mitigate and adapt to the effects of climate change.

Securitization: The process by which an issue is transformed from a purely political matter into a security concern. It involves framing the issue as a threat to security, making it urgent and bypassing normal democratic processes to address it.

UN Security Council: One of the six main organs of the United Nations responsible for maintaining international peace and security. The Security Council has 15 member states, including five permanent members (China, France, Russia, the United Kingdom, and the United States) with veto power and ten non-permanent members elected for two-year terms. It has the authority to discuss and act on various global issues, including conflicts, threats to peace, and emerging security challenges.

Chapter 4
Implementation of Carbon Tax and Emissions Trading System in Türkiye

Aysel Varoglu
Ministry of Trade, Turkey

İzzet Ari
Social Sciences University of Ankara, Turkey

ABSTRACT

The industrial revolution, which started with the invention of coal-fired steam engines, led to the intensive consumption of fossil fuels and environmental pollution all over the world. In the 1960s, the first international steps were taken to prevent environmental pollution. The main ones are the United Nations Framework Convention on Climate Change, the Kyoto Protocol, and the Paris Agreement. Building on the Paris Agreement, the European Union announced the Green Deal and prepared the carbon border adjustment mechanism in line with the objectives of the Deal. The peculiarity of this mechanism is that it will price carbon not only for European producers, but also for the countries with which Europe trades. Large economies that do not want to lose the European Market are updating their own emissions trading systems in line with the European Union emissions trading system. The aim of this study is to propose a model for a carbon market to be established in Türkiye based on the carbon markets implemented in selected large countries.

1. INTRODUCTION

In order to prevent climate change, many countries have started to price carbon. This is done through the Emissions Trading System (ETS), which sets a cap on greenhouse gas (GHG) emissions, or through a direct carbon tax. Since carbon taxes increase production costs, it is a fact that multinational companies that do not want to pay carbon taxes continue their production in developing countries (DCs) or less

DOI: 10.4018/978-1-6684-9272-7.ch004

developed countries (LDCs). By June 2023, 195 countries had signed the Paris Agreement. With the Agreement, efforts to prevent climate change in the world have increased.

In the 1960s, increasing environmental pollution called into question the use of fossil fuels. Since the problem concerns the whole world, the first attempt to reduce emissions was the United Nations Framework Convention on Climate Change (UNFCCC), followed by the Kyoto Protocol. But the protocol failed to achieve its goal when the countries that emit the most emissions did not join. Unlike the Kyoto Protocol, the Paris Agreement allowed countries to submit declarations of intent and set a clear international deadline for zero emissions. With the participation of all countries of the world in the Paris Agreement, the EU and all countries trading with the EU aim to phase out the use of fossil fuels with a net zero (emission-free) target by 2050. In particular, most countries have set a date for coal phase-out. In China, which is rich in coal reserves, many of the world's largest companies produce and continue to use coal-generated electricity in their production (Urgewald, 2021). As published by the IEA, China ranks first in global coal consumption for 2020-2023, while India ranks second (IEA, 2022). Nevertheless, the countries included in the agreement have committed to carbon neutrality by 2050, while China has committed to carbon neutrality by 2060 and India by 2070 (Vinay, et al., 2023).

Voluntary carbon markets have been implemented in Türkiye so far.[1] However, these voluntary markets have not been effective in reducing emissions and are not an adequate method for the CBAM announced by the EU. There is no established carbon tax or Emissions Trading System in the country. Considering that Türkiye is a party to the Kyoto Protocol and ratified the Paris Agreement on the one hand and a Customs Union Partner of the EU on the other, the absence of an Emissions Trading System in the country is a major shortcoming. If Türkiye, which is already working to establish an Emissions Trading System, fails to implement it as soon as possible, it will lose revenue from steel and aluminum exports in particular, as it will be more costly to export to the EU. The aim of this paper is to analyze the carbon markets in Canada, the UK, the US, the EU, and China and to propose a model for the first carbon market to be established in Türkiye.

2. CARBON PRICING

There are two main types of carbon pricing (The World Bank, 2022a). One of these is the ETS. In an ETS, a cap is placed on emissions. Within this upper limit, allocations are distributed free of charge or by auction. The price is determined by the market's supply and demand for emission allowances. The second type of carbon pricing is the carbon tax. In this tax, the government places a fixed price on emissions. The polluter (producer or consumer) pays this price. In other words, the carbon tax method intervenes in the market through a price mechanism (The World Bank, 2022a).

Figure 1. Map of carbon tax and ETS
(The World Bank, 2023)

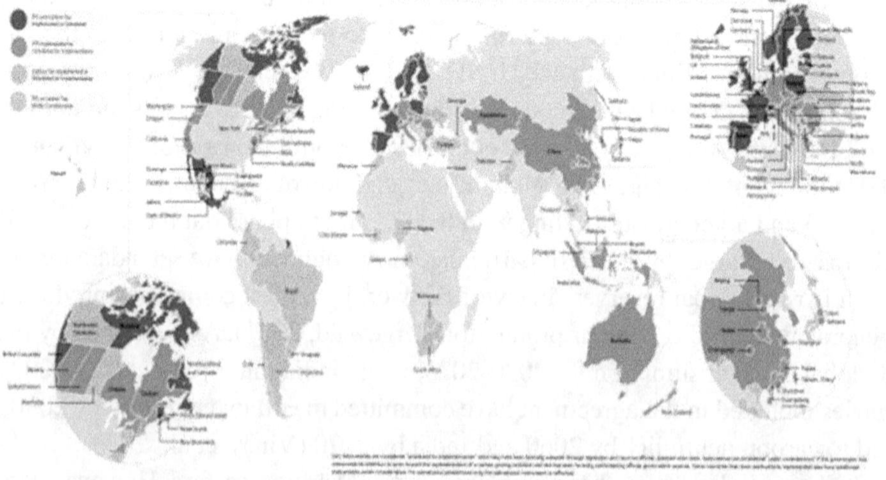

The carbon market is the market where carbon credits and emission allowances are traded. These markets can be regional, national, and global. Carbon markets are divided into mandatory and voluntary markets. Mandatory markets implement mandatory emissions set under an international agreement. The Kyoto Protocol and the ETSs established in countries are examples of this. Voluntary markets are markets that aim to reduce GHG independently of international agreements. Examples include voluntary over-the-counter markets and the Chicago Climate Exchange (EEX) (Özcan, Ergün Yüksel, & Ocaklı, 2022).

Individuals and businesses are discouraged from greenhouse gas-emitting production and consumption by putting a price on carbon in the carbon trading market. With this price applied at every stage from production to consumption, environmental pollution, which is an external cost, is internalized (The World Bank, 2022a). Worldwide, there are 68 carbon pricing instruments (CPIs). These operate as carbon taxes and emissions trading systems (ETSs). And Global carbon pricing revenue reached nearly US$84 billion last year, up almost 60% from the previous year. CPIs in operation account for about 23% of total global greenhouse gas (GHG) emissions (The World Bank, 2023). However, carbon pricing to prevent pollution and thus climate change negatively affects low-income households. Low-income people, especially in rural areas, have to use carbon-intensive products for cooking, heating, and transportation. (Caranci & Econ, 2021). Another problem is that a country that unilaterally imposes a carbon price will lose competitiveness in Emissions Intensive Trade Exposed Industries (EITE). The reduced competitiveness of EITE businesses will force them to produce in countries that do not put a price on carbon, creating the risk of carbon leakage. Many countries provide free allowances to carbon-intensive sectors under the ETS to prevent this. One of the objectives of the EU's Carbon Border Adjustment Mechanism (CBAM) is to protect domestic producers whose ability to compete in EITEs within the EU is reduced. Because the EU has been implementing unilateral carbon pricing since 2005 (Caranci & Econ, 2021).

2.1. Emissions Trading System (ETS)

An emissions trading scheme (ETS) sets a cap on GHG emissions that can be emitted in defined sectors and scopes (ICAP, 2023). In the ETS, emissions can be traded to meet emission targets. Emission permits can be traded within the cap. Supply and demand for emission allowances determine the emission price. Allocations are initially given free of charge but are later auctioned. Emission credits are also given to organizations that reduce their emission levels below the upper limit. These credits can be sold to other entities that exceed baseline emission levels (The World Bank, 2022a). When compatible ETSs are linked, participants in one system can use units of the other system. This lowers the cost of reducing emissions and increases liquidity, making the carbon price more stable (European Commission, 2022).

Table 1. The ETS has advantages and disadvantages

Advantages	Disadvantages
Provides cost-effectiveness	Fixing emissions at the upper limit prevents emission reductions
Provides flexibility	Creates a risk of carbon leakage
Provides transparency in the market	The system becomes open to the outside world as the price is determined by supply and demand in the market
Free allocations encourage companies to participate	Free distribution of allocations within the system may reduce demand

If we briefly explain the disadvantages; the fact that the ETS fixes the emission at the upper limit and businesses can buy and sell emission permits within the upper limit prevents emission reductions (Yılmazcan & Çakmak, 2018). Since the ETS creates the risk of carbon leakage when the carbon cap and carbon price are not set correctly, the method used by countries to prevent carbon leakage is to provide free allowances. These free allocations could translate into a subsidy to domestic producers under border carbon regulations. This is contrary to the rules of the World Trade Organization (WTO). Because incentives lead to imbalances in mutual trade and competition (Jegou & Rubini, 2011).

The fact that the price in the ETS system is determined according to supply and demand in the market may create risks as it makes the system open to the outside world. This is because an excessive increase in supply or demand due to external intervention would cause instability in the market. Free distribution of allocations within the system may reduce demand. An example of this is seen in the EU ETS. In 2005-2007, the first phase of the EU ETS, demand fell due to initial free allocations and carbon prices falling to zero (European Commission, 2022). To avoid a similar situation in Türkiye, it is important to provide free allocations when needed. In terms of advantages, the ETS provides market-based mechanisms for cost-effective emission reductions. Companies have the flexibility to choose what is cost-effective in reducing emissions. The ETS provides a transparent mechanism for monitoring and reporting emissions. Free allowances incentivize companies to join the ETS.

2.2. Carbon Tax

Carbon tax is based on the polluter pays principle (Hotunluoğlu & Tekeli, 2007-2). The carbon tax has the advantage of being a fiscal instrument. Because the government's rate of revenue generation is high.

Setting the tax at the beginning of the year avoids future uncertainty in the carbon market (Yılmazcan & Çakmak, 2018). If the carbon tax is applied together with the emission target, the correct carbon tax rate can be determined according to the result. For example, if emission levels are lower than expected, carbon tax revenues will also be lower than expected (Kaufman, Krause, & Desousa, 2018).

2.3. Carbon Border Adjustment (CBA)

Import duties are imposed on goods imported into a country that puts a price on carbon in border regulations, on the scale of the emissions content of those goods, thus protecting the domestic producer. In exports, domestically produced goods are exported to foreign countries without a carbon price, while the domestic producer recovers carbon costs as a rebate. Thus, by reducing carbon costs domestic producers, gain an advantage over their foreign competitors who will be subject to increased import duties. This avoids the risk of carbon leakage from carbon pricing and overcomes competition barriers (Caranci & Econ, 2021). In a CBA, low-income countries and low-emission countries could be exempted from the system. But imposing import duties on some countries but not others creates trade discrimination, which is against WTO rules (Holzer, 2016).

Another aspect is that the CBA-imposing country imposes an import tax equal to the carbon price of domestic products. This increases carbon costs for exporters. An example of what is considered a local subsidy is Canada's Output-Based Pricing System (OBPS). The system covers the production of cement, natural gas, aluminum, and refined products, which are particularly carbon-intensive sectors. In the OBPS, domestic firms are protected from carbon prices by giving emission credits to domestic EITE firms (Turcotte, Gorski, & Riehl, 2019). Providing emission credits and free allowances to domestic producers in EITE is also a form of subsidy.[2] A CBA between some countries would also violate WTO rules as it would be an import tariff. Because WTO rules prohibit preferential treatment of domestic products over imported products (Caranci & Econ, 2021). Nevertheless, the European Commission plans to phase out free allocations in CBAM from 2026 to 2034, which it claims is in line with WTO rules. Moreover, this will start at a low rate and gradually increase, ending in 2034 (ICAP, 2023).

On the other hand, the EU, which has been implementing an ETS within the union since 2005, has exposed its domestic producers to unfair competition for more than fifteen years due to cheaper imports from countries not subject to carbon taxes. To remedy this, the EU will implement CBAM. Another reason for the CBAM regulation is Europe's goal of becoming a climate-neutral continent to prevent climate change under the Paris Agreement (European Commission, 2021). The Union initially defined CBAM to cover six carbon-intensive products and some of the inputs used in their production. If the system runs smoothly, it is planned to be applied to all sectors. Starting in 2023, the pilot phase will cover these selected sectors. These sectors account for more than 45% of CO_2 emissions. From October 1, 2023, importers will report embedded emissions of imported goods but will not pay the carbon tax. CBAM will not apply to goods from Switzerland, Norway, Iceland, and Liechtenstein, which are not EU members but have an ETS linked to the EU ETS (Ari & Varoglu, 2022).

CBAM will initially apply to imports of goods and selected precursors from carbon-intensive sectors with a high risk of carbon leakages, such as cement, iron and steel, aluminum, fertilizer, electricity, and hydrogen. However, when fully phased in, the CBAM will cover more than 50% of emissions from sectors covered by the ETS. CBAM will enter into force from October 1, 2023, during the transitional phase, and will move from the transitional phase to the permanent phase on January 1, 2026. The first reporting period for importers in transition will end on January 31, 2024. From 1 January 2026, importers will annually declare the number of goods imported into the EU in the previous year and their embedded greenhouse gases and will surrender the corresponding number of CBAM certificates. The price of the certificates will be calculated based on the average weekly auction price of EU ETS allowances (European Commission, 2023). CBAM's ability to eliminate the risk of carbon leakage depends on not putting too much pressure on importers or EU producers. This will be possible if the European Commission abolishes free allowances altogether in 2034. Because only then will importers be treated impartially compared to domestic producers within the EU. However, the retention of the EUA free allocation for European domestic producers in the CBAM also contradicts the principles set out in the UNFCCC . While European producers are supported by EUAs, producers in countries vulnerable to climate change will not benefit from these free allocations (United Nations, 1992). Another important issue is that the mechanism violates the principle of "non-discrimination" in the General Agreement on Tariffs and Trade (GATT) by differentiating between low and high-carbon products (GATT, 2022).

3. SELECTED COUNTRIES İMPLEMENTING ETS

3.1. EU ETS

The EU ETS, established in 2005 within the EU, is the world's first international ETS. The system is currently in its fourth phase, from 2021 to 2030. Under the system, an upper limit is imposed on the amount of GHG emissions of emission-intensive sectors in the Union and companies are obliged to hold an EUA for every ton of CO_2 they emit. Companies that emit more CO_2 than their emission permits cover are liable to pay fines. Firms can also receive emission credits from developing countries other than EU ETS allocations. The system that gives companies this right is the Clean Development Mechanism (CDM) in the Kyoto Protocol (Appunn, Clean Energy Wire, 2021).

The EU ETS includes a green finance system that establishes financing mechanisms for the transition of energy-intensive industrial sectors to a low-carbon economy. The innovation fund in the system is used to support innovative technologies, while the modernization fund is used to modernize energy systems, especially in the electricity sector, and to increase energy efficiency. The system supports green investments in low-income Member States. This ensures a fair transition (European Commission, 2022). These low-income Member States are also supported with auction revenues and free allocations to support their investments. These supports enable these countries to diversify their energy supply sources, upgrade their infrastructure and modernize their energy generation, transmission, and distribution lines (European Commission, 2022). Since the start of the third phase of the EU ETS in 2013, a certain amount of EUAs is auctioned each year, excluding the surplus allocations in the Union portfolio, and each year the allocation amount and the cap are reduced. No increase in investment in industry as low-allocation EUAs failed to make electricity generation from fossil sources more expensive and failed to incentivize low-carbon innovation. The EU has therefore temporarily withdrawn 900 million permits from auction between 2014 and 2016. As of 2019, part of the surplus of circulating allocations is transferred to the Market Stabilization Reserve (MSR), EUAs are auctioned when the number of allocations in the market falls below a certain level (Appunn, Clean Energy Wire, 2019). The ETS Market Stabilization Reserve will reduce allocations by more than 272 million from September 2023 to August 2024 (European Commission, 2023).

The first phase was implemented between 2005 and 2007, during which emissions from generators and energy-intensive industries were included in the system. In addition, the system provided all allowances free of charge, imposed a €40 per tonne penalty for non-compliance, and liberalized emissions trading across the EU. Emissions were determined through Monitoring, Verification, and Reporting (MRV) and the upper limit was estimated in the absence of reliable emission data. However, as the total amount of allowances issued in these years exceeded emissions, the price of allowances dropped to zero in 2007 (European Commission, 2022a). "The sectors in the first phase are power plants, hazardous waste, some incineration plants, oil refineries, coke ovens and iron and steel mills, cement, glass, lime, brick, ceramic and paper sectors" (ICAP, 2022).

The second phase was implemented between 2008 and 2012, with Iceland, Liechtenstein, and Norway included in the system and the free allocation rate reaching 90%. The penalty for non-compliance was increased to €100 per ton. On January 1, 2012, the aviation sector was included in the system (including flights within Europe only) and the cap on allowances was lowered based on the actual emissions achieved in the first phase. In 2008, due to the economic crisis, there was a glut of allowances and credits due to high emission reductions (European Commission, 2022a). The third phase was implemented between 2013 and 2020 and allocations were auctioned. Free allocations were subject to certain rules and the number of sectors and gas in the system was increased (European Commission, 2022a). "Sectors in the third tier are petrochemicals, ammonia, non-ferrous metals and ferrous metals, gypsum, aluminum, nitric, adipic, and some glyoxylic acid production. From this stage, in addition to emission monitoring and reporting, data verification was also carried out" (ICAP, 2022). The fourth phase started in 2021 and will continue until the end of 2030 (European Commission, 2022a). "In the EU ETS, MRV is issued annually and verification is required before March 31st of each year. After verification, operators must deliver the equivalent number of allowances by the end of April" (ICAP, 2022).

As the EU plans to become a net-zero continent by 2050 under the European Green Deal, sectors covered by the EU ETS need to reduce their emissions by 55% compared to 2005 levels. In addition, the free allowance system will be extended for ten years and allowances will be given free of charge to emission-intensive sectors and new businesses (Council of The European Union, 2023). Free allowances in low-emission sectors will be phased out from 2027 and completely removed by 2032 (KPMG, 2023). To reduce the surplus of allowances, from 2023 onwards, retained EUAs will be canceled and excess allowances that lead to higher emissions in the long term will be returned to the market (Appunn, Clean Energy Wire, 2019).

3.2. UK ETS

The ETS of the country that left the European Union entered into force on January 1, 2021. However, under the Ireland/Northern Ireland Protocol, electricity producers in Northern Ireland remained in the EU ETS. The UK ETS covers energy-intensive industries, electricity generation, and aviation. The aviation sector includes domestic flights within the United Kingdom, flights between the United Kingdom and Gibraltar, and flights from the United Kingdom to the countries of the European Economic Area (UK Government, 2023).

3.3. Canadian ETS

On October 3, 2016, the Government of Canada announced the Pan-Canadian Approach to Pricing Carbon Pollution, setting out Canada's approach to carbon pricing for the period 2018-2022. This year, updates were made to the system. The new system includes a price-based system, i.e. a carbon tax on fossil fuels, or a hybrid system consisting of a carbon tax on fossil fuels and an output-based pricing system for industry or, a cap and trade system.

According to the new regulation; The federal fuel surcharge will continue to apply in Alberta, Saskatchewan, Manitoba, Nunavut, Ontario, and Yukon. It will also cover Newfoundland and Labrador, Nova Scotia, and Prince Edward Island as of July 1, 2023. And Canadians in these provinces will receive their first quarterly Climate Action Incentive payments. On the other hand, British Columbia, New Brunswick, Northwest Territories, and Quebec will continue to implement their own pollution pricing systems. For polluters from large industries, the Federal Output-Based Pricing System will continue to apply in Manitoba, Prince Edward Island, Yukon, and Nunavut, but will no longer apply in Saskatchewan. On the other hand, Alberta, British Columbia, New Brunswick, New Brunswick, Newfoundland and Labrador, Northwest Territories, Nova Scotia, Ontario, Quebec, and Saskatchewan will continue to implement their own pollution pricing systems for industrial emissions. Many provinces, such as Quebec and British Columbia, have established their own carbon tax systems to fulfill the OBPS. Covers industrial polluters that emit 50,000 tons or more of annual GHG emissions in the OBPS (Government of Canada, 2022).

The Government of Canada's Federal System most of the revenue collected in the system is paid to households as carbon tax support. This is done to prevent the public from being negatively affected by carbon taxes. The remaining is spent on clean energy projects. A carbon tax is levied according to household size and refunded to all households. In addition, revenues are distributed only in the states where the system is implemented (Government of Canada, 2022). Quebec ETS became operational in 2013 and integrated with the California ETS in 2014. This system covers energy, buildings, transportation, and industrial emissions. The system is estimated to cover more than 80% of GHG emissions from the industry, energy, heating, and transportation sectors (ICAP, 2023). Comparing carbon markets in two countries on the basis of price alone may yield inaccurate results. The countries with the highest carbon prices worldwide are Sweden, Switzerland, Finland, and Norway, followed by Canada. Of these, Switzerland has no domestic fossil fuel production, so all fuels are imported, hence the carbon tax is applied at the border. Given the abundance of fossil fuel reserves in Canada, a higher carbon price in the oil and gas sector could act as a disincentive to fossil fuel use (Caranci & Econ, 2021).

3.4. US ETS

There is only one ETS in the USA. California is the only state in the country with an ETS. The California ETS became operational in 2012 and was connected to the Quebec ETS in 2014. The system is committed to being carbon-neutral by 2040 (ICAP, 2023). "California's climate laws require that at least 35% of investments from the GHG mitigation fund go to projects that benefit disadvantaged communities and at least 25% to projects located in these communities" (Lashof, 2019). At the COP26 Climate Summit in Glasgow, it was raised that EU steel and aluminum produced under the ETS could enter the US duty-free (Hay, 2021). This is only possible if the California ETS is harmonized with the EU ETS. Because a national ETS has not yet been implemented in the US. It will be easy for the California ETS, which has been integrated with the Quebec ETS for years, to adapt to the EU ETS. In light of this information, in the event of such an agreement between the US and the EU, Türkiye needs to establish an ETS integrated with the EU ETS in order for Turkish steel to enter the US market. On the other hand, if this turns into an FTA, it will benefit Türkiye. Because under the Customs Union Agreement, Türkiye has the right to conclude free trade agreements with countries with which the EU has free trade agreements (Uzun & Doğan, 2014).

In addition, the US states of Connecticut, Delaware, Maine, Maryland, Massachusetts, New Hampshire, New Jersey, New York, Pennsylvania, Rhode Island, Vermont and Virginia are implementing the Regional Greenhouse Gas Initiative (RGGI), a joint program to limit and reduce CO_2 emissions in the energy sector. RGGI is the first market-based, cap-and-invest regional initiative in the United States. Under RGGI, each state limits CO_2 emissions from power plants, awards CO_2 allowances, and participates in regional CO_2 allowance auctions. In RGGI states, fossil-fuel electricity generators with a capacity of 25 megawatts or more are required to hold allowances equal to their CO_2 emissions over a three-year control period (RGGI, 2023).

Another recent step forward on the carbon market in the US is US President Biden's Reconciliation Act. This law aims to put a price on carbon pollution and thus close the emissions gap (The White House, 2022). The US Department of Energy's Loan Programs Office (LPO) finances large-scale energy infrastructure projects in the US, providing support for transforming existing energy infrastructure, revitalizing nuclear construction, accelerating publicly-sourced solar and wind power, expanding domestic electricity generation, etc (Jordan & Cunningham, 2023).

3.5. China ETS

China ETS is the world's largest ETS, launched in 2021. In addition, there are eight regional ETSs established under the Paris Agreement within the China ETS, which are gradually joining the national ETS (ICAP, 2021d). Between 2014 and 2017, the European Commission ran a 3-year project to support the design and implementation of emissions trading in China. The project provided technical assistance to China for capacity building. This supported the linking of regional ETSs to the National ETS (European Commission, 2023).

Beijing switched to the ETS in November 2013 and covered emissions from direct and indirect electricity users for seven years. Heating, cement, petrochemicals, and services are covered, and in 2016 the transportation sector was also covered. The system is managed by the Beijing Municipal Bureau of Ecology and Environment. Beijing ETS was connected to the national ETS in 2021 (ICAP, 2023). In Chongqing, another pilot region, the ETS system started in 2014 and the sectors in the system are electricity, aluminum, ferroalloys, calcium carbide, cement, caustic soda, and iron and steel (ICAP, 2023). On a sectoral basis, the scope of this ETS is almost identical to the EU ETS. China managed to set it up in 2014. Launched in December 2013, the Guangdong ETS is the largest ETS in the country and has covered the power, cement, steel, petrochemical, paper, and local aviation sectors since 2016 (ICAP, 2023). Hubei ETS started in April 2014 and has the largest market in the spot futures secondary market. It also covers 38% of emissions from carbon-intensive companies. The Hubei ETS is also linked to the national ETS (ICAP, 2023). Launched in November 2013, the Shanghai ETS covers the electricity, industry, construction, aviation, shipping, and transportation sectors and has a highly successful emissions allowance system with credit trading and term allowances, and financing opportunities such as green bonds and carbon credits are widespread in the system (ICAP, 2023). Launched in June 2013, the Shenzhen ETS is the first pilot ETS in the country and covers the energy, industry, construction, and transportation sectors (ICAP, 2023).

The Tianjin ETS was launched in December 2013. The system covers the heat, electricity, iron and steel, petrochemicals, chemicals, oil and gas exploration, paper, aviation, and building materials sectors (ICAP, 2023). China, the world's most active producer, does not want to risk its economic future, so it is establishing local ETSs and gradually transitioning them to national ETS. If China, not wanting to lose the large European market, fully integrates its ETS into the EU ETS (which is exactly the purpose of the EU's support to China to establish local ETSs), Türkiye will lose the EU market to China in some sectors. Worse, it is quite easy for China's ETS to be fully integrated into other ETSs around the world. This is because different financial steps and methods have been used in China's domestic ETSs. Integrating all these into the national system will make China the world's strongest ETS owner.

4. TÜRKİYE'S CARBON MARKET MODEL

In Türkiye, voluntary carbon markets are being implemented in wind, geothermal, small hydroelectric power plants, solid waste disposal, etc. These markets certify and trade greenhouse gas emissions. Since 2006, these emission certificates have been traded on spot markets and are called VERs. However, the voluntary nature of this market and the lack of a legal infrastructure prevents access to information such as transaction volume, parties and emission reductions achieved (Arı, 2010). Türkiye's delay in establishing an ETS is seen as a disadvantage. However, this delay can be turned to advantage by modeling systems that have been integrated locally, nationally and globally for years in many countries. First of all, Türkiye needs to make infrastructure investments suitable for the new production and consumption system. Revenue from carbon pricing can be used to build climate-smart infrastructure. Second, as decarbonization technologies require significant infrastructure, these sectors need to be supported. In addition, revenue from the carbon market can be used to provide rebates to low-income households. Another important aspect is that businesses and households should be allowed to choose their own carbon pricing systems. This will ensure a fair transition in the system. Otherwise, social and economic injustice will result.

In addition, non-profit institutions and organizations should be exempt from the carbon tax (Caranci & Econ, 2021). In Canada, for example, revenues from federal taxes are redistributed to provincial citizens within the system. In California, it uses the proceeds to give discounts on electric cars, provide affordable housing, build energy-efficient homes, plant trees, reduce fire risk, etc (Mountford & McGregor, 2018).

In this section, based on the "Emissions Trading in Practice Design and Implementation Manual" prepared by the World Bank Secretariat and ICAP, the necessary infrastructure and financial institutions for a carbon market to be established in Türkiye and which carbon market would be more suitable for Türkiye are analyzed. Türkiye should first establish a greenhouse gas pricing law. It should also establish a climate services center. These centers should work in close collaboration with science, industry, and policy. Thus, it can be made aware of climate change adaptation needs in the industrial sector and investigate their political and scientific feasibility. Because adaptation to climate change requires detailed climate information. Once climate services are established, a carbon market should be established.

A carbon tax is a fiscal instrument. With this tax, the government sets the price, but the quantity is determined by the market itself. ETS is an economic instrument, the government sets the emission cap, and the price is determined by supply and demand in the market. In mixed systems, there is an ETS with a price cap and a tax system that also reduces emissions (World Bank Group and International Carbon Action Partnership, 2022). Türkiye's primary objective is to maintain its share of the EU market in selected sectors covered by the EU CBAM. To achieve this goal, it is essential that an ETS is established in Türkiye and integrated into the EU ETS. Because more than USD 13 billion worth of SDCC products exported from Türkiye to the EU in 2022. This figure corresponds to 42% of our total exports to the world in these products (IMMIB, 2023). However, as the ETS will be open to the outside world, this may lead to external intervention in the ETS market. In other words, it would be risky for Türkiye to set the price entirely in the market. Given the purchasing power of the Turkish lira, a mixed system would be more appropriate in Türkiye.

It makes the most sense to establish local ETSs with different scopes, such as the local ETSs implemented by China, and incorporate them into the national ETS. However, a direct national ETS in selected sectors, aligned with the EU ETS, would pave the way for Türkiye to continue exporting to the EU in selected sectors. In practice, a high proportion of fluorinated greenhouse gases that trigger climate change should be included in the system. Among sectors, the electricity sector should be the first in the carbon pricing system. In addition, industrial sectors that use the most electricity and emit high levels of emissions, the transport sector (especially transport and airlines), and the agricultural sector should also be included, as fertilizers are covered by the EU CBAM, and agricultural vehicles continue to use fossil fuels.

The first question to be determined in this sector is whether the point of regulation will be at the source of the fuel, producer-based or consumer-based. Türkiye needs to use a mixed system in the electricity sector. Because some of the electricity produced in Türkiye is generated from imported natural gas and imported coal. It is therefore necessary to regulate at the import stage, production stage, or distribution stage. In other words, regulation should be done at the source. Electricity generated from domestic renewable resources should be regulated at the production stage. In the EU and Beijing ETS, electricity is regulated at the generation stage. This is because administrative costs are lower in this system (World Bank Group and International Carbon Action Partnership, 2022). Another option is to regulate the consumption stage. This system is used in Tokyo, Beijing, and Saitama. This is because it focuses on large energy consumers (World Bank Group and International Carbon Action Partnership, 2022). Consumers should be given the opportunity to choose which electricity to use. This would protect low-income households from high carbon taxes.

Regulation at source is essential when it comes to fossil fuel use. For example, California and Quebec use this method. The EU, China, and Korea regulate the consumption side (World Bank Group and International Carbon Action Partnership, 2022). Considering that Türkiye is a major producer of steel and cement, it would be more appropriate to monitor emissions at source, especially in these sectors. Because the number of producers is small. Therefore, monitoring, reporting, and evaluation will be easy. According to data from Turkish Cement, the countries importing cement from Türkiye are Bulgaria, Italy, Romania, Greece, and other EU countries. In addition to cement, clinker exports from Türkiye to EU countries are also high (Turkish Cement Manufacturers' Association, 2022). Türkiye's cement exports to the EU-27 in 2022 were worth USD 265,851 billion (Trade Map, 2023).

Similarly, according to statistics published by the Steel Exporters' Association, Türkiye's main export market in 2022 is the European Union, which accounts for 29% of Türkiye's total steel exports with 5.7 million tons. In 2022, the most remarkable increase in Turkish steel exports in terms of tonnage was realized to Other European Regions by 21% (Steel Exporters Association, 2022). The steel sector has a

5% share in total exports and an export value of around USD 9 billion in 2020. Türkiye's main trading partner is the EU. USD 2.7 billion worth of exports, representing 31% of Türkiye's total steel exports. Since around 75% of steel production in Türkiye is done in electric arc furnaces and integrated plants, Türkiye is a carbon-efficient steel producer compared to its competitors (Sefia, 2022). Türkiye's crude steel production was 40.4 million tons in 2021. World's 7th largest steel producer. The largest producer of steel in Europe (Steel Exporters' Association, 2021). In 2021, Israel (1887 thousand tons), Spain (1380 thousand tons), Italy (1379 thousand tons), the USA (1186 thousand tons) and Romania (1059 thousand tons) took the first five places in Türkiye's steel exports in terms of tonnage (Turkish Steel Steel Exporters' Association, 2021). Another sector covered by the EU CBAM is the fertilizer sector. According to the 2022 Fertilizer Sector Report, Romain ranks first in our fertilizer exports with 174.8 Million $. In addition, other EU countries Irland and Italy also import large quantities of fertilizer from Türkiye (Sancı, 2022). Table 1 from İDDMİB shows the countries to which Türkiye exported aluminum in 2020.

Table 2. Countries to which Türkiye exported aluminum, in 2020

Number	Country	Volume (KG)	Value FOB $	Price $/KG	Export Share
1	Germany	130.782.761	445.497.620	3,41	0,15
2	USA	66.887.917	202.337.543	3,03	0,07
3	Iraq	53.154.235	172.530.304	3,25	0,06
4	United Kingdom	52.406.710	171.644.934	3,28	0,06
5	Poland	44.150.859	131.843.648	2,99	0,04
6	Italy	43.862.574	120.589.790	2,75	0,04
7	France	33.183.791	114.914.996	3,46	0,04
8	Israel	31.275.911	98.581.999	3,15	0,03
9	Netherlands	29.012.944	97.547.854	3,36	0,03
10	Egypt	18.872.030	95.590.105	5,07	0,03
11	Austria	22.548.272	70.123.694	3,11	0,02
12	Swetzerland	24.810.721	69.199.080	2,79	0,02
13	Bulgaria	21.709.266	62.542.670	2,88	0,02
14	Czechia	17.216.931	57.587.885	3,34	0,02
15	Spain	19.242.072	56.779.853	2,95	0,02
16	Belgium	13.290.326	53.681.865	4,04	0,02
17	Romania	13.493.505	51.840.246	3,84	0,02
18	Canada	18.834.084	49.073.721	2,61	0,02
19	Hungary	10.751.347	47.462.939	4,41	0,02
20	Georgia	10.077.927	37.768.037	3,75	0,01

(IDDMIB, 2020)

As seen in Table 1, EU countries and the UK have an important place in our aluminum exports. Therefore, in the ETS that Türkiye should establish, the industrial sector should be included in the system first. Because the industrial sector is covered by the EU CBAM. This would allow Türkiye to maintain its market share in these sectors in the EU and not lose the UK market, which has already established an ETS compatible with the final phase of the EU ETS. Similarly, As of February 2023, the top five countries in Türkiye's aluminum exports were Germany (12,874,927 Kg), the USA (6,808,881 Kg), Poland (5,329,621 Kg), Italy (5,408,592 Kg), France (3,890,165 Kg).

New Zealand, Quebec, and California regulate the transportation sector at the source. The Republic of Korea and China regulate on a business-by-business basis (World Bank Group and International Carbon Action Partnership, 2022). In Türkiye, especially in Istanbul as a pilot region, regulation at the fuel production or fuel import stage would be effective. In a large industrial city like Istanbul, it would be difficult to follow the regulation on an enterprise-by-enterprise basis as there are many companies and facilities. In addition, the domestic transportation and aviation sectors should also be included in the system.

"This sector is included in the system in Korea and New Zealand. Because methane gas from solid wastes is difficult to control as it is released after a long period of time" (World Bank Group and International Carbon Action Partnership, 2022). Instead of controlling emissions from waste, Türkiye could benefit from more stringent waste recycling.

"Forestry is only included in New Zealand. Because emission reduction in forestry is difficult. In agriculture, on-farm electricity use is included in the ETS in China and Korea. Emissions from agricultural machinery using liquid fuels are included in the system in California, Quebec, and New Zealand" (World Bank Group and International Carbon Action Partnership, 2022). Electricity used by agricultural vehicles and farms using fossil fuels in agriculture in Türkiye should also be included in the system.

Countries with large oil and gas refineries prefer source-side regulation. Fossil fuel terminals and refineries are another points of regulation at source. The EU is not a fossil fuel producer. The ETS is therefore regulated on the consumption side (World Bank Group and International Carbon Action Partnership, 2022). Administrative costs are lower on a resource basis. This is because few enterprises are responsible for the extraction and processing of the resource and the proportion of emissions covered is high. In New Zealand, 102 companies have source-side regulation, but this covers 100% of emissions. In the EU ETS, on the other hand, more than 11,500 enterprises regulate the consumption side, but this number covers only 45% of emissions (World Bank Group and International Carbon Action Partnership, 2022). Therefore, a source-side arrangement is initially more suitable for Türkiye as the costs are lower and the scope is wider.

"The absolute emission cap reports the number of emission allowances from inception, while the intensity emission cap covers the number of allowances per production or input. In linking two ETSs, ETSs with the same emission cap structure are more easily harmonized" (World Bank Group and International Carbon Action Partnership, 2022). Therefore, as the EU ETS has an absolute emission cap, Türkiye should use a corresponding ETS (ADB, 2016). Türkiye needs to harmonize with the EU ETS in terms of the intervals for setting the emission cap. It should therefore update the emission cap before each phase.

Sectors entering and leaving the ETS change the participation threshold. The emission cap should therefore be updated frequently. For example, the EU ETS updated its emissions cap when the aviation sector joined the system. Another action to be taken when determining the threshold level is to exclude small enterprises from the system based on their GHG emissions, electricity consumption, production, and import levels. This reduces monitoring, reporting, and verification costs. It is also necessary to determine in advance whether the reporting obligation belongs to the company or the facility (World Bank Group and International Carbon Action Partnership, 2022).

When the ETS was first established, allowances were given free of charge in the market where allowances were traded. This is to avoid the risk of carbon leakage. Moreover, free emission allowances facilitate data collection by increasing the number of participants. However, allowances are valuable when the ETS is first established. This is an opportunity for the government to generate revenue. This revenue can be used to support sectors exposed to leakage and to support emission taxes for low-income households. California and Quebec have used this method (World Bank Group and International Carbon Action Partnership, 2022). Auctioning allowances is a preferred method as it reduces the volatility of carbon prices. In addition, banking-free allocations during auctions increase cash flow (World Bank Group and International Carbon Action Partnership, 2022). Türkiye should first protect the sectors that will be exposed to carbon leakage identified under the EU CBAM by distributing free allowances. Because this is the only way to avoid the risk of carbon leakage due to high EU carbon border taxes.

"Sectors not covered by the ETS give credits to sources covered by the ETS to support their emission reductions. This is called "offsetting". Equalizations will reduce investments in low-carbon products by lowering allowance prices, but they will also create carbon credits. These credits can be national and global credits" (World Bank Group and International Carbon Action Partnership, 2022). Reliable climate-related financial information is important for financial markets. Financial institutions provide preliminary information on investment opportunities and risks in the markets (TCFD, 2022). Because investment decisions should also take carbon pricing into account. For this purpose, financial institutions are being established to guide investors. The Financial Stability Board's Task Force on Climate-related Financial Disclosures (TCFD) was also established in 2017. The organization collects data from the market to determine the carbon prices needed to meet the Paris Agreement targets and provides guidance to investors based on this data (The World Bank, 2022b). TCFD supporter banks in Türkiye are Garanti BBVA, Türkiye Vakıflar Bankası TAO, and The Industrial Development Bank of Turkey (TSKB) (TFCD, 2022).

Türkiye should urgently establish similar local financial stability boards. This is because there are financial risks associated with increasing carbon emissions. While physical risks include various natural events related to climate change, transition risks include problems arising from the process of adaptation to a low-carbon economy. Liability risk, on the other hand, financially compensates for climate-related losses through compensation from responsible parties for those who suffer from the impacts of climate change. The management of liability risks caused by global climate change falls within the mandate of central banks and regulatory authorities seeking financial stability (Yılmaz & Çakaloğlu, 2021). In Türkiye, the Green Economy and Climate Change Directorate was established within the Central Bank in 2021. This Department is responsible for formulating and implementing the Bank's green economy and climate change policy (TCMB, 2023). However, local financial stability boards could be tasked with informing investor firms about the financial risks associated with carbon emissions and green bonds.

5. DISCUSSION AND CONCLUSION

There are two different possibilities for the establishment of a carbon market in Türkiye. The first possibility is based on the assumption that Türkiye establishes a carbon market and links its ETS to the EU ETS. Under this assumption, Türkiye could initially establish ETS in pilot regions in selected sectors identified under the EU CBAM. In this way, source mixing can be done. In other words, only by exporting to the EU from these regions can CBAM compliance be achieved. In addition, in the ETS to be established in Türkiye, producers should be given free allowances or allowance discounts in proportion to their initial risk exposure. This is how many countries prevent the risk of carbon leakage in carbon-intensive sectors. Considering the purchasing power of the Turkish Lira against the Euro, if the domestic producer is not supported by free allocations and allocation discounts, it will not be able to meet the (+/-) 50 Euro per ton demanded under the Sovereign Debt Restructuring Mechanism (SDRM) and will not be able to continue exporting. In the long run, when we take into account the falling export rates, Türkiye will come out of this process with serious economic losses.

If Türkiye does not provide an allowance discount to domestic producers, there may be a risk of reverse carbon leakage in carbon-intensive sectors. For example, a steel producer may prefer to continue production in a country where it can receive an allowance, rather than in Türkiye where it cannot receive an allowance. Moreover, no matter what type of carbon tax is implemented in Türkiye, if it is imposed on consumers, consumers who cannot afford it will be harmed. To prevent this, a portion of the fines levied on businesses should be paid to low-income families as carbon tax relief, as in the Canadian ETS. The second possibility is based on the assumption that a few countries, including Türkiye, reject the EU CBAM. In other words, countries trading with the EU will not comply with the CBAM, and carbon haven countries will emerge like tax haven countries. What makes China so big today is not only that multinational companies want to continue production in China with cheap labor, but also that they produce in China in order to escape the carbon tax burden in their countries. While many countries have set 2050 as a deadline for carbon neutrality, an emission haven like China has committed to be carbon neutral by 2060. This is contrary to global competition.

As stated in the Paris Agreement, developed countries are the first polluters of the world. They have become powerful economies by polluting the world. It is also an inequality that developing countries and LDCs are not exempted from CBAM. This inequality will hinder the development of Developing or LDCs that are suppliers to powerful countries within the EU. The selected sectors are industrial sectors with high carbon content, where large quantities are produced. Therefore, decarbonization technologies in these sectors are also expensive. The economies of LDCs and Developing Countries that cannot afford these technologies are exposed to unfair competition. If some developing countries like India, Brazil, Türkiye, Russia, etc. reject CBAM, the EU will not be able to achieve its climate goal alone and will lose its cheap and continuous suppliers. As a result, the EU economy will also suffer. As cheap suppliers to the EU, these countries, like China, may choose not to engage in climate-friendly production until 2060. Rejection of CBAM by Developing Countries and Least Developed Countries will trigger producers within the EU and the risk of carbon leakage will turn into investment leakage in the long run and the EU economy will lose strength. In short, the EU's imposition of CBAM, ignoring its trading partners, could plunge the EU into difficult economic times.

Another risk of CBAM is its vulnerability to source mixing. Recognizing this weakness of the system, countries have already taken action and started to create clean zones where the ETS is in place. Another question is whether the EU will use the revenues from CBAM to prevent climate change or to provide incentives to its own investors. Because the EU, which sets out with the goal of climate change, protects the rights of domestic producers both in imports and exports. For example, when exporting a product produced under CBAM, the carbon costs paid by the domestic producer are deducted from the amount. To turn this into an opportunity, domestic producers can increase the emissions intensity of their export activities. In other words, the EU that wants to be carbon neutral could turn into a carbon-intensive EU. The EU CBAM plans to include all sectors in the system in the coming years. Including more countries and sectors would reduce the risk of carbon leakage, but it is not easy to implement. It would be difficult or even impossible to assess the emissions of thousands of different commodities. For example, when determining the embedded emissions of an electric vehicle to be imported into the EU under CBAM, the emissions of the lithium used in the vehicle imported from another country, the emissions of the electricity used in the production of each component used in the manufacture of the vehicle, the emissions of the fuel used by the transportation vehicle that transports the vehicle to the EU, etc. must be included in the MRV. should be included in the MRV. This is a very difficult process to implement. In addition to transforming itself, the EU wants to transform all the countries with which it trades. It is difficult to convince many countries of this.

As mentioned in the introduction, India, which is known as the second most polluting country in the world with coal, has committed to be carbon neutral by 2070. Multinational Corporations may continue to pollute the world by producing in China between 2050 and 2060 and in India between 2060 and 2070. On the other hand, Developing Countries and LDCs will be forced to protect the climate. Türkiye, one of these countries, is rich in coal reserves. So, while India, which continues its production by importing coal, is given until 2070, will Türkiye, which has abundant coal reserves, be given an additional period to become carbon neutral? Türkiye, which can produce with its own coal in thermal power plants but needs to switch to renewable energy, should be given a reasonable period of time to consume its coal reserves or be provided with the technology and financial support to transform coal into a clean energy system. Türkiye could initially exempt coal from the carbon tax in its ETS or carbon taxation system, and electricity from coal could not be used to produce products in certain sectors to be exported to the EU. However, Türkiye, which ratified the Paris Agreement, has limited time. Under the agreement, it must stay away from initiatives that cause climate change and rapidly phase out coal use.

Ultimately, if the countries of the world remain committed to the Paris Agreement, the first of two things will happen. Therefore, under this scenario, Türkiye should urgently establish an ETS integrated into the EU ETS. If some of the world's countries reject the EU ETS, the world will continue to become more and more polluted, and efforts to prevent climate change will stall.

REFERENCES

ADB. (2016). *Emissions Tradingschemes And Their Linking: Challenges And Opportunities In Asia And The Pacific.* Asian Development Bank.https://www.adb.org/sites/default/files/publication/182501/emissions-trading-schemes.pdf

Appunn, K. (2019, April 04). *Clean Energy Wire.* National climate measures and European emission trading: Assessing the 'waterbed effect': https://www.cleanenergywire.org/factsheets/national-climate-measures-and-european-emission-trading-assessing-waterbed-effect

Appunn, K. (2021, July 20). *Clean Energy Wire.* Understanding the European Union's Emissions Trading System (EU ETS). https://www.cleanenergywire.org/factsheets/understanding-european-unions-emissions-trading-system

Arı, İ. (2010). Emıssıon Tradıng For Combatıng Wıth The Clımate Change And Its Implementatıon In Turkey. *Planning Expertise Thesis.* Ankara: State Planning Organization.

BBC. (2021). *COP26: India PM Narendra Modi Pledges Net Zero By 2070.* BBC. https://www.bbc.com/news/world-asia-india-59125143#:~:text=Detailing%20what%20he%20termed%20were,the%20country's%20electricity%20from%20coal.: BBC.

Caranci, B., & Econ, C. (2021). A Primer on Carbon Pricing and Carbon Border Adjustments. *TD Economics.* https://economics.td.com/domains/economics.td.com/documents/reports/ff/carbon_border_adjustments.pdf

Council of The European Union. (2023, January 12). *Fit for 55.* Council of The European Union.. https://www.consilium.europa.eu/en/policies/green-deal/fit-for-55-the-eu-plan-for-a-green-transition/ ı

Energy.Gov. (2023). *About Energy.Gov.* Loan Programs Office. https://www.energy.gov/lpo/about-us-home

Ari, I., Varoglu, A. (2022). Erupean Union'S Carbon Border Adjustement Mechanism And Its Impact On Turkey. In A. Bektaş (Ed.), Global Climate Change and Sosyo-Economic Impacts (p. 217). Tasav.

European Commission. (2021, July 14). *Regulation Of The European Parliament And Of The Council establishing a carbon border adjustment mechanism.* European Commission. https://eur-lex.europa.eu/legal-content/EN/TXT/HTML/?uri=CELEX:52021PC0564&rid=9

European Commission. (2022). *Climate Action.* International carbon market. https://ec.europa.eu/clima/eu-action/eu-emissions-trading-system-eu-ets/international-carbon-market_en

European Commission. (2022). *Climate Action.* European Commission. https://ec.europa.eu/clima/eu-action/eu-emissions-trading-system-eu-ets/revision-phase-4-2021-2030_en

European Commission. (2022). *Development of EU ETS (2005-2020).* European Commission. https://ec.europa.eu/clima/eu-action/eu-emissions-trading-system-eu-ets/development-eu-ets-2005-2020_en

European Commission. (2022). *Free allocation for the modernisation of the energy sector.* European Commission. https://ec.europa.eu/clima/eu-action/eu-emissions-trading-system-eu-ets/free-allocation/free-allocation-modernisation-energy-sector_en

European Commission. (2022a). *Climate Action.* European Commission. https://ec.europa.eu/clima/eu-action/eu-emissions-trading-system-eu-ets/development-eu-ets-2005-2020_en

European Commission. (2023, May 15). *ETS Market Stability Reserve to reduce auction volume by over 272 million allowances between September 2023 and August 2024.* European Commission. https://climate.ec.europa.eu/news-your-voice/news/ets-market-stability-reserve-reduce-auction-volume-over-272-million-allowances-between-september-2023-05-15_en

European Commission. (2023). *International carbon market.* European Commission. https://ec.europa.eu/clima/eu-action/eu-emissions-trading-system-eu-ets/international-carbon-market_en)

European Commission. (2023). *Taxation and Customs Union.* Carbon Border Adjustment Mechanism. https://taxation-customs.ec.europa.eu/carbon-border-adjustment-mechanism_en

Favasuli, S., & Sebastian, V. (2021, June 10). *Voluntary carbon markets: how they work, how they're priced and who's involved.* S&P Global. https://www.spglobal.com/commodityinsights/en/market-insights/blogs/energy-transition/061021-voluntary-carbon-markets-pricing-participants-trading-corsia-credits

GATT. (2022). *WTO rules and environmental policies: GATT exceptions*. World Trade Organization. https://www.wto.org/english/tratop_e/envir_e/envt_rules_exceptions_e.htm

Government of Canada. (2022). *Carbon Pollution Pricing Systems Across Canada*. Government of Canada. https://www.canada.ca/en/environment-climate-change/services/climate-change/pricing-pollution-how-it-will-work/industry.html

Government of Canada. (2022). *Carbon Pollution Pricing Systems Across Canada*. Government of Canada. https://www.canada.ca/en/environment-climate-change/services/climate-change/pricing-pollution-how-it-will-work.html

Government of Canada. (2022). *The Government of Canada strengthens pollution pricing across the country*. Government of Canada. https://www.canada.ca/en/environment-climate-change/news/2022/11/the-government-of-canada-strengthens-pollution-pricing-across-the-country.html

Governmment of Canada. (2011, July). *Canada's Emissions Trends*. Environment Canada. https://www.ec.gc.ca/doc/publications/cc/COM1374/ec-com1374-en-s3.html

Hay, G. (2021, November 2). *Retrieved from EU-U.S. Green Steel Deal Shows Way For COP26*. Reuters. https://www.reuters.com/breakingviews/eu-us-green-steel-deal-shows-way-cop26-2021-11-02/

Holzer, K. (2016). *WTO Law Issues Of Emissions*. https://www.wti.org/media/filer_public/6e/88/6e884b29-f5e2-4a25-85a6-a6edb5c25ed9/working_paper_short_version.pdf: World Trade Institut.

Hotunluoğlu, H., & Tekeli, R. (2007-2). Economic Analysis and Impacts of the Carbon Tax: Does a Carbon Tax Have an Emission Reducing Effect? *Sosyoekonomi*, 107-126.

ICAP. (2021a, November 17). *ICAP Carbon Action*. Retrieved from Canada-Quebec Cap-and-Trade System: https://icapcarbonaction.com/en/ets-map?etsid=88

ICAP. (2021b, November 17). *ICAP Carbon Action*. Retrieved from Canada-Nova Scotia: https://icapcarbonaction.com/en/ets-map?etsid=88

ICAP. (2021d, November 17). *ICAP Carbon Action*. China National ETS. https://icapcarbonaction.com/en/ets-map

ICAP. (2022). *ICAP*. European Emission Trading System (EU ETS). https://icapcarbonaction.com/en/ets-map?etsid=88

ICAP. (2023). *ICAP*. About Emissions Trading Systems: https://icapcarbonaction.com/en/about-emissions-trading-systems

ICAP. (2023). *ICAP*. Canada - Québec Cap-and-Trade System: https://icapcarbonaction.com/en/ets/canada-quebec-cap-and-trade-system

ICAP. (2023, November 2023). *ICAP Carbon Action*. California Cap-and-Trade Program: https://icapcarbonaction.com/en/ets-map

ICAP. (2023, November 17). *ICAP Carbon Action*. Guamgdong ETS: https://icapcarbonaction.com/en/ets-map

ICAP. (2023). *ICAP Carbon Action*. Tianjin Pilot ETS. https://icapcarbonaction.com/en/ets-map

ICAP. (2023). *ICAP Carbon Action*. Shenzen Pilot ETS. https://icapcarbonaction.com/en/ets-map

ICAP. (2023). *ICAP Carbon Action*. Shangai Pilot ETS. https://icapcarbonaction.com/en/ets-map

ICAP. (2023). *ICAP Carbon Action*. Hubei Pilot ETS. https://icapcarbonaction.com/en/ets-map

ICAP. (2023). *ICAP Carbon Action*. Chongqinq Pilot ETS. https://icapcarbonaction.com/en/ets-map

ICAP. (2023). *ICAP Carbon Action*. Beijing Pilot ETS. https://icapcarbonaction.com/en/ets-map

ICAP. (2023, May 03). *International Carbon Action Partnership (ICAP)*. EU adopts landmark ETS reforms and new policies to meet 2030 target. https://icapcarbonaction.com/en/news/eu-adopts-landmark-ets-reforms-and-new-policies-meet-2030-target

IDDMIB. (2020). *Aluminum Sector Meeting*. Istanbul Ferrous and Non-Ferrous Metals Exporters' Association. https://immib.org.tr/files/metaller/IDDMIB_Aluminium_Sektor_Bulusmas%C4%B1_Rapor_A4%20g%C3%BCncel%202li%20sayfa.pdf

IEA. (2022, October 26). *Global coal consumption, 2020-2023*. IEA. https://www.iea.org/data-and-statistics/charts/global-coal-consumption-2020-2023

IMMIB. (2023, March 13). *Istanbul Mineral and Metals Exporters' Associations (IMMIB)*. European Union Carbon Border Adjustment Mechanism. https://immib.org.tr/tr/avrupa-birligi-sinirda-karbon-duzenleme-mekanizmasi

Jegou, I., & Rubini, L. (2011). *The Allocation of Emission Allowances Free of Charge: Legal and Economic Considerations*. ICTSD Programme on Competitiveness and Sustainable Development. doi:10.7215/CO_IP_20110826

Jordan, C., & Cunningham, L. (2023). *Renewable Energy and Energy Efficiency Incentives: A Summary of Federal Programs*. Congressional Research Service.

Kaufman, N., Krause, E., & Desousa, K. (2018). *Achıevıng U.S. Emıssıons Targets Wıth A Carbon Tax*. World Resources Institute. https://files.wri.org/d8/s3fs-public/us-emission-targets-with-carbon-tax.pdf

KPMG. (2023). *KPMG*. ETS, CBAM nad Social Climate Fund. https://home.kpmg/xx/en/home/insights/2022/05/ets-cbam-and-social-climate-fund.html

Lashof, D. (2019, February 04). *World Resources Institut*. 5 Things To Look For In The Green New Deal. https://www.wri.org/insights/5-things-look-green-new-deal

Mountford, H., & McGregor, M. (2018, November 15). *World Resources İnstitut*. A Carbon Price Can Benefit the Poor While Reducing Emissions. https://www.wri.org/insights/carbon-price-can-benefit-poor-while-reducing-emissions

Özcan, M., Ergün Yüksel, B., & Ocaklı, E. (2022). Evaluation of voluntary carbon markets in Turkey. *Duzce University Journal of Science & Technology*, 10-25.

RGGI. (2023). *Elements of RGGI*. The Regional Greenhouse Gas Initiative (RGGI) an initiative of Eastern States of the EUS. https://www.rggi.org/program-overview-and-design/elements

Sancı, S. (2022). *2022 Fertilizer Report.* Istanbul Chemicals and Chemical Products Exporters' Association.

Sefia. (2022). *Turkey Steel Sector Report: Production, Trade and Decarbonization Process.* Sustainable Economy and Finance (Sefia).

Steel Exporters' Association. (2021). *2022 Shape The World With Turkish Steel.* Steel Exporters' Association.

Steel Exporters Association. (2022). *Steel Exporters Association.* Statistics. https://www.cib.org.tr/en/statistics.html

TCFD. (2022). *The challenge we're addressing.* Task Force on Climate-related Financial Disclosures. https://www.fsb-tcfd.org/about/#task-force-members

TCMB. (2023). *Central Bank of the Republic of Turkey.* Central Bank of the Republic of Turkey. https://www.tcmb.gov.tr/wps/wcm/connect/EN/TCMB+EN/Main+Menu/About+the+Bank/Organization/Head+Office/

TFCD. (2022). *Task Force on Climate-Related Financial Disclosures.* Climate Change Presents Financial Risk To The Global Economy. https://www.fsb-tcfd.org/

The White House. (2021, October 28). *President Biden Announces the Build Back Better Framework.* The White House. https://www.whitehouse.gov/briefing-room/statements-releases/2021/10/28/president-biden-announces-the-build-back-better-framework/

The White House. (2022, August 16). *The White House.* Bill Signed: H.R. 5376. https://www.whitehouse.gov/briefing-room/legislation/2022/08/16/bill-signed-h-r-5376/

The World Bank. (2022a). *What Is Carbon Pricing?* Pricing Carbon. https://www.worldbank.org/en/programs/pricing-carbon

The World Bank. (2022b). *Carbon Pricing Dashboard.* What is Carbon Pricing? https://carbonpricing-dashboard.worldbank.org/what-carbon-pricing

The World Bank. (2023). *State and Trends of Carbon Pricing 2023.* The World Bank.

Trade Map. (2023). *TradeMap.* Trade Map. https://www.trademap.org/Product_SelCountry_TS.aspx?nvpm=1%7c792%7c%7c%7c%7c2523%7c%7c%7c4%7c1%7c1%7c1%7c2%7c1%7c1%7c1%7c1%7c1

Turcotte, I., Gorski, J., & Riehl, B. (2019). The Pan-Canadian Price On Pollution. In *A New Era Of Climate Policy In.* Pembina Institute.

Turkish Cement Manufacturers' Association. (2022). *Statistics.* Turkish Cemenr Manufacturers' Association. https://www.turkcimento.org.tr/en/statistics/exports

Turkish Steel Steel Exporters' Association. (2021). *Turkish Steel Steel Exporters' Association 2021 Working Report.* Turkish Steel Steel Exporters' Association.

UK Government. (2023, Apr 17). *Department for Business, Energy and Industrial Strategy.* Guidance Participating in the UK ETS. https://www.gov.uk/government/publications/participating-in-the-uk-ets/participating-in-the-uk-ets

United Nations. (1992). *United Nations Framework Convention.* UNFCCC. https://unfccc.int/resource/docs/convkp/conveng.pdf

Urgewald. (2021). Groundbreaking Research Reveals the Financiers of the Coal Industry. *Urgewald.* https://coalexit.org/sites/default/files/download_public/Financing%20GCEL%202020_Press%20Release_urgewald.pdf

Uzun, A., & Doğan, A. (2014). The Effects of FreeTrade Agreements on Turkey's Foreign Trade. *Cumhuriyet University Journal of Economics and Administrative Sciences*, 325-344.

Vinay, S., Parikh, K., Parikh, J., Ghosh, P., Tot, M., & Das, A. (2023). *Pathways to net zero emissions for the Indian power sector*. Elseiver.

World Bank Group and International Carbon Action Partnership. (2022). *A Handbook on Design and Implementation.* World Bank Group. https://documents1.worldbank.org/curated/en/541731484292546048/pdf/108879-TURKISH-PUBLIC-ETSHandbookTurkishFullReport.pdf

Yılmaz, O., & Çakaloğlu, M. (2021). The Transformation of Central Banks In Response To Climate Change: Green Central Banking. *Business, Economics and Management Research Journal*, 135-156.

Yılmazcan, H., & Çakmak, H. (2018). As A Financial/Effective Vehicle In The Prevention Of Climate Change "Carbon Emission Tax Or Carbon Emission Trading? ". *Proceeding of the İnternational Congress on Business and Marketing,* Maltepe University.

ENDNOTES

1. The markets where the credits obtained as a result of the flexibility mechanisms of the countries party to the Kyoto Protocol are traded are defined as mandatory carbon markets. The voluntary carbon market is a market created to facilitate individuals, institutions, organizations and non-governmental organizations to voluntarily reduce and compensate their greenhouse gas emissions (Favasuli & Sebastian, 2021).
2. Canadian law defines Emissions-Intensive and trade-exposed industries as Iron Ore Mining, Non-Metal Mining, Pulp and Paper, Cement, Lime & Gypsum, Chemicals and Fertilizers, Iron and Steel, Aluminum and Base Metal Smelting (Governmment of Canada, 2011).

Chapter 5
The Synergistic Effect of Institutional Quality and Remittances on Africa's Low-Carbon Transition

Ibrahim Nandom Yakubu
https://orcid.org/0000-0003-4424-996X
University for Development Studies, Ghana

Alhassan Bunyaminu
University of Professional Studies, Accra, Ghana

Ibrahim Mohammed
https://orcid.org/0000-0002-9583-7078
University of Professional Studies, Accra, Ghana

ABSTRACT

This study explores the factors influencing energy transition in Africa, specifically focusing on the impact of institutional quality and remittances on renewable energy consumption. Using a comprehensive dataset covering 45 African countries from 2000 to 2020 and employing the generalized method of moments (GMM) technique, the analysis controls for industrialization, financial development, and population growth. The results demonstrate a significant negative effect of institutional quality and remittances on renewable energy consumption. However, the finding reveals a positive and significant interactive effect between institutional quality and remittances, indicating that the favourable alignment of these factors promotes the demand for renewable energy. Additionally, the study highlights a positive impact of industrialization and population growth on renewable energy consumption, while financial development has a significant negative effect. These findings provide valuable insights for policymakers in developing effective strategies for a sustainable energy transition in Africa.

DOI: 10.4018/978-1-6684-9272-7.ch005

INTRODUCTION

The unsustainable escalation in energy consumption and the depletion of natural resources have exacerbated the environmental challenges resulting from human activities. The increasing threat of global warming poses a severe danger to human existence, evident in the form of rising temperatures, heightened sea levels, prolonged drought periods, and the degradation of ecosystems (Burke et al., 2018). Traditional energy sources, notably the combustion of fossil fuels like oil and coal, have consistently been identified as major contributors to environmental deterioration (Yakubu et al., 2022). Fossil fuels hold a significant share of global primary energy consumption, accounting for approximately 80% of the world's energy supply (Environmental and Energy Study Institute, 2021). However, recognizing the adverse impacts of these conventional energy sources, global treaties and agreements such as the Kyoto Protocol, the United Nations Framework Convention on Climate Change, and the Paris Agreement have underscored the critical importance of environmental sustainability. These international agreements stress the need for implementing measures that aim to mitigate and decrease human-generated greenhouse gas (GHG) emissions in the atmosphere. In this regard, the adoption of renewable energy has the potential to serve as a significant driver in enhancing the overall state of the environment.

Over the years, governments have endeavoured to implement policy frameworks that facilitate the expansion of renewable energy usage and diversification of the energy portfolio in response to the challenges posed by global climate change (Bkun & Alola, 2022). The transition to a low-carbon economy is more pertinent for Africa due to its vulnerability to the adverse consequences of climate change. The Word Bank (2020) reported that despite the continent's lowest contribution to global greenhouse gas emissions, it is among the regions most affected by climate change. Among others, the extreme poverty level and the dependency on rain-fed agriculture exacerbate its susceptibility to climate change.

Acknowledging the pressing need to tackle climate change, African governments, within the framework of the Paris Agreement, have pledged to shift towards low-carbon economies. This commitment entails implementing climate change adaptation strategies and adopting renewable energy sources (United Nations, 2015).

Harnessing renewable energy sources can be crucial in mitigating climate change (Zhao et al., 2023), but it necessitates substantial upfront investments in infrastructure and technology. In the context of Africa, this presents a unique challenge. However, a potential solution lies in utilizing remittances as a viable funding option for facilitating the continent's sustainable energy transition. Remittances, which involve financial transfers from migrants to their home nations, offer a promising avenue for supporting renewable energy projects in Africa (Das et al., 2021). However, for remittances to have a profound and enduring impact on the energy transition agenda, it becomes imperative to consider the quality of institutional structures in the recipient nations. Institutions can be pivotal in determining a country's ability to attract and effectively employ remittances for sustainable development, particularly within the energy sector (Moskalenko et al., 2022). Effective governance, for instance, assumes a critical role in establishing an enabling environment for investments in renewable energy and ensuring the efficient implementation of energy policies (Vakulchuk et al., 2023).

Based on the preceding discussion, this study asserts that the interplay between institutional quality and remittances holds significant importance in shaping the path toward a low-carbon future in Africa. While previous studies have investigated the impact of remittances and institutional quality on economic development (see Nguyen et al., 2018; Eggoh et al., 2019; Maruta et al., 2020; Utile et al., 2021; Ahmed et al., 2022; Islam, 2022; Mohamed Aslam & Alibuhtto, 2023; Raza et al., 2023), there is limited research on their impact on the energy transition. Therefore, this study aims to fill this gap by investigating the role of institutional quality in moderating the relationship between remittances and the transition to renewable energy in Africa. Specifically, the researchers examine how institutional quality moderates the relationship between remittances and renewable energy consumption in African countries. By doing so, the study provides insights into the role of institutional quality in achieving a low-carbon future in Africa and informs policies aimed at promoting renewable energy transition in the continent.

The remainder of this chapter is structured as follows: Section 2 provides a comprehensive review of the existing literature. Section 3 outlines the methodology employed in this study, while Section 4 presents and discusses the findings. Finally, Section 5 concludes the study by offering pertinent policy recommendations.

LITERATURE REVIEW

Given the objectives of this study, this section is divided into two subsections. Firstly, the researchers provide a theoretical and empirical review of the impact of institutional quality on renewable energy consumption. The second subsection reviews the literature on the link between remittances and energy consumption.

The Impact of Institutional Quality on Renewable Energy Consumption

The institutional theory is a plausible theory for investigating the nexus between institutional quality, and renewable energy consumption. This theory, according to Scott (2013, p. 1), "focuses on the role of formal and informal rules, regulations, and norms in shaping behaviour and outcomes within a specific social context". On the premise of this theory, institutional quality impacts the adoption and diffusion of innovations, such as renewable energy technologies, through a stable and supportive environment (DiMaggio & Powell, 1983). High-quality institutions foster investment, support policy stability, and enable the efficient execution of renewable energy development legislation. These institutions also ease access to finance, offer incentives for the utilization of renewable energy, and set up open and accountable decision-making procedures.

Empirically, several studies have examined how institutional quality drives renewable energy consumption. For instance, Wu and Broadstock (2015) investigated the effect of institutional quality and financial development on renewable energy consumption employing data from emerging economies covering 1990-2010. The findings revealed that institutional quality positively drives the consumption of renewable energy. Uzar (2020) investigated the relationship between renewable energy and institutional quality in a sample of 38 countries from 1990 to 2015. The research revealed a positive long-run impact of institutional quality on renewable energy consumption. In a panel threshold analysis, Chen et al. (2021) found that countries with democratic institutions have higher renewable energy consumption. Asongu and Odhiambo (2021) assessed how governance quality impacts renewable energy consumption in 44 countries in Sub-Saharan Africa. Applying Tobit regressions, the authors documented a negative relationship between political and institutional governance and renewable energy consumption in the sampled countries. In the OECD, Wang et al. (2022) empirically explored the impact of institutional quality and political risk on renewable energy consumption from 1997 to 2019. The researchers discovered that higher levels of institutional quality are associated with increased adoption of renewable energy sources. Conversely, the study also revealed a negative long-term link between political risk and renewable energy consumption. Using the Pool Mean Group technique, Rahman and Sultana (2022) found a significant positive effect of institutional quality on renewable energy consumption in a sample of emerging economies. Saadaoui and Chtourou (2022) examined how Tunisia's financial development, institutional quality, economic growth, and renewable energy consumption are interconnected. Their findings suggested that stronger institutions play a significant role in promoting renewable energy consumption, contributing to a more sustainable energy sector. Vatamanu and Zugravu (2023) examined the dynamic link between institutional quality and renewable energy consumption in European Union countries with data covering 2000 to 2020. The research revealed that institutional quality has a positive impact on energy consumption and strengthens efforts to reduce carbon emissions.

The Impact of Remittances on Renewable Energy Consumption

In recent years, there has been a growing research interest in understanding the impact of remittances on various aspects of development, including environmental sustainability. While the literature has extensively investigated how remittances affect environmental pollution (Ahmad et al., 2019; Khan et al., 2020; Wang et al., 2021; Ali et al., 2022; Islam, 2022; Jafri et al., 2022; Yakubu et al., 2022; Adebayo et al., 2023; Chishti, 2023; Umair et al., 2023), there is still much to be known about the impact of remittances on the adoption of renewable energy as part of measures to ensure environmental quality. Specifically, studies investigating the link between remittances and renewable energy consumption have received relatively little attention in the literature. Among the limited number of studies conducted in this area, Das et al. (2021) revealed a unidirectional causality from remittances per capita to renewable energy consumption in Bangladesh. Subramaniam et al. (2022), using data from the top recipient developing countries, examined the influence of remittances on renewable energy consumption and found a positive impact of remittances on the use of renewable energy. Similarly, Zhao et al. (2022) provided evidence of a direct link between remittances and renewable energy consumption in the Belt and Road countries. These studies highlight the importance of further research in understanding the relationship between remittances and renewable energy adoption, particularly in different contexts and regions.

RESEARCH METHODOLOGY

Data

This study utilizes data from 45 countries in Africa, covering the period from 2000 to 2020. The selection of sample countries is based on data availability. The primary data sources for this study are the World Development Indicators and the World Governance Indicators provided by the World Bank.

Description of Variables

Renewable energy consumption serves as the dependent variable in this study. Following the methodology of Yakubu et al. (2022), renewable energy consumption (% of total final energy consumption) measures renewable energy consumption. The main independent variables examined in this study are institutional quality and remittance. To account for potential confounding factors, the study also controls for the effects of industrialization, financial development, and population. In order to measure institutional quality, the researchers employ principal component analysis to construct an index based on several sub-measures. These sub-measures include control of corruption, voice and accountability, the rule of law, and regulatory quality, which collectively form the institutional quality sub-indices. The remittance variable is assessed using personal remittances received as a percentage of GDP. This measures the financial flows from individuals living abroad to their home countries. Consistent with the approach taken by Akçay (2019), industrialization is quantified using manufacturing value added as a percentage of GDP. This indicator helps capture a country's industrial activity and economic diversification level. To capture the level of financial development, the study utilizes domestic credit to the private sector (% of GDP) as an indicator (Musah & Yakubu, 2022). This variable reflects the availability and accessibility of credit for private businesses and individuals. Lastly, population is gauged by population growth (annual %) for a specific period. This variable provides insights into the demographic dynamics within the countries under study.

Model Specification

The fundamental empirical model for analyzing the influence of institutional quality and remittance on renewable energy is outlined as follows:

$$Y_{it} = \alpha + \beta' X_{it} + v_{it} + \varepsilon_{it} \tag{1}$$

In the given context, the subscripts *i* and *t* correspond to the specific country and year, respectively. The constant term is denoted as α, representing the intercept in the model. The independent variables are represented by *X*, while their corresponding coefficients are denoted by β. The letter v signifies the unobservable characteristics specific to each country, and finally, the error term is represented as ε.

By incorporating the variables of interest, equation (1) can be redefined as follows, thereby examining the direct effect of the independent variables on renewable energy consumption:

$$REN_{it} = \beta_0 + \beta_1 INSQ_{it} + \beta_2 REM_{it} + \beta_3 INDS_{it} + \beta_4 FID_{it} + \beta_5 POP_{it} + v_{it} + \varepsilon_{it} \tag{2}$$

The acronyms REN, INSQ, REM, INDS, FID, and POP represent renewable energy consumption, institutional quality, remittance, industrialization, financial development, and population, respectively.

To examine the interactive effect of institutional quality and remittance on renewable energy consumption, the following equation is presented:

$$REN_{it} = \beta_0 + \beta_1 INSQ_{it} + \beta_2 REM_{it} + \beta_3 INSQ_{it} {*} REM_{it} \, \beta_4 INDS_{it} + \beta_5 FID_{it} + \beta_6 POP_{it} + v_{it} + \varepsilon_{it} \tag{3}$$

Model Estimation Technique

The study utilizes the Generalized Method of Moments (GMM) technique to address potential endogeneity and dynamic panel data issues in the analysis. Endogeneity arises when the independent variables are correlated with the error term, leading to biased and inconsistent estimates (Arellano & Bover, 1995 cited in Yakubu et al., 2021). In the context of this study, it is possible that institutional quality, remittances, and other control variables are endogenous, as they may be influenced by unobserved factors that also affect renewable energy consumption. Furthermore, in comparison to other techniques, the GMM estimator has the advantage of generating estimates that are consistent with respect to heteroskedasticity and autocorrelation (Roodman, 2009 cited in Bunyaminu et al., 2022).

By employing the GMM technique, the model incorporates the lagged value of the dependent variable. As a result, equation (1) is modified and redefined as follows:

$$REN_{it} = \alpha + \gamma REN_{it-1} + \beta' X_{it} + v_i + \varepsilon_{it} \quad (4)$$

RESULTS AND DISCUSSION

Descriptive Statistics

Table 1 presents descriptive statistics for the variables in the study, offering a comprehensive overview of their characteristics. The mean value of renewable energy consumption (REN) is 66.0298, indicating a moderate level of renewable energy usage among the countries studied. However, the minimum and maximum values of 3.5400 and 97.4200, respectively, suggest a significant range of consumption levels. The standard deviation of 25.4628 reinforces the considerable variability. Institutional quality (INSQ) has a mean of 0.2399, implying a moderate level of institutional quality across the sample. The distribution shows a wide range of scores, with a minimum of -3.3642 and a maximum of 4.6052. Remittances (REM) exhibit a mean of 3.4004, reflecting a moderate level of remittance inflows as a percentage of GDP. However, the distribution shows significant variability, with a minimum of 0.0000 and a maximum of 53.8262. For the control variables, industrialization (INDS), financial development (FID), and population (POP) have mean values of 10.1702, 20.3537, and 2.5195, respectively. The distributions of the control variables display varying degrees of skewness and kurtosis, with industrialization and financial development showing positive skewness and higher kurtosis values, suggesting right-skewed distributions with heavier tails. The Jarque-Bera tests indicate significant departures from normality for all variables.

Table 1. Descriptive statistics

	REN	*INSQ*	*REM*	*INDS*	*FID*	*POP*
Mean	66.0298	0.2399	3.4004	10.1702	20.3537	2.5195
Maximum	97.4200	4.6052	53.8262	25.7506	142.4220	5.6050
Minimum	3.5400	-3.3642	0.0000	0.2326	1.1235	-0.6164
Std. Dev.	25.4628	1.7686	6.0228	4.7799	23.6292	0.8680
Skewness	-0.9164	0.4031	4.2383	0.5090	3.0313	-0.8536
Kurtosis	2.6155	2.7128	27.0314	2.8710	12.5722	4.6097
Jarque-Bera	98.1969	20.5061	18182.05	29.4877	3594.690	154.1577
Probability	0.0000	0.0000	0.0000	0.0000	0.0000	0.0000

Correlation Analysis

The correlation and variance inflation factor (VIF) analyses presented in Table 2 provide insights into the relationships between the variables and their potential collinearity issues. Starting with the correlation coefficients, it can be observed that there is a weak positive correlation between institutional quality (INSQ) and remittances (REM) with a coefficient of 0.1284. Similarly, a moderately positive correlation of 0.6060 exists between institutional quality (INSQ) and financial development (FID). On the other hand, there is a negative correlation between population (POP) and the remaining variables, ranging from -0.4675 to -0.5042. These correlation coefficients indicate some degree of a linear relationship between the variables but are not strong enough to suggest multicollinearity concerns. Turning to the VIF analysis, each independent variable's VIF values are provided. Generally, VIF values below 10 are considered acceptable, while values above 10 indicate high multicollinearity (Gujarati, 2003). In this case, all VIF values in Table 2 are below 10, ranging from 2.3096 to 7.1904. This suggests that multicollinearity is not a major concern among the independent variables.

Table 2. Correlation analysis

	INSQ	*REM*	*INDS*	*FID*	*POP*
INSQ	1.0000				
REM	0.1284	1.0000			
INDS	0.0193	0.1691	1.0000		
FID	0.6060	-0.0257	0.1522	1.0000	
POP	-0.4675	-0.4275	-0.1928	-0.5042	1.0000
VIF	3.3737	2.3096	4.4202	5.8446	7.1904
Tolerance (1/VIF)	0.2964	0.4330	0.2262	0.1711	0.1391

Regression Results

Table 3 presents the regression results obtained using the GMM technique in this study. The analysis encompasses three distinct models. Model 1 focuses on assessing the direct impact of institutional quality on renewable energy consumption, while Model 2 examines the direct impact of remittance on renewable energy consumption. Model 3 explores the interactive effect of institutional quality and remittance on renewable energy consumption.

Before delving into the main findings of this study, it is important to briefly discuss the diagnostic tests, which offer valuable insights into the statistical properties and validity of the estimated models. In this case, three tests have been conducted: the Wald test, the Arellano-Bond AR(2) test, and the Hansen test. The Wald test assesses the joint significance of the coefficients in the model. In this analysis, the test statistic (λ^2) is quite large for all variables, indicating strong evidence against the null hypothesis of no joint significance. The Arellano-Bond AR(2) test is used to check for the presence of serial correlation in the model's residuals. The test results indicate small and non-significant coefficients for the lagged residuals, suggesting no evidence of serial correlation. The associated p-values (all above 0.95) further support this conclusion. Furthermore, the Hansen test shows that the over-identifying restrictions of the models are not violated. Overall, based on the diagnostic tests, the models appear to be well-specified and statistically sound.

Table 3. Regression results

Variables	*Model 1*	*Model 2*	*Model 3*
REN_{t-1}	0.8123***	0.7924***	0.7674***
	(0.0024)	(0.0405)	(0.0426)
INSQ	-0.4662***		-0.8278***
	(0.0096)		(0.0934)
REM		-0.3906***	-0.3549***
		(0.1004)	(0.0501)
INSQ*REM			0.042254**
			(0.0208)
INDS	0.0295***	0.0750**	0.0517*
	(0.0029)	(0.0326)	(0.0306)
FID	-0.0965***	-0.0600*	-0.0635
	(0.0017)	(0.0331)	(0.0617)
POP	0.1162***	-0.2254	-0.1008
	(0.0120)	(0.3634)	(0.5474)
Diagnostics			
Wald (λ^2)	3913095.0	1352.075	16366.95
(*p*-value)	[0.0000]	[0.0000]	[0.0000]
Arellano–Bond AR(2) test	-0.0546	-0.0013	-0.0003
(*p*-value)	[0.9565]	[0.9990]	[0.9998]
Hansen test	39.3977	36.2761	26.5196
(*p*-value)	[0.4972]	[0.5493]	[0.8993]

Standard errors in parentheses *** $p<0.01$ ** $p<0.05$ * $p<0.1$ p-values are in [ ]

From the regression results, the coefficient of the lag of renewable energy consumption (RENt−1) is positive and highly significant for all the models. This indicates a strong persistence in renewable energy consumption over time, suggesting that past REN levels substantially influence current levels. It highlights the importance of considering the historical trajectory of renewable energy consumption when examining its determinants.

In Model 1, the coefficient of institutional quality is negative and highly significant (-0.4662, $p<0.001$). This suggests that higher institutional quality is associated with lower levels of renewable energy consumption. The negative impact may be attributed to several factors. It could indicate that African countries with stronger institutions rely more on traditional energy sources or face challenges in adopting and implementing renewable energy policies and technologies. Additionally, it could be attributed to the limited institutional capacity, bureaucratic inefficiencies, and lack of supportive policies that are prevalent in most African countries, hindering the development and utilization of renewable energy sources in these nations. This finding contradicts most previous studies that have established a positive influence of institutional quality on renewable energy consumption (see Uzar, 2020; Rahman & Sultana, 2022; Saadaoui & Chtourou, 2022; Vatamanu & Zugravu, 2023). Industrialization has a positive and significant impact on renewable energy consumption. This indicates that higher levels of industrialization are associated with increased renewable energy consumption. This finding aligns with the notion that industrial sectors are typically energy-intensive and may contribute to the demand for renewable energy sources as a cleaner alternative to traditional fossil fuels. Financial development exerts a negative and highly significant effect on renewable energy consumption, indicating that countries with higher levels of financial development have lower levels of renewable energy consumption. This result may be counterintuitive, as one would expect financial development to facilitate investment in renewable energy projects. However, it is important to consider possible underlying factors that could influence this relationship, such as the availability and accessibility of financial resources specifically directed toward renewable energy initiatives. Furthermore, population growth is found to have a significant positive impact on renewable energy consumption, implying that higher population growth rates are associated with increased levels of renewable energy consumption. As the population grows, there is likely an increased demand for energy, and renewable sources may serve as an attractive option to meet this growing demand.

In Model 2, the study establishes a negative and highly significant impact of remittances on renewable energy consumption. This suggests that higher levels of remittance are associated with lower levels of renewable energy consumption. This result possibly indicates that remittance inflows in Africa may not be adequately channelled towards renewable energy projects or may be used for immediate consumption rather than long-term sustainable investments in the energy sector. The result sharply contrasts with prior studies (Das et al., 2021; Subramaniam et al., 2022; Zhao et al., 2022). Similar to Model 1, industrialization has a positive and significant effect on renewable energy consumption in Model 2. The impact of financial development remains negative and significant, while the effect of population growth is insignificant.

Turning to Model 3, institutional quality and remittance maintain their respective signs, as in Models 1 and 2. However, the coefficient of the interaction term INSQ*REM is positive and moderately significant (0.042254, $p < 0.01$). This suggests that the interactive effect of institutional quality and remittance has a positive impact on renewable energy consumption in Africa. This finding implies that when both institutional quality and remittance inflows are favourable, the potential for increased renewable energy consumption is enhanced. It underscores the importance of aligning institutional frameworks and financial resources to foster sustainable energy practices and investments.

CONCLUSION

In conclusion, this study investigates the determinants of energy transition in Africa, with a specific focus on the impact of institutional quality and remittance on renewable energy consumption. By analyzing a comprehensive dataset spanning 45 African countries from 2000 to 2020 and utilizing the generalized method of moments (GMM) technique, the researchers controlled for the effects of industrialization, financial development, and population growth. The study findings reveal that institutional quality and remittance negatively and significantly impact renewable energy consumption in Africa. This implies that countries with stronger institutional frameworks and higher levels of remittance inflows tend to exhibit lower levels of renewable energy consumption. However, the study also uncovers an interesting interactive effect between institutional quality and remittance, indicating that when these factors align favourably, they promote the demand for renewable energy consumption. Furthermore, the study establishes that industrialization and population growth positively and significantly contribute to Africa's renewable energy consumption. This suggests that as countries experience higher levels of industrialization and population growth, there is an increased demand for renewable energy as a cleaner alternative to traditional fossil fuels. On the other hand, the effect of financial development on renewable energy consumption is negative and significant, highlighting potential barriers or inefficiencies in allocating financial resources towards renewable energy projects in the region.

IMPLICATIONS FOR POLICY AND PRACTICE

The findings of this study have important implications for policy and practice in promoting renewable energy consumption and fostering sustainable development in Africa. Firstly, policymakers must prioritize the strengthening of institutional quality. The study reveals that institutional quality without remittance hurts renewable energy consumption, emphasizing the need for governance reforms, transparent policies, and effective regulatory frameworks. Policymakers should focus on creating an enabling environment for renewable energy development by promoting investment-friendly policies, establishing clear guidelines for renewable energy integration, and ensuring efficient implementation and enforcement of renewable energy policies.

Secondly, policymakers should consider the potential of remittance as a driver for renewable energy development. The study reveals that remittances *per se* without institutional quality harm renewable energy consumption. To harness the potential of remittance inflows, policymakers should design targeted policies and awareness campaigns to encourage the allocation of remittance funds towards sustainable energy projects. This can involve providing incentives for remittance recipients to invest in renewable energy technologies or supporting community-based renewable energy initiatives that involve remittance-receiving households. Strengthening financial literacy and promoting investment opportunities in renewable energy can also maximize the positive impact of remittance inflows.

Furthermore, addressing financial barriers is essential to accelerating renewable energy adoption. Policymakers should explore innovative financing mechanisms and incentives to attract investments in renewable energy projects. This can include establishing green investment funds, providing subsidies or tax incentives for renewable energy investments, and facilitating access to affordable financing options for renewable energy initiatives. Engaging with financial institutions and fostering public-private partnerships can also mobilize the necessary funds for renewable energy projects.

In addition, policymakers should support sustainable industrialization and ensure that population growth is accompanied by investments in renewable energy infrastructure. Strategies should be developed to promote sustainable industrial practices and encourage industries to transition to cleaner and more energy-efficient technologies. This can be achieved by incentivizing the adoption of renewable energy technologies in urban planning, promoting energy-efficient practices, and raising awareness about the benefits of renewable energy among industrial and residential sectors.

Lastly, regional collaboration and knowledge sharing plays a vital role in accelerating the energy transition in Africa. Policymakers should prioritize collaboration among African countries to share best practices, experiences, and lessons learned. Regional initiatives can focus on harmonizing renewable energy policies, fostering technology transfer, and promoting joint research and development efforts. Collaboration with international partners and organizations can provide additional support in terms of funding, expertise, and capacity building.

LIMITATIONS AND SUGGESTIONS FOR FURTHER RESEARCH

While this research provides valuable insights into the determinants of energy transition in Africa, it is important to acknowledge some limitations that should be considered when interpreting the findings. Firstly, the study relies on a specific time frame and dataset covering the years 2000-2020. The dynamic nature of renewable energy markets and the evolving policy landscape may warrant further analysis with more recent data to capture any potential changes in the relationships between variables.

Secondly, the study utilizes the generalized method of moments (GMM) technique for estimation. While GMM is a widely used method for addressing endogeneity and dynamic panel data issues, it has certain assumptions and limitations. Alternative econometric approaches or robustness checks could be employed to validate the findings and ensure the robustness of the results.

In addition, the researchers focus on a specific set of independent variables, namely institutional quality, remittance, industrialization, financial development, and population. There may be other relevant factors that were not included in the analysis but could potentially impact renewable energy consumption in Africa. Future studies could consider incorporating additional variables such as policy support, technological advancements, and environmental awareness to provide a more comprehensive understanding of the factors influencing energy transition.

REFERENCES

Adebayo, T. S., Ghosh, S., Nathaniel, S., & Wada, I. (2023). Technological innovations, renewable energy, globalization, financial development, and carbon emissions: Role of inward remittances for top ten remittances receiving countries. *Environmental Science and Pollution Research International*, *30*(26), 69330–69348. doi:10.100711356-023-27184-x PMID:37133657

Ahmad, M., Ul Haq, Z., Khan, Z., Khattak, S. I., Ur Rahman, Z., & Khan, S. (2019). Does the inflow of remittances cause environmental degradation? Empirical evidence from China. *Economic research-. Ekonomska Istrazivanja*, *32*(1), 2099–2121. doi:10.1080/1331677X.2019.1642783

Ahmed, F., Kousar, S., Pervaiz, A., & Shabbir, A. (2022). Do institutional quality and financial development affect sustainable economic growth? Evidence from South Asian countries. *Borsa Istanbul Review*, *22*(1), 189–196. doi:10.1016/j.bir.2021.03.005

Ahmed, F., Kousar, S., Pervaiz, A., & Shabbir, A. (2022). Do institutional quality and financial development affect sustainable economic growth? Evidence from South Asian countries. *Borsa Istanbul Review*, *22*(1), 189–196. doi:10.1016/j.bir.2021.03.005

Akçay, S. (2019). Do industrialization, democracy, and financial openness promote financial development? Evidence from Turkey. *Turkish Studies*, *20*(5), 708–727. doi:10.1080/14683849.2018.1537752

Ali, M., Kirikkaleli, D., Sharma, R., & Altuntaş, M. (2022). The nexus between remittances, natural resources, technological innovation, economic growth, and environmental sustainability in Pakistan. *Environmental Science and Pollution Research International*, *29*(50), 75822–75840. doi:10.100711356-022-21228-4 PMID:35661303

Arellano, M., & Bover, O. (1995). Another look at the instrumental variable estimation of error-components models. *Journal of Econometrics*, *68*(1), 29–51. doi:10.1016/0304-4076(94)01642-D

Asongu, S., & Odhiambo, N. M. (2022). Governance and renewable energy consumption in Sub-Saharan Africa. *International Journal of Energy Sector Management*, *16*(2), 209–223. doi:10.1108/IJESM-10-2020-0009

Bunyaminu, A., Mohammed, I., Yakubu, I. N., Shani, B., & Abukari, A. L. (2022). The effect of health expenditure on average life expectancy: Does government effectiveness play a moderating role? *International Journal of Health Governance*, *27*(4), 365–377. doi:10.1108/IJHG-03-2022-0027

Chen, C., Pinar, M., & Stengos, T. (2021). Determinants of renewable energy consumption: Importance of democratic institutions. *Renewable Energy*, *179*, 75–83. doi:10.1016/j.renene.2021.07.030

Chishti, M. Z. (2023). Exploring the dynamic link between FDI, remittances, and ecological footprint in Pakistan: Evidence from partial and multiple wavelet based-analysis. *Research in Globalization*, *6*, 100109. doi:10.1016/j.resglo.2022.100109

Das, A., McFarlane, A., & Carels, L. (2021). Empirical exploration of remittances and renewable energy consumption in Bangladesh. *Asia-Pacific Journal of Regional Science*, *5*(1), 65–89. doi:10.100741685-020-00180-6

DiMaggio, P. J., & Powell, W. W. (1983). The iron cage revisited: Institutional isomorphism and collective rationality in organizational fields. *American Sociological Review*, *48*(2), 147–160. doi:10.2307/2095101

Eggoh, J., Bangake, C., & Semedo, G. (2019). Do remittances spur economic growth? Evidence from developing countries. *The Journal of International Trade & Economic Development*, *28*(4), 391–418. doi:10.1080/09638199.2019.1568522

Environmental and Energy Study Institute. (2021). *Fossil Fuels*. EESI. https://www.eesi.org/topics/fossil-fuels/description

Gujarati, D. (2003). Basic Econometrics. Singapura: McGraw-Hill.

Islam, M. S. (2022). Do personal remittances cause environmental pollution? Evidence from the top eight remittance-receiving countries. *Environmental Science and Pollution Research International*, *29*(24), 35768–35779. doi:10.100711356-021-18175-x PMID:35060043

Islam, M. S. (2022). Do personal remittances influence economic growth in South Asia? A panel analysis. *Review of Development Economics*, *26*(1), 242–258. doi:10.1111/rode.12842

Jafri, M. A. H., Abbas, S., Abbas, S. M. Y., & Ullah, S. (2022). Caring for the environment: Measuring the dynamic impact of remittances and FDI on CO2 emissions in China. *Environmental Science and Pollution Research International*, *29*(6), 1–9. doi:10.100711356-021-16180-8 PMID:34495470

Kaufmann, D., Kraay, A., & Mastruzzi, M. (2011). The worldwide governance indicators: Methodology and analytical issues1. *Hague Journal on the Rule of Law*, *3*(2), 220–246. doi:10.1017/S1876404511200046

Khan, Z. U., Ahmad, M., & Khan, A. (2020). On the remittances-environment led hypothesis: Empirical evidence from BRICS economies. *Environmental Science and Pollution Research International*, *27*(14), 16460–16471. doi:10.100711356-020-07999-8 PMID:32124280

Maruta, A. A., Banerjee, R., & Cavoli, T. (2020). Foreign aid, institutional quality and economic growth: Evidence from the developing world. *Economic Modelling*, *89*, 444–463. doi:10.1016/j.econmod.2019.11.008

Mohamed Aslam, A. L., & Alibuhtto, M. C. (2023). Workers' remittances and economic growth: new evidence from an ARDL bounds cointegration approach for Sri Lanka. *Journal of Economic and Administrative Sciences*.

Moskalenko, B., Lyulyov, O., Pimonenko, T., & Kobushko, I. (2022). Institutions' Effect on a Country's Investment Attractiveness within Sustainable Development. *Virtual Economics*, *5*(4), 50–64. doi:10.34021/ve.2022.05.04(3)

Musah, A., & Yakubu, I. N. (2022). Exploring industrialization and environmental sustainability dynamics in Ghana: A fully modified least squares approach. *Technological Sustainability*, *2*(2), 142–155. doi:10.1108/TECHS-06-2022-0028

Nguyen, C. P., Su, T. D., & Nguyen, T. V. H. (2018). Institutional quality and economic growth: The case of emerging economies. *Theoretical Economics Letters*, *8*(11), 1943–1956. doi:10.4236/tel.2018.811127

Rahman, M. M., & Sultana, N. (2022). Impacts of institutional quality, economic growth, and exports on renewable energy: Emerging countries perspective. *Renewable Energy*, *189*, 938–951. doi:10.1016/j.renene.2022.03.034

Raza, M. A. A., Yan, C., Abbas, H. S. M., & Ilahi, S. (2023). Do Remittance Inflows, Investment Attributes, and Regional Integration Accelerate Sustainable Economic Growth in Asia? *Journal of the Knowledge Economy*, 1–16. doi:10.100713132-023-01126-x

Roodman, D. (2009). How to do xtabond2: An introduction to difference and system GMM in Stata. *The Stata Journal*, *9*(1), 86–136. doi:10.1177/1536867X0900900106

Saadaoui, H., & Chtourou, N. (2022). Do institutional quality, financial development, and economic growth improve renewable energy transition? Some evidence from Tunisia. *Journal of the Knowledge Economy*, 1–32. doi:10.100713132-022-00999-8

Scott, W. R. (2013). *Institutions and organizations: Ideas, interests, and identities*. Sage publications.

Subramaniam, Y., Masron, T. A., & Loganathan, N. (2022). Remittances and renewable energy: an empirical analysis. *International Journal of Energy Sector Management*.

Umair, M., Yousuf, M. U., Ul-Haq, J., Hussain, Z., & Visas, H. (2023). Revisiting the environmental impact of renewable energy, non-renewable energy, remittances, and economic growth: CO2 emissions versus ecological footprint for top remittance-receiving countries. *Environmental Science and Pollution Research International*, *30*(23), 1–15. doi:10.100711356-023-26812-w PMID:37055685

United Nations. (2015). *Paris Agreement*. UN. https://unfccc.int/process-and-meetings/the-paris-agreement/the-paris-agreement

Utile, T. I., Ijirshar, V. U., & Adoo, S. E. M. (2021). Impact of institutional quality on economic growth in Nigeria. *Gusau International Journal of Management and Social Sciences*, *4*(3), 21–21.

Uzar, U. (2020). Political economy of renewable energy: Does institutional quality make a difference in renewable energy consumption? *Renewable Energy*, *155*, 591–603. doi:10.1016/j.renene.2020.03.172

Vakulchuk, R., Overland, I., & Suryadi, B. (2023). ASEAN's energy transition: How to attract more investment in renewable energy. *Energy, Ecology & Environment*, *8*(1), 1–16. doi:10.100740974-022-00261-6

Vatamanu, A. F., & Zugravu, B. G. (2023). Financial development, institutional quality and renewable energy consumption. A panel data approach. *Economic Analysis and Policy*, *78*, 765–775. doi:10.1016/j.eap.2023.04.015

Wang, E., Gozgor, G., Mahalik, M. K., Patel, G., & Hu, G. (2022). Effects of institutional quality and political risk on the renewable energy consumption in the OECD Countries. *Resources Policy*, *79*, 103041. doi:10.1016/j.resourpol.2022.103041

Wang, Z., Zaman, S., Zaman, Q. U., & Rasool, S. F. (2021). Impact of remittances on carbon emission: Fresh evidence from a panel of five remittance-receiving countries. *Environmental Science and Pollution Research International*, *28*(37), 52418–52430. doi:10.100711356-021-14412-5 PMID:34008066

World Bank. (2020). *Climate Change*. World Bank. https://www.worldbank.org/en/topic/climatechange

Wu, L., & Broadstock, D. C. (2015). Does economic, financial and institutional development matter for renewable energy consumption? Evidence from emerging economies. *International Journal of Economic Policy in Emerging Economies*, *8*(1), 20–39. doi:10.1504/IJEPEE.2015.068246

Yakubu, I. N., Kapusuzoglu, A., & Ceylan, N. B. (2020). Determinants of Working Capital Management of Manufacturing Firms in Ghana Under Innovative Work Behaviour Perspective. *Strategic Outlook for Innovative Work Behaviours: Interdisciplinary and Multidimensional Perspectives*, 235-252.

Yakubu, I. N., Kapusuzoglu, A., & Ceylan, N. B. (2022). ICT trade and energy transition in the BRICS economies. In *Sustainability in Energy Business and Finance: Approaches and Developments in the Energy Market* (pp. 13–24). Springer International Publishing. doi:10.1007/978-3-030-94051-5_2

Yakubu, I. N., Kapusuzoglu, A., & Ceylan, N. B. (2022). Investigating the Role of Export Diversification, Remittances, and Environmental Sustainability in Accordance with Clean Energy and Zero Emission. In *Circular Economy and the Energy Market: Achieving Sustainable Economic Development Through Energy Policy* (pp. 51–65). Springer International Publishing. doi:10.1007/978-3-031-13146-2_5

Zhao, J., Zhang, T., Arshad, A., Chen, J., Ji, H., & Wang, T. (2023). An empirical investigation of the impact of renewable and non-renewable energy consumption and economic growth on climate change, evidence from emerging Asian countries. *Frontiers in Environmental Science*, *10*, 1–16. doi:10.3389/fenvs.2022.1085372

Zhao, L., & Qamruzzaman, M. (2022). Do urbanization, remittances, and globalization matter for energy consumption in belt and road countries: Evidence from renewable and non-renewable energy consumption. *Frontiers in Environmental Science*, *10*, 723. doi:10.3389/fenvs.2022.930728

Chapter 6
Domestic Policies for Sustainable and Economic Development in Countries With Emerging Economies:
A Case Study of Mexico

María E. Raygoza-L.
Universidad Politécnica de Baja California, Mexico

Roxana Jiménez-Sánchez
Universidad Politécnica de Baja California, Mexico

Jesús Heriberto Orduño-Osuna
https://orcid.org/0009-0004-4850-7481
Universidad Politécnica de Baja California, Mexico

Abelardo Mercado-Herrera
Universidad Politécnica de Baja California, Mexico

Miguel E. Bravo-Zanoguera
Universidad Politécnica de Baja California, Mexico

Guillermo M Limón-Molina
https://orcid.org/0000-0002-5445-8928
Universidad Politécnica de Baja California, Mexico

Ivette Cota-Rivera
Universidad Politécnica de Baja California, Mexico

Diego Bonilla-García
Universidad Autónoma de Baja California, Mexico

Fabian N. N. Murrieta-Rico
https://orcid.org/0000-0001-9829-3013
Universidad Politécnica de Baja California, Mexico

ABSTRACT

The current era of globalization has exacerbated the problem of climate change, affecting all ecosystems, The anthropogenic footprint has been the leading cause of the current environmental impact on the planet, and socioeconomically developed countries have implemented various strategies to mitigate

DOI: 10.4018/978-1-6684-9272-7.ch006

the environmental impact of anthropogenic damage on marine and terrestrial ecosystems. The two main challenges are environmental protection and education. It is necessary to develop a linkage between education, government, society, and industry to address climate change as the principal measure for creating programs with international reach. Governmental and educational institutions must develop quality educational policies. The implementation of a triad between public institutions, private institutions, and education, which collaborate with society and the government through programs that integrate institutional internal plans and programs with economic support for the incorporation of public educational policies, the promotion of R&D projects.

INTRODUCTION

One of the biggest problems that arise worldwide is global warming due to the high rate of emissions from the industrial, electrical, and transportation sectors mainly, this has proven the formulation of a set of strategies delivered by the United Nations Organization (UN), as an international agenda seeking to align the countries that belong to this alliance. One of the biggest problems that arise worldwide is global warming due to the high rate of emissions from the industrial, electrical, and transportation sectors mainly, this has proven the formulation of a set of strategies issued by the United Nations Organization (UN), as an international agenda seeking to align the countries that belong to this alliance. Mexico has participated in these initiatives to mitigate climate change and has directed its efforts to implement and develop Clean Development Mechanism (CDM) projects.

However, it must offer more strategies to promote the energy transition to clean and efficient technologies necessary for a low-carbon economy. Prospects have been more campaign-oriented or for the benefit of large concessionaires in the country, without focusing on continuity between governments that have alternated in the change of government. Among the initiatives that Mexico has participated in is the Kyoto Protocol, despite implementing different strategies to achieve the goals, which were not enough.

This chapter aims to propose the integration of domestic and fiscal policies for the sustainable development of countries with Emerging Economies: Case Study Mexico, considers including economic and environmental policies through the involvement of stakeholders, based on the assumption that these strategies would allow countries with emerging economies to have economic and social development.

Currently, the search for sustainable development in the country is hindered by economic and political support for conventional energy, where the installed capacity's participation in the energy matrix is over 90%, with a high percentage of fossil fuel extraction of over 50%, natural gas with a greater than 37% share, coal with around 6%, and large hydroelectric plants that have a negative impact on aquatic flora and fauna (IRENA, 2023)

In the year 2013 government period, modifications were made to Mexico's laws, seeking the economic opening of new markets. Energy perspectives continued to mark an over-exploitation of fossil resources by more than 100% and natural gas in more than 50% of the generation percentage (SENER, 2016). Modifications were made to several normative and institutional laws, such as the Mexican political constitution and the electric industry law. This political proposal, the Energy Reform, did not contain indicators or incentives for reducing carbon footprint and developing green projects in different economic sectors (Torne, 2019). Regardless of changes in government, it was contained without fulfilling its established objectives.

Instead, the policies that directed government efforts towards sustainable development sought deep oil well extraction. Still, the country's legal framework modifications had the advantage of foreign economic inclusion for promoting renewable energy generation projects for more significant sustainable development. Due to the potential of renewable energy in Mexico, the central technological transfers that have been enabled in projects with investment from the Mexican government in the foreign private initiative have been wind energy generation in the main area of the country and photovoltaic energy in the northeast, not reaching the generation of electricity with the sum of all renewable energies, nor even 10% of the country.

Currently, due to Mexico's socioeconomic situation, where its economy is in an emerging conjectural moment, and due to various economic crises, the government has opted for subsidies in the electricity tariff system, such as the agricultural and the domestic sector, especially in some border areas of the country due to extreme climates, where temperatures reach up to 50° Celsius in the summer.

Due to the country's geopolitical conditions, subventions favor the well-being of vulnerable groups. They have also maintained little interest in creating public policies and developing programs that promote using renewable energies as an alternative to diversify the country's energy matrix with green options that contribute to reducing greenhouse gases. Developing countries have the greatest opportunities for capitalizing on environmental and economic sustainability synergies. A green growth approach is a chance for emerging and developing economies to leapfrog unsustainable and wasteful production and consumption patterns (UN Environmental Programme, 2022).

The goals in institutional policies and prospective plans in the electricity sector require greater institutional participation from both public and private sectors of environmental care. This is necessary for the development of climate, environmental, and energy policies that have an ecological impact, with objectives aimed at promoting a culture of environmental awareness and measures that initiate the development of laws that incentivize and penalize actions that reduce carbon footprint and anthropogenic damage, as well as the irrational use of natural resources.

Government strategies have included energy plans and prospective plans issued by Energy Secretary SENER (from Spanish: Secretaría de Energía), that imply ambitious goals in the installed capacity of renewable energies and clean energy generation. However, these goals have been issued and worked on individually and in isolation within various government institutions, without strategic linkage and joint efforts for their achievement among society, government, industry, and educational institutions. As a result, the energy transition has been delayed so far due to the failure to meet the objectives of energy development plans.

Developing economies should evaluate having a vision focused on meeting the 17 objectives issued by the UN for sustainable development. To align with this global strategy, the importance of quality government measures in environmental matters must be recognized to promote laws with relevant scope, to encourage research and development projects with public, private, and mixed funds, with a low-interest rate regime and subsidies primarily to educational institutions for the creation of sustainable programs. This should involve society, industry, government, and educational institutions, with educational institutions having the most significant impact concerning cultural change, dissemination, and generation of innovation and technology, with research, innovation, and development (R&D) projects, in green technology theme that accelerates sustainable development in countries with emerging markets.

PUBLIC POLICIES INTEGRATED WITH FISCAL, ECONOMIC, AND ENVIRONMENTAL POLICIES FOR EMERGING ECONOMIES

Developing countries should continue to implement measures that activate the development and implementation of environmental laws and the context of ecological issues, the regulations that support bonuses or penalties for the proper management of natural resources should continue to be implemented. In addition, fiscal incentives, and revenue-raising measures for non-compliance with the percentage of clean energy consumption according to its installed capacity should continue with the objective defined to meet goals that help mitigate environmental impact.

For a relevant socio-economic development and energy transition, developing economies such as Mexico must seek to exercise equitable socio-economic development and resume proposals such as those pronounced in the Energy Reform, which was not executed due to various interests and visions of the government. Among the strategies, there were objectives for high electricity consumers, especially in the industrial sector. The Energy Reform enacted regulatory initiatives, including providing Clean Energy Certificates (CEL). The objective of CEL was to provide either a bonus for energy-efficient use of clean energy consumption or a penalty in case of non-compliance with the targets contemplated in the Energy Reform (Torne, 2019).

The sustainable development of Mexico as a country with an emerging market requires a quality government organization, where, based on efficient public policies, a structure is executed that manages to make a connection between fiscal, economic, and environmental policies.

To introduce ourselves to this chapter, we will begin with the basic definition of public policies. "Public policy is whatever governments choose to do or not do; it can be seen in the behavior of government officials and agencies; it defines the relationship of government to its environment. A policy is a purposeful course of action taken to deal with a problem or concern". Public policymaking is a complex process that involves many participants with different roles, interests, and resources. The study of public policy is the study of who gets what, why, and what difference it makes.

To develop quality governments in developing countries, the different groups that intervene in society must be considered to know their needs and work together with them. This joint work is done through the development of public policies, which are the precursors of the changes in the countries when they are developed appropriately.

The public administration is the organic structure of the State, it is saying a set of organizations, ministries, public companies, etc., which combine human, financial, technological, and regulatory, which are transformed into public policies, to address the problems of the citizens, control their behavior, satisfy their needs, or demands.

Table 1. Shows the structure of the objectives of public policies and some of their scope within the state and society.

Table 1. The objective of the government in public policies

Coerce	Persuade	Educate	Strengthen	Rewards
Prohibit, compel Criminalize	Register of the public policy proposal License, Certified. Report Tax Investigative. -Mediate -Discussion / Debate	Exhort Educate. Standards. The study, inform Publicize Manage Coordinate	Grants, loans. Equal Protection. Reduce risk Transfer payments In-kind benefits.	Hire & pay Contract. Guarantee profi

Source: Saint Germain (2007)

STEPS FOR THE DEVELOPMENT OF THE METHODOLOGY FOR THE DEVELOPMENT OF PUBLIC POLICIES:

Step 1. Problem Identification: Getting Government to See the Problem

A problem is a situation that produces a human need, deprivation, or dissatisfaction, such as pollution, inflation, poverty, etc. However, only those needs and wants that are articulated by people demanding action become problems eligible for public policy solutions.

Step 2. Agenda: Getting Government to Consider the Problem

The policy agenda consists of items that receive serious attention from official policymakers. Only a small number of needs and wants ever to attain a place on the policy agenda of an executive, legislative, or judicial branch of government.

Step 3. Policy Formulation: Getting Government to Consider Solutions

Courses of action for dealing with public problems must be developed that will be acceptable to official policymakers. Proposals may be put forward by a chief executive, a legislator, an administrative agency, interest groups, think tanks, individual citizens, etc.

Step 4. Policy Adoption: Getting Government to Adopt a Solution

For a policy to be adopted, a majority coalition that supports the alternative must be constructed. This depends on the official actors involved, as well as their beliefs, and intentions.

Step 5. Policy Implementation: Getting the Government to Apply the Solution to the Problem

The law, rule, or order that results from the adoption stage can be called a public policy. Without implementation, there is virtually no effect, but the act of implementation may change the nature of the policy itself. Public administrators are the primary implementers of public policy, congress has oversight responsibility, and the courts could exercise judicial review.

Step 6. Policy Evaluation

Did It work? What was the policy content? What was the output, the outcome, and the impact? Did it work? To what degree were the objectives of the policy met? To what extent was the problem solved? (Saint-Germain, 2007).

Table 2. Shows the methodology that domestic policies follow from their identification to the execution process, exemplifying a general case for Low-Carbon

Table 2. Methodology for the efficient development of domestic and public policies

1 Problem ID	2 Agenda	3 Formulation	4 Adoption	5 Implementation	6 Evaluation
What is the problem? Public policies are required for Low-Carbon and sustainable development.	Where is the problem presented? Countries with developing markets.	What are the proposed solutions? Integration with economic, fiscal, and environmental policies, to develop sustainable projects.	What is done about the problem? Countries with developing markets.	How does the government do what it decides to do? Currently under a vertical scheme not linked between the stakeholders.	Did it work? The objective (Low-Carbon) has not been reached.

Own development

Types of Policies According to Inference

- **Regulatory:** a policy that imposes limits on the behavior of some identifiable groups or individuals; reduces the freedom or discretion to act or not act; Example: regulation of criminal activity, business activity, access to public goods; FDA regulation of drugs, etc.
- **Distributive**: a policy that benefits some people but at not discernable costs to others; allocates government benefits to individuals and groups; uses public funds; little direct competition or challenge from other groups; no direct costs to any identifiable group; clear winners but no clear losers; Example: agricultural subsidies, government-sponsored research; river improvements.
- **Re-distributive:** a polity that makes a deliberate re-allocation of resources among identifiable social groups; Examples: welfare, housing subsidies, progressive income tax, social security, etc.

Integration of Public Policies With Policies of the Different Disciplines

Normally, the models are descriptions of phenomena that abstract the details of reality and that try to highlight the significant elements of said problem. In the case of the integration of public policies for socioeconomic development and low carbon, the contributions generated by the different disciplines such as economics, public administration, political sciences, and environmental sciences, etc. must be used.

In recent times, organizations such as the Inter-American Development Bank have indicated that public policies have their instrumentation, at least six indicators: stability, adaptability, implementation and effective application, coordination and coherence, orientation to the public interest, and efficiency.

One of the sciences with an integral character is environmental science which incorporates, in a transversal way, elements of sustainability in its different aspects such as socioeconomic development. On the other hand, there is a model that integrates three world views on environmental problems that include: stewardship of the planet, leadership, and environmental wisdom. These three visions have been determining factors for the design, application, and evaluation of public policies in this area (Huerta & Guzmán, 2020).

Public policies, due to their interaction, can be called vertical and horizontal policies, called "horizontal" if the interactions occur at the same government level or "vertical" if they relate to two different governmental tiers (Saint-Germain, 2007).

As mentioned, the policies can be stratified by different techniques, by their subject of interest, their objective, as well as by their hierarchical structure, in table 3, their hierarchical division is shown.

Table 3. Scheme of policies according to the hierarchical system that is disseminated and promulgated in different political contexts

Coerce	Horizontal coordination	Vertical coordination
Internal coordination within the government	Coordination between agencies or public sectors	coordination between subordinate agencies
External coordination between the government and the public and private sector	Coordination with civil society organizations and the private sector	Coordination: a) Upwards with international organizations b) Down with the local and regional government

Source: Christensen and Laegrein (2008)

In the process of planning and strategies for sustainable development, the incorporation of quality public policies of the "Distributive type" is required. These policies establish what concerns the issues of agricultural subsidies, government-sponsored research, and other problems of world priority such as environmental issues and the distribution of economic resources (UNDP, 2017).

In Mexico, most public policies are developed and promoted under a vertical scheme, where government authorities publicize public policies based on world organizations such as the UN; Mexico is governed under a centralized political system, therefore public policies are also constantly distributed from the center of the country, spreading to the states, and finally the county with a vertical political system, they are disseminated and executed in educational systems, civil society, and various organizations.

Currently, the centralized political system has supported the incorporation into the national agenda of Mexico of the goals issued by the UN in terms of sustainable development, allowing planning and development of policies aligned with international objectives, achieving from the current organizational structure. the different public organizations, it has also been a disadvantage in the participation and commitment of civil society and non-governmental associations, since they do not have leadership in establishing goals and objectives relevant to the social and environmental needs of local community groups (Harrop, 2004).

Mexico is working as part of the Organization for Economic Development Co-operation and Development (OECD), Participation of Mexico in the OECD Public Policy Agenda: contributions and benefits, the work, and recommendations of public policies of the OECD. These commissions are attended by expert officials from all member countries and from some non-member countries, invited for their importance and experience.

Where in meetings Mexico contributed to ministerial meetings regarding employment, environment, and social development policies. Mexico made interesting contributions to committees related to issues where valuable experiences to contribute. In others where we were further behind, we derived important knowledge from other countries. In a moment I will list some of the main contributions.

A quality government continuously works to improve the effectiveness of policymaking: what mechanisms for addressing coordination and capacity difficulties across levels of government with objectives in fiscal, economic, and environmental policies. The next point in this chapter provides information on the importance and function of fiscal policies for countries with emerging markets such as Mexico.

Political Economists

Political economy is the study of the relationship between the market and powerful actors, such as a country's government. This almost always involves the forces of supply and demand and the allocation of resources through private economic decision-making. The interaction between the state and the market through political, economic, and societal institutions can frame deliverable outcomes, such as public goods. This can occur not only within a country but between them as well. Public goods are defined as goods and services provided by the state that are available for everyone in society. Political economy will involve the mixing of political and economic policy goals. Finally, the political economy also studies how individuals interact with the market and society (FRIEDEN, 2020).

Political economists are tasked with understanding how the state affects the market. A good example is the concept of wealth distribution within a country.

Wealth distribution is defined as how investments, properties, and resources, or wealth, are divided amongst its population. In some countries, wealth is distributed quite evenly, whereas, in other countries, wealth is distributed unevenly. Countries with uneven wealth distribution are more susceptible to political tension. Similarly, political economists look at how the market affects the state and its society (Cingano, 2014).

Fiscal Policy

For the region's economies to recover and meet investment needs and social demands, proactive public policies will be required. This calls for a new fiscal pact that lays the foundations for a fiscal sustainability framework focused on increasing permanent revenues to meet well-being, investment, and environmental sustainability needs. Public spending should not only be oriented to conjunctural needs but must also drive sustainable development. This would mean boosting public investment to boost economic growth and achieving the Sustainable Development Goals (SDGs) (Salazar-Xirinachs, 2023). Since the late 80s, the Mexican government has drawn up a decree for tax incentives to prevent environmental pollution, but the integration of laws that execute these regulations and follow-up for efficient results with corporate and social responsibility is still required.

Environmental Policy

The evolution of environmental policy In Mexico occurs in three stages. The first stage had a "sanitary" approach if we understand by health both knowledge and improvement of sanitary conditions in the natural environment of the population.

In the second stage, environmental policy acquired a comprehensive approach to the preservation and restoration of the ecological balance, creating in 1982 the Federal Law of Protection of the Environment, and in 1983 the Secretary of Urban Development and Ecology SEDUE (from Spanish: Secretaría de Desarrollo Urbano y Ecología), whose faculties were preserving forest resources, flora, and fauna wild and counteract the harmful effects of excessive industrial concentration (Tamargo, 2002).

In the third stage, environmental policy acquires a "Sustainable Development" approach, which raises the need to plan resource management natural resources, and environmental policies in our country from an integral point of view, articulating the objectives economic, social, and environmental (from Spanish: Secretaría del Medio Ambiente y Recursos Naturales) (CONGRESO DE LA UNIÓN, Secretaría General, 2015).

As mentioned, the current structure of public policies is vertical as shown in Fig. 1, the results of maintaining vertical police have not had relevant results, because there has not been much involvement by civil society, so in This chapter proposes a horizontal structure as shown in Fig. 2, so that civil society can take leadership in local problems.

Figure 1. Current policy system

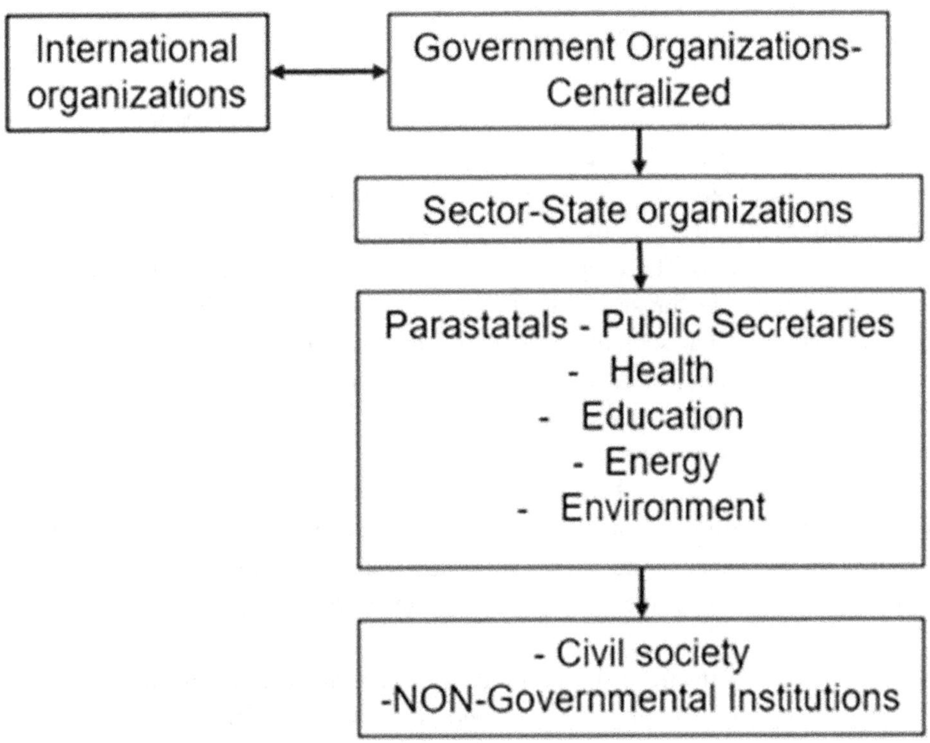

Figure 2. Domestic and public policy proposal for sustainable development

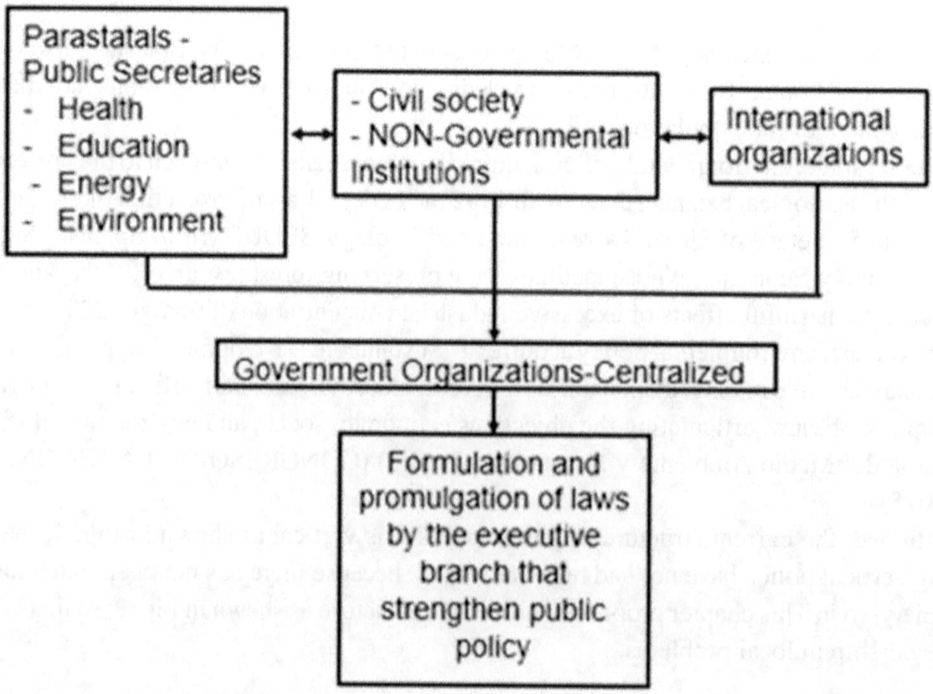

PUBLIC POLICY INICIATIVES AND SUCCESS STORIES OF EMERGING ECONOMIES

Sustainable development ought to mean the creation of a society and an economy that can come to terms with the life-support limits of the planet. The institutions of the social and economic order have yet to respond in any meaningful way, but a beginning has been made, and that beginning has brought with it some institutional changes, for these changes indicate both the nature of the response and the impediments to further progress. These early changes also clarify what further institutional adjustments will be desirable to continue the transition, what they might look like, and how they might be achieved.

Individuals will have to act as socially responsible citizens, not self-gratifying consumers, and care for their neighbors near and far. The amount of waste created to produce any useful item will have to be cut by at least half and preferably more. Energy and materials usage will also have to be reduced by almost as much per unit of value used.

Prices will reflect the full ecological and social 'footprint' of economic activity, and the precautionary principle will become the holy grail of management and science. Equity issues, notably the improvement of the well-being of both ecosystems critically endangered, and human populations threatened, by unmanageable catastrophe, will come to dominate efficiency rules in the determination of valuation, risk avoidance, and cost-benefit analysis.

Citizens will have to 'get involved' in the process of governance, the sustainable policy will be a collectivist polity, indentured to tending the global commons (Voisey, 2007).

Markets refer to arrangements in the competitive economy ensuring that ecological and social tolerances to expansion and change are not exceeded. Though the mechanism of control may also be regulatory, the process of implementation is competitive and market-driven.

Regulations apply to patterns of control and guidance imposed either by the state in the form of legal rules, or various formal restrictions or by collective action supported by voluntary agreements or legal norms.

Equity relates to distributional fairness in dealing with both non-human and human life but mainly the latter and encompasses both rights and duties towards future as well as present generations and ecosystems. Within equity will be legal norms that guide such institutional arrangements as monitoring, protecting, evaluating, and compensating, either in cash or in kind.

Revelation encompasses the idea of capturing the spirit of communal obligation and citizenship (O'Riordan,1997).

As a means of identifying how far any country studied has moved in its institutional re-design for the transition to sustainable development, we proposed eight 'indicators' for testing response and adaptation:

- The language and meaning of sustainable development.
- The scope for policy integration where heretofore policies were neither united nor mutually reinforcing.
- The nature of inter-departmental coordination promoting and reflecting these new policy alliances.
- The role of legislative (parliamentary) surveillance of both policy integration and administrative cohesion, including improved means of identifying targets and performance indicators.
- The compilation of environmental and social indicators of quality of life and ecological tolerance as a basis for legitimizing action and evaluating the sustainability transition.
- The creation of 'green' accounts covering indicators of resource depletion, environmental disruption, price incompatibilities, inappropriate subsidies, and measures of human welfare and social justice, coupled with tentative moves towards ecological tax reform.
- The involvement of the business community in addressing sustainability through full cost accounting, internal housekeeping, full regulatory compliance, product stewardship, supply chain audits, and sustainability awareness-raising for shareholders and customers; and the emergence of local action, to bring about a locally responsive version of all the above points, set in a drive for fresh democratic mandates (Lundqvist, 2001).

The potential economic and social impacts of environmental degradation are particularly serious for developing countries given their dependence on natural resources for economic growth and their vulnerability to energy, food, water security, climate change, and extreme weather risks. All these factors are challenging their ability to develop (OECD, 2021).

Developing countries have the greatest opportunities for capitalizing on environmental and economic sustainability synergies. A green growth approach is a chance for emerging and developing economies to leapfrog unsustainable and wasteful production and consumption patterns. They can still factor environmental issues into their infrastructure investment decisions and can further develop agriculture and other natural resources in a way that improves livelihoods, creates jobs, and reduces poverty.

They are less constrained than developed countries, which are now locked into investment choices and sunk capital from previous decades. Adequate financing and capacity would offer developing economies the opportunity to lay down the infrastructure and networks needed to support a sustainable development path.

National development strategies must be based on each country's strengths, bottlenecks, and constraints Developed, emerging, and developing countries will face different challenges and opportunities in greening growth, as will countries with differing economic and political circumstances (OCDE, 2006).

According to OECD data, Mexico is the member country with the lowest environmental taxes, it was the only country with a negative relationship of -0.8% on average as a percentage of Gross Domestic Product (GDP), a situation that contrasts with developed countries such as Japan, Germany, Finland, Denmark, and the Netherlands range from 3% to 4.4%.

The government of Mexico as a developing country since the end of the 80s elaborated in a decree of fiscal incentives for the prevention of environmental pollution, but the integration of laws is required through the executive branch, which obliges the public and private sectors, with the taking for carbon emissions of actions to follow the rules and achieve efficient results through tax and incentives with inciting sanctions. These incentives as mechanisms can be established as taxis and green bonds.

Taxis and discounts must be an efficient instrument in terms of low carbon and the environment, administrative processes are carried out that provide efficient follow-up with the cooperation and responsibility, and commitment of the pro-life companies and society. The countries of the European continent are at the forefront of initiatives and implementation of mechanisms for the protection of the environment.

Proposals for Initiatives From European Countries for the Energy Transition and Care for the Environment

- Defend ecological and social sustainability as a central collective objective and must be a backbone of the Constitution.
- Ecological and social sustainability must have a rank of the maximum hierarchy.
- In case of incompatibilities between economic development and ecological sustainability, the latter must come first.
- Include the analysis of ecological economics in economic proposals, recognizing the limits of resources and the dependence of societies and their economies.
- Protect local and global sustainability in international treaties.
- Take a proactive role in the fight against climate change, the energy transition.
- Defend the precautionary principle in the extraction, production, and emission of waste.
- Development of alternative and renewable energies.
- Development of sustainable technologies, the right to environmental information.
- Promotion of research in sustainability, and the development of education for sustainability.
- Defend the participation of the population in environmental management.

The instruments and mechanisms of a fiscal nature such as taxis for carbon emissions and green bonuses, as well as resuming the initiative of the Clean Energy Certificates (CEL) proposed by the Energy Reform. These strategies must be aligned with the environmental policy to reduce the carbon footprint, and the country's economic policy through public policies for economic development that take initiatives from civil society and the educational system, from a perspective of local economic growth. to global.

Success Stories of Initiatives in Countries With Emerging Economies to Mitigate Environmental Impact

Under the support and supervision of international organizations such as the UN, the World Bank, and the Word Resources Institute (WRI) have developed different initiatives to mitigate the impact on the environment by supporting countries with emerging economies. Table 4 contains information on initiatives and success stories of countries with emerging economies for the mitigation of environmental.

Table 4. Initiatives to reduce environmental impact in countries with emerging economies

Country	Initiative	Impact on the environmental
China	China Renewable Energy Law serves as the main framework for the development of the sector.	The law offers a variety of financial incentives, such as a national fund to foster renewable energy. A combination of investments and policy incentives has encouraged major advances in the development of both wind power and solar power. Policy-led growth in renewable energy has created jobs, income, and revenue streams for nascent low-carbon industries
Kenya	Feed-in Tariff (FIT) is a policy instrument that makes it mandatory for energy companies	Responsible for operating the national grid to purchase electricity from renewable energy sources at a pre-determined price. The Government has taken a critically important step in the development of the country's significant potential for renewable energy generation while pursuing equally important economic, environmental, and social policy objectives
Uganda	organic farming with economic, social, and environmental benefits, the draft policy	The objective was self-sustaining growth as it provides mechanisms for individual farmers to improve productivity, and "Poverty Eradication Action Plan objectives". Policy and city planning for ecological infrastructure and industrial activity, sustainable planning, city management, transport planning, and economic and environmental benefits to reduce CO^2
India	MGNREGA - Strengthen rural natural resource management	This is achieved by financing rural works that address causes of drought, deforestation, and soil erosion, thus restoring the natural capital base on which rural livelihoods depend. Water conservation, silted water harvesting infrastructure, alleviating their water shortage
India	climate risks	Drought and weather fluctuations are employing a Climate Change Adaptation project to analyze the costs and benefits of the approach and the use of climate change adaptation treatments to manage risks.
Brazil	Sustainable Urban Planning	Brazilian Curitiba city has implemented several innovative systems to create jobs, improve public transportation accessibility, promote housing development, and improve waste management, and strict environmental regulations and does not allow "polluting" industries.
Mexico	Mexico Environmental Sustainability Development Policy Loan	The objective of the DPL operation is to balance socio-economic development with environmental protection and improvement by integrating environmental concerns in the sectoral policies and programs of key development sectors (tourism, energy, forestry, water, agriculture, and housing).

Elaboraci6n propia con datos del The Word Bank & WRI

In Mexico, in matters of public policy for sustainability, other internal initiatives for low carbon were framed under different programs of which some examples are presented below:

- Use of Renewable Energies and Energy Efficiency
- Sustainable Use of Energy
    - Environmental sustainability
    - Employment generation
- Prospects of the energy sector

- Law for the use of renewable energies and financing of the energy transition (SENER, 2023)
- National Development Plan 2013 - 2018
- Energy Sector Program 2013 – 2018
- National Energy Strategy 2013-2027

International Collaborations and Partnerships to Support Mexico's Sustainability Efforts

These plans and programs have as their fundamental purpose that the energy sector serves as a lever for the development of the country and that at the same time incorporates all Mexicans in the benefits derived from access to and consumption of energy (SENER, 2023).

According to report number PGD210, of the World Bank Environmental Sustainability and Urban Resilience, it is mentioned that the authorities make the decision to focus on environmental and sustainability problems, as well as climate change, situations where recovery efforts are taken into consideration in a comprehensive manner, which manage to protect the country's natural resources and biodiversity, as well as the action to promote initiatives that achieve adaptation to climate change and their respective mitigation measures, which are reflected in the sector programs related to the environment as is the case of (PROMARNAT).

Therefore, through the government agency called the Secretary of the Environment and Natural Resources (SEMARNAT), the following goals were established, which are a priority to follow:

- The conservation, protection, restoration, and use of ecosystems, as well as biodiversity.
- Strengthening of the action for the transition towards a low carbon economy, as well as a resilient population, ecosystems, and infrastructures.
- Manage through transparent policies the water resource as a pillar of well-being, as well as honest, effective, and efficient institutions in this regard.
- Promote a pollution-free environment that can contribute to the action of the right for a healthy environment.
- Strengthening of government through free, effective, and meaningful participation.

On the other hand, the Mexican authorities also include the issue of urban infrastructure, as well as social housing, among their priorities, seeking inclusion and resilience, with a special interest in the poorest and most vulnerable groups, who have been excluded from public assistance programs. Currently, Mexico is committed to reducing GHG by the year 2030, through nationally determined contributions to climate change (NDC), within the reforms include support for the implementation of the emission rights trading regime (ETS), and carbon taxes.

The policies that have been supported are aimed at protecting forests, which are essential components of national efforts to mitigate climate change through carbon sequestration and thus improve the environment and, consequently, health. They also support the adaptive capacity of the municipalities most vulnerable to climate change (The World Bank, 2020).

Political, Economic, and Fiscal Transition and the Role of Education in Achieving Sustainable Development

As previously mentioned, the main proposal of this chapter is the integration of public, economic, fiscal, and environmental policies, this management must take strategies such as research and development of projects whose main objective is to avoid, reduce and control environmental pollution. to develop renewable energy mechanisms and sources, where the executive branch achieves a detection strategy to detect private companies for industrial processes and achieve improvement to a less polluting process, following the guideline of SDG 9 regarding industry, innovation, and infrastructure; with a vision of low carbon and energy transition, allocating part of public spending to the incorporation of quality education, which belongs to SDG 4 of the UN objectives as a source of knowledge and research for the development of renewable and sustainable technologies.

It is necessary to create a system that manages all the guidelines and boosts the growth potential of the economies of developing countries to reduce the social gaps that also allow the creation of a strategy for the first of the 17 Sustainable Development Goals (SDG). of the UN "End of poverty".

The efforts of developing countries to achieve low carbon and sustainable development must be aligned with guidelines that seek the sustainability of public finances and attention to investment needs in well-being, investment, and sustainability. Environment, integrating and aligning the low carbon guidelines, as well as the efficient administration of these policies, a greater scope of the percentages of the objectives at the national level should be envisioned from the perspective of the requirements of civil society for a changing culture that encompasses all of society, public and private institutions, and the government, managing to execute pertinent measures and the creation of future laws that require sustainable practices, where each stakeholder takes responsibility (Nurmi, 2017).

The ecological rationality tradition investigates the preconditions and processes of evolution or emergence of social systems out of the interaction of individuals and groups following their behavioral norms and strategies. These individuals and groups may not have any idea of the order or system emerging out of this interaction. There are also institutional designs that bring about unintended changes in other institutions. For example, the abandonment of trade barriers in Europe over the past decades is changing the organization of the labor markets.

Similarly, the establishment of the European Parliament and the growth of its importance in the Union legislation will undoubtedly be reflected in the national parliaments. So, the constructivist rationality represents an unduly narrow view of institutions: very few of them, probably none, have been designed to their last detail anticipating all effects on other institutions.

As the term suggests this approach traces the over-time variation of economic behavior, structures, and most importantly institutions. Its focus is on processes whereby standards, customs, norms, and behavior patterns emerge over time out of interactions between individuals going about their business not necessarily realizing that what they are involved in is an institution-building process (Allan, 2010).

Regarding the educational system, in 1975, in Belgrade, Yugoslavia, the International Seminar on Environmental Education took place, intending to incorporate it into the definition of goals and the objectives and principles of environmental education. The Mexican Federal Government currently maintains a special interest in each of its programs, focusing on developing just, sustainable, and democratic societies. Considering the principle of "Leaving No One Behind" (LNOB) as outlined in the transformative 2030 Agenda for Sustainable Development and its Sustainable Development Goals (SDGs), where UN member states commit to eradicating poverty, eliminating discrimination, and exclusion, it has become a significant challenge. To achieve this, it is imperative to have teachers who possess the relevant competencies and profiles, who contribute to a comprehensive education that addresses various existing issues and proposes multiple short, medium, and long-term solutions as appropriate.

Furthermore, working with different learning styles strategically and innovatively, where the critical thinking of each member of diverse communities is developed from their perspectives, provides a significant advantage in the timely identification of situations that may jeopardize universal values.

In addition to that, the proper use of cutting-edge tools derived from ICT (Information and Communication Technologies) and artificial intelligence (AI) is of vital importance to achieving environmental awareness and sustainability in our society. This starts in educational centers with governmental support that provides clear and decisive instructions on educational programs that promote environmental education and raise awareness about climate change. This can be done through the transmission of knowledge and techniques regarding the design and modeling of renewable energy systems and sustainable technologies (Subosa, 2019).

By conducting prototypes and models as teaching and learning tools, the basic principles of green technologies and sustainable energy can be explained and exemplified, broadening students' horizons. They can experiment with various approaches and propose diverse solutions to the environmental issues of today. For example, designing and building prototypes of renewable energy systems such as wind turbines and solar panels can provide valuable information about their functioning and capacity to generate sustainable energy.

The use and application of modeling tools and simulators can greatly benefit students, allowing them to estimate different scenarios and refine their designs, considering various factors in terms of performance, efficiency, and environmental impact. This enables students to gain a deeper understanding of the subject matter and develop practical skills in sustainable energy.

Integrating ICT and AI in educational matters offers opportunities for students to use various online applications and platforms that provide access to real-time data related to electricity usage, energy consumption, and greenhouse gas emissions. It is important to consider the relevance of these tools as they can facilitate connections with experts worldwide, enabling knowledge exchange and discussions about projects and research related to the topics described in this document.

As an educational outcome, this approach cultivates future leaders who are equipped with knowledge, capabilities, and skills, and, most importantly, empowered, and conscious about generating innovative and sustainable outcomes in their daily work. They contribute to developing a more responsible society and a more sustainable future.

ANALYSIS OF THE CHALLENGES, CHALLENGES, AND OPPORTUNITIES ASSOCIATED WITH THE IMPLEMENTATION OF PUBLIC POLICIES

Responsible consumption implies a new culture and a different understanding of society-nature relationships. A change of culture can take generations, the current environment and development have turned consumerism into an essential part of culture. Sustainable alternatives, which bring economic and environmental visions closer, have formulated new perspectives, such as environmental economics (Acquatella, J., & Bárcena Ibarra, 2005).

Environmental economics raises the need for economic growth, job and income generation with technological innovations and changes in consumption patterns, proposing economic policies and instruments for cultural change. The environmental economy and green economy suggest economic models that maintain stable growth within the ecological limits necessary to guarantee the renewability of natural resources (Carabias, 2019).

One of the main strategies for the development of the economy is the efficient management of public policies, which are considered the design of collective action; the course taken because of the decisions, is what you want to achieve and what is done or carried out, they are also courses of action aimed at solving problems.

Challenges to the Efficient Management of Public Policies in Countries With Emerging Economies

- Coordination failures in the formulation, design, and implementation of public policies on environmental matters.
- The economic, social, and environmental dimensions of development are disjointed.
- Need to create public awareness.
- Design of efficient regulatory institutions (relationship between environmental and fiscal authorities).
- Weak institutional framework established to respond to environmental management needs.
- Fragility and instability of budget resources as political support granted at various levels of government.
- The low political priority between the structure of macroeconomic and sectoral incentives for economic and environmental regulation.
- Existence of fiscal restrictions (Taxes and environmental fiscal reforms).
- Design of environmental management instruments that are effective and economically efficient to achieve environmental goals.
- The limitation of self-financing advances in environmental management with an impact on emerging economies.
- The generation and availability of information for environmental management.
- The initiatives and technical-bureaucratic activities required are excessive and the authorities maintain fluid relations with political markets.

Opportunities for the Development of Public Policies for the Socioeconomic Development of Countries With Emerging Economies

- The use of environmental taxes as instruments to internalize the social cost of economic activities that entail environmental impacts,
- Apply taxes to internalize the social cost of activities that cause environmental externalities.
- Induce a better environmental performance of the economic agents and develop a "Pigouvian" tax.
- Develop an incentive structure whose purpose is to reduce environmental degradation through the price system.
- Design a tax regime applicable to the exploitation of natural resources to induce a use in accordance with the national objectives of sustainable development and environmental management.
- Territorial wealth of natural resources

Opportunities for economic growth must be based on the use of efficient and sustainable energy development for local economic development, together with technological development with a political framework for environmental protection (Garrido, 2020), Mexico has the potential to attract large projects, which can help meet the increase in energy demand and diversify its production matrix, while building energy security and reducing GHG emissions, with significant positive impacts on the environment, the economy and society (Mendivil, & Child, (2016).

Sociocultural Factors That can Influence the Adoption and Effectiveness of These Policies

- Productive activities established for decades that imply a negative environmental impact as part of the economic development of countries with emerging economies.
- High demand for polluting products due to consumer culture trends.
- Deforestation than poverty implies the use of firewood for cooking, increasing pollution.
- Globalization and neoliberalism. The economic range on many occasions does not want to follow institutional or governmental rules, so there is no commitment to the environment.
- Lack of awareness of millions of inhabitants of the planet, due to lack of culture or negative habits regarding care for the environment.
- Economic and political interests of some governments.
- There are governments that do not commit to important international agreements for economic reasons (Lara, 2021).

Mexico´s Electricity Rate System, Challenges, and Opportunities

In 1960, Mexico made a significant move by taking control of the national electric industry. For the next fifty years, the industry remained under state control, with the government acting as a key player and supervisor. However, recognizing the need for change and the benefits of private sector participation, Mexico embarked on a transformative journey of liberalization and deregulation in the energy sector. This marked a significant shift in the country's approach to its electric industry, opening doors for private entities to contribute while still maintaining state involvement. A pivotal moment in this process came in 2013 with the constitutional energetic reform, with constitutional changes which set the stage for a new era in Mexico's energy landscape.

Numerous persuasive justifications were posited to substantiate the relaxation of trade and investment regulations in the electricity industry. Initially, advocates of this initiative underscored deficiencies in the state's monopolistic practices, primarily about tariff rates. It was posited that the embracement of the growth of the sector would catalyze expanded prospects regarding economic progress and societal well-being. Mexico aimed to cultivate a more robust and active electricity sector that would invigorate the economy and have positive outcomes for the populace in its entirety, utilizing the implementation of competition and drawing in private investments as means to achieve this end goal (Rodríguez Padilla, 2016).

With the implementation of liberalization in 2013, the focus of public policy in the electricity sector shifted towards the promotion of private generation and the encouragement of a parallel electricity market and the use of natural gas and electrification as part of its energy agenda. sustainable, the government offered several incentives and guarantees. These included guarantees in the purchase of electricity, fuel supply, reimbursement of investments and assumption of commercial and market risks. (Rodriguez Padilla, 2016).

Currently an active tariff scheme by the Federal Electricity Commission CFE (from Spanish: Comisión Federal de Electricidad) in Mexico, which is divided into eight tariffs: Domestic Rates: 1, 1A, 1B, 1C, 1D, 1E, 1F (The letters indicate the different regions in Mexico, as each region varies in terms of its average monthly minimum temperature, and the applicable subsidy depends on the tariff type), High-consumption Domestic Tariff: DAC. Domestic Tariff 1F, that applies in cities with temperatures higher than 32 degrees Celsius. The electricity rate of the agricultural system, has a government subsidy, where there have been various proposals so that the user is the one who is subsidized and can cover their energy demand, since this has meant a delay in sustainable development and the incorporation of efficient and renewable technologies to the country's energy matrix, continuing with the increase in carbon emissions from the generation of the conventional electricity industry.

It is necessary to identify the economic strata with the highest proportion of energy-poor, when implementing reforms in the electricity sector, it is crucial to take appropriate measures to protect the well-being of poor and marginalized households, or at least maintain it at the current level. The elimination of electricity subsidies may require compensating households' income deciles due to their vulnerability to basic electricity and energy poverty resulting from the loss of government subsidies.

As mentioned by Navarrete et al (2023) Mexico's energy reforms, approved in 2013, aimed to gradually liberalize energy prices to align them with production costs and encourage investment in clean and renewable energy. Although electricity subsidies benefit the majority of low-income households by offering affordable prices, they also impact households with medium and high incomes.

Integration and Based on the Participation of all Stakeholders to Develop Public Policies

- Integration of public policies and fiscal, and environmental policies for the generation of plans, strategies, and actions that promote fiscal stimuli or penalties for the use of energy.
- Development and enforcement of laws and regulations to monitor GHG emissions.
- Use of resources for the development of R&D projects aligned with energy efficiency and renewable technologies.
- Involvement of universities and research centers through grants to promote R&D.
- Involvement of large energy consumers such as industry so that they can link up with research centers and generate clean projects.
- Incentive for cultural change to minimize excessive energy use and high consumption to reduce environmental impact. Encourage and provide by civil society and universities for cultural change for socioeconomic and sustainable development.

Policies cannot be isolated elements, they are complex systems that need each other, to achieve objectives, as well as a good development and actions of a policy will imply other results.

Each interested party must participate in the cultural changes, with integration and commitment between all the elements, Fig. 3 shows the representation of an integrated system of the different policies with the stakeholders to achieve low carbon emissions, mitigate environmental impact and achieve sustainable development, this scheme of public policies applies to the internal policies of developing countries, where a quality government and an environmentally conscious society are key elements for this purpose where the main proposed guidelines are the following:

Figure 3. The integrated management system of public policy for sustainable development

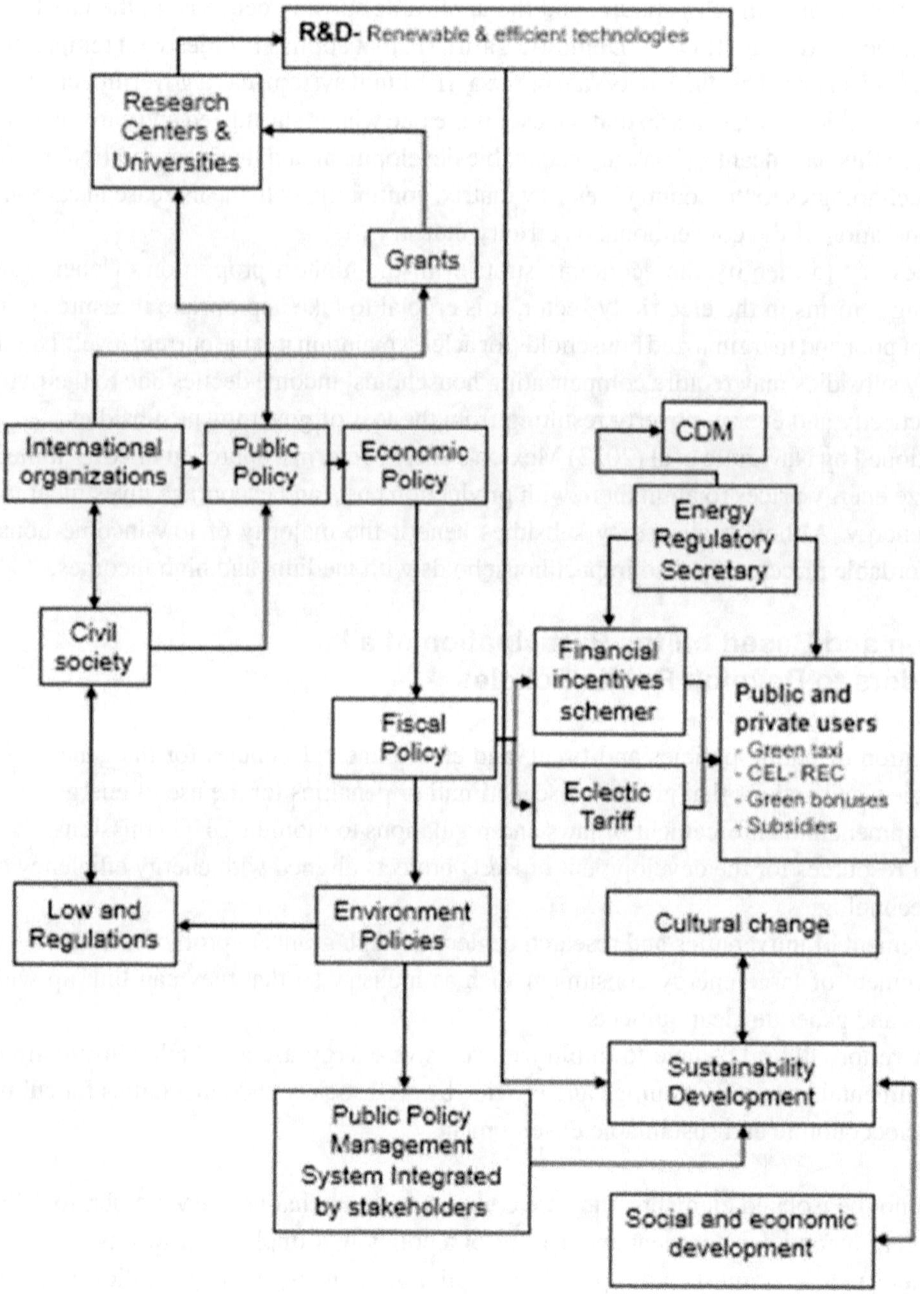

CONCLUSION AND FUTURE RESEARCH DIRECTIONS

Greening the growth path of an economy depends on the institutional settings, level of development, resource endowments, and particular environmental pressure points. For development and low carbon, it must be sustainable to prioritize greening as a path of economic growth within institutional frameworks, the level of development, the endowment of resources, and environmental points from individuals as change culturally, with the leadership of civil society and global, education with international funds arranged to support with grants to strengthen the scientific base with research and development of efficient and green technologies, giving a sustainable administration system, which provides technical assistance to developing governments for improving their capacity to strengthen and implement environmental legislation, give access to information from international bases and multilateral environmental agreements with dialogues for decision-making.

Incorporating horizontal domestic and public policies into the national agenda is a strategy that would support meeting the adapted needs of communities, collectively with the educational system from levels before research institutes, which permits the resolution of environmental needs and creating an environmental culture based on the involvement of the stakeholders.

A mixed system of domestic and public policies should be sought to allow developing countries to align with international objectives and create a true leadership of civil society for cultural change, especially in the environmental field.

In the current governance system that works in isolation without joint guidelines in sustainable development, the main vector for sustainable development is the environmental market, globalization must be implicit in regional economic growth, and natural diversity for the energy matrix, to stop global warming that grows accelerated.

REFERENCES

Acquatella, J., & Bárcena Ibarra, A. (2005). *Política fiscal y medio ambiente: bases para una agenda común*. Cepal.

Allan, S. (2010). *Perspectivas OCDE: México Políticas Clave para un Desarrollo Sostenible*. OCDE.

Calderón, J. P. (2010). La política ambiental en México: Gestión e instrumentos económicos. *El cotidiano*, (162), 91-97.

Carabias, J. (2019). Economic policies with environmental sustainability. *Economía UNAM*, *16*(46), 118–125.

Christensen, T., & Lægreid, P. (2007). *The Challenge of Coordination in Central Government Organizations*.

Cingano, F. (2014). *Trends in Income Inequality and its Impact on Economic Growth*. France: (OECD Social, Employment and Migration Working Papers). CONGRESO DE LA UNIÓN.

Comisión Federal de Electricidad. (2023). *Esquema tarifario vigente*. CFE.mx. https://app.cfe.mx/Aplicaciones/CCFE/Tarifas/TarifasCRECasa/Casa.aspx

Frieden, J. (2020). *International Monetary Fund*. International Monetary Fund web. https://www.imf.org/en/Publications/fandd/issues/2020/06/political-economy-of-economic-policy-jeff-frieden

Garrido, S. M., Lalouf, A., & Moreira, A. J. (2020). *Energías renovables y procesos de desarrollo inclusivo y sustentable: de las políticas públicas puntuales a los abordajes sistémicos.*

Hague, R., & Harrop, M. (2004). *Comparative government and politics* (Vol. 6). Palgrave Macmillan.

Harrop, R. H. (2004). *Comparative Government and Politics*. PALGRAVE MACMILLAN.

Huerta, M. M., Guzmán, O. V., & Gonzále, S. F. (2020). *Retos de las políticas públicas para el desarrollo regional sostenible en una sociedad incluyente y solidaria*. Montiel & Soriano.

IRENA. (2023, July). *World Energy Transitions Outlook 2022 Executive Summary and Introduction*. International Renewable Energy Agency. https://www.irena.org/Digital-Report/World-Energy-Transitions-Outlook-202

Lara, B. M. (2021). Calentamiento global y desarrollo sostenible, avances y retos actuales en la política pública de México. *Ciencia económica, 15*, 25-41.

Lundqvist, L. J. (2001). A Green Fist in a Velvet Glove: The Ecological State and Sustainable Development. *JSTOR Collection*, 472-475.

Mendivil, A., & Niño, G. (2016). *Una política energética sustentable: Un pendiente en México*. México, F. D. L. O.

Micheli, J. (2002). Política ambiental en México y su dimensión regional. *Región y Sociedad, 14*(23), 129–170.

Navarrete Ávila, H., & Sun, L. X. (2023). *Pobreza de la energía eléctrica en México y sus perspectivas ante la eliminación de subsidios. Hatso-Hnini*. Revista De Investigación De Paisajes Y Espacio Construido, 1-15. revistahatsohnini.com.mx/index.php/inicio/article/view/16

Nurmi, H. (2017). *Models of Political Economy*. Routledge.

O'Riordan, T., & Voisey, H. (1997). The political economy of sustainable development. *Environmental Politics*, *6*(1), 1–23. doi:10.1080/09644019708414309

OCDE. (2006). *Políticas Públicas para un Mejor Desempeño Económico*. Centro de la OCDE en México para América Latina.

OECD. (2021). *Green Growth and Developing- A Summary for Policy Makers.* 2012: Green Growth and Development.

OECD. (2023, 05 15). *Green Growth Indicators*. OECD.Stat. https://stats.oecd.org/Index.aspx?DataSetCode=GREEN_GROWTH

Pedro, F., Subosa, M., Rivas, A., & Valverde, P. (2019). *Artificial intelligence in education: Challenges and opportunities for sustainable development.* UNESCO.

Rodríguez Padilla, V. (2016). Industria eléctrica en México: Tensión entre el Estado y el mercado. *Problemas del Desarrollo*, 33–55.

Saint-Germain, P. M. (2007, 08 02). *Faculty Integrating Technology*. CSULB. home.csulb.edu: https://home.csulb.edu/~msaintg/ppa590/intro.htm

Salazar-Xirinachs, J. M. (2023). *Fiscal Panorama of Latin America and the Caribbean*. Santiago: United Nations PUblication.

Secretaría General. (2015). *Ley general del equilibrio ecológico y la protección al ambiente*. Mexico: Secretaría de Servicios Parlamentarios.

SENER. (2016). *Prospectiva de Energías Renovables 2016-2030*. Gobierno de México.

SENER. (2023, July). *GOBIERNO DE MEXICO*. Sener. https://www.gob.mx/sener/articulos/politicas-publicas-del-sector-energetico

Tamargo, J. L. (2002). *La gestión ambiental en México*. Semarnat.

The World Bank. (2020). Environmental Sustainability and Urban Resilience (P174000). United Mexicans States: International Bank.

Torne, C. (2019). *ENERGY TRANSITION IN MEXICO: THE SOCIAL DIMENSION OF ENERGY AND THE POLITICS OF CLIMATE CHANGE*. Federal Ministry for the Environment, Nature Conservation, and Nuclear Safety.

UN Environmental Programme. (2022, October). *Environmental Governance*. UNEP. https://www.unep.org/regions/west-asia/regional-initiatives/environmental-governance

UNDP. (2017). *INSTITUTIONAL AND COORDINATION MECHANISMS*. United Nations Development Programme.

Voisey, H. (2007). The political economy of sustainable development. *Environmental Politics*, 1743–8934.

ADDITIONAL READING

Atkinson, B., & Milward, B. (1996). *Economic policy*. Bloomsbury Publishing. doi:10.1007/978-1-349-24876-6

Dearlove, J. (2011). *The politics of policy in local government: the making and maintenance of public policy in the Royal Borough of Kensington and Chelsea*. Cambridge University Press.

Enríquez-Díaz, J., Castro-Santos, L., & Puime-Guillén, F. (Eds.). (2021). *Financial management and risk analysis strategies for business sustainability*. IGI Global. doi:10.4018/978-1-7998-7634-2

Fields, Z., & Atiku, S. O. (2019). Collective green creativity and eco-innovation as key drivers of sustainable business solutions in organizations. In Green Business: Concepts, Methodologies, Tools, and Applications (pp. 415-439). IGI Global. doi:10.4018/978-1-5225-7915-1.ch022

Kingdon, J. W. (2013). Agendas, alternatives, and public policies, update edition, with an epilogue on health care: Pearson new international edition. 2nd editor. Pearson Education Limited.

Martinez-Vazquez, J. (2011). *Taxation in Asia*. Asian Development Bank.

McGregor, G. I. (2021). *Environmental law and enforcement*. CRC Press. doi:10.1201/9781003210573

Palmer, J. (2002). *Environmental education in the 21st century: Theory, practice, progress, and promise*. Routledge. doi:10.4324/9780203012659

KEY TERMS AND DEFINITIONS

Clean Development Mechanism (CDM): This mechanism allows a country with a commitment to reduce or limit emissions under the Kyoto Protocol to implement a project to reduce emissions in developing countries. Such projects can earn marketable Certified Emission Reduction (CER) credits, each equivalent to one ton of CO_2.

Clean Energy Certificates (CEL - REC): A market based instrument that represents the property rights to the environmental, social, and other non-power attributes of renewable electricity generation. RECs are issued when one megawatt-hour (MWh) of electricity is generated and delivered to the electricity grid from a renewable energy resource.

Electric Tariff: The electricity tariff is defined as the rate at which the electrical energy is sold to a consumer, the tariff is the method of charging a consumer for consuming electric power. The tariff covers the total cost of producing and supplying electric energy plus a reasonable cost.

Emerging Markets: An emerging market economy is the economy of a developing nation that is becoming more engaged with global markets as it grows.

Fiscal policy: Describes changes to government spending and revenue behavior to influence the economy. By adjusting its level of spending and tax revenue, the government can affect economic outcomes by either increasing or decreasing economic activity.

Footprint: The Ecological Footprint measures how fast we consume resources and generate waste compared to how fast nature can absorb our waste and generate resources.

Grant: The grant data is collected at scheme programmers and awards level where the scheme is related to an overarching policy area and grant award is given out to meet the objectives of the grant scheme.

Political economy: This is a cross-disciplinary field that combines economics, political science, and sociology to understand the role or roles of the economy, political systems, law, government, institutions, and culture, their interactions, and the impact that they have on the agents within society.

Research and Development (R&D): This is creative and systematic work undertaken to increase the stock of knowledge including knowledge of humankind, culture, and society, and to devise new applications of available knowledge.

Sustainable development: Development that meets the needs of the present without compromising the ability of future generations to meet their own needs.

Chapter 7
Charting a New Course:
Inclusive Finance, Corruption Control, and Environmental Sustainability in Ghana

Alhassan Musah
https://orcid.org/0000-0002-4416-6526
University for Development Studies, Ghana

Seydou Oumarou
Université Abdou Moumouni, Niger

ABSTRACT

This study examines the impact of inclusive finance and control of corruption on environmental pollution in Ghana from 2000 to 2020, considering the effects of remittances and renewable energy consumption. The results indicate that both inclusive finance and control of corruption have a significant negative influence on CO2 emissions, emphasizing the importance of promoting financial inclusion and combating corruption to reduce environmental pollution. However, the study finds that remittances have a positive but insignificant impact on pollution. Additionally, there is a negative relationship between renewable energy consumption and pollution, highlighting the role of renewable energy in mitigating environmental harm. Policy recommendations include enhancing financial inclusion, intensifying anti-corruption efforts, and promoting renewable energy sources.

INTRODUCTION

The pursuit of industrial growth and modern lifestyles has had ramifications on the ecosystem. For instance, excessive combustion of fossil fuels like coal, oil, and gas emits massive volumes of carbon dioxide (CO_2) and other greenhouse gases (GHG) into the atmosphere (Yakubu et al., 2021). Similarly, agricultural activities such as the uncontrolled use of chemical fertilizers lead to the release of GHGs such as methane (CH_4) and nitrous oxide (N_2O). In recent years, the international community has come to the realization that addressing concerns relating to environmental sustainability and biodiversity conservation is critical in enhancing progress and well-being. The demand for energy in emerging and

DOI: 10.4018/978-1-6684-9272-7.ch007

developed countries has grown due to industrial growth and the surge in technical innovation. Although energy consumption contributes to economic advancement, it is also a major source of environmental degradation (Saidi & Mbarek, 2016). To achieve carbon neutrality and improve environmental sustainability, it is necessary to understand the factors that drive CO2 emissions.

Despite the extensive body of literature exploring the influence of various factors, such as macroeconomic variables, on environmental pollution, the role of finance has been relatively understudied. While a few studies have shed light on the impact of financial development on environmental pollution (Le & Ozturk, 2020, Pata & Yilanci, 2020; Amjad et al., 2021; Deng et al., 2022; Ahmad et al., 2022; Das & Sethi, 2023; Shahzadi et al., 2023), it remains an area that warrants further investigation and analysis given its multidimensionality. In recent years, inclusive finance, a critical component of the finance ecosystem, has emerged as a significant driver of environmental sustainability. Inclusive finance has the potential to play a crucial role in achieving environmental sustainability by providing financial services to underrepresented and underprivileged communities. It accomplishes this by facilitating access to necessary resources, fostering the establishment of environmentally responsible enterprises, and promoting community resilience.

Despite its promise to improve environmental sustainability, inclusive finance encounters significant hurdles, particularly in nations plagued by corruption. Corruption weakens the efficacy and confidence of financial institutions by diverting money away from intended recipients and prolonging inequity (Yakubu, 2019). In Ghana, corruption comes in many forms and shapes, including bribery, embezzlement, and misappropriation of money, erecting a substantial barrier in the process of initiating and sustaining inclusive finance programs. The resultant effect has been a weak inclusive finance architecture, limiting its ability and potential to tackle environmental concerns.

The main objective of this research is to investigate the effects of inclusive financing and corruption control on environmental pollution in Ghana. Studies on inclusive finance have been primarily focused on its impact on economic growth (Singh & Stakic, 2021; Van et al., 2021; Yakubu & Bunyaminu, 2021; Pal & Bandyopadhyay, 2022; Chinoda & Kapingura, 2023; Ndombi Avouba et al., 2023). Therefore, this research offers a unique perspective by emphasizing the impact of inclusive finance in fostering environmental sustainability in Ghana, a topic that has not previously been fully researched. The study's findings and insights will be of great interest to policymakers and stakeholders in Ghana and other developing nations interested in fostering sustainable energy development. Additionally, by shedding light on the link between inclusive finance, corruption control, and environmental pollution, this study intends to contribute significantly to the achievement of the United Nations Sustainable Development Goals, notably Goal 13: Climate Action.

In the next section, the researchers review related literature. Section three explains the methodology of the study and Section 4 discusses the main findings. The final section presents the conclusion and recommendations.

LITERATURE REVIEW

The analysis of environmental pollution is a complex task that requires a comprehensive examination of various factors. To better understand the causes and effects of pollution, researchers have studied the interaction between social and economic factors. For instance, Adebayo et al. (2020) conducted a study to investigate the impact of various variables on CO2 emissions in Thailand. Using the Autoregressive

Distributed Lag (ARDL) technique, the authors revealed that gross capital formation and energy usage have a positive effect on CO2 emissions. In the European Union (EU), Neves et al. (2020) found that renewable energy-supportive policies and environmental regulations contribute to the reduction of CO2 emissions. Shaheen (2020) examined the drivers of environmental degradation in Pakistan using the ARDL method. The authors provided evidence that energy consumption and GDP positively affect CO2 emissions. Ayobamiji and Kalmez (2020) pursued similar themes and found a positive relationship between economic growth and CO2 emissions in both the long and short run. Energy consumption showed a positive impact on CO2 emissions in the long run, while foreign direct investment has a negative effect on CO2 emissions. It has also been suggested that financial development could have implications on pollution levels. Not surprisingly, Khalid et al. (2021) revealed that financial development significantly increases pollution levels in Bangladesh and Sri Lanka. Whereas trade openness only improves environmental quality in Nepal. In another interesting study, Sharma et al. (2021) employed panel regression and found that energy consumption leads to environmental pollution at lower income levels, but its harmful effect weakens at higher income levels. Extending the discourse to cover other variables and themes, Bhujabal et al. (2021) used the Pooled Mean Group (PMG) method to investigate how information technology and foreign direct investment (FDI) affect environmental pollution in major Asia-Pacific countries. The results indicated that both ICT and FDI have a negative impact on carbon emissions or environmental pollution, implying that as ICT infrastructure and FDI inflows increase, environmental pollution decreases significantly in the long run. Anwar et al. (2023) conducted a study to examine the relationship between various factors and CO2 emissions in the E-7 countries. Their findings suggested that an increase in renewable energy consumption, technological innovations, and institutional quality is associated with a reduction in CO2 emissions. However, they also found that sustained economic growth and population increase contribute to environmental degradation in these countries. Similarly, Caglar et al. (2022) investigated the determinants of CO2 emissions in the BRICS economies. Their empirical analysis revealed that positive changes in trade openness and economic complexity have a stimulating effect on environmental quality. Conversely, they found that economic growth, natural resources, and public-private partnerships contribute to environmental degradation. Burki and Tahir (2022) researched the ASEAN economies to explore the impact of energy consumption and trade openness on environmental degradation. Their findings indicated that increasing energy consumption and trade openness are positively associated with environmental degradation in these economies. Examining the relationship between economic growth, globalization, renewable energy, non-renewable energy, and environmental pollution in South America, Ali et al. (2023) utilized various econometric techniques. Their results suggested that while environmental pollution increases with economic growth, it decreases with an increase in renewable energy consumption in both the short and long term. Farooq et al. (2023) investigated the factors influencing CO2 emissions in the GCC region. Their study revealed that economic growth, foreign investment, tourism investment, electricity production, and population density have a positive impact on CO2 emissions in this region. Using the ARDL technique, Yakubu et al. (2021) examined the relationship between urbanization and CO2 emissions in Ghana. Their analysis demonstrated that urbanization has a negative significant influence on CO2 emissions in both the short and long term. Additionally, they observed that while fossil fuel consumption leads to pollution in the short term, it hinders CO2 emissions in the long run.

The relationship between financial inclusion and environmental pollution has received limited attention in the literature. However, a few studies have explored this nexus. Le et al. (2020) conducted a study focusing on Asia and found that financial inclusion is associated with increased CO2 emissions during the period from 2004 to 2014. Similarly, Ozturk and Ullah (2022) provided evidence suggesting that digital financial inclusion contributes to a decline in environmental quality by increasing CO2 emissions. Fareed et al. (2022) conducted research in the Eurozone and established a link between financial inclusion and environmental deterioration. In a cross-country analysis, Rehman et al. (2023) examined the role of financial inclusion in environmental sustainability and found a negative association in countries with both higher and lower carbon emission levels. Additionally, Hussain et al. (2023) identified financial inclusion and corruption as significant factors contributing to environmental degradation in OECD countries.

In summary, the limited studies on the impact of financial inclusion on environmental pollution suggest mixed results. While most of the studies indicate a positive association between financial inclusion and CO2 emissions, others highlight the negative role of financial inclusion in environmental sustainability and its contribution to environmental degradation.

METHODOLOGY

Data

The study utilized annual data from 2000 to 2020, specifically focusing on Ghana. The data for the research were obtained from the International Monetary Fund and the World Bank. To fulfill the study's objective, carbon dioxide emission (CO2) in metric tons per capita was used as a measure of environmental pollution. The main independent variables considered in the study were inclusive finance and the control of corruption. Inclusive finance (INCF) was evaluated using an index constructed from various sub-measures of financial inclusion, drawing from the research conducted by Yakubu and Musah (2022). Following the World Bank's definition, control of corruption (COC) "captures perceptions of the extent to which public power is exercised for private gain, including both petty and grand forms of corruption, as well as capture of the state by elites and private interests". The study also included remittances (REMIT) and renewable energy consumption (REN) as control variables. Remittance inflow is measured as personal remittances received as a percentage of GDP, providing insight into the financial inflows from individuals residing outside the country. Renewable energy consumption was expressed as a percentage of total final energy consumption, serving as an indicator of the country's reliance on sustainable energy sources.

Specification and Estimation of the Empirical Model

The empirical model specification based on the selected variables is as follows:

$$CO_{2t} = \beta_0 + \beta_1 INCF_t + \beta_2 COC_t + \beta_3 REMIT_t + \beta_4 REN_t + \varepsilon_t \quad (1)$$

In this model, CO2, INCF, COC, REMIT, and REN were previously defined. β1, β2, β3, and β4 are the coefficients that measure the relationship between the variables and CO2 emissions. *ε* represents the error term, accounting for unobserved factors and measurement errors, and *t* is the period.

The Canonical Cointegrating Regression (CCR) is utilized to estimate the model. This technique provides efficient estimates of the model parameters, accounting for the potential presence of endogeneity and spurious regression issues that may arise in the presence of nonstationary variables. Before conducting the model estimation, the study performed a unit root test using the Phillips-Perron (PP) method to assess the stationarity level of the variables. Subsequently, cointegration analysis was carried out to examine the long-run association between the variables.

RESULTS AND DISCUSSIONS

Descriptive Statistics of the Variables

The descriptive statistics provide insights into the characteristics of the variables. The mean CO_2 emissions per capita in Ghana are 0.457 metric tons, indicating the average level of environmental pollution. Inclusive finance (INCF) shows a balanced distribution around zero. Control of corruption (COC) has a negative mean (-0.176), suggesting perceived corruption. Remittances (REMIT) represent an average of 3.001% of GDP, while renewable energy consumption (REN) stands at 53.828% of total final energy consumption. The variables exhibit varying levels of dispersion, skewness, and kurtosis, with COC displaying the highest kurtosis, indicating a heavy-tailed distribution. The Jarque-Bera test confirms the departure from normality for COC.

Table 1. Descriptive statistics

	CO_2	INCF	COC	REMIT	REN
Mean	0.457	4.23E-17	-0.176	3.001	53.828
Maximum	0.659	3.111	0.039	10.085	71.620
Minimum	0.298	-4.172	-0.996	0.422	41.480
Std. Dev.	0.120	2.435	0.217	2.821	9.468
Skewness	0.197	-0.646	-2.658	0.772	0.398
Kurtosis	1.545	2.254	10.843	2.662	1.891
Jarque-Bera	1.895	1.949	78.547	2.184	1.553
Probability	0.388	0.377	0.000	0.336	0.460

Unit Root Test Results

The unit root test results presented in Table 2 using the Phillips-Perron (PP) method show the variables are integrated. In the level form, the CO2 variable has an adjusted t-statistic of -2.083, suggesting that it is not stationary at conventional significance levels. Similarly, the INCF variable also fails to exhibit stationarity, with an adjusted t-statistic of -1.820. However, the COC, REMIT, and REN variables show stronger evidence of stationarity at the 1% significance level, as indicated by their significantly adjusted t-statistics of -4.048, -3.451, and -2.547, respectively. When considering the first difference, all variables exhibit strong evidence of stationarity with highly significant adjusted t-statistics, reflecting their integration properties. These results indicate that the variables in their level form are non-stationary, but become stationary after differencing.

Table 2. Phillips-Perron (PP) unit root test results

Variables	Level Adj. t-Statistic	First Difference Adj. t-Statistic
CO_2	-2.083	-5.647***
INCF	-1.820	-9.133***
COC	-4.048**	-12.814***
REMIT	-3.451*	-11.113***
REN	-2.547	-21.714***

Note: *, **, *** indicate stationarity at 10%, 5%, and 1% respectively

Cointegration Test Results

The cointegration test results presented in Table 3 indicate the presence of cointegration among the variables. The test is performed based on the trace statistic and maximal eigenvalue of the stochastic matrix. According to the trace statistic, the null hypothesis of no cointegrating equations is rejected at all levels, indicating the existence of cointegration. The eigenvalues also support this finding, as the null hypothesis of no cointegration is rejected at the 0.05 level for all cases. Both the trace and maximal eigenvalue tests suggest the presence of two cointegrating equations. The significance of the results implies that the variables under investigation have long-run relationships, suggesting that changes in one variable are associated with changes in the others in a stable manner.

Table 3. Cointegration results

Cointegration test based on Trace of the Stochastic Matrix.				
Hypothesized No. of CE(s)	*Eigenvalue*	*Trace Statistic*	*0.05 Critical Value*	*Prob.***
None*	0.982	146.125	69.819	0.000
At most 1*	0.865	74.203	47.856	0.000
At most 2*	0.682	38.132	29.797	0.004
At most 3*	0.503	17.498	15.495	0.025
At most 4*	0.239	4.9123	3.841	0.027
Cointegration test based on Maximal Eigenvalue of the Stochastic Matrix				
Hypothesized No. of CE(s)	*Eigenvalue*	*Max-Eigen Statistic*	*0.05 Critical Value*	*Prob.***
None *	0.982	71.922	33.877	0.000
At most 1 *	0.865	36.071	27.584	0.003
At most 2	0.682	20.634	21.132	0.059
At most 3	0.503	12.586	14.265	0.091
At most 4*	0.239	4.912	3.841	0.026

Trace test and Max-eigenvalue test indicate 2 cointegrating equations
* denotes rejection of the hypothesis at the 0.05 level
**MacKinnon-Haug-Michelis (1999) p-values

Regression Results

The regression results based on the Canonical Cointegrating Regression (CCR) technique are shown in Table 4. The R-squared value in the table is reported as 0.948, indicating that approximately 94.8% of the variation in the carbon dioxide emissions (CO2) can be explained by the independent variables (inclusive finance, control of corruption, remittances, and renewable energy consumption) included in the model. The results from the regression analysis indicate that inclusive finance exerts a significant negative influence on CO2 emissions, implying that greater emphasis on promoting financial inclusion is associated with lower levels of carbon dioxide emissions. This finding could be attributed to the fact that improved access to financial services and resources enables individuals and businesses to adopt cleaner technologies and sustainable practices, thus reducing their carbon footprints. This result contrasts most prior studies suggesting that financial inclusion increases pollution (Le et al., 2020; Ozturk & Ullah, 2022; Fareed et al., 2022). This finding differs from previous studies, possibly due to differences in the measurement of financial inclusion, the country of analysis, or methodological approaches. The negative coefficient for control of corruption highlights that efforts to combat corruption contribute to a decrease in environmental pollution in Ghana. This suggests that as corruption levels decrease, environmental sustainability improves. Consequently, minimizing corruption can lead to better environmental outcomes. We also infer from this finding that, anti-corruption efforts may lead to improvements in enforcement mechanisms on environmental regulations, thereby contributing to environmental sustainability. Regarding remittances, the results show a positive but statistically insignificant impact on pollution, indicating that the influence of remittances on environmental pollution is not significant within the context of this study. Furthermore, the analysis reveals a negative relationship between renewable energy consumption and pollution, underscoring the role of renewable energy sources in reducing environmental pollution. The negative coefficient suggests that as the use of renewable energy increases, pollution levels decrease. This finding emphasizes the importance of transitioning to renewable energy sources as a means of mitigating pollution and achieving environmental sustainability.

Table 4. Canonical cointegrating regression (CCR) results

Variables	*CCR Estimates*
INCF	-0.027***
	(0.009)
COC	-0.105*
	(0.059)
REMIT	0.007
	(0.005)
REN	-0.019***
	(0.003)
Constant	1.436***
	(0.151)
R-squared	0.948
Adjusted R-squared	0.933
S.E. of regression	0.030
Long-run variance	0.001

Standard errors in parentheses *** p<0.01, * p<0.10

CONCLUSION AND RECOMMENDATIONS

This study investigates the influence of inclusive finance and control of corruption on environmental pollution in Ghana from 2000 to 2020, while also considering the effects of remittances and renewable energy consumption. The findings demonstrate that both inclusive finance and control of corruption exert a significant negative impact on CO2 emissions, indicating that efforts to promote financial inclusion and combat corruption contribute to reduced environmental pollution. Conversely, the analysis reveals that remittances have a positive but statistically insignificant impact on pollution, suggesting that their influence is not substantial within the scope of this study. Furthermore, the results highlight a negative relationship between renewable energy consumption and pollution, underscoring the role of renewable energy in mitigating environmental pollution.

Several policy recommendations can be made to promote environmental sustainability in Ghana given the findings of the study. Firstly, policymakers should prioritize initiatives that enhance financial inclusion, such as expanding access to affordable financial services and promoting financial literacy. This can empower individuals and businesses to adopt eco-friendly technologies and practices, thereby reducing CO2 emissions. Additionally, efforts to combat corruption should be intensified through transparency and accountability measures. Strengthening anti-corruption institutions and promoting ethical practices in both the public and private sectors can contribute to a decrease in environmental pollution. Furthermore, the promotion of renewable energy sources should be a key policy focus. This can be achieved through incentives for renewable energy investments, the development of renewable energy infrastructure, and the formulation of supportive regulations.

It is important to acknowledge the limitations of this study. Firstly, the analysis is based on data from Ghana only, limiting the generalizability of the findings to other countries or regions. Moreover, the study focused on a specific set of variables, and there may be additional factors influencing environmental pollution that were not considered. Future studies could incorporate a broader range of variables, such as technological innovation, industrial structure, and government policies, to provide a more comprehensive understanding of the determinants of environmental pollution. Furthermore, longitudinal studies with longer timeframes and panel data analysis could provide more robust insights into the long-term effects of inclusive finance, corruption control, and other factors on environmental sustainability.

REFERENCES

Adebayo, T. S., Akinsola, G. D., Odugbesan, J. A., & Olanrewaju, V. O. (2021). Determinants of environmental degradation in Thailand: Empirical evidence from ARDL and wavelet coherence approaches. *Pollution*, *7*(1), 181–196.

Ahmad, M., Ahmed, Z., Yang, X., Hussain, N., & Sinha, A. (2022). Financial development and environmental degradation: Do human capital and institutional quality make a difference? *Gondwana Research*, *105*, 299–310. doi:10.1016/j.gr.2021.09.012

Ali, E. B., Shayanmehr, S., Radmehr, R., Amfo, B., Awuni, J. A., Gyamfi, B. A., & Agbozo, E. (2023). Exploring the impact of economic growth on environmental pollution in South American countries: How does renewable energy and globalization matter? *Environmental Science and Pollution Research International*, *30*(6), 15505–15522. doi:10.100711356-022-23177-4 PMID:36169822

Amjad, M. A., Asghar, N., & Rehman, H. U. (2021). Can financial development help in raising sustainable economic growth and reduce environmental pollution in Pakistan? Evidence from non linear ARDL model. *Review of Economics and Development Studies*, *7*(4), 475–491. doi:10.47067/reads.v7i4.406

Anwar, A., Chaudhary, A. R., & Malik, S. (2023). Modeling the macroeconomic determinants of environmental degradation in E-7 countries: The role of technological innovation and institutional quality. *Journal of Public Affairs*, *23*(1), e2834. doi:10.1002/pa.2834

Ayobamiji, A. A., & Kalmaz, D. B. (2020). Reinvestigating the determinants of environmental degradation in Nigeria. *International Journal of Economic Policy in Emerging Economies*, *13*(1), 52–71. doi:10.1504/IJEPEE.2020.106680

Bhujabal, P., Sethi, N., & Padhan, P. C. (2021). ICT, foreign direct investment and environmental pollution in major Asia Pacific countries. *Environmental Science and Pollution Research International*, *28*(31), 42649–42669. doi:10.100711356-021-13619-w PMID:33818724

Burki, U., & Tahir, M. (2022). Determinants of environmental degradation: Evidenced-based insights from ASEAN economies. *Journal of Environmental Management*, *306*, 114506. doi:10.1016/j.jenvman.2022.114506 PMID:35051821

Caglar, A. E., Zafar, M. W., Bekun, F. V., & Mert, M. (2022). Determinants of CO2 emissions in the BRICS economies: The role of partnerships investment in energy and economic complexity. *Sustainable Energy Technologies and Assessments*, *51*, 101907. doi:10.1016/j.seta.2021.101907

Chinoda, T., & Kapingura, F. M. (2023). Digital financial inclusion and economic growth in Sub-Saharan Africa: The role of institutions and governance. *African Journal of Economic and Management Studies*. doi:10.1108/AJEMS-09-2022-0372

Das, A., & Sethi, N. (2023). Modelling the environmental pollution-institutional quality nexus in low-and middle-income countries: Exploring the role of financial development and educational level. *Environment, Development and Sustainability*, *25*(2), 1492–1518. doi:10.100710668-021-02105-5

Deng, Q. S., Alvarado, R., Cuesta, L., Tillaguango, B., Murshed, M., Rehman, A., Işık, C., & López-Sánchez, M. (2022). Asymmetric impacts of foreign direct investment inflows, financial development, and social globalization on environmental pollution. *Economic Analysis and Policy*, *76*, 236–251. doi:10.1016/j.eap.2022.08.008

Fareed, Z., Rehman, M. A., Adebayo, T. S., Wang, Y., Ahmad, M., & Shahzad, F. (2022). Financial inclusion and the environmental deterioration in Eurozone: The moderating role of innovation activity. *Technology in Society*, *69*, 101961. doi:10.1016/j.techsoc.2022.101961

Farooq, U., Tabash, M. I., Anagreh, S., Al-Rdaydeh, M., & Habib, S. (2023). Economic growth, foreign investment, tourism, and electricity production as determinants of environmental quality: Empirical evidence from GCC region. *Environmental Science and Pollution Research International*, *30*(16), 45768–45780. doi:10.100711356-023-25545-0 PMID:36707478

Hussain, M., Ye, C., Ye, C., & Wang, Y. (2021). Impact of financial inclusion and infrastructure on ecological footprint in OECD economies. *Environmental Science and Pollution Research International*, 1–8. PMID:34775558

Khalid, K., Usman, M., & Mehdi, M. A. (2021). The determinants of environmental quality in the SAARC region: A spatial heterogeneous panel data approach. *Environmental Science and Pollution Research International*, *28*(6), 6422–6436. doi:10.100711356-020-10896-9 PMID:32997249

Khan, N., Zafar, M., Okunlola, A. F., Zoltan, Z., & Robert, M. (2022). Effects of Financial Inclusion on Economic Growth, Poverty, Sustainability, and Financial Efficiency: Evidence from the G20 Countries. *Sustainability*, *14*(19), 12688. doi:10.3390u141912688

Le, H. P., & Ozturk, I. (2020). The impacts of globalization, financial development, government expenditures, and institutional quality on CO 2 emissions in the presence of environmental Kuznets curve. *Environmental Science and Pollution Research International*, *27*(18), 22680–22697. doi:10.100711356-020-08812-2 PMID:32323231

Le, T. H., Le, H. C., & Taghizadeh-Hesary, F. (2020). Does financial inclusion impact CO2 emissions? Evidence from Asia. *Finance Research Letters*, *34*, 101451. doi:10.1016/j.frl.2020.101451

Ndombi Avouba, F. G., Akougbe, A. I. S., & Ndombi Ondze, C. L. I. L. (2023). Non-linearity between financial inclusion and economic growth in sub-saharan Africa: What implications for the West African Economic and Monetary Union (WAEMU)? *Cogent Economics & Finance*, *11*(1), 2158630. doi:10.1080/23322039.2022.2158630

Neves, S. A., Marques, A. C., & Patrício, M. (2020). Determinants of CO2 emissions in European Union countries: Does environmental regulation reduce environmental pollution? *Economic Analysis and Policy*, *68*, 114–125. doi:10.1016/j.eap.2020.09.005

Ozturk, I., & Ullah, S. (2022). Does digital financial inclusion matter for economic growth and environmental sustainability in OBRI economies? An empirical analysis. *Resources, Conservation and Recycling*, *185*, 106489. doi:10.1016/j.resconrec.2022.106489

Pal, S., & Bandyopadhyay, I. (2022). Impact of financial inclusion on economic growth, financial development, financial efficiency, financial stability, and profitability: An international evidence. *SN Business & Economics*, *2*(9), 139. doi:10.100743546-022-00313-3

Pata, U. K., & Yilanci, V. (2020). Financial development, globalization and ecological footprint in G7: Further evidence from threshold cointegration and fractional frequency causality tests. *Environmental and Ecological Statistics*, *27*(4), 803–825. doi:10.100710651-020-00467-z

Rehman, A. U., Malik, A. H., Md Isa, A. H. B., & Jais, M. B. (2023). Dynamic impact of financial inclusion and industrialization on environmental sustainability. *Social Responsibility Journal*, *19*(5), 906–929. doi:10.1108/SRJ-07-2021-0275

Saidi, K., & Mbarek, M. B. (2016). Nuclear energy, renewable energy, CO2 emissions, and economic growth for nine developed countries: Evidence from panel Granger causality tests. *Progress in Nuclear Energy*, *88*, 364–374. doi:10.1016/j.pnucene.2016.01.018

Shaheen, A., Sheng, J., Arshad, S., Muhammad, H., & Salam, S. (2020). Forecasting the determinants of environmental degradation: A gray modeling approach. *Energy Sources. Part A, Recovery, Utilization, and Environmental Effects*, 1–21. doi:10.1080/15567036.2020.1827090

Shahzadi, H. N., Sheikh, S. M., Sadiq, A., & Rahman, S. U. (2023). Effect of Financial Development, Economic Growth on Environment Pollution: Evidence from G-7 based ARDL Cointegration Approach. *Pakistan Journal of Humanities and Social Sciences*, *11*(1), 68–79. doi:10.52131/pjhss.2023.1101.0330

Sharma, R., Shahbaz, M., Kautish, P., & Vo, X. V. (2021). Does energy consumption reinforce environmental pollution? Evidence from emerging Asian economies. *Journal of Environmental Management*, *297*, 113272. doi:10.1016/j.jenvman.2021.113272 PMID:34280860

Singh, D., & Stakic, N. (2021). Financial inclusion and economic growth nexus: Evidence from SAARC countries. *South Asia Research*, *41*(2), 238–258. doi:10.1177/0262728020964605

Van, L. T. H., Vo, A. T., Nguyen, N. T., & Vo, D. H. (2021). Financial inclusion and economic growth: An international evidence. *Emerging Markets Finance & Trade*, *57*(1), 239–263. doi:10.1080/1540496X.2019.1697672

Yakubu, I. N. (2019). Does corruption grease or sand the wheels of bank profitability in Ghana? *Cogent Economics & Finance*, *7*(1), 1701909. doi:10.1080/23322039.2019.1701909

Yakubu, I. N., & Bunyaminu, A. (2021). Financial Inclusion and Economic Growth in West Africa: The Moderating Effect of Financial Openness. *Empirical Economics Letters*, *20*(2), 155–164.

Yakubu, I. N., Kapusuzoglu, A., & Ceylan, N. B. (2021). Environmental impact of economic globalization and renewable energy consumption in the OPEC countries. *Strategic Approaches to Energy Management: Current Trends in Energy Economics and Green Investment*, 155-171.

Yakubu, I. N., Kapusuzoglu, A., & Ceylan, N. B. (2021). Urbanization, fossil fuel consumption and carbon dioxide emission in Ghana: the STIRPAT model approach. *Strategic Approaches to Energy Management: Current Trends in Energy Economics and Green Investment*, 201-216.

Yakubu, I. N., & Musah, A. (2022). The nexus between financial inclusion and bank profitability: a dynamic panel approach. *Journal of Sustainable Finance & Investment*, 1-14.

Chapter 8
The Road to a Greener Future:
How Government Expenditure and Effectiveness Drive Renewal Energy Consumption

Alhassan Bunyaminu
University of Professional Studies, Accra, Ghana

Shani Bashiru
Accra Technical University, Ghana

Wahab Abdul Iddrisu
https://orcid.org/0000-0001-7543-1794
Ghana Communication Technology University, Ghana

Adibura Baba Seidu
https://orcid.org/0000-0002-3592-7856
University of Professional Studies, Accra, Ghana

Ahmed Jamal Iddrisu
University of Professional Studies, Accra, Ghana

ABSTRACT

This study examines the impact of government expenditure and government effectiveness on renewable energy consumption in Africa from 1990 to 2021. Utilizing the fixed effects technique, the findings indicate a positive significant relationship between government expenditure and renewable energy consumption, while government effectiveness demonstrates a significant negative influence. Additionally, trade openness and urbanization exhibit a negative impact on renewable energy usage. The effect of foreign direct investment (FDI) on renewable energy consumption is found to be mixed. To facilitate the transition towards a greener energy future in Africa, the study recommends several measures including increasing government expenditure on renewable energy, enhancing government effectiveness, promoting sustainable trade practices, and prioritizing sustainable urban planning.

DOI: 10.4018/978-1-6684-9272-7.ch008

1.0 INTRODUCTION

Development of a green economy has become a key approach for stimulating social and economic growth worldwide. There is a growing conviction that, protecting and improving natural habits require engaging in practices and investing in economic activities that will advances environmental sustainability (Sarwar et al., 2019).

The concept of "green economy" denotes a change toward a more comprehensive strategy for growth, one that recognizes the connection of economic development, social improvement, and environmental preservation. The green economy aims to achieve a healthy balance between human wellbeing and the preservation of ecosystems by incorporating sustainability concepts into economic decision-making processes (Sooducho-Pelc & Sulich, 2020; Sulich et al., 2021).

Using this perspective, a green economy connects with and expands on the goals outlined in Agenda 21, the United Nations' comprehensive action plan adopted at the 1992 Earth Summit. Agenda 21 highlights the necessity of handling social, economic, and environmental concerns leveraging on a holistic approach (Tao & Wang, 2020).

Furthermore, the green economy is inextricably linked to the United Nations' Sustainable Development Goals (SDGs) set in 2015. The SDGs provide a roadmap for a more sustainable future, embracing a diverse set of interrelated goals such as poverty eradication, quality education, gender equality, climate action, and responsible consumption and production. The green economy, which promotes environmentally friendly technology, renewable energy sources, sustainable agriculture, and green innovation, is critical to achieving these goals (Iqbal et al., 2021).

Countries could reap significant benefits by making efforts to switch to a greener economy. For example, green growth has the potential to create new jobs in domains such as renewable energy and eco-tourism. These industries do not only foster social inclusion and poverty reduction but also generate employment and economic prosperity that are environmentally sustainable. Navigating towards greener economy has the propensity to considerably boosts innovation and sophisticated technology. Furthermore, a green economy yields improve quality of the environment by lowering pollution.

However, the transition to a green economy is not devoid of immense challenges and necessitates robust measures such as strong political determination, supportive policies, and effective institutional frameworks. Government investment decisions play a pivotal role in shaping the future trajectory of economies (Chien et al., 2021). Nonetheless, the implementation of the green economy concept encounters hurdles due to political complexities and substantial transaction costs. Effectively transforming the economy and achieving green targets require innovative approaches in terms of government backing, governance frameworks, accessible technology, and propitious market conditions.

Numerous economies are currently grappling with fiscal crises, as governments struggle to strike a balance between public spending and taxation, resulting in budget cuts to green economy initiatives and environmental risks mitigation (Hou et al., 2019b; Fu et al., 2021b; Iqbal et al., 2021c). The extent of government expenditure within a green economy, the effectiveness of government actions, and the relationship between the composition of government spending and economic growth collectively influence the implementation of fiscal policies. Altering the level and composition of overall government expenditure, along with enhancing its efficacy, can bolster a country's adoption of renewable energy.

This study investigates how government expenditure and the effectiveness of government actions can facilitate the transition to a green economy in Africa. The study's contributions to literature and policy discussions are multifaceted. Firstly, it addresses a notable gap in existing literature by investigating the simultaneous impact of government spending and effectiveness of governmental tactics on renewable energy adoption in developing economies—an area that has received limited attention to date. Secondly, by exploring the influence of government effectiveness on the green economy movement, the study offers valuable insights into governance strategies that can facilitate a successful transition. Finally, this research underscores the importance of allocating resources and investing in environmentally friendly initiatives, emphasizing the pivotal role of public funding in promoting sustainable economic growth.

The subsequent sections of this chapter are organized as follows: Section 2 offers a review of the existing literature. Section 3 outlines the research data and methods employed in this study. In Section 4, the findings of the research are presented and thoroughly discussed. Finally, Section 5 presents the concluding remarks of the study, summarizing the key findings alongside key policy recommendations.

2.0 LITERATURE REVIEW

2.1 Effect of Government Expenditure on Renewal Energy Consumption

Several empirical studies have been conducted by in examining the effect of government expenditure on renewal energy consumption. For instance, the study by Molefe and Choga (2017) delved into the association between government expenditure and economic growth among South African companies within the period 1990 to 2015. Employing the Vector Error Correction Model and Granger Causality Test methods, the research used Gross Domestic Product, government expenditure, national savings, government debt and consumer price index or inflation as variables for the research. The findings of the research revealed a negative relationship between government expenditure and economic growth in the long run. Furthermore, the outcome of the research revealed a causal relationship from economic growth to government expenditure, implying that economic growth affects government expenditure in South Africa. The study by Sharmin and Khan (2016) assessed the nexus between public health expenditures, logistics performance indices, renewable energy, and ecological sustainability using the Association of Southeast Asian Nations member countries. The study utilized secondary data to examine the hypotheses by employing the structural equation modeling as a method. The findings of the study revealed that using renewable energy in logistics operations increases environmental and economic performance and decreases carbon emissions. Alternatively, environmental performance revealed a negative relationship with public health expenditures, signifying that better environmental stability can improve human health and economic growth. The results further indicates that a surge in spending in public health and low environmental performance reduce economic performance with low effectiveness and little productivity of labour, resulting in declining the rapidity of economic activity. Conversely, using renewable energy in logistics similarly results in better national image and enhances exports in environmentally friendly nations. The research suggested initiatives that will assist policy makers in designing policy schemes and fashioning investment and resource allocations that will precipitate sustainable economic growth.

Sekantsi and Timuno (2017) conducted a research on the drivers of electricity demand in Botswana. The study used the Autoregressive Distributive Lag (ARDL) bounds testing method and the Error Correction Model (ECM) ranging from the period 1981 to 2011. The research assessed the role of financial development, industrialization, government expenditure and urbanisation in Botswana's energy. The outcome of the study demonstrated that economic growth, government expenditure, financial development, and industrialisation have a positive effect on electricity consumption, whereas urbanisation has negative effect on electricity consumption in the long run. The study recommends that policy makers should factor increasing demand for electricity arising from financial development, urbanisation, increase government expenditure and industrialisation in their energy policy formulation in order to avoid energy crisis in future and emphasized that, policy makers should invest in renewable energy to obtain inexpensive energy.

2.2 The Effect of Government Effectiveness on Renewal Energy Consumption

In recent times, varying empirical researches have been conducted to assess the effect of governance on economic growth. The outcome of these studies indicate that the quality of governance has a positive relationship with sustainability and renewal nergy strategy (Mauro, 1995; Ades & Di Tella, 1999; Wei, 2001; Fredriksson and Svensson, 2003). The subject of pervasive corruption bedevilling national governance in Africa has led to stunted economic growth. This has aggravated stagnant growth rates due to the waste of limited economic resources and misdirection of productive resources, which upscale poverty and adversely affect investment in renewable energy. This research seeks to fill the void in literature regarding the effect of quality of governance on renewable energy. Fredriksson et al. (2004) examined the effect of corruption on energy efficiency using 12 OECD countries. The study covers a period from 1982 to 1996. The outcome of the study revealed that corruption stifles the effectiveness of energy policy. The study concluded that the higher the corruptibility of policy makers, the greater the reduction of the quality and quantum of energy policy and expenditure which results in reduction of energy efficiency. Their study further hinted that the greater the corruption implies stringent pro-environment policies. Damania et al. (2003) investigates the connection between corruption, trade and environmental policy using panel data from a combination of developed and developing countries within the period 1982 to 1992. The study disclosed that greater corruption gives birth to fewer environmental regulations, while the effect of trade liberalization on the strictness of environmental policy relies on the extent of corruption.

Stern (2012) conducted a study to assess the energy efficiency trends in 85 countries using the cross-section of time-averaged data for 37 years. The study used a stochastic production frontier model and the results indicate that energy efficiency is greater in nations with greater total factor productivity, devalued currencies and little fossil fuel reserves. Furthermore, the study discovered that enhancing quality governance by reducing corruption will result in increasing energy efficiency. Additionally, Stern (2012) contends that technological change is a cardinal factor in offsetting the energy-use and carbon emissions which leads to strong impacts of economic growth. Nicolli and Vona (2015) investigated the effect of corruption on resource allocated to renewable energy in OECD countries from 1970 to 2005. The outcome of the study indicated that erosion of effectiveness in the level of governance through widespread corruption has disturbing bearing on renewable energy policy. The findings of their study are consistent with forecasts of political-economy models of environmental policies. Butler et al. (2018) explore the effects of governance on the energy sector by emphasizing on four different means in which non-energy interrelated issues on governance can have impact on energy issues. The main input of their research was to set out a unique analytic framework for showcasing 'non-energy' policy effects, which might otherwise be obscured within an analysis. Their study suggests that policy makers should configure their governance strategy on energy demand to be in consonance with prevailing challenges.

Sekrafi and Sghaier (2018) examine the effect of energy consumption, corruption, environmental quality, and political instability on economic growth in 13 MENA countries within the time span of 1984 to 2012. The research used both the static and dynamic panel data techniques. The study discovered that increased corruption impacts economic growth, environmental quality and energy consumption and argued that corruption has an indirect impact on economic growth through energy consumption and environmental quality. It was also discovered that corruption has an indirect effect on environmental quality through economic growth and an indirect effect on energy consumption through CO2 emissions and GDP.

In a study conducted by Arminen and Menegaki (2019), they investigate the causal relationships between economic growth, energy consumption and carbon dioxide (CO2) emissions in developed economies and developing economies by employing the simultaneous equations framework using the data from the period 1985 to 2011. The study used institutional quality, measured using the level of corruption and climate using average temperatures over the winter and summer months into consideration. The results of the study revealed that there is a correlation between GDP and energy consumption. The study further contended that developed economies and developing economies focus their economic growth on a feedback relationship with energy consumption. The study established that in those countries, ensuing pollution has not yet reached a maximum point. Additionally, the study discovered that climate and weather differences are vital factors of energy consumption and CO2 emissions than corruption. The study recommends that changes in institutional quality are probably going to have a limited effect on energy and environmental policies. Bercu et al. (2019) carried a study using panel data for 14 Central and Eastern European countries within the time span from 1995 to 2017. The research examines the relationship between energy consumption, economic growth and good governance. The study reveals that good governance affects electricity and Gross Domestic Product (GDP) consumption. The research suggests that governments from Central and Eastern European countries need to strengthen good governance in the economy, thereby ensuring an enabling environment favorable for investment in the energy industry. This will propel competition and curb inadequacies in the production, transmission, and distribution of energy sector in those economies.

3.0 METHODOLOGY AND DATA

3.1 Data and Selection of Variables

This study examines the relationship between government expenditure, government effectiveness, and renewable energy consumption in 40 African countries with data spanning from 1990 to 2021. The data for each variable is sourced from the World Development Indicators of the World Bank. The main dependent variable, renewable energy consumption (RENE), is measured as the proportion of total energy consumption derived from renewable sources. The independent variables include government expenditure (GOVEX) and Government effectiveness (GEFF). Government expenditure is measured as general government final consumption expenditure as a percentage of GDP. Government effectiveness (GEFF) is assessed using a World Bank indicator that captures perceptions of public service quality, civil service independence, policy formulation and implementation, and government commitment to these policies, ranging on an aggregate scale from approximately -2.5 to 2.5. Additionally, other control variables such as trade openness (TRADE), foreign direct investment (FDI), and urbanization (URB) are considered. FDI is measured as the percentage of GDP representing inflows of foreign direct investment, while trade is represented by the import and export of goods and services as a percentage of GDP. Urbanization is assessed using the proportion of the total population residing in urban areas.

3.2 Empirical Model Specification

The general specification of the panel data model can be represented as follows:

$$Yit = \alpha + \beta Xit + \varepsilon it \quad (1)$$

where the index *i* denotes the cross-sectional dimension, and *t* represents the time dimension. The dependent variable is denoted by Y, while X represents the independent variables included in the model. The constant term is captured by α, and the vector coefficients are denoted by β. The error term is represented by ε.

The specific panel data model for this study, incorporating the variables considered can be represented as follows:

$$RENEit = \alpha + \beta 1GOVEXit + \beta 2TRADEit + \beta 3FDIit + \beta 4URBit + \varepsilon it \quad (2)$$

$$RENEit = \alpha + \beta 1GEFFit + \beta 2TRADEit + \beta 3FDIit + \beta 4URBit + \varepsilon it \quad (3)$$

3.3 Model Estimation Method

The developed equations in the models are derived from the ordinary least squares (OLS) method, which treats all observations across time periods as a single sample. However, the OLS model overlooks the panel nature of the data and assumes no serial correlation in the error term (Ünvan & Yakubu, 2020). Panel data, on the other hand, may exhibit group effects, time effects, or both. These effects can be either fixed or random. In this study, both the random effects and fixed effects methods are employed to estimate the models. To determine which model is appropriate for equation estimation, the Hausman test will be conducted. If the test statistic of the Hausman test is significant at a 5% level of significance, the fixed effects estimator is favoured, rejecting the random effects model.

Fixed-effects (FE) models are a type of statistical models in which the levels (i.e., values) of independent variables are assumed to be fixed (i.e., constant), and only the dependent variable changes in response to the levels of independent variables. The rationale behind FE estimation is simple and persuasive, which explains why it is so regularly used in many disciplines. To avoid the problem of heterogeneity bias, all higher-level variance, and with it any between effects, are controlled out using the higher-level entities themselves (Allison, 2009).

One of the limitations of FE model is that it loses a large amount of important information. No inferences can be made about that higher-level variance, including whether or not it is significant (Schurer & Yong, 2012). Thus it is impossible to measure the effects of time-invariant variables at all, because all degrees of freedom at the higher level have been consumed. Where time-invariant variables are of particular interest, this is obviously critical. And yet even in these situations, researchers have suggested the use of FE, on the basis of a Hausman test.

4.0 PRESENTATION AND DISCUSSION OF RESULTS

4.1 Summary Statistics

The summary statistics presented in Table 1 provide insights into the distribution and variation of the variables under study. The mean renewable energy consumption (RENE) is 70.008, indicating a relatively moderate level across the observations. Government expenditure (GOVEX) has a mean of 14.297, suggesting that, on average, governments allocate a relatively small portion of their final consumption expenditure to the green economy. Government effectiveness (GEFF) has a negative mean of -0.756, which implies that, on average, there are challenges in the quality of public services and policy implementation. Trade (TRADE) has a mean of 63.654, indicating a relatively high level of import and export activity. Foreign direct investment (FDI) has a mean of 3.639, suggesting a moderate level of inflows relative to the GDP. Urbanization (URB) has a mean of 37.506, indicating a substantial proportion of the total population residing in urban areas. The maximum and minimum values of the variables show considerable variability, reflecting significant differences among the observations.

Table 1. Summary statistics

	RENE	GOVEX	GEFF	TRADE	FDI	URB
Mean	70.008	14.297	-0.756	63.654	3.639	37.506
Maximum	98.340	43.484	1.161	163.619	161.824	90.423
Minimum	3.540	0.911	-1.887	16.352	-18.918	5.416
Std. Dev.	23.969	6.247	0.593	28.356	9.080	16.405
Observations	1189	1107	917	1145	1269	1280

4.2 Correlation Analysis

The correlation analysis is presented in Table 2. Upon examining the table, it can be observed that there is a moderate positive correlation between government expenditure (GOVEX) and trade (TRADE), as well as between government expenditure and urbanization (URB) with correlation coefficients of 0.422 and 0.425, respectively. Additionally, a weak positive correlation is found between government effectiveness (GEFF) and trade, with a correlation coefficient of 0.213. However, there is a lack of substantial correlations between government effectiveness and the other variables. The correlations between government expenditure or government effectiveness and foreign direct investment (FDI) are negligible, indicating a weak relationship.

Table 2. Correlation analysis

	GOVEX	GEFF	TRADE	FDI	URB
GOVEX	1.000				
GEFF	0.343	1.000			
TRADE	0.422	0.213	1.000		
FDI	0.063	0.006	0.329	1.000	
URB	0.048	0.184	0.425	0.107	1.000

4.3 Multicollinearity Analysis

The multicollinearity analysis in Table 3 provides information on the Variance Inflation Factor (VIF) and Tolerance values for each variable included in the analysis. The VIF measures the degree of correlation between an independent variable and the other independent variables in the model. Generally, a VIF value above 10 indicates high multicollinearity (Yakubu, 2019). In this analysis, all the variables have VIF values below 2, suggesting a low level of multicollinearity. The Tolerance values (1/VIF) indicate the proportion of variance in a variable that is not explained by the other variables. Here, the Tolerance values are all above 0.5, which indicates that less than 50% of the variance is shared among the variables. Overall, the multicollinearity analysis suggests that there is no significant issue of multicollinearity among the variables in the model, allowing for reliable interpretation of their individual effects on the dependent variable.

Table 3. Multicollinearity analysis

Variable	Variance Inflation Factor (VIF)	Tolerance (1/VIF)
GOVEX	1.422	0.703
GEFF	1.187	0.842
TRADE	1.781	0.561
FDI	1.148	0.871
URB	1.335	0.749

4.4 Empirical Findings

The empirical findings presented in Table 4 reveal the estimated coefficients for the impact of government expenditure, government effectiveness, and other variables on renewable energy consumption. The significant Hausman test result suggests that the fixed effects estimation technique is preferred, and the interpretations of the findings are based on this approach.

In terms of the specific variables, government expenditure shows a positive and statistically significant impact on renewable energy consumption. This implies that increased government spending on environmentally friendly initiatives can contribute to higher levels of renewable energy adoption. Similarly, government effectiveness demonstrates a negative and statistically significant effect on renewable energy consumption. This implies that countries with higher levels of government effectiveness may have lower renewable energy consumption levels, indicating a potential need for policy reforms or better implementation strategies.

As several studies show evidence of the negative effect of weak governance on RE investment, some papers show that trade openness may decrease this negative effect, signifying that countries not in favor of institutional improvements can establish a policy of open market (Ades and Di Tella, 1999; Blake and Martin, 2002). Principally, Damania et al (2003) show that trade liberalization weakens the effect of corruption on environmental policy formation. Mukherjee and Chakraborty (2013) think that government systems might affect pollution haven hypothesis effects, predominantly in countries where democracy and freedom of speech is missing. However, it is imparative to take into account the interaction effect between trade and governance when studying RE investment.

For the control variables, trade openness has a negative and significant impact on renewable energy consumption, suggesting that countries with higher levels of trade may prioritize economic activities that are less environmentally sustainable. Consistent with the finding of Bunyaminu and Yakubu (2022), foreign direct investment exhibits mixed effect on renewable energy consumption, indicating that there is a limited impact of FDI on renewable energy consumption. There is a significantly negative effect of urbanization on renewables. This raises concerns about the environmental impact of rapid urban development and emphasizes the importance of sustainable urban planning and infrastructure.

Table 4. Regression results

Variables	Pooled OLS		Random Effects		Fixed Effects	
GOVEX	-0.934***		0.202***		0.228***	
	(0.105)		(0.060)		(0.060)	
GEFF		-19.734***		-3.236***		-2.520***
		(0.980)		(0.787831)		(0.805)
TRADE	-0.213***	-0.279***	-0.042***	-0.044***	-0.037**	-0.035**
	(0.027)	(0.024)	(0.015)	(0.014)	(0.015)	(0.014)
FDI	0.395***	0.501***	-0.067	-0.030	-0.075*	-0.039
	(0.125)	(0.115)	(0.045)	(0.037)	(0.045)	(0.038)
URB	-0.623***	-0.474***	-0.731***	-0.803***	-0.727***	-0.797***
	(0.042)	(0.039)	(0.042)	(0.045)	(0.043)	(0.047)
C	118.721***	88.183***	96.024***	99.246***	96.239***	99.570***
	(1.957)	(2.032)	(3.483)	(3.096)	(1.934)	(2.012)
R^2	0.425	0.610	0.269	0.306	0.946	0.971
Adjusted R^2	0.423	0.608	0.266	0.302	0.943	0.969
Hausman test χ^2 [Prob.> χ^2]					15.914 [0.003]	31.692 [0.000]
Number of Countries	40	40	40	40	40	40

5.0 CONCLUSION AND RECOMMENDATIONS

This study investigates how government expenditure and effectiveness drive renewable energy consumption in Africa from 1990 to 2021. The analysis is conducted using the fixed effects technique. The findings indicate that government expenditure has a positive and statistically significant impact on renewable energy consumption. Conversely, government effectiveness shows a negative and statistically significant effect on renewable energy consumption. Furthermore, trade openness and urbanization have a negative and significant impact on renewable energy consumption, while the impact of foreign direct investment (FDI) on renewable energy consumption is mixed.

The findings of this study suggest several key policy recommendations to promote renewable energy consumption in Africa. First and foremost, policymakers should prioritize increasing government expenditure on renewable energy initiatives. This entails allocating more resources towards research and development, providing subsidies and incentives for renewable energy technologies, and investing in the necessary infrastructure. Additionally, efforts should be directed towards enhancing government effectiveness in the renewable energy sector. This involves improving policy formulation and implementation, ensuring the quality of public services, and fostering the independence of the civil service from political pressures. Moreover, sustainable trade practices should be encouraged, incorporating environmental considerations into trade agreements, implementing green trade policies, and promoting eco-friendly technologies in trade-related industries. Sustainable urban planning and infrastructure development should also be a priority, focusing on energy-efficient building designs, integrating renewable energy systems, and prioritizing the preservation of green spaces. Lastly, further research is needed to understand the impact of foreign direct investment (FDI) on renewable energy consumption, allowing policymakers to identify strategies to attract sustainable FDI and maximize its positive impact.

REFERENCES

Ades, A., & Di Tella, R. (1999). Rents, competition, and corruption. *The American Economic Review*, *89*(4), 982–993. doi:10.1257/aer.89.4.982

Arminen, H., & Menegaki, A. N. (2019). Corruption, climate and the energy-environment-growth nexus. *Energy Economics*, *80*, 621–634. doi:10.1016/j.eneco.2019.02.009

Bercu, A. M., Paraschiv, G., & Lupu, D. (2019). Investigating the energy-economic growth-governance nexus: Evidence from central and eastern European countries. *Sustainability*, *11*(12), 3355. doi:10.3390u11123355

Bunyaminu, A., & Yakubu, I. N. (2022). Green Energy Demand and Financial Development: Evidence from Africa. In Finance for Sustainability in a Turbulent Economy (pp. 26-48). IGI Global.

Butler, C., Parkhill, K. A., & Luzecka, P. (2018). Rethinking energy demand governance: Exploring impact beyond energy policy. *Energy Research & Social Science*, *36*, 70–78. doi:10.1016/j.erss.2017.11.011

Chien, F. S., Kamran, H. W., Albashar, G., & Iqbal, W. (2021). *Dynamic planning, conversion, and management strategy of different renewable energy sources: A sustainable solution for severe energy crises in emerging economies*. Int. J. Hydrog. Energy. doi:10.1016/j.ijhydene.2020.12.004

Damania, R., Fredriksson, P. G., & List, J. A. (2003). Trade liberalization, corruption, and environmental policy formation: Theory and evidence. *Journal of Environmental Economics and Management, 46*(3), 490–512. doi:10.1016/S0095-0696(03)00025-1

Fredriksson, P. G., & Svensson, J. (2003). Political instability, corruption and policy formation: The case of environmental policy. *Journal of Public Economics, 87*(7-8), 1383–1405. doi:10.1016/S0047-2727(02)00036-1

Fredriksson, P. G., Vollebergh, H. R., & Dijkgraaf, E. (2004). Corruption and energy efficiency in OECD countries: Theory and evidence. *Journal of Environmental Economics and Management, 47*(2), 207–231. doi:10.1016/j.jeem.2003.08.001

Fu, F. Y., Alharthi, M., Bhatti, Z., Sun, L., Rasul, F., Hanif, I., & Iqbal, W. (2021a). The dynamic role of energy security, energy equity and environmental sustainability in the dilemma of emission reduction and economic growth. *Journal of Environmental Management, 280*, 111828. Advance online publication. doi:10.1016/j.jenvman.2020.111828 PMID:33360740

Hou, Y., Iqbal, W., & Shaikh, G. M. (2019a). Measuring energy efficiency and environmental performance: A case of South Asia. *Processes (Basel, Switzerland), 7*(6), 325. Advance online publication. doi:10.3390/pr7060325

Iqbal, S., Bilal, A. R., Nurunnabi, M., Iqbal, W., Alfakhri, Y., & Iqbal, N. (2021a). It is time to control the worst: Testing COVID-19 outbreak, energy consumption and CO < inf > 2 < /inf > emission. *Environmental Science and Pollution Research International, 28*(15), 19008–19020. doi:10.100711356-020-11462-z PMID:33184786

Mauro, P. (1995). Corruption and growth. *The Quarterly Journal of Economics, 110*(3), 681–712. doi:10.2307/2946696

Molefe, K., & Choga, I. (2017). Government expenditure and economic growth in South Africa: A vector error correction modelling and Granger causality test. *Journal of Economics and Behavioral Studies, 9*(4 (J)), 164–172. doi:10.22610/jebs.v9i4(J).1831

Nicolli, F., & Vona, F. (2015). The evolution of renewable energy policy in OECD countries: Aggregate indicators and determinants. In F. Schneider, A. Kollmann, & J. Reichl (Eds.), *Political Economy and Instruments ofEnvironmental Politic* (pp. 117–148). The MIT Press. doi:10.7551/mitpress/10274.003.0009

Sarwar, S., Farooq, M. U., Shahzad, U., & Zaijun, L. (2019). The impact of carbon emission and forest activities on health outcomes: Empirical evidence from China. *Environmental Science and Pollution Research International, 26*(13), 12894–12906. doi:10.100711356-019-04779-x PMID:30888615

Sekantsi, L. P., & Timuno, S. (2017). Electricity consumption in Botswana: The role of financial development, industrialisation, and urbanization. *Review of Economic and Business Studies, 10*(1), 75–102. doi:10.1515/rebs-2017-0049

Sekrafi, H., & Sghaier, A. (2018). Examining the relationship between corruption, economic growth, environmental degradation, and energy consumption: A panel analysis in MENA region. *Journal of the Knowledge Economy, 9*(3), 963–979. doi:10.100713132-016-0384-6

Sharmin, F., & Khan, M. R. (2016). A causal relationship between energy consumption, energy prices and economic growth in Africa. *International Journal of Energy Economics and Policy*, *6*(3), 477–494.

Sołoducho-Pelc, L., & Sulich, A. (2020). Between sustainable and temporary competitive advantages in the unstable business environment. *Sustain*, *12*(21), 32–88. doi:10.3390u12218832

Stern, D. I. (2012). Modeling international trends in energy efficiency. *Energy Economics*, *34*(6), 2200–2208. doi:10.1016/j.eneco.2012.03.009

Sulich, A., & Sołoducho-Pelc, L. (2021). Renewable energy producers' strategies in the Visegrád group countries. *Energies*, *14*(11), 30–48. doi:10.3390/en14113048

Tao, C., & Wang, Y. (2020). The spatial spillover effect of China's government health expenses on the regional economy: Empirical analysis based on the spatial panel model. *Journal of Coastal Research*, *103*(sp1), 95–100. doi:10.2112/SI103-020.1

Ünvan, Y. A., & Yakubu, I. N. (2020). Do bank-specific factors drive bank deposits in Ghana? *Journal of Computational and Applied Mathematics*, *376*, 112827. doi:10.1016/j.cam.2020.112827

Wei, S. J. (2001). *Corruption in Economic Transition and Development: Grease or Sand?* United Nations.

Yakubu, I. N. (2019). Does corruption grease or sand the wheels of bank profitability in Ghana? *Cogent Economics & Finance*, *7*(1), 170–190. doi:10.1080/23322039.2019.1701909

Chapter 9
Evaluating the Policy-Making Framework Around Climate-Induced migration

Akash Bag
https://orcid.org/0000-0001-8820-171X
Amity University, India

Prateek Mishra
https://orcid.org/0000-0002-3262-1173
KIIT University, India

Shashank Nande
KIIT University, India

Vishal Kumar Rai
O.P. Jindal Global University, India

ABSTRACT

Climate change significantly affects climate-induced migration, particularly on low-lying atoll islands in the Pacific. This impact is particularly relevant for Kiribati, a country highly affected by climate change and expected to experience climate-induced migration. A study conducted a comparative analysis of the problem representations of climate-induced migration in Kiribati and New Zealand's national policies. The study, grounded in post-structuralism and post-colonialism, examined how the issue is portrayed in policy and how migrants are constructed as subjects. The analytical framework used was 'What's the problem represented to be?' (WPR). The findings revealed that climate-induced migration is depicted as both a challenge and an adaptation strategy. Transnational climate-induced migration is portrayed as a strategy for increased resilience, while internal migration is seen as challenging.

DOI: 10.4018/978-1-6684-9272-7.ch009

INTRODUCTION

Climate change is not a future problem but affects people's lives today. One consequence of climate change that is increasingly discussed is its effect on increased migration. The climate-induced migration mainly occurs within countries and in cities, but when borders are crossed, it is usually done to neighboring states (Ash & Campbell, 2016). The countries hit disproportionately hard, considering their small populations are island nations in the South Pacific. The Pacific islands are particularly vulnerable as the entire existence of certain states is threatened due to rising sea levels. In these areas, climate change's effect on migration is also feared to be evident (Hugo, 2010, p. 10). Kiribati is a country in the Pacific Ocean that, due to its status as a low-lying island, experiences increased vulnerability and poorer conditions for adaptation because the habitable land area is slowly but surely decreasing (Thornton et al., 2021, p. 2). Talking about "sinking islands" may be considered alarmist, but asking how climate-induced migration to and from Kiribati is managed in policy is well worth asking.

Based on the problems described above, there is a great need for policy in the area. As internal migration continues to be the most common form of climate-induced migration, the policy at the national level is central, but also migration policy in countries less affected by climate change is important (Brown, 2008, p. 39). Given Kiribati's particularly vulnerable situation as a low-lying island with limited opportunities for internal migration, the relationship between the country and neighboring states is of great relevance. Kiribati's relationship with New Zealand is particularly important, as it is where most transnational migration occurs today (Thornton et al., 2021, p. 11). A comparison between these countries is interesting regarding their different roles – Kiribati as a potential sending country of climate migrants and New Zealand as a likely recipient. The countries' different relationship to the phenomenon means that the essay also sheds light on the more worldwide power asymmetries between nations in the global North and South. Power asymmetries are based on past colonial experiences, current and historical contributions to greenhouse gas emissions, and the consequences countries are expected to suffer due to climate change. The existing research that studies the view of climate-induced migration in the Pacific is currently scarce, and examining how the phenomenon is represented within the region is therefore important (Remling, 2020, p. 2). Several representations of climate-induced migration have previously been identified in the research, of which two central to the study are climate-induced migration as a challenge or an adaptation measure.

How the phenomenon is represented affects which policies are proposed and constructs the migrant as a subject (Methmann & Oels, 2015; Ranson-Cooper et al., 2015). Examining problem representations of climate-induced migration in government policy is crucial because governments have a privileged role in creating these as their understanding of a "problem" is used as a policy tool and cemented through legislation (C. Bacchi, 2009, p. 33). Therefore, Examining the problem representations found in the countries' policies and whether they differ is interesting. By examining the relationship between migration and climate change, the essay also highlights the conflict regarding governance and sovereignty that arises when dealing with the phenomenon. The conflict arises as climate change is a global and cross-border problem that is largely managed through international cooperation (Vogler, n.d., p. 388), while there is a lack of global governance mechanisms for the management of transnational migration, where national sovereignty and national borders are highly valued (Castles, 2014, p. 202). The interlinking of these two phenomena forms an interesting starting point in analyzing policy in the area.

PURPOSE AND ISSUES

The essay aims to analyze and compare how climate-induced migration is represented in Kiribati and New Zealand national policy. The study, therefore, aims to identify and analyze the two countries' policy material regarding climate-induced migration. The primary purpose of the study is thus to investigate problem representations of climate-induced migration, which is done by identifying how the "problem" is described, which "solutions" are presented to the "problem," and what implications this has. The essay also examines Kiribati and New Zealand as a case of how two countries with different relationships to climate-induced migration represent it. To make the purpose researchable, it is broken down into two questions:

- How is climate-induced migration represented in Kiribati's and New Zealand's national policy documents?
- What are the implications of the identified problem representation?

BACKGROUND

The chapter briefly describes Kiribati's and New Zealand's socio-economic and geopolitical conditions. This is done to gain an expanded understanding of how Kiribati and its people may be affected by climate-induced migration and the relationship between Kiribati and New Zealand. Next, the international and regional policy context of relevance to the study is explained.

Kiribati And New Zealand

The Republic of Kiribati is located in the Pacific Ocean and consists of the three island groups Gilbert, Phoenix, and Line (Oakes et al., 2016, p. 21). The country consists of a raised coral island and 32 low-lying atolls, of which the average height of the atolls above the water is 2 to 4 meters. This means that the island is in a particularly vulnerable situation regarding increased sea levels, "king tides," and cyclones, and the country is also affected by more and more extreme weather events such as drought and flooding (Clement et al., 2021, p. 222; Oakes et al., 2016, p. 22). The rising sea levels risk leading to a large part of the country becoming uninhabitable within a few decades, but threats such as drought and water insecurity risk displacing the population before then (Foreign Policy Institute (UI) 2021). In addition, Kiribati is classified by the UN as a Small Island Developing State (SIDS) and one of the world's least developed countries. The designation SIDS was established to clarify the common social, economic, and environmental challenges this country group faces (Clement et al., 2021, p. 218). Kiribati shares many of these vulnerabilities as the country's economy, livelihoods, and employment depend highly on its marine resources, an activity particularly affected by climate change (Clement et al., 2021, p. 217).

Namely, more than 70% of the country's total income comes from the sale of fishing licenses abroad, and Kiribati is largely dependent on aid for its livelihood, of which New Zealand is a crucial partner. The possibility of diversifying the country's income is also limited due to the large distances between the islands and the lack of agricultural resources (Clement et al., 2021, p. 228). The country thus has limited development opportunities. Kiribati is one of the countries that is often raised in debates regarding climate-induced migration. The country has previously promoted a "migration with dignity" policy based on managing its climate-induced migration from the country on its terms (Clement et al., 2021, p. 235). The policy has been promoted by providing students in the country with internationally accredited education, allowing them to seek work abroad (Oakes et al., 2016, p. 28). Kiribati has also purchased 5460 hectares of land in Fiji to secure its food security and a location for possible future migration (Oakes et al., 2016, p. 28). However, the Government of Kiribati has clarified that migration abroad should be seen as a last resort and that adaptation in situ is prioritized (Clement et al., 2021, p. 235). Part of the country's population also risks being prevented from migrating due to a lack of resources, which confirms previous research that shows that those most in need of movement also have the least opportunity to migrate (Oakes et al., 2016, p. 57). Even though no policy exists specifically for climate-induced migration, Kiribati has made the issue visible and drawn attention to the fact that policy in the area is an important proactive adaptation strategy (Oakes et al. 2016, p. 28f).

Most of Kiribati's internal migration occurs to the southern part of the capital atoll of Tarawa, where 51.5% of the country's population resides. This atoll is more developed than the others, and many people move here in search of livelihood, which has led to the creation of slums (UI 2021). The country's Government has tried to reduce overpopulation by advocating migration to the country's more sparsely populated and less vulnerable islands (Oakes et al., 2016, p. 27). Unfortunately, the country's internal migration is also limited. The population of Kiribati's outer islands is particularly vulnerable, some of whom have already had to move from their home environments (Smith & McNamara, 2015, p. 55). The main destination for transnational migration is New Zealand, followed by Fiji and Australia (Oakes et al., 2016, p. 27). New Zealand has a low population density, a strong economy, and close ties to Kiribati, both historical and contemporary. As previously mentioned, the country is today the largest recipient of I-Kiribati (Kiribati population) migrants and has a long history of seeking migrants to meet the demand for labor, which according to some researchers, makes the country suitable as a recipient country for climate migrants as well (Oakes et al., 2016, p. 70; Wyett, 2014, p. 177). New Zealand has two agreements that include migration from Kiribati. Partly, seasonal labor immigration to New Zealand occurs through the "Recognized Seasonal Employer Scheme," which Kiribati joined in 2011 (Oakes et al., 2016, p. 28). Here, the opportunity is given to work in the country's agricultural, horticultural, and viticultural sectors for up to nine months (Oakes et al., 2016, p. 28). In 2002, the "Pacific Access Category Scheme" (PAC) was also established, which annually gives 75 of Kiribati's citizens a work permit and the opportunity to permanent residence in New Zealand (Oakes et al., 2016, p. 28). even though this regulation is quota-based and the migrants are met with requirements for full-time jobs, minimum income, and English requirements, PAC is an important migration route (Thornton et al., 2021, p. 13). The forms of migration currently regulated regionally within the Pacific are thus mainly focused on temporary educational or employment opportunities. It has been argued that these agreements can also be expanded to include climate-induced migration, but this would mean that these need to evolve from agreements that regulate temporary migration to permanent settlement (Smith & McNamara 2014, p. 52). Thus, there is currently no agreement regarding specifically climate-induced migration between the countries.

International And Regional Policy Context

The essay focuses on the countries' national policy material in its analysis, but one should not ignore the guidelines and recommendations produced at the international and regional levels, as these also have consequences for the management of the phenomenon in Kiribati and New Zealand (Thornton et al., 2021, p. 13). Initially, the United Nations Framework Convention on Climate Change is an important starting point for international governance. Under this convention, the Cancun Agreement has been established, which is one of the largest collective attempts the world has taken in the hope of global emission reductions. Under the Cancun Agreements, the process of creating national adaptation plans was established, whereby the member states reported on their strategies for reduced emissions. Equally important are the UN's "Guiding Principles of Internal Displacement," non-binding principles that regulate internal migration, the most common form in this context (Smith & McNamara 2014, p. 48). The principles contain 30 recommendations that guide states in developing legislation affecting the protection and security of internally displaced persons (Smith & McNamara 2014, p. 48). It is, therefore, important that there is no international framework for the protection of climate migrants (Smith & McNamara 2014, p. 48). Given the major climate challenges SIDS faces, they have been leaders and have worked proactively to integrate climate resilience and mobility into national, regional, and international climate discussions (Clement et al., 2021, p. 218).

At a regional level, several frameworks aim to strengthen resilience to climate change and improve disaster risk management, for example, the Framework for Resilient Development in the Pacific and the SAMOA Pathway (Clement et al., 2021, p. 235). Within the Pacific area, there are also the regional and transnational alliances Alliance of Small Island States and Small Island Developing States (Klepp & Herbeck, 2016, p. 65). Among other things, these have established the Male Declaration, highlighting how the member countries in the alliances have contributed little to climate change while largely being affected by its consequences (Klepp & Herbeck, 2016, p. 65). The declaration clarifies their demand to be provided with the right tools to manage the effects of climate change and maintain their self-determination (Klepp & Herbeck, 2016, p. 65). In conclusion, there are more international and regional developments in the field that it is impossible to discuss in this essay due to its practical limitation. It should also be mentioned that much of this material is non-binding. However, the relationship between international and national policy formulation may constitute an area worth investigating in further research.

Theory And Previous Research

The chapter describes the essay's theoretical starting points, which creates a framework for the rest of the essay. The purpose is to discuss how climate-induced migration is represented in Kiribati's and New Zealand's policies and the implications of the problem representations. The essay is based on post-structuralism and post-colonialism, which is motivated by the theories' helpfulness in elucidating alternative approaches to climate-induced migration and in critically analyzing the problem representations in the policy material. In this case, discourse, problem representation, and "othering" are central concepts. An account of previous research connected to the phenomenon is then given. Based on the purpose of the study, previous research linked to representations is of the greatest importance. The chapter thus describes various representations of climate-induced migration found and established within academic literature and policy formulation (Bettini et al., 2016, p. 349).

THEORETICAL UNDERPINNINGS

Post-Structuralism

Using an analytical discourse method, and specifically the WPR approach, entails basic theoretical assumptions of a post-structuralist nature. According to post-structuralist theorizing, the role of language is emphasized, which is based on social constructivist epistemology. Language is not considered neutral but meaning-making because discussing various phenomena carries political implications (Hansen, 2019, p. 180). This is also done through the formulation of policy. From this starting point, there is no natural way to define climate-induced migration, but how we do it makes certain policies appear more natural and thus legitimate. By asking ourselves how "problems," in this case climate-induced migration, are represented in policy, it becomes possible to examine the underlying assumptions that make these representations seem natural and the implications the Problem representations entail (Bacchi & Goodwin, 2016, p. 6). Within post-structuralism, the concepts of power and discourse are central. Discourse analysis starts with the constitutive role of language, where the language we use also reflects a certain perspective on the world. From a power perspective, only a piece of certain knowledge is recognized as the correct and "true" knowledge and constitutes the dominant discourse. The paper's power perspective is based on examining which is the dominant problem representation and what underpins this, as well as the implications of the problem representations. Since different representations lead to different solution proposals seeming reasonable, it entails consequences for which these proposals favor and disadvantage, which further links to the power aspect of discourse analysis. The formation of theory is thus useful as it contributes to critical and analytical thinking about policy development (C. Bacchi & Goodwin, 2016, p. 4).

Post-Colonialism

A post-colonial way of thinking assumes that the world as it looks today is influenced by previous colonial experiences and power relations, both as colonizers and colonized (Sabaratnam, 2020, p. 161). Thus, the perspective contributes with a critical starting point in the study of knowledge production and offers an opportunity for alternative approaches to various phenomena through an account of how the imperialist hierarchies still shape policy today (Sabaratnam, 2020, p. 161). The post-colonial approach is thus useful in comparing policy material from New Zealand in the global North and Kiribati in the South, given that our understanding and representation of the world are largely based on historical hierarchies and experiences.

A concept of great importance in post-colonial theory and for the study is "othering." The concept has been further developed by Gayatri Spivak but is based on Edward Said's theorizing about the construction of the "Orient" as opposed to the "Occident" (Said, 2014). Through this dichotomy, Said examines the double discursive practice whereby the West, the Occident, produces its self-image through a contemporary construction of the East, the "Orient." By representing the "Orient" as "irrational, depraved (fallen), childlike, "different," Said means that the West is constructed as "rational, virtuous, mature, "normal." (Said, 2014, p. 40). This discursive construction of "the other" is double, as it legitimizes domination and imperial control while presenting this action as rational (Velho & Thomas Olalde, 2016, p. 29). The perspective was based on a geographical division of the world into "West" and "East," but can be applied to more contemporary social relations to analyze the processes that recreate the production of "the other" (Velho & Thomas-Olalde, 2016, p. 34). The dichotomy of an "us" and a "them" is also found in research regarding climate-induced migration, where different representations of the phenomenon and the migrant as a subject are also considered to contribute to a form of "othering."

Furthermore, the dichotomy of a "we" and a "them" can be found in the conceptualization of the global North and South, where the global North is presented as a knowledge holder and a dominant center, which intends to "solve" "problems" in the global South (Hartmann, 2010, p. 23; Ranson-Cooper et al., 2015, p. 109). A post-colonial framework is thus justified based on the purpose of the study as the perspective helps make visible if and how the power relationship between Kiribati and New Zealand is reflected in the problem representations. This is relevant regarding the countries' unequal contribution to emissions and the representation of the climate-driven migrant. The perspective is thus helpful in politicizing the policy proposals found in the material and connecting this to the broader discussion about who should bear the burden of this adaptation (Klepp & Herbeck, 2016, p. 54).

The Study's Theoretical Starting Point

The study starts with the post-structuralist understanding of language, contributing to a view of policy as meaning-making. Post-structuralism also contributes to a critical examination of the policy material where its underlying assumptions are examined and highlights the problem representations from a power perspective. Furthermore, the study is grounded in post-colonialism, which means a view of the countries' realities, problem representations, and power relations as colored by their colonial history. A post-colonial perspective helps understand how climate-induced is represented within policy, what underpins the problem representations, and makes alternative approaches to the phenomenon visible. Through these theoretical starting points, the hope is to emphasize the role of discourses in our understanding of the world and its implicit effects. Another hope is to analyze if and how the power relationship between the countries is reflected in the problem representations.

PREVIOUS RESEARCH

migration as a consequence of changes in the climate is something that has been studied for a long time because people have always used movement as an adaptation measure when their immediate environment has changed (Klepp, 2017, p. 11). However, the specific relationship between migration and human-induced climate change was only noticed in the research world during the 1980s, and a greater connection between the environment and migration began when the term "environmental refugee" was used in a UN report in 1985 (Klepp, 2017, p. 2). After the IPCC described in 1990 that the greatest impact of climate change might be on migration, the topic has grown in popularity (Brown, 2008, p. 9).

Representations of Climate-Induced Migration

Researchers and other actors have long tried to define and categorize climate-induced migration to find "solutions" to the "problem" that the phenomenon represents (Ransan-Cooper et al., 2015, p. 106). The representations are not neutral modes of expression but are based on normative assumptions and bring consequences for policy making (Ransan-Cooper et al., 2015, p. 106f). The representations mainly found within policy-making circles are the representation of climate-induced migration as a security threat, an adaptation measure, or the migrant as a victim. Therefore, these are discussed more thoroughly (Ransan-Cooper et al., 2015, p. 113). My analysis is based on Staempfli's (2017) division of the representations of climate-induced migration as a challenge or an opportunity, which in the study is referred to as an adaptation strategy. However, it is important to highlight that the same form of representation can lead to different policy proposals, and it is thus not given which solutions are proposed only based on a certain representation (Ransan-Cooper et al., 2015, p. 113).

Different Types of Climate-Induced Migration

Analysis of the policy material requires understanding the connection between climate change and migration and the different types of mobility that can arise concerning this. (Piguet et al., 2011, p. 14; Ranson-Cooper et al., 2015, p. 14) Describe three categorizations: migration as short-term or long-term, migration that takes place over short or long distances, and migration as forced or voluntary. The first categorization concerns the link between migration that occurs due to natural disasters or a slower environmental change, where those who migrate due to a slow change in the environment tend to make a longer-term movement (Piguet et al., 2011, p. 15). The second categorization is mainly linked to the difference between an internal and an international movement, where internal migration, as previously mentioned, is most common. The last variable refers to the discussion around the term "climate refugee" vs. "climate migrant" and the difficulty in capturing the exact reason behind migration as it is often multidimensional and strongly linked to the vulnerability of the migrant and society in general. Furthermore, it also connects to the distinction often made between a rapid and a slow environmental change, where the former is mainly linked to a forced movement and the latter to a higher degree of voluntariness. These categorizations become useful to distinguish when climate-induced migration is referred to in the material, as the phenomenon is rarely named directly.

Understanding how the driving forces for climate-induced migration are conceptualized also becomes relevant to distinguishing representations of climate-induced migration in the material. Brown (2008, p. 9) describes climate change as a driving force for migration that can be divided into two categories: partly climate processes, such as increased sea levels or desertification, and partly climatic events, such as floods and storms. These can be linked to the distinction often made between fast-coming disasters and slow-coming disasters, where it is mainly the first-mentioned variant treated in policy (Hugo 2012, p. 11). McLeman explains in Brown (2008, p. 17) that climate processes and events can be classified as "climate drivers" to climate-induced migration. McLeman highlights, however, that climate-induced migration is also driven by "non-climate drivers," which refer to the effect that climate change has on society to a large extent and also depends on society's vulnerability (Brown 2008, p. 18). Since a society's vulnerability to future climate-induced migration is not static but changeable and dependent also on factors that are not directly linked to increased emissions, consideration of "non-climatic drivers" is crucial (Brown 2008, p. 20). In agreement with this, many researchers highlight migration as a result of several factors or so-called "mixed flows" (Smith & McNamara, 2015, p. 49). Consequently, it is important to consider the phenomenon's complexity in the analysis.

Climate-Induced Migration as a Challenge

A prominent representation of climate-induced migration found in policy, media, and research is a challenge that needs political attention (Methmann & Oels, 2015, p. 55). Climate-induced migration is presented in this context as a failure regarding adaptation and "mitigation" (Felli, 2013, p. 340). The representation of the Problem rests largely on sensational language and is often presented in terms of a mass movement of climate refugees, where these are portrayed as a threat to global, regional, and national security (Bettini et al., 2016, p. 349; Methmann & Oels, 2015, p. 55; Ranson-Cooper et al., 2015, p. 110). One of the most well-known and well-used calculations predicting the amount of climate migrants is that of researcher Myers (1993, p. 759), who estimated that 150 million people would be forced to migrate due to climate change. Thus, the representation portrays migration as forced rather than a voluntary choice (Felli, 2013, p. 340). A myth that the challenge representation largely relies on is the connection between climate-induced migration and conflict, as migration is considered to increase conflicts over natural resources (Ransan-Cooper et al., 2015, p. 110). The solutions produced are, therefore, usually within the framework for the military, where the protection of the northern sovereign state is prioritized (Ransan-Cooper et al., 2015, p. 108ff). Some researchers believe that the representation further contributes to the already ongoing securitization of migration within the global North, which legitimizes increasingly exceptional measures, for example, in the form of tougher migration legislation and border controls (Kelman 2015, Bettini 2012:68). Even policy proposals with demands for an expanded international legal framework are advocated by actors within the representation (Bettini et al., 2016, p. 67; Felli, 2013, p. 340). By this means Bettini et al (2016, p. 352) that one of the core elements of the representation is its attention to (in)justice, where the global North is advocated to take more responsibility in dealing with the phenomenon, even if, according to the authors, the representation is still considered problematic.

In addition, one of the cornerstones of the challenge representation is a geopolitical view of the world where the rational global North is placed concerning a chaotic South in need of control (Ransan-Cooper et al., 2015, p. 110). Through this, there is a convergence between the challenge representation and the victim representation, where the affected populations are represented as victims, either in need of protection or to be feared (Bettini, 2013, p. 63; Ranson-Cooper et al., 2015, p. 110). Against this background, the migrants are constructed as passive and helpless in need of rescue from the outside. In this painted situation, the global North is often portrayed as a possible protector of helpless racialized "others" (Ransan-Cooper et al., 2015, p. 109f, Felli, 2013, p. 340). The representation itself is thus based on deep-rooted racist ideas and stereotypes about the "other" and an "us" vs. "them" dichotomy that risks replicating colonial notions of northern actors as developed and experts concerning disaster-prone countries in the South (Hartmann, 2010, p. 23; Ranson-Cooper et al., 2015, p. 109). Against the background of painting northern ideas as superior to others and creating an image of external help as necessary, the challenge representation can be considered to disregard other policy proposals.

Researchers believe there is a risk that policymakers ignore alternative policy proposals and local perspectives, leaving little room for support for the affected countries and people (Klepp & Herbeck, 2016, p. 73; Ranson-Cooper et al., 2015, p. 109). Bettini (2013, pp. 63, 69) also believes that this perspective depoliticizes and deprives the affected populations of political subjectivity by both victimizing the climate migrant and, in the same way de-individualizing him, as he is seen as just one in the large mass of "refugees." In this way, the narrative ignores the socio-ecological context that often lies behind the basic vulnerability of migrants (Bettini, 2013, p. 69). When the migrants are thereby painted as silenced "others" and helpless victims needing foreign assistance, researchers believe that the need for adaptation to climate change can be overlooked (Felli, 2013, p. 338; Remling, 2020, p. 6). Finally, according to many researchers, the challenge representation has been brought forward to increase attention to the subject. Many authors highlight, for example, how the narrative is primarily developed in and by northern actors, but that one must not forget that the representation can also be used strategically by actors who instead want to demand responsibility from Western states (Hartmann, 2010, p. 239). However, researchers warn that the representation is counterproductive as it contributes to the increased securitization of migration (Hartmann 2010). Furthermore, critics of the perspective believe that the representation is based on weak empirical evidence, a simplified understanding of climate-induced migration and that it ignores the fact that the affected populations themselves do not want to be called "refugees" (Bettini et al., 2016, p. 352; Felli, 2013, p. 338; Kelman, 2015, p. 134).

Climate-Induced Migration as an Adaptation Measure

In response to the pessimism of the challenging discourse, researchers believe that a representation of climate-induced migration as an adaptation measure has emerged in policy, media, and research (Ransan-Cooper et al., 2015, p. 112). Through this representation, climate-induced migration is no longer seen as a challenge or a security threat but is presented as a "solution" that in itself makes populations more resilient (Ransan-Cooper et al., 2015, p. 110; Methmann & Oels, 2015, p. 58). The solutions primarily generated by this representation are linked to work, circular migration, skill enhancement, and remittances (Ransan-Cooper et al., 2015, p. 111; Remling, 2020, p. 3). More specifically, migration as adaptation can be achieved by reducing movement restrictions within countries and providing infrastructure to enable movement, and internationally also by expanding the free movement of people, goods, and money (Black et al., 2011, p. 448). To further increase migration's potential, researchers believe that migration can be linked to recipient countries with a shortage of labor to create "win-win" situations where both the sending country and the receiving country benefit (Black et al., 2011, p. 449; Felli 2013., p. 351). Kiribati's former president, Anote Tong, has been considered to present this representation through his "migration with dignity" concept, where labor emigration, skill enhancement, and remittances were prioritized (Ransan-Cooper et al., 2015, p. 108, 111).

In this way, migration is presented as bringing with it several advantages. Climate-induced migration is seen, among other things, as a way to increase society's resilience by diversifying household income and generating remittances (Bettini et al., 2016, p. 352; Black et al., 2011, p. 449; Felli, 2013, p. 353). It is also highlighted that migration reduces pressure on the environment in the home countries (Ash & Campbell, 2016, p. 3). In the long run, the hope is that migration will establish networks abroad and thus simplify future migration and postpone large-scale climate-induced migration (Remling, 2020, p. 5). A premise for migration to be seen as an adaptation strategy is that it is effectively managed to minimize the risk of humanitarian crises and conflicts, as well as increase the benefits that migration can contribute (Ash & Campbell, 2016, p. 3; Black et al., 2011, p. 448). Through the representation of adaptation, the migrant is also constructed as a certain type of subject. Migrants are no longer seen as victims in need of compensation but as entrepreneurs who, with the help of their responsibility, can improve their situation, and migration is presented as a rational and voluntary choice rather than a forced movement (Felli, 2013, p. 350; Methmann & Oels, 2015, p. 59). The responsibility for creating increased resilience is placed on the individual, which is done through a connection to the global capitalist market (Methmann & Oels, 2015, p. 51; Ranson-Cooper et al., 2015, p. 111). With this, it has there has been a transition from trying to prevent movement, establishing international protection mechanisms for those who move, and assisting affected populations to increasingly formulating policies that enable and allow mobility and let them take care of themselves (Bettini et al., 2016, p. 354; Felli, 2013, p. 345; Methmann & Oels, 2015, p. 63). With this, states are no longer active actors in this process but only enablers, while the market and self-organization are the governing mechanisms (Bettini et al., 2016, pp. 351–354; Methmann & Oels, 2015, p. 60).

Although the adaptation representation is often portrayed positively, it has faced much criticism from researchers. Much of the criticism is aimed at the representation's depoliticization of climate-driven migration (Bettini, 2013; Bettini et al., 2016; Felli, 2013; Klepp, 2017). Depoliticization is seen as a result of placing the responsibility on the individual migrant to migrate, participate in the labor market, and increase their and their society's resilience. Trust in the concept of resilience is the basis for this, whereby climate-induced migration is seen as a natural consequence of climate change and thus also presented as a rational adaptation strategy (Methmann & Oels, 2015, p. 51; Remling, 2020, p. 3). This is considered to eliminate the political, as climate change is seen as a "matter of fact" rather than a social problem that can be changed through reduced emissions (Methmann & Oels, 2015, p. 51). Thus, researchers believe that a consequence of migration being represented as a natural and inevitable result of climate change may be that solutions that focus on international efforts to alleviate climate change and to adapt "in situ" may be de-prioritized (Ransan-Cooper et al., 2015, p. 111; Methmann & Oels, 2015, p. 51; Bettini et al., 2016, p. 350). Researchers also highlight that international actors thereby abdicate their responsibility for handling the situation as an unfairly large responsibility is placed on the migrants (Felli, 2013, p. 341, Bettini et al., 2016, p. 349).

As the representation is largely based on the incorporation of migrants into a wage labor market, the representation is considered to reflect neoliberal values (Ransan-Cooper et al., 2015, p. 112; Felli, 2013, p. 337; Felli & Castree, 2012, p. 3). The reason for this is that the representation attaches great importance to the responsibility of individuals in "creating a future," mainly by contributing to their workforce abroad. The neoliberal tendencies of the representation are also demonstrated in the very understanding of the concept of resilience, which has shifted from an aspiration for a collective transformation of entire systems to an individualization of the concept with a focus on individuals and households (Methmann & Oels, 2015,p. 60; Felli, 2913, p. 339). In addition, the adaptation representation has been criticized by researchers for increasing inequalities. Because the perspective primarily promotes labor migration, the recipient country's Government determines who and under what conditions people have the right to migrate (Remling, 2020, p. 6). Migration is thus preceded by a "migrant selectivity" where only those migrants who can maximize and diversify income are considered desirable (Bettini et al., 2016, p. 353). It is, therefore, mainly a small group of young, healthy, better-educated men who participate in this circular form of migration both within and from the global South, which further reinforces already existing inequalities (Bettini et al., 2016, p. 353, Remling, 2020, p. 6). In addition, the costs of migration are also high, and remittances rarely benefit the poorest communities, which can further exacerbate and cement inequalities within the population (Bettini et al., 2016, p. 353). Klepp (2017, p. 12) also believes that populations can be divided into resilient or non-resilient based on their competence, creating new discrimination against "non-resilient others."

METHOD

The What's the Problem Represented (*hereinafter* WPR) approach is an analytical discourse method that enables a critical examination of policy by examining how "problems" are represented within them (C. L. Bacchi, 2019, p. 21). The approach critically examines taken-for-granted ideas about social and political problems and the power relations these ideas create and maintain. This thinking can be applied to policy, as the policy is a proposal for change and thus a certain representation of a "problem" (Bacchi & Goodwin, 2016, p. 16). Creating a policy means that the Government has identified a particular "problem" that requires a solution, where the proposed solutions also indicate what the Government believes needs change and what constitutes a problem (Bacchi & Goodwin, 2016, p. 16). The analytical task thus becomes to question specific problematizations in policy and reveal which implicit assumptions the problem representation contains, as policy formulation is not a neutral practice (Bacchi & Goodwin, 2016, p. 16; Bacchi, 2012, p. 21). The hope is not to reveal new "truths" as this would contradict the post-structuralist foundations but rather to allow questioning (Bacchi & Goodwin, 2016, p. 16). The method is largely based on the concepts of "problematization" and "problem representation." In this context, problematization can be seen as a general questioning of something and understanding how a phenomenon is problematized (Bacchi & Goodwin, 2016, p. 16). A problem representation is, in turn, the form of problematization that is found in a certain place (Bacchi & Goodwin, 2016, p. 16). Bacchi believes that these govern us constituted problems in many ways, as a certain representation has discursive, subjectifying, and lived effects (Bacchi & Goodwin, 2016, p. 14,17). Bacchi's method allows us to access the discourse's substantial effects by showing how a certain problem representation can create both "winners" and "losers."

ANALYSIS

How does climate-induced migration appear in Kiribati's and New Zealand's national policy documents? What does the problem representation mean? Text excerpts and quotations support my interpretations. The remaining three questions analyze the assumptions, unproblematized elements, and impacts of problem representations; therefore, the study builds on previous research and the theoretical framework outlined before. Climate-induced migration policy material As indicated, neither country has a policy paper on climate-induced migration. Instead, it appears in other policy documents. The poll starts with migration and climate change policy recommendations because the analysis material doesn't always make the relationship obvious. The approach posits that climate change "solutions" and proposals simultaneously establish climate-induced migration as a "problem" to discover problem representations. Policy descriptions of problems have also influenced the analysis.

How Does Kiribati and New Zealand Policy Address Climate-Induced Migration?

The first question identifies the problem representation and shows how climate-induced migration is recognized and classed as a "problem" in the material. To identify the prevailing problem representation, work "from behind" the proposed solution to the "problem" (Bacchi & Goodwin, 2016, p. 20). The first stage is to find the "solutions" in the material that address climate-induced migration and build the phenomena as a "problem." This problem representation starts the study, although policy can have several contradictory problem representations (Bacchi & Goodwin, 2016, p. 20). The country splits problem representations for clarity.

Kiribati

Despite not mentioning climate-induced migration, Kiribati offers numerous "solutions" for managing it. This starts with identifying private and public land and property "at risk of reduction/ disappearance due to climate change impact." Strategies to financially compensate landowners for climate-related property losses are recommended to address this. Using state-owned land outside the risk zone, the land swap is another option. Identify and value non-at-risk state-owned areas for land swap compensation. Strategies for reconstructing or moving schools and essential service facilities to adapt to climate change and harsh weather occurrences are frequently documented. Throughout the content, climate change affects structures and infrastructure, not individuals. These policies involve people's movement because they mention private buildings. Thus, climate migrants are compensated. The document also addresses internal migration, the most common climate-induced movement. Urbanization drives internal migration.

"Disparities between the different islands of Kiribati" cause internal migration, displacement, and Urbanization, although the material does not specify these differences. However, the information indicates how the country's outer islanders have restricted access to labor, health, and education, making them more vulnerable. Thus, vulnerability may be a factor in island urbanization. "Urban development has been a pull factor for those seeking better job and living opportunities" is another pushing cause for internal mobility. Climate change and the desire for better jobs and living conditions drive people away from the coasts. Climate change and coastal development, notably on South Tarawa and Betio, have caused coastal erosion, forcing residents away from the coast. According to the instances above, climate change is a "push factor" to internal migration, whereas jobs and living circumstances are "pull factors." Thus, climatic change may drive internal migration and Urbanization. Urbanization is a key policy area because most internal migration occurs in cities. To decentralize the population, a "Rural Land Development Plan" is planned to encourage the growth of the country's outer islands by employing neglected land on other islands. Urban/rural profiling studies for the Rural Land Development Plan advocating the Outer Islands Growth Center Concept use neglected outer island lands to solve food security and decentralization. In addition to this decentralization plan, the Government's proposal for three "land reclamation" sites and a displacement plan to raise the earth by two meters to alleviate overpopulation promote internal displacement.

The Government has suggested three land reclamation areas in South Tarawa and Betio and a resettlement plan to raise land by two meters to address overpopulation. The paper does not elaborate on these recommendations but suggests a planned population shift within the country, which climate change may be pushing. External migration is another climate adaptation method. Despite not directly addressing climate-induced migration, Kiribati suggests many policy "solutions" for internal and external migration. The policy promotes internal and external migration, as seen above. Many internal displacement policies support housing and human displacement. Instead of Urbanization, rural migration is encouraged. This makes internal climate-induced migration difficult since it increases Urbanization, which causes water shortages and sanitation problems. Climate adaptation policies encourage labor emigration. External migration is depicted as a proactive plan to strengthen Kiribati and I-Kiribati's resilience, not as a direct result of climate change. Thus, this migration is becoming an adaptation strategy. Both views are based on a perceived lack of resilience in Kiribati and thus view the "problem" as internal.

New Zealand

Unlike Kiribati's, New Zealand's policy explicitly mentions "climate-related human mobility." The policy document emphasizes aiding Kiribati as part of the Pacific region to avoid, delay, and prepare for climate-induced migration (New Zealand Ministry of Foreign Affairs and Trade. [...] help the Pacific area prevent, delay, and prepare for climate-related human movement. To do this, Kiribati decision-makers must have access to the knowledge and science they need "to make informed decisions including on climate-related human mobility." Leaders must participate in global and regional policy talks to address regional issues like climate-induced migration. "Increase in several overseas labor markets that I-Kiribati are accessing" is one Kiribati migration target. A "skilled, competitive human resource base" allows I-Kiribati to enter more labor markets. This migration is only referenced concerning migration, not climate change. Kiribati's policy describes foreign labor migration as a climate adaptation tool, but otherwise identical. New Zealand's major climate change management "solution" emphasizes enhancing Kiribati's adaptation ability. We enhance climate change adaptation [...]. Kiribati's development depends on its adaptive capacity, which increases resilience. New Zealand believes it can enable Kiribati's climate resilience through data, lobbying, and regional dialogue. To better respond to climate change, governments need more technology and innovation.

In conclusion, New Zealand has numerous "solutions" for climate-induced migration. Most policy material seeks to help Kiribati control the situation by providing more information and science. New Zealand also wants to prevent, delay, and prepare for climate-induced migration, recognizing its difficulty. This implies that the "problem" is again "within" Kiribati. The policy emphasizes I-Kiribati's access to foreign labor markets as a positive adaptation measure, like Kiribati. Even though Kiribati lists this as an important climate adaptation method, it is not highlighted concerning climate change. New Zealand's policies don't mention climate migrants.

What Are These Climate-Induced Migration Assumptions?

The analysis question determines which taken-for-granted truths and assumptions made these problem representations feasible by finding the assumptions and discourses that make them acceptable and understandable (Bacchi & Goodwin, 2016, p. 21). Examining binary oppositions, like Said's (2014) discussion of the Occident and the Orient, and categorizations (Bacchi, 2009, p. 7) can help.

Binary

Climate-induced migration is both a problem and a solution. Both countries' materials and policy documents have this opposite pair.

Kiribati

In Kiribati, internal and external migration are depicted differently, yet both have positive and negative characteristics. Urbanization drives internal migration. Given its many drawbacks, Urbanization is generally portrayed negatively. It reduces fresh water and land availability. The inflow of outer islanders seeking better living circumstances worsens South Tarawa's water problems. Urbanization is both a threat and a vulnerability for the nation. However, internal migration for jobs and better living conditions drives

Urbanization. However, internal migration "creates problems" rather than "solves" them. For instance, moving private and public buildings may exacerbate landowner disputes.

If private buildings are moved, private landowners will fight. The policy mentions private buildings, implying people movement again. Thus, climate-induced migration may produce conflict. This suggests that climate-induced migration is seen as a challenge rather than an adaptation. Kiribati's workforce emigration strategy is increasingly seen as a beneficial adaptation measure. External migration is described by its benefits, such as improved remittances and resilience. The migration can produce "win-win" circumstances for Kiribati and the receiving country. However, some groups have "limited employment opportunities in-country and overseas, especially for youth, women, and their families." People go abroad due to a shortage of jobs in the country. Thus, external migration is both a beneficial adaptation technique and a need.

New Zealand

New Zealand policy describes climate-induced as a "challenge" and climate change as a source of conflict and uncertainty. Climate change is now a conflict and security concern because it can raise resource competition and destabilize weak governance. Kiribati's policy material implicitly links climate-induced migration and war. To "avert, delay and prepare for climate-related human mobility," Kiribati, a Pacific nation, must be supported. This shows that the policy material prevents Kiribati displacement rather than promoting migration. Thus, New Zealand policy views climate-induced migration as a problem. Labor emigration, however, can boost society's resilience. I-Kiribati should have access to more overseas labor markets. Thus, external migration is seen as a positive phenomenon that boosts economic resilience and mitigates climate change. The adaptation representation also emphasizes enhancing Kiribati's overall adaptive capacity. New Zealand's policy reflects this side of the split. Materially, the binary is apparent, but countries express it differently. Internal and external migration is increasingly portrayed as challenges and adaptation measures in Kiribati. In New Zealand, "climate-induced migration," whether internal or external, is seen as a challenge, while labor emigration from Kiribati is seen as an adaptation measure. Thus, the countries have policy material from both sides of the dichotomy, making it impossible to divide them. However, whether countries' policies view climate-induced migration as a challenge or an opportunity depends on the belief that Kiribati will be affected, that it exists and that climate change is a reality that must be addressed. Most representations assume many sites will decline and become uninhabitable (Ransan-Cooper et al., 2015, p. 113).

Topics

"Climate migrant" is a key study category. The content rarely mentions climate-induced migration or the migrant as a theme. However, the problem representations and binaries show how the migrant becomes a topic. Based on prior studies, transnational climate-induced migration is typically portrayed as an adaptation measure in the material, which may contribute to migrant subject formation. In both nations, external migration from Kiribati is seen as an adjustment tactic tied to labor emigration, whereas internal migration is linked to improved livelihood and work prospects. This depiction matches earlier research on migration as an adaptation metric. According to prior research, the adaptation representation views the migrant as an economic actor and entrepreneur who can and should integrate into the global labor market through personal responsibility and action (Methmann & Oels, 2015, p. 60, Felli 2013, p.

350). Migration is marketed as a "triple-win" that helps individuals, their home nation, and the recipient country by providing work, as demonstrated in the policy material (Felli, 2013, p. 350). The migrant is shown as a subject with agency and choice, not a victim needing compensation. Representation fits the prevailing neoliberal narrative (Ransan-Cooper et al., 2015, p. 113, Felli, 2013, p. 337).

However, both countries' policy materials portray climate-induced migration as a challenge, which many believe portrays migrants as victims needing rescue or as people to be feared (Bettini, 2013, p. 63, Ransan-Cooper et al., 2015, p. 110). Unlike the adaption story, the migrant is passive. New Zealand's portrayal of migration prevention initiatives, both countries' linking climate-induced migration to conflict, and the term "challenge" are examples of this representation. This mostly concerns internal migration in Kiribati but climate-induced migration in New Zealand. Challenge representation also portrays the global North as a prospective protector of racialized "others" as an expert and transmitter of knowledge. Thus, the portrayal can reproduce colonial views about Northern players in disaster-prone South countries (Ransan-Cooper et al., 2015, p. 109). The material largely uses this discourse to construct Kiribati and New Zealand as subjects. New Zealand has a crucial "facilitation role" in transmitting knowledge, technology, information, and money to Kiribati. Kiribati also acknowledges New Zealand's financial and technical assistance. In both situations, Kiribati is portrayed as the actor who needs outside support and must "solve" the "problem," even if New Zealand contributes. New Zealand's response to climate-induced migration receives less attention. New Zealand lacks a climate migration policy and a climate perspective on labor migration.

Instead, the countries' unity and history are emphasized. "Shared Pacific identity, historical connections, and mutual trust and respect" underpin New Zealand's material on the two countries' relationship. NZMFAT 2021:3,6. Kiribati says labor migration can benefit both countries, implying that they supply labor. Finally, Kiribati's policy material emphasizes gender. The policy literature emphasizes that climate change affects the most disadvantaged and disenfranchised, particularly women. The strategy also highlights women's limited possibilities and resources, particularly their underrepresentation in short-term agricultural labor in New Zealand and as "seafarers." Women are also one of the essential groups to build resilience. Supporting women's economic empowerment helps them and their families improve resilience to climate change by diversifying livelihoods and revenue sources. Women's and men's climate adaptation needs must be recognized to reduce climate change vulnerability. Kiribati's strategy emphasizes women's needs and possibilities, but New Zealand's does not.

What Isn't a Problem?

This inquiry helps us identify what is left out of the problem representation and, consequently, not needing change. The goal is to highlight representation silences and undermine the dominant problem representation (Bacchi & Goodwin, 2016, p. 22). To answer the question. We must compare Kiribati's and New Zealand's problem representations to understand how they differ in various situations. My interpretation is based on my past analysis, theoretical starting points, and research since what is left unproblematized can be interpreted in many ways. Policy for Kiribati's uninhabitability and displacement is omitted. Both governments ignore this. As previously indicated, New Zealand and Kiribati do not explicitly include climate-induced migration as a method for coping with this "worst-case scenario."

However, Kiribati states that "the most serious concern is that sea level rise will threaten the very existence of Kiribati as a nation," but the document does not offer any solutions. "Negative messages on the impacts of climate change (e.g., "Kiribati is sinking") [...]" can hurt investments in the country.

Thus, neither country adopts actions that might endanger Kiribati's existence. Global North's duty is also unquestioned due to New Zealand's lack of policy. Both countries' policies acknowledge that climate change is real and that Kiribati is especially affected.

The global North emitted more greenhouse gases than the Pacific islands (Clement et al., 2021, p. 226). However, the problem representation considers climate-induced migration a "problem" that can be solved in Kiribati. New Zealand surrenders some of the responsibility for managing climate-induced migration by portraying itself as an "enabler" who will help Kiribati become more resilient. "Avert, delay, and prepare for climate-related human mobility" is their policy. Labor emigration is mostly promoted as a positive adaptation option, shifting climate adaptation duty to the individual migrant. Even though geopolitical and diplomatic ties will largely determine I-Kiribati's migration options, global responsibility and "loss and damage" are not addressed in the content.

Finally, the material ignores non-migrants. Kiribati's strategy recognizes disadvantaged populations' limited adaptation capacity but does not label them as unable to move. New Zealand policy lacks this viewpoint. The previous study demonstrates that the most marginalized in communities have the least chance of migrating, creating "trapped populations" (Oakes et al., 2016, p. 57). This demands more on citizens by pushing labor emigration as an adaptive strategy and opportunity. Transnational migration excludes those without resources or international networks (Hugo, 2012, p. 26). Remling (2020, p. 6) claims that such policies benefit a youthful, well-educated elite and overlook the most vulnerable. Thus, most of the people who need migration are unproblematized.

This Climate-Induced Migratory Portrayal Has What Effects?

The inquiry investigates the consequences of the problem representation and is crucial to resolving the second research question (Bacchi & Goodwin, 2016, p. 20). Bacchi distinguishes discursive, subjectifying, and lived consequences. Discursive effects are studied to highlight which action options are less plausible based on representation. Because problem representations produce unique subject positions, they suggest how climate-induced migration management should be distributed (Bacchi, 2009, p. 17). The problem representation has lived impacts, showing how discourses affect people's lives. Bacchi (2009) emphasizes policy implications rather than measured outcomes. I answer the question using past analysis, theory, and research. Based on the prevalent representation of climate-induced migration as an adaptation mechanism, transnational migration policy progressively enables, promotes, and permits mobility (Bettini et al., 2016, p. 354, Felli, 2013, p. 345). In the descriptions above, external migration is emphasized as an adaptation technique, but internal displacement in Kiribati is also mentioned. Migration is depicted as a natural result of climate change, which researchers feel can lead to an excessive acceptance of climate change as a "matter of fact" that cannot be prevented (Ransan-Cooper et al. 2015:111). This can distract from international climate change mitigation and in-situ adaptation efforts by encouraging impacted populations to help themselves (Ransan-Cooper et al., 2015, p. 111; Methmann & Oels, 2015, p. 63). Discursive effect

If migration is the only adaptation strategy, numerous mitigating and adaptation alternatives are missed. The problem depiction of climate-induced migration as an adaptation strategy subjectifies. As previously stated, the problem representation views the migrant as an "entrepreneurial subject" who must adjust to a changing climate by working overseas. Subjectifying effects result from presenting climate change as inevitable rather than a societal problem that wealthy economies can solve by reducing their emissions (Methmann & Oels, 2015, p. 51). The subject structure implies that those affected by the Problem must modify their situation rather than the global North's lifestyles and energy systems (Methmann & Oels, 2915, p. 53). Thus, affected communities, not states in the global North, adapt to climate change. The portrayal does what Bacchi (2009, p. 17) warns against making impacted communities responsible for "their own" "problems." Because discursive and subjectifying effects have lived effects, Bacchi (2009:xviii) emphasizes the need to research discourses' tangible repercussions. In this scenario, problem representations affect migration chances and are carried to their extreme. It may affect people's life and death. I-Kiribati, who rarely migrate, are most affected by this. According to the adaptation representation, each migrant is responsible for their adaptation. However, research has shown that people most in need of migration rarely have the chance to migrate (Oakes et al., 2016, p. 57; Hugo, 2010, p. 26; Remling, 2020, p. 6).

Since the receiving state sets migration conditions, migrants' freedom to choose and a chance to migrate are likewise limited (Remling, 2020, p. 6). The marginalized groups' ability to migrate when their home environments become uninhabitable due to climate change is affected when the adaptation representation places the responsibility for adaptation on the individual and the market rather than the sending state and the international community. Policy approaches highlighting climate-induced migration as an issue generally call for international accountability and a legal framework (Bettini, 2012, p. 67, Felli, 2013, p. 340). "Solutions" are generally military-based (Ransan-Cooper et al., 2015, p. 110). However, these solution offers are not found in the policy literature, which mostly aligns with the adaptation representation. However, New Zealand's intention to restrict migration, both countries' connection between climate-induced migration and conflict, and a general categorization of the Problem as a "challenge" depict it. The challenge representation can have discursive repercussions since it elevates northern ideas and actors. Policymakers ignore 'alternative policy proposals' because they ignore the local context and the impacted populations' perspectives (Klepp & Herbeck, 2016, p. 55,73; Ransan-Cooper et al., 2015, p. 109). The post-colonial creation of a "us" and a "them" where the migrant is also represented as passive, without agency, and in need of external help differs from the representation of adaptation in such a way that a greater part of the responsibility is transferred to the global North, despite the problematic construction of the migrant as a subject. Effects last. Even if the global North is encouraged to take more responsibility, migration requirements, and border controls are strengthened when migrants are portrayed as a threat, making migration for I-Kiribati more difficult (Bettini 2012, p. 68). Thus, both representations have serious ramifications.

DISCUSSION AND CONCLUSION

The chapter discusses the analysis results and further develops its most important findings. Furthermore, the essay's two questions are answered in the conclusion, and suggestions for further research are given.

Closing Discussion

The analysis results show that the problem representations previously identified in the research, where climate-induced migration is seen as a challenge and an adaptation strategy, can be found in the countries' policy materials but are expressed differently. The representation of climate-induced migration as a challenge is manifested primarily in policy concerning Kiribati's internal migration and the country's Urbanization and New Zealand's more general description of the phenomenon. The representation of climate-induced migration as an adaptation strategy is found primarily in policies regarding transnational migration in Kiribati and New Zealand's policy materials and is primarily linked to labor migration. However, that the countries' policy materials would contain these representations is not surprising, as previous studies have identified the representations as dominant in policy (Ransan-Cooper et al., 2015, p. 113). Furthermore, Bacchi (2019) also highlights that several different and often conflicting problem representations are common, and the existence of both representations was thus conceivable.

The analysis results presented above indicate that it is impossible to make a clear division between the countries' representations of climate-induced migration, but they hold policy material linked to both representations. This suggests that the countries' different relationship to the phenomenon does not seem to affect the problem representation found in the policy. Drawing this conclusion based on the essay's limited analysis, in terms of scope and material, is not considered fully fair. An explanation for the result could be based on the fact that the representations of climate-induced migration were largely developed in the global North and then reflected in the representations of the global South (Ransan-Cooper et al., 2015, p. 113). This would thus explain the presence of similar problem representations in Kiribati and New Zealand. Even though similar problem representations are found in the countries, they take different expressions and carry implications. The analysis highlights, for example, how they found challenge representation contributes to a certain subject construction of the countries as actors. The problem representation presents the relationship between New Zealand and Kiribati as unequal. New Zealand represents the phenomenon as a challenge rather than an adaptation strategy to a greater extent than Kiribati. This is exemplified by the representation of climate-induced migration as a 'problem' found 'within' Kiribati, whereby New Zealand presents itself as an 'expert.'

To some extent, this can be considered to reflect and replicate colonial notions of a developed and rational global North concerning an underdeveloped global South, similar to Said's (2014) dichotomy of the Occident and the Orient. Remling (2020:6) believes, for example, that through this climate, migrants are once again reduced to "recipients of help" rather than actors with choices, as they continue to be portrayed as needing help from the outside. Through this representation, New Zealand thus creates its self-image in the contemporary construction of Kiribati as needing help, and vice versa. Concerning this, other differences in the countries' policy material and problem representations become important, such as the amount of policy material that concerns the phenomenon. Kiribati's policy in the area is more comprehensive than New Zealand's, even though both countries lack policies specifically for climate-induced migration. This speaks for the importance of the phenomenon and the country's intention in dealing with it. Equally important is that labor migration between countries is described from different perspectives. Kiribati describes labor migration as a proactive climate adaptation strategy, while New Zealand omits the climate link in its policy. This is of particular importance as the problem representation of transnational migration primarily affects the relationship between the countries. Through this, it is possible to show how the phenomenon is increasingly left unproblematized in New Zealand's policy and how the identified problem representations thus reflect a post-colonial power asymmetry.

The analysis also highlights how the migrant is constructed as a certain type of subject through the problem representation that sees climate-induced migration as an adaptation strategy. Since, as previously mentioned, it is mainly the problem representation with connection to transnational migration that affects the relationship between the countries, it is mainly this that is discussed below. As previously explained, this representation rests largely on a neoliberal framework, where the "solution" to climate-induced migration is individualized by making the individual migrant bear responsibility for the creation of their resilience through participation in a global capitalist market ((Methmann & Oels, 2015, p. 51; Ransan-

Cooper et al., 2015, p. 111). This is why the policy is increasingly formulated that enables, promotes, and permits mobility (Bettini et al., 2016, p. 354, Felli, 2013, p. 345). This means that the responsibility for handling climate-induced migration is transferred from being handled at an international level to being transferred to the global South and the individual migrant. This implies that Kiribati and New Zealand are no longer active actors in this process but only enablers, while the market and self-organization are the governing mechanisms (Bettini et al. 2016:351-4; Methmann & Oels 2015:60). This can be considered to reflect the depoliticization mentioned before in the context, where less focus is placed on the Global North's ability to reduce emissions because the responsibility is placed on the migrant as an individual (Bettini 2013; Bettini et al. 2016; Felli 2013; Klepp 2017).

This is also demonstrated by the fact that global responsibility is left unproblematized in the material. As it is mainly countries in the Global North that have contributed to the global emissions of greenhouse gases, while Pacific islands like Kiribati are exposed to the greatest risks in terms of a changed climate, the question of how responsibility should be distributed for the effects this entails becomes particularly relevant (Klepp 2017:12f; Clement et al. 2021:226). Researchers have previously argued for the benefits of the adaptation representation, as it attributes greater agency to the migrant. Despite this seemingly positive aspect, the representation of adaptation entails other discriminatory practices and life effects, especially for the often-marginalized groups who do not have the opportunity to migrate. The neoliberal perspective does not portray the migrant as a victim needing compensation but as a rational, entrepreneurial actor (Felli, 2013, p. 350). Klepp (2017, p. 12) believes, for example, that populations can be divided into either resilient or non-resilient based on their competence, which is considered to create new discrimination against "non-resilient others." This can be linked to the post-colonial theoretical framework and the creation of an "us" and a "them." One can also discuss how much "freedom" the migrant has when it is still the receiving country that determines the conditions for the migration, according to the "migrant selectivity" described earlier.

The (un)ability of marginalized groups to migrate was also left unproblematized in the policy material. On the one hand, no policy directly deals with climate-induced migration, and it is not even mentioned as a phenomenon in Kiribati's policy material. This shows major shortcomings in the handling of the phenomenon. In addition, the countries' policy proposals also reflect a broader trend of depoliticization and neo-liberalization of adaptations to climate change. This trend is illustrated, for example, in the understanding of the concepts of adaptation and resilience, which no longer refer to a collective, political, and social process, but to a transformation of individuals to adapt better and become more resilient (Felli, 2013, p. 350). In this context, we see increasing importance placed on individual climate adaptation through lifestyle changes while companies and states continue with "business as usual." In this context, this can be interpreted as the need for "mitigation" to climate change being put aside when climate change and its consequences are understood as a natural and unstoppable phenomenon, where more focus is placed on adaptation measures (Castles, 2014, p. 240). That the management of the phenomenon is left to the individual goes against the global and cross-border nature of both climate change and migration, and thus also the need for global and cross-border policy proposals to manage these.

CONCLUSION

The study's primary purpose was to examine and compare how climate-induced migration is represented in Kiribati's and New Zealand's national policy documents and the implications of the identified problem representations. The study was based on Kiribati's particularly vulnerable situation as a low-lying island nation in the Pacific and the country's relationship with New Zealand. The analysis was based on two previously established representations of climate-induced migration: a challenge and an adaptation measure. To examine the countries' problem representations, Bacchi's (2012) approach, "What's the problem represented to be?" was used. In an analysis of four public policy documents from the countries. The analysis was guided throughout by the two research questions:

- How is climate-induced migration represented in Kiribati's and New Zealand's national policy documents?
- What are the implications of the identified problem representation?

In light of the analysis and discussion above, it appears that representations of climate-induced migration as a challenge and an adaptation measure were identified in Kiribati's and New Zealand's problem representations. The challenge representation was primarily identified in policy concerning Kiribati's internal migration and New Zealand's more general description of the phenomenon. The adaptation representation was mainly found in policy regarding transnational migration, specifically labor migration, in both countries. Despite the similar representations of the countries, the concluding discussion highlights how these carry implications. The essay partly shows how the countries' problem representations replicate colonial tendencies and the creation of "the other" by presenting the relationship between the two countries. The neoliberal foundations of problem representation, which place the responsibility for creating increased resilience and adaptation on the individual, also risk creating new forms of discrimination, particularly affecting already marginalized groups. The problem representation thus also reflects a broader trend of neo-liberalization and depoliticization of climate adaptation measures. This clearly shows the implications of Problem representations, which constitute important starting points in the continued study of climate-induced migration and the management of the phenomenon.

The study has contributed to understanding the relationship between policy and climate-induced relationship, which is of great importance in terms of the continued impact of climate change on the environment and societies. However, the essay's analysis is only a snapshot of the countries' representations, as discourses constantly change (Bacchi & Goodwin, 2016, p. 4). This, combined with the fact that only a few official policy documents were analyzed, limits the ability to draw general conclusions about the countries' full problem representations based on this paper alone. The analysis results should therefore be understood concerning the essay's limitations and boundaries. Furthermore, the results have been largely influenced by the choice of conceptual framework, i.e., the representations on which the analysis was based. When choosing other representations as a starting point, other perspectives could also have been found and thus other analysis results. The same can be said regarding the essay's theoretical starting point. Overall, the essay has contributed to a deeper understanding of the relationship and dynamics between two countries with different relationships to climate-induced migration and whether and how it is reflected in problem representations in the policy.

FURTHER RESEARCH

Finally, expanding knowledge regarding the assumptions and limitations of problem representations is of great importance to understanding climate-induced migration, and research in the subject area needs further development. It would be interesting to expand the material to other than official policy documents to gain a more extensive understanding of the country's problem representations and the larger discourse. An analysis that includes the media debate and interviews with relevant actors would have been fruitful as a suggestion. Furthermore, it would have been interesting to investigate the management of climate-induced migration at different levels of governance and in a larger geographical scope, for example, by comparing regional or international policy frameworks and national policy within the Pacific region.

REFERENCES

Ash, J., & Campbell, J. (2016). Climate change and migration: The case of the Pacific Islands and Australia. *Pacific Studies, 36*(1), 36. doi:10.33318/jpacs.2016.36(1)-4

Bacchi, C. (2009). *Analysing Policy: What's the Problem Represented To Be?* Bacchi, C., & Goodwin, S. (2016). *Poststructural Policy Analysis: A Guide to Practice*. Palgrave Macmillan.

Bacchi, C. L. (2019). Introducing the 'What's the Problem Represented to be?' Approach. In Introducing the 'What's the Problem Represented to be?' Approach (pp. 427–430). Verlag. doi:10.1515/9783839437322-031

Bettini, G. (2013). Climate Barbarians at the Gate? A critique of apocalyptic narratives on 'climate refugees.'. *Geoforum, 45*, 63–72. doi:10.1016/j.geoforum.2012.09.009

Bettini, G., Nash, S. L., & Gioli, G. (2016). One step forward, two steps back? The fading contours of (in)justice in competing discourses on climate migration. *The Geographical Journal, 183*(4), 348–358. doi:10.1111/geoj.12192

Black, R., Bennett, S. R. G., Thomas, S. M., & Beddington, J. R. (2011). Climate change: migration as adaptation. *Nature, 478*(7370), 447–449. doi:10.1038/478477a PMID:22012304

Brown, O. (2008). *Migration and Climate Change*. IOM migration Research Series. doi:10.18356/26de4416-en

Castles, S. (2014). International migration at a crossroads. *Citizenship Studies, 18*(2), 190–207. doi:10.1080/13621025.2014.886439

Clement, V., Rigaud, K. K., de Sherbinin, A., Jones, B., Adamo, S., Schewe, J., Sadiq, N., & Shabahat, E. (2021). *Groundswell Part 2: Acting on Internal Climate migration*. World Bank. https://openknowledge.worldbank.org/handle/10986/36248

Felli, R. (2013). Managing Climate Insecurity by Ensuring Continuous Capital Accumulation: 'Climate Refugees' and 'Climate Migrants.'. *New Political Economy, 18*(3), 337–363. doi:10.1080/13563467.2012.687716

Hansen, L. (2019). Post-structuralism. In *The Globalization of World Politics* (pp. 177–191). Oxford University Press. https://www.oxfordpoliticstrove.com/display/10.1093/hepl/9780198825548.001.0001/hepl-9780198825548-chapter-11 doi:10.1093/hepl/9780198825548.003.0011

Hartmann, B. (2010). Rethinking climate refugees and climate conflict: Rhetoric, reality and the politics of policy discourse. *Journal of International Development*, *22*(2), 233–246. doi:10.1002/jid.1676

Hugo, G. (2010). Climate change-induced mobility and the existing migration regime in Asia and the Pacific. In J. McAdam (Ed.), *Climate change and displacement: Multidisciplinary Perspectives*. Hart Publishing. http://hdl.handle.net/2440/63904

Kelman, I. (2015). Difficult decisions: migration from Small Island Developing States under climate change. *Earth's Future*, *3*(4), 133–142. doi:10.1002/2014EF000278

Klepp, S. (2017). *Climate Change and migration—An overview, Oxford Research Encyclopedia of Climate Science*. Oxford Research Encyclopedia of Climate Science.

Klepp, S., & Herbeck, J. (2016). The politics of environmental migration and climate justice in the Pacific region. *Journal of Human Rights and the Environment*, *7*(1), 54–73. doi:10.4337/jhre.2016.01.03

Methmann, C., & Oels, A. (2015). From 'fearing' to 'empowering' climate refugees: Governing climate-induced migration in the name of resilience. *Security Dialogue*, *46*(1), 51–68. https://www.jstor.org/stable/26292938. doi:10.1177/0967010614552548

Myers, N. (1993). Environmental Refugees in a Globally Warmed World. *Bioscience*, *43*(11), 752–761. doi:10.2307/1312319

Oakes, R., Milan, A., & Campbell, J. (2016). *Kiribati: Climate Change And Migration Relationships Between Household Vulnerability, Human Mobility And Climate Change Report*. Research Gate. doi doi:10.13140/RG.2.2.11824.05122

Piguet, E., Pécoud, A., & de Guchteneire, P. (2011). migration and Climate Change: An Overview. *Refugee Survey Quarterly*, *30*(3), 1–23. https://www.jstor.org/stable/45054544. doi:10.1093/rsq/hdr006

Ranson-Cooper, H., Farbotko, C., & McNamara, K. (2015). Being(s) framed: The means and ends of framing environmental migrants. *Global Environmental Change*, *35*, 106–115. doi:10.1016/j.gloenvcha.2015.07.013

Remling, E. (2020). migration as climate adaptation? Exploring discourses amongst development actors in the Pacific Island region. *Regional Environmental Change*, *20*(1), 3. doi:10.100710113-020-01583-z

Sabaratnam, M. (2020). Post-colonial and decolonial approaches. In *The Globalization of World Politics* (pp. 160–176). Oxford University Press., https://www.oxfordpoliticstrove.com/display/10.1093/hepl/9780198825548.001.0001/hepl-9780198825548-chapter-10

Said, E. W. (2014). *Orientalism*. Knopf Doubleday Publishing Group.

Smith, R., & McNamara, K. (2015). Future migrations from Tuvalu and Kiribati: Exploring Government, civil society and donor perceptions. *Climate and Development*, *7*(1), 47–59. Advance online publication. doi:10.1080/17565529.2014.900603

Staempfli, F. (2017). *Framing Environmental migration—An Analysis of Indian Government Policies*. Semantic Scholar. https://www.semanticscholar.org/paper/Framing-Environmental-migration-An-Analysis-of-Staempfli/feae85c24f8897610171e5389b545c9296f196b6

Thornton, F., James, S., Dun, O., Farbotko, C., McNamara, K. E., McMichael, C., Coelho, S., Kim, R. M., Ngo, L., & Westbury, T. (2021). *Policy developments and options to address human mobility in the context of climate risk in the Pacific Islands region*. eSpace Library. https://espace.library.uq.edu.au/view/UQ:f9872cf

Velho, A., & Thomas Olalde, O. (2016). *Othering and its effects: Exploring the concept*.

Vogler, J. (n.d.). Environmental issues. In J. Baylis, S. Smith, & P. Owens (Eds.), *The Globalization of World Politics* (pp. 387–403). Oxford University Press. https://www.oxfordpoliticstrove.com/display/10.1093/hepl/9780198825548.001.0001/hepl-9780198825548-chapter-24

Wyett, K. (2014). Escaping a Rising Tide: Sea Level Rise and migration in Kiribati. *Asia & the Pacific Policy Studies*, *1*(1), 171–185. doi:10.1002/app5.7

ADDITIONAL READING

de Sherbinin, A., Grace, K., McDermid, S., van der Geest, K., Puma, M. J., & Bell, A. (2022). Migration Theory in Climate Mobility Research. *Frontiers in Climate, 4*. https://www.frontiersin.org/articles/10.3389/fclim.2022.882343

Ghosh, R. C., & Orchiston, C. (2022). A systematic review of climate migration research: Gaps in existing literature. *SN Social Sciences*, *2*(5), 47. doi:10.100743545-022-00341-8

Hari, V., Dharmasthala, S., Koppa, A., Karmakar, S., & Kumar, R. (2021). Climate hazards are threatening vulnerable migrants in Indian megacities. *Nature Climate Change*, *11*(8), 8. doi:10.103841558-021-01105-7

Hoffmann, R., Šedová, B., & Vinke, K. (2021). Improving the evidence base: A methodological review of the quantitative climate migration literature. *Global Environmental Change*, *71*, 102367. doi:10.1016/j.gloenvcha.2021.102367

Jaswal, P. S., & Jolly, S. (2013). Climate Refugees: Challenges and Opportunities for International Law. *Journal of the Indian Law Institute*, *55*(1), 45–58. https://www.jstor.org/stable/43953626

Leal-Arcas, R. (2012). Climate Migrants: Legal Options. *Procedia: Social and Behavioral Sciences*, *37*, 86–96. doi:10.1016/j.sbspro.2012.03.277

Milán-García, J., Caparrós-Martínez, J. L., Rueda-López, N., & de Pablo Valenciano, J. (2021). Climate change-induced migration: A bibliometric review. *Globalization and Health*, *17*(1), 74. doi:10.118612992-021-00722-3 PMID:34217341

KEY TERMS AND DEFINITIONS

Climate-Induced Migration: The process of human migration that is primarily motivated by the impacts of climate change, such as rising sea levels, extreme weather events, and environmental degradation. It refers to the movement of individuals or communities from one location to another in response to the adverse effects of climate change.

Internal Migration: The movement of people within the borders of a country from one region or place to another. In the context of climate-induced migration, internal migration refers to the relocation of individuals or communities within their own country due to the effects of climate change.

Neoliberalization: The process of adopting and promoting neoliberal economic policies, which emphasize free markets, privatization, deregulation, and individual responsibility. Neoliberalization in the context of climate-induced migration refers to the tendency to place the burden of resilience and adaptation on individuals and communities, potentially exacerbating inequalities and discriminations, particularly affecting marginalized groups.

Power Asymmetries: Unequal distribution of power and influence between different individuals, groups, or countries. Power asymmetries in the context of climate-induced migration refer to the disparities in resources, capabilities, and decision-making authority between nations in the global North (developed countries) and South (developing countries) regarding their historical contributions to greenhouse gas emissions and the consequences they face due to climate change.

Problem Representations: The ways in which an issue or problem is conceptualized, understood, and presented in policy documents, public discourse, and academic research. Problem representations shape policy responses and public perceptions, influencing how the phenomenon of climate-induced migration is addressed and the measures that are proposed to manage it.

Transnational Migration: The movement of people across international borders, involving the change of residence and often the change of citizenship. In the context of climate-induced migration, transnational migration refers to the movement of individuals or communities from one country to another, primarily driven by climate-related factors.

Chapter 10
Shaping and Reshaping Legislators' Understanding and Forecasting Capacity to Vote Legal Instruments for Sustainable Energy

Isidore E. Agbokou
https://orcid.org/0000-0003-1225-9311
Ecole des Hautes Etudes Internationales et Politiques de l'académie de Paris, France

ABSTRACT

The development of renewable energies and technological progress offer new possibilities for project operators. In particular, the gradual interconnection of off-grid systems and mini-grids could prove to be more suited to economic constraints and local socio-demographic specificities, leading to long-term energy systems that differ from the current centralized systems of industrialized countries. The objective of universal access to energy poses the challenge of disseminating large-scale competitive, sustainable, and affordable energy solutions for end users. Thus, legislators must fully understand issues and challenges within the energy sector and post-2030 development prospects. This chapter will cover areas in Benin to guide legislators on robust and relevant energy acts for the future. This includes commitments for the sound implementation of the Paris Agreement and sustainable development.

INTRODUCTION: SHAPING AND RESHAPING LEGISLATORS' UNDERSTANDING AND FORECASTING CAPACITY TO VOTE LEGAL INSTRUMENTS TO THE BENEFIT OF SUSTAINABLE ENERGY IN THE POST-2030 ERA IN BENIN

Sustainable development has undergone a paradoxical evolution over the last few decades. It became an unavoidable watchword in the 1990s. However, in the 2000s, it experienced a certain decline. Following

DOI: 10.4018/978-1-6684-9272-7.ch010

the failure of the Rio+20 Conference, the movement seems to be accelerating and the term "sustainable development" is gradually being replaced by "ecological transition" (Boutaud, 2013). The latter seems marked by a transformational principle that trends to a "greening of the economy" rather than an "economization of ecological issues." Indeed, the development model of the past is resource-intensive accompanied by rising costs, lost productivity, and disrupted economic activity.

Estimates based on the International Labour Organization's Global Economic Linkages (GEL) model show that if the scenario remains unchanged, productivity levels in 2030 will be 2.4% lower than today and 7.2% lower by 2050. These estimates are consistent with the findings of several studies that assess the economic damages associated with environmental degradation and loss of basic ecosystem services. The result is a shake-up of the world economy, with slowing effects on the major variables of the short-term economic policy of many countries.

According to Kaldor's magic square theory, the cyclical policy of a country is represented graphically by four variables: (1) economic growth; (2) employment; (3) trade balance; and (4) prices. Governments normally set a target for each variable, including strong growth, full employment, trade surplus, and price stability. By connecting these variables (or objectives), it can be easy to obtain a quadrilateral that represents a favorable economic situation. Yet, it is difficult to achieve all four objectives simultaneously. Strong growth, for example, leads to an overheating of the economy and, therefore, inflation. Thus, there exists a "conflict of objectives" that political authorities must arbitrate. Obviously, by locking ourselves into this theory, it is noticeable that any disturbance at the global level of the economy will have consequences on each of the variables and would, therefore, constitute a major deficiency in the unbridled search for development. In addition, there would be impacts to the economic growth of countries, with adverse environmental effects and a pronounced depletion of natural resources. Thus, alongside the results of development and strong growth by national economies, there are degrading environmental exploits and a certain collapse of the environmental ecosystem (ILO, 2013).

The political economy of Benin integrates in its architecture the various factors of the transformation of the traditional economic logic toward a more rational, respectful logic of the environment with a pronounced impact on public policies like the energy policy. Without being mistaken, Benin has understood that access to energy is the foundation of economic development. In fact, the transformational process of the economy calls for an energy transition adapted to current realities. However, the implementation of the energy transition aims to influence the trajectory of the economy to reduce greenhouse gas (GHG) emissions compared to its spontaneous evolution. This policy can mobilize a variety of instruments, including taxation of carbon emissions, quota trading system, regulation, and financial incentives to guide behavior. This reflection is produced to enlighten decisionmakers—legislators, technical and financial partners, and private sector actors—on the potential risks and obstacles likely to hinder initiatives to accelerate the energy transition and increase access to energy.

This insight targeted parliamentarians due to their range of tools to promote the development of renewable energy generation and, where policy space permits, establish the framework required to mitigate or remove obstacles. The entry points of legislators in renewable energy are linked to key functions of parliamentarian actions that consist of:

- Legislative: Parliamentarians examine bills and amendments submitted to the vote of their institution. In parliamentary systems like Benin, parliamentarians also take an active part in the elaboration of new laws.

- Oversight: This is the process by which parliamentarians oversee the activities and executive power expenditures. This action ensures accountability and the implementation of effective implementation of laws passed by Parliament.
- Representational: As elected members, parliamentarians are accountable to citizens. It is their responsibility to engage in dialogue with citizens to ensure that their parliamentary actions reflect the concerns and aspirations of their constituents.

This analysis seeks to highlight risks or obstacles (political, commercial, and market) to the intensification of actions aimed at closing the energy access deficit and accelerating the energy transition. Uncertainties and hazards in the sustained system of energy transition in Benin will be explored. First, the diagnostic examination highlights the role of energy in the economy. Second, it correlates current and future vulnerability of the energy sector and energy transition parameters to identify constraints related to transforming energy into a cleaner, more environmentally and ecologically responsible system. This perspective aims to guide legislators' actions as they boost the energy transition in Benin in the post-2030 agenda.

POLITICAL ECONOMY OF THE ENERGY SECTOR

Energy in the Economy

Access to energy determines the satisfaction of meeting basic social needs related to water, food, health, and education. The African continent, however, lags in access to energy in rural areas (extremely low electrification rates) and urban areas (security problems surrounding supply).

Although Africa boasts 14% of the world's population, the continent consumes only 3% of the world energy. In sub-Saharan Africa, average consumption is 92% lower than the world average. It is 97% lower than European consumption (Ministry of Energy Strategic Plan, 2020-2024). This observation provides a glimpse of the energy barrier that separates Africa from the rest of the world, especially from developed countries.

The energy sector of Benin, a country in sub-Saharan Africa, is characterized by high dependence on the traditional use of biomass (firewood and charcoal), high dependence on sources for electrical energy supplies, low access to electricity (particularly in rural areas), total dependence on the outside world for supplies of petroleum products, and a significant untapped potential for renewable energies. Indeed, like most countries in sub-Saharan Africa, Benin's energy sector is dominated by petroleum products and traditional energy sources. The use of traditional biomass products like wood energy and charcoal represent about 46% of Benin's energy balance per data from the Benin 2017 Energy Information System (EIS) report. This falls just behind products consumed at 52%. Electricity use is about 2%, while butane gas remains minor and limited to urban areas. According to the results of the fourth General Population and Housing Census (RGPH 4, 2013), only 5% of households use gas for cooking, while 84.8% use wood or charcoal.

This situation creates constant pressure on forest resources, with serious consequences for the environment and health of populations, mainly women and children. In fact, the adverse effects of climate change have become important issues, impacting areas of development like agriculture, water, health, and the environment.

Electricity plays a crucial role in the provision of basic social services, including education and health, where lack of energy is often an obstacle to sterilization, water supply and purification, sanitation and hygiene, and the refrigeration of essential drugs. Electricity can also run machinery that supports income-generating opportunities. Examples include pumping water in agriculture, food processing, garment manufacturing, and light industries.

In rural areas, the lack of modern energy services can discourage skilled workers (i.e., teachers, doctors, nurses, and extension workers) from settling, further limiting the services and opportunities available to local populations. Villages, towns, and cities experience an insufficient supply of reliable and affordable energy, braking income-generating industrial, commercial, and service activities.

The juxtaposition of these elements allows us to explore different types of renewable energy in use or in sight in Benin. Indeed, renewable energies include those that result from natural, renewable processes as opposed to fossil, non-renewable, exhaustible energy sources. Renewable resources include biomass, hydraulic, geothermal, wind, solar, and marine. Benin has great potential in renewable energies; however, this is under-exploited except for the traditional form of biomass-energy that constitutes firewood. The penetration rate of renewable energies, therefore, remains low. In 2017, renewable energy accounted for only 9.84% of total electricity supply. The share of solar represents 0.48%. Hydroelectric power plants represent 9.36% (DGE, SIE Report 2017).

In 2018, 45% of Africa's primary energy demand was met by biomass, mainly in the form of firewood and charcoal for cooking (IEA, 2019b). This, however, has serious negative repercussions. Indoor air pollution causes 490,000 premature deaths per year in sub-Saharan Africa (WHO, 2018). The risk of exposure is particularly high among women and young children, who spend the most time in the household. On the other hand, non-sustainable logging leads to deforestation and environmental degradation. See Figure 1.

Figure 1. Primary energy demand in africa by source
Source: From La transition vers les énergies renouvelables en Afrique, 2021

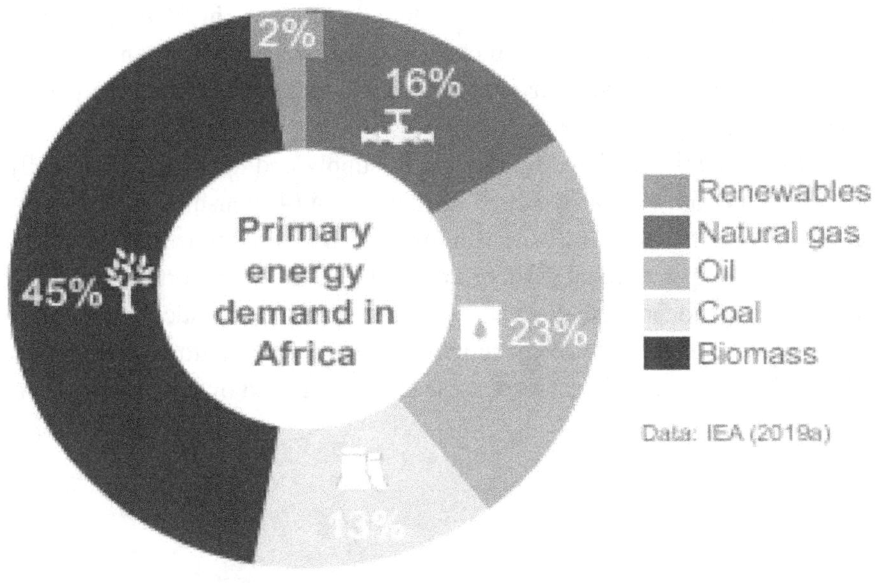

CLIMATE CHANGE: CURRENT AND FUTURE VULNERABILITY AND VARIABILITY OF THE ENERGY SECTOR

Climate change affects macroeconomic outcomes through physical and transition risks. Physical risks arise from gradual changes in temperature or rainfall and seasonal patterns that impact crops and labor productivity. In addition, sudden events, such as extreme weather (i.e., droughts, forest fires, hurricanes, and floods) are becoming more frequent and severe. These can directly affect consumption, investment, and trade. Transition risks arise from the adjustment of asset prices in response to climate policies and technological changes during the transition to a low-carbon economy. Many countries like Benin are facing transition challenges to manage the potential negative impacts of national and international adaptation and mitigation policies on equity, labor markets, or external competitiveness. The introduction of global carbon prices and other mitigation efforts have negative effects on fossil fuel exporters and carbon-intensive activities.

Thus, the analysis of physical and transition risks must be systematically included in macroeconomic management. The diagnostics in this policy brief will help governments design and implement smart macroeconomic policies in the face of climate change. First, it will integrate climate considerations into main macroeconomic work and macro projections through the development of macro-models at the national level. Using a climate lens, it will assess the impact of climate shocks and climate policies on macroeconomic outcomes and fiscal sustainability. Second, it will design fiscally viable climate strategies through the introduction of tailored and politically viable environmental tax reforms that use revenues to maximize the ancillary benefits of development. Third, it will link environmental tax reforms to public investments in adaptation and measures aimed at maintaining budgetary room for maneuvers and alleviating borrowing constraints.

By focusing on the diagnosis of current and future climate vulnerability of the energy sector in relation to agriculture, food, water, land, towns, transportation, and the manufacturing industry, we put our finger on the global climate problem from which the planet suffers. These prioritized sectors, thus, contribute the most to emissions by generating more than 90% of global emissions gas.

The lack of just transition measures to reduce global emissions threatens economic and political stability. We must urgently address these problems, as world leaders find themselves confronted with a convergence of crises related to the climate emergency, a global pandemic, inequalities, and loss of confidence in democracy.

The energy sector, which is regulated by the law of supply and demand, is generally grouped into four segments: (1) production; (2) transport; (3) demand; and (4) consumption. The Beninese energy sector is characterized by a strong dependence on imports and a preponderance of the consumption of biomass energy (fuelwood and charcoal). According to the 2015 EIS report, energy performance indicators show an energy dependency rate of 41.3% and an electricity dependency rate of 76%. Regarding consumption, the structure of the net energy supply shows a complete dominance by biomass energy, with 59% justifying the pressure on forest resources. This is followed by petroleum products, representing 38% (see Figure 2).

Figure 2. Energy consumption by type

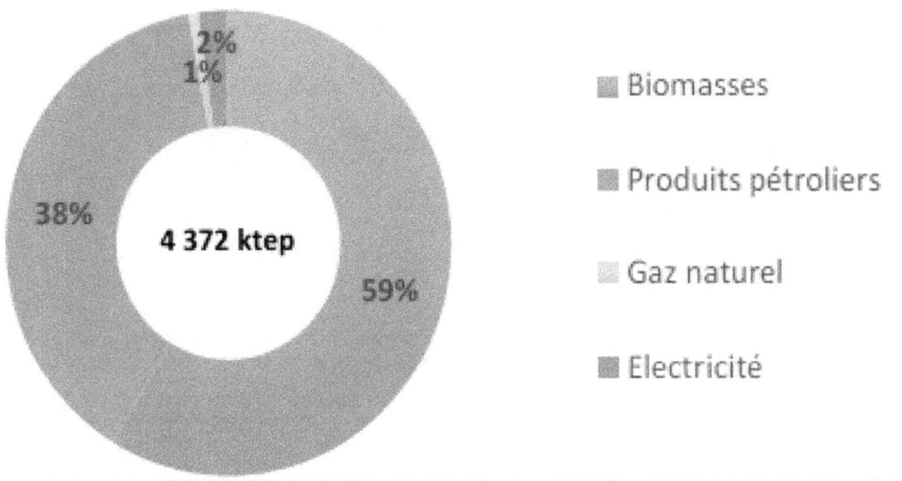

The electricity sub-sector is characterized by a demand for electrical energy that is far greater than the supply available for consumption. Electric energy consumption per capita estimated in 2018 is 0.10 (MWh), one of the lowest in the sub-region (SIE-UEMOA, 2020). See Figure 3 and Figure 4.

The state of vulnerability is characterized by cumulative losses (carbonization-electric - petroleum products) [3] 1000 ktep per year, totaling a carbon dioxide emission of 20,651.53 in 2020 against 19,842 in 2019. This is critical and calls for rapid action. Figures 3 and 4 show the vulnerabilities of the energy sector and the need to reduce its carbon footprint.

Figure 3. Total electricity demand in Benin in MWh (2018-2035) by scenario
(Source: RECASEB, 2019)

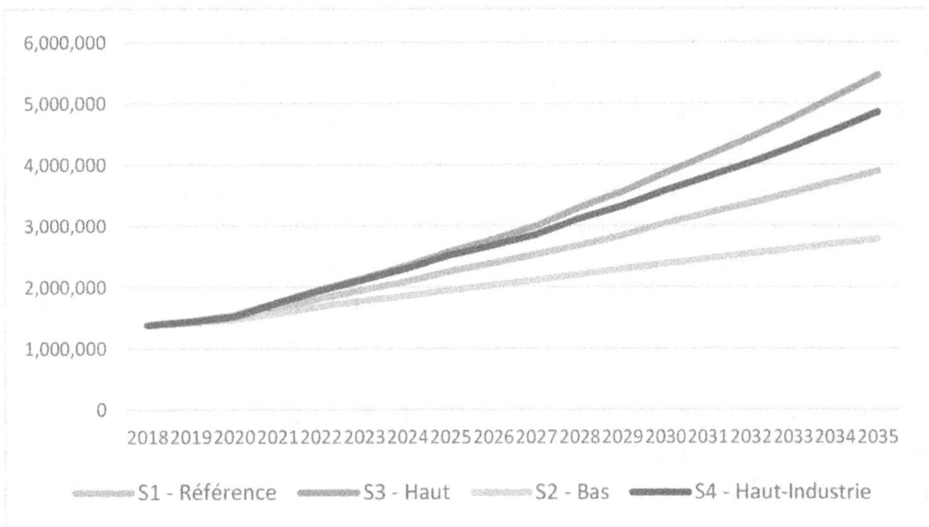

Figure 4. SIE 2021 Ministry of Energy, Benin

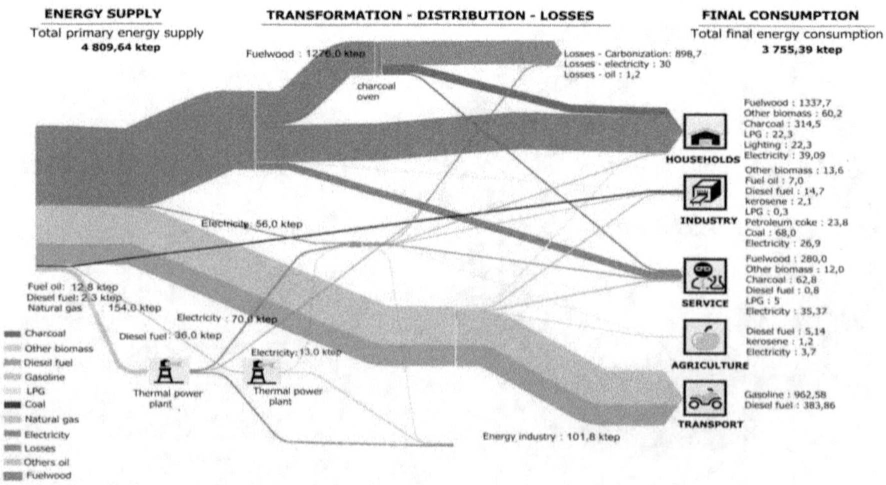

In terms of functionality, demand plays a central role because it drives development and investments in production and transport (Burillo, 2018). This demand depends on socio-economic variables (i.e., gross domestic product [GDP], income, population, urbanization, and penetration of certain devices) and climatic variables (i.e., temperature and humidity). The chain of impacts of climate change for the energy sector was developed based on an analysis of the results of empirical studies, data from the vulnerability and adaptation (VA) study, and through a participatory approach with experts and stakeholders in the sector.

Exposure and sensitivity factors that may decrease or worsen the degree of impact, as well as the current adaptive capacity of the sector, have been identified. The identified climatic hazards that may affect the sector include variations in ambient temperature, rains and extreme events that could cause flooding, drought or heat waves, rising sea levels, and strong winds. Sensitivity factors that can accentuate or mitigate the impact will affect these hazards. These factors also depend on the physical or social environment of the energy sector. For example, the dilapidated state of the transport infrastructure can contribute to supply disruptions when devices are subject to strong winds. Indeed, a large share of renewable energies makes the production system, transmission, distribution, and consumption of energy inefficient, low in carbon, and unstable.

In Benin, the energy consumed is often subject to significant losses and waste. To curb this trend, the government of Benin has carried out reforms, one of which focuses on minimum energy performance standards for systems like lighting and air conditioning. Technologies in the industrial sector are often outdated and carry significant energy losses. Companies faced with high energy production costs may experience significant problems related to competition. Thus, the system must have spare capacity or storage systems capable of responding at any time to the shortage of production that may be created by their intermittent nature and sensitivity to weather conditions. Sensitivity and exposure factors, when combined, determine the impact that key segments of the sector (i.e., generation, transmission, distribution, and demand) will suffer.

Regarding production, the different sources in the energy system mix were analyzed. Attention was given to sources sensitive to climate change and those that inject power into the Benin Electric Community's (CEB) current distribution network. The plants that supply electrical energy to Benin include hydroelectric, thermal, and solar energy. They also rely on strong importation from neighboring countries. Based on current and future climate variability, the potential impacts to which each segment of the sector is subject are discussed. The production of biomass energy is also discussed. The vulnerability of the energy sector is determined by the intrinsic capacity of the sector to cope with these impacts. For each segment of the system, vulnerability indicators are observed to assess the potential impacts.

PRODUCTION

Due to energy dependence of the importing country, the quality and stability of the electricity supply is dependent on the production status of suppliers. The reasons are linked to climatic and non-climatic factors.

Regarding climatic factors, droughts have severely affected the production of hydroelectric dams. Under an international agreement signed in August 1969, the Volta River Authority (VRA) of Ghana has been providing electric power through the CEB to neighboring countries, including Togo and Benin, since December 1972. The VRA supplies electrical energy from its Akosombo hydroelectric dam to the CEB with a capacity of between 80 and 100 MW through a 161 kV transmission line, comprising a 130 km line from Akosombo to Lomé in Togo and a 176 km line to Cotonou in Benin. However, this production has not been stable in view of the sensitive nature of this source to climatic variability, especially the water supply from the rains. In recent years, the Akosombo dam has suffered droughts, resulting in a drastic reduction in production and barriers in meeting the needs of the Benin populations. The years 1977, 1983, 1988, 1992, 1998, 2001, and 2006 were the most severe. Benin has resorted to the rental of groups that run on diesel to cover the gap. This, in turn, weighs on the finances of the Electricity company (Société Béninoise d'Energie Electrique - SBEE). For example, in fiscal year 2017/2018, the state had to inject nearly 21 billion Central African CFA franc (FCFA) into the finances of the SBEE for the company to pay the invoices for the purchase of fuel and the rental of groups generators from private operators (e.g., AGGREKO, MRI, and APR).

TRANSPORT AND DISTRIBUTION

Heavy rains, excessive temperatures, and strong winds caused significant damage to the transport infrastructure. This led to the deployment of financial resources for their support. For example, in Figure 5, an electric pole almost collided with a passing couple (http://pressedubenin.over-blog.com, 2014).

Figure 5. Electric pole on ground

The high number of incidents on the network suggests close links with climatic extreme events, particularly temperature and heavy rains (NAPA ENERGY, 2019). From 1970 to 2018, maximum temperatures increased by around +1°C and minimum temperatures increased by around +2°C. This affected the transmission capacity and caused cables to sag. The performance indices speak volumes, demonstrating improvements that can be made in terms of reducing supply disruptions for customers (see Figure 6 and Figure 7).

Figure 6. Projection of annual precipitation of the average of the four climate models (2020 to 2050)

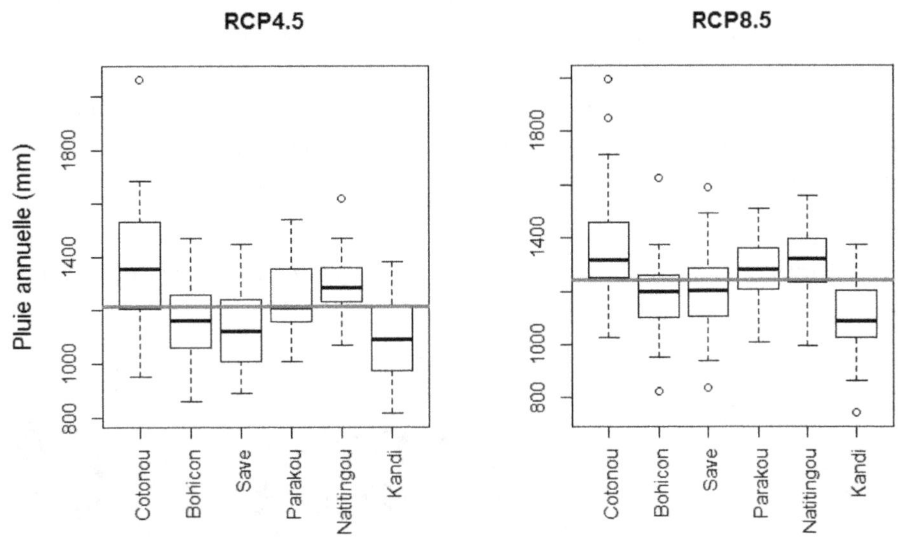

Figure 7. Number of incidents per month
(PANA-ENERGIE, 2019)

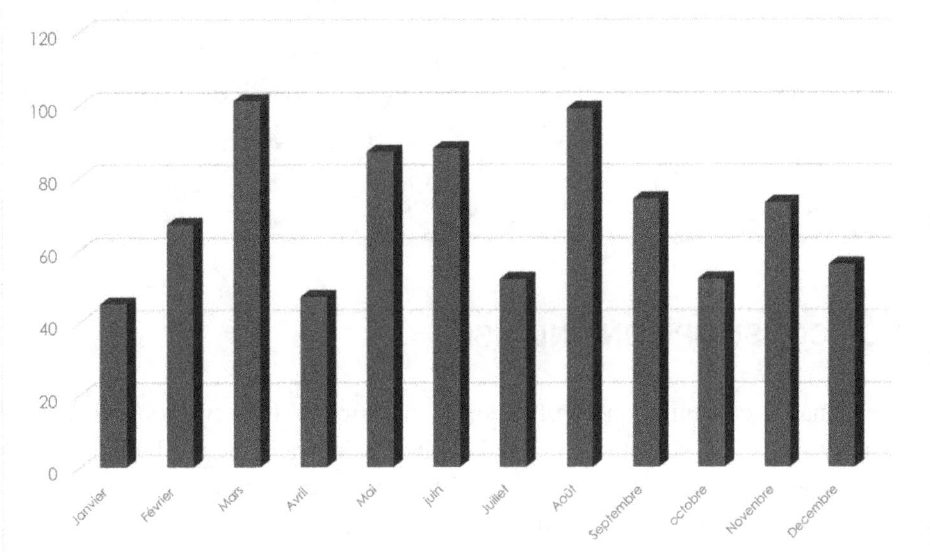

DEMAND

Benin has many renewable energy and resources (i.e., solar, micro-hydroelectric, and biomass). Still, the country has faced more than two decades of an energy crisis. Nevertheless, privileged environments like urban areas (with strong electrical coverage) note an increase in loads, especially during high temperature months. This trend is confirmed by a recent study on the influence of heat waves on electricity demand in the mega-cities of West Africa, including Cotonou, which has a strong correlation with the increase in consumption (Kondi et al., 2019). The study also shows that the fraction of consumption due to weather variations is approximately 20% on an annual scale compared to 26% considering the maximum daily consumption (Kondi et al., 2019). Moreover, due to the limits of production capacity, load shedding in favor of priority lines is carried out to cope with sudden increases in demand. Indeed, efforts to strengthen the country's production capacity are underway (see Figure 8).

Figure 8. Visibly aggressive erosion phenomenon on electricity production and distribution facilities along the coasts of Benin

PATTERNS OF CONSUMPTION AND USE

Peaks in poorly managed consumption involve costly investments in networks and pose risks to the continuity of supply. While consumption is very low, it is being rationalized by consumers who face regular energy shortages, load shedding problems, and energy price volatility. As a country dominated by biomass in the data structures of the EIS, wood, fire, and charcoal constitute the main uses in urban areas.

Almost all the vulnerable communities are dependent on traditional biomass like fuelwood and charcoal. Despite progress in the use of improved stoves, the energy systems remain inefficient, which has negative consequences on the health of the population and the ecosystems (for example, deforestation). It also weighs on certain categories (for example, women are in charge of collecting wood). While the central and northern regions of Benin are self-sufficient, an increase in demand in the southern cities puts pressure on the forest resources of central and northern Benin.

Future demands for biomass energy are expected to increase, while the supply of sustainable biomass should, according to these same forecasts, decrease slightly (NAPA-ENERGY, 2019). Developing energy efficient nature-based solutions (SbNs) like clean energy and modern cooking can create green jobs and lower costs of producing electricity. Energy efficiency is, therefore, key in low-carbon development, according to the Paris Agreement. Controlling energy demand, structuring the supply of energy services, and ensuring efficient access of communities to the resource would allow energy savings at the global level. These energy savings would positively impact development by contributing to the reduction of social inequalities. This analysis is supported by the fact that a rapid review of 20 years of measurements and struggles against climate variability and change shows that energy efficiency integrating SbNs has received little support and funding from donors. In fact, its potential is underestimated within the framework of the United Nations Framework Convention on Climate Change negotiations on future actions to reduce GHG emissions.

ACCESS TO ENERGY

Energy and Challenges of Sustainable Development Goals in Benin

The main orientations of the Sustainable Development Goals No. 7 (SDG No. 7) of the United Nations are, by 2030, are as follows (see Figure 9):

Figure 9. Impact of access to modern energy services on sustainable development
Source: Excert from ''La transition vers les énergies renouvelables en Afrique, 2021''

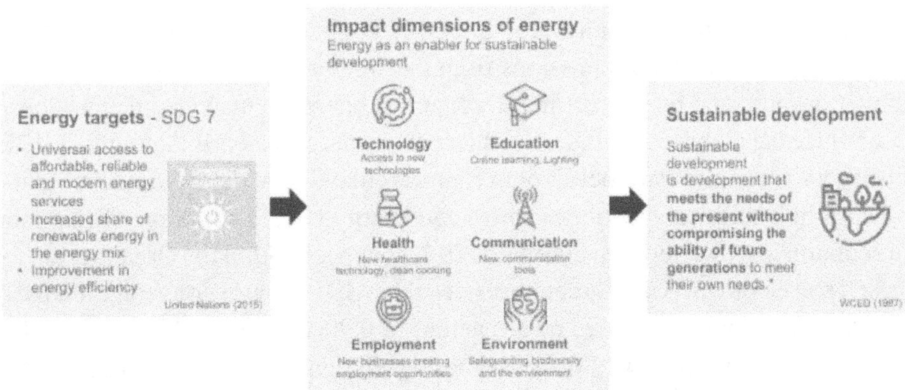

- Guarantee access for all to reliable and modern energy services at an affordable cost.
- Significantly increase the share of renewable energy in the global energy mix and double the global rate of improvement in energy efficiency. Apart from directly improving livelihoods, access to modern and sustainable energy services is also generally seen as a prerequisite for achieving all the other SDGs. Lack of access to modern energy sources disproportionately harms women and girls, who are often the primary household energy stewards.

ENERGY TRANSITION

Principles of Energy Transition

Energy transition is based on principles that justify its implementation. Thus, the following principles are those on which the establishment of energy transition policies is based:

- Reduce Carbon Intensity: Through this principle, the objective of energy transition is to decarbonize the "current" energy mix by modifying energy sources and moving from a mix dominated by fossil energy sources to a low-carbon energy mix.
- Decrease Energy Intensity: Efficiency in the context of energy production can be summed up as "doing more with less" or producing more (or as much) with less energy (and, therefore, less GHG).
- Increase Sobriety: Between 1965 and 2019, GHG emissions increased by 224%, particularly due to the increase in population (+130%) and increase in the average standard of living (+155%). Indeed, progress in energy efficiency (-46% energy intensity) and the decarbonization of energy production (-13% carbon intensity) have not been enough to compensate for neither the increase in population nor the standard of living. Sobriety, therefore, is another lever that seems necessary to support the energy transition and reduce GHG emissions. We must keep in mind that sobriety is the reduction of energy consumption through lifestyle changes and social transformations.

Importance of Energy Transition

In 2016, energy-related activities accounted for around 73% of global GHG emissions (World Resource Institute, 2020). This figure includes emissions from the combustion of fossil fuels in electricity, heating and cooling, transport, and manufacturing. Decoupling energy demand from emissions is central to efforts to decarbonize the global economy and achieve the goals of the Paris Agreement (IRENA, 2021).

In developed economies and some developing countries like China, there is evidence that it is possible to break the causal link between economic growth and energy-related emissions. Emissions are falling even as these economies grow. Between 2008 and 2017, countries within the Organisation for Economic Co-operation and Development (OECD) countries saw their GDP grow at an average annual rate of 1.3%, while energy-related emissions decreased by an average of 0.9% each year. On average, GHG emissions in African countries grew more slowly than in other developing economies from 2008 to 2017. Still, total energy-related emissions increased by almost 20% (even if the starting level was very low). Even with efficiency measures in place, energy demand in African economies is expected to nearly double by 2040 alongside rising populations and rising living standards (IRENA, 2019a). Therefore, making the vision of zero-emission African power sectors a reality by 2050 is primarily about preventing the growth of emissions as demand increases. Hence, the importance of enabling developing economies to shift from fossil fuels to low-carbon energy sources, including renewables (see Figure 10).

Figure 10. Share of energy-related carbon dioxide emissions in Africa by Sector, 2018
Source: Excerpt from "La transition vers les énergies renouvelables en Afrique, 2021"

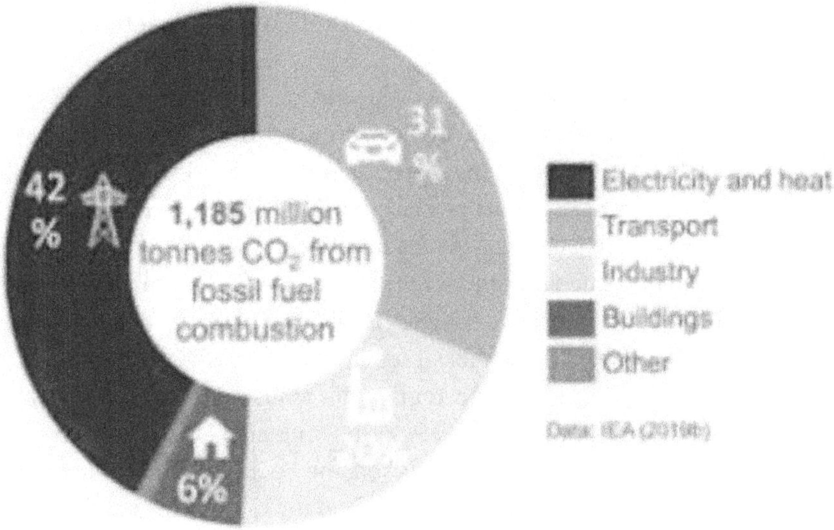

Between 2010 and 2019, the world saw a dramatic decline in the levelized cost of electricity (LCOE) produced from renewable sources. The cost of utility-scale solar photovoltaic (PV) 4 fell by 82%, while onshore wind fell by 40% (IRENA, 2020a). This means that in 2020, in most cases, renewables are the lowest cost option for bringing in new electricity generation capacity globally. In 2018, almost 25% of electricity was generated from renewable sources. In addition, 71% of generation capacity added in 2019 was based on renewable technologies, mainly solar and wind (IRENA, 2020b). Upfront capital and logistics can result in slightly higher than average costs for renewables and storage in some parts of Africa. However, to some extent, this is often offset by the excellent resources available on the market continent.

Post-2030 Energy Requires Acceleration of the Energy Transition

This portion will discuss the potential risks and obstacles related to the initiatives of accelerating the energy transition in Benin.

Acceleration of the Energy Transition

Benin, like many countries, is experiencing an energy transition. It has not yet left its old production system because it wants to meet the growing needs of its population by exploiting the means at its disposal. To this end, according to data from the Energy Dashboard, in 2005, wood fuels (firewood and charcoal) accounted for approximately 60% of the final energy consumed. Petroleum products accounted for 38% and electricity accounted for 2%. Despite the strong use of wood energy, there has been a slight change in the country's energy structure, which went from 67% (2002) to 59.4% (2005) for the share of biomass energy. At the same time, the consumption of petroleum products went from 31% (2002) to 38.4% (2005).

This development indicates a general drop in the relative participation of traditional energies in the country's energy consumption due to a better availability of domestic gas. According to a categorization by sector of activity, the structure of energy consumption is marked by a predominance of the household sector (64%), transport sector (23%), and service sector (10%) due to the consumption of petroleum products. Energy consumption in the industrial sector remains the lowest (2%) due to an industrial fabric that is still embryonic (if not underdeveloped).

Despite its dependence on electrical energy vis-à-vis the outside, Benin displays the same situation in terms of oil. Thus, in 2005, 100% of the petroleum products consumed were imported because Benin did not have an oil refinery. This situation remains the same today; however, a refinery installation project is on the table of those in power. An SDG report produced in 2022 indicates that electricity generation comes almost entirely from fossil fuels and must be decarbonized.

According to the information presented Figure 11, the proportion of energy production by solar (0.7%) remains very low. However, oil (23.6%) and natural gas (75.7%) are high. This, therefore, confirms that the production of electricity comes largely from fossil fuels. The same SDG report made one clarification, revealing that Benin is the country in the sub-region that emits the most carbon dioxide from the combustion of fuels for electricity and heating. In 2019, Benin emitted 34 megatonnes of carbon dioxide for each terawatt-hour of electricity produced. In comparison, the Economic Community of West African States (ECOWAS) emit an average of 5 megatonnes of carbon dioxide in the same year (IEA, 2021b). Faced with such a situation and aware of the challenges this presents, the government is committed to initiating the transformation of its energy mix by implementing a national policy for the development of renewable energies (PONADER 2020-2030).

Figure 11. Electricity production by energy source in Benin (2020)
Source: Authors' calculation based on data from SE4All (2021), RAPPORT SUR LE DÉVELOPPEMENT DURABLE POUR LE BÉNIN - Rapport pilote de référence (2022).

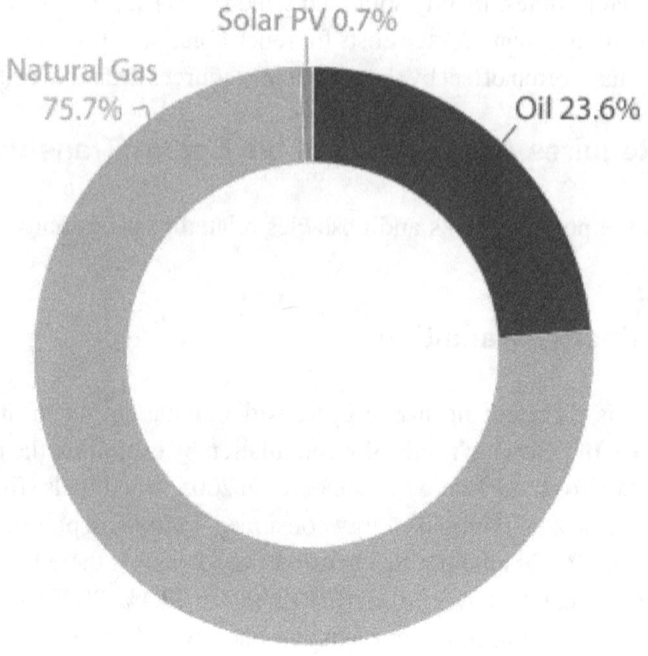

As a reminder, the vision of the energy transition has been a matter of concern for the Beninese government for years. In 2005, it was announced that alternative energy sources like solar energy and biomass will be explored in rural energy. In the Growth Strategy for the Reduction of Poverty (SCRP), the government declines in strategic axis No. 2 (the main objectives in terms of energy):

- Creation of an adequate institutional, legal, and regulatory framework
- Consolidation of the establishment of an energy information system with a view to acquiring decision-making support tools in terms of energy policy
- Promotion of the rational use of energy in all sectors of activity
- Diversification of domestic energy sources and development of economically profitable national energy resources
- Improvement of the pricing system
- Reduction of electrical connection time

In 2016, as part of its action program (PAG), the government planned reforms like the establishment of a financing instrument for renewable energies. The PAG also highlighted projects like the Dogo bis dam project and the construction of five solar power plants that totaled 100 MWp. However, these projects do not directly target the development of zero-emissions transport (Reference Pilot Report, 2022).

THE BENINESE AGENCY FOR RURAL ELECTRIFICATION AND ENERGY MANAGEMENT (ABERME)

The creation of ABERME, a long-awaited structure for the impetus of a real energy management strategy, took place in August 2004. Its purpose is to implement state policy in the areas of rural electrification and energy management (ABERME, 2009). The times, circumstances, state institutions, and regimes have undergone significant changes. However, certain structures still exist under other names (or even the same). Still, this policy of energy transition has not been abandoned and remains a priority for current rulers. Thus, the desired energy transition could be manifested by the territorialization of the photovoltaic solar resource from the municipalities and the implementation of incentive measures with a view to better disseminating solar photovoltaic technology. The purpose of this system is to facilitate the Beninese population's access to electrical energy (Kohomlan & Yehouénou, 2020).

Benin has the potential and opportunity to plan a zero-carbon energy mix and electrification. Transport and households represent nearly 90% of total energy consumption. This transformation must aim to improve their energy efficiency and accelerate the adoption of technologies that run on renewable energy. Indeed, although the share of renewable energies in the total supply of primary energy was 54.6% in 2019 (OECD, 2022), it has been decreasing since 2000. Also, almost all the renewable energies come from biomass (IEA, 2021b), although it is an energy potential that could be diversified in favor of solar, wind, and hydraulic energies (PONADER, 2020).

In view of the facts presented on the energy transition in Benin, it appears that a process of transformation focused on renewable energies (i.e., biomass and photovoltaic energy) is underway at a slower "speed." Internal factors are disrupting the desired momentum and undermining the commitment to a deeper revolution in the transition to cleaner energy. These factors are linked to potential risks and the political, economic, sociological, and environmental constraints to which the various initiatives, actions, and strategies of the trajectory of this energy transition are subject.

POTENTIAL RISKS

The implementation of actions and strategies to accelerate access to energy and intensify the energy transition is not on the sidelines of internal and external risks. This section presents risks through a map, considering socio-economic and socio-political parameters, partnership and commercial agreements, and international circumstances (see Table 1).

Table 1. Summary of risks: intensification of access to energy and acceleration of the energy transition

Internal Risks	
Socio-Economic and Operational Risks	• Colossal investments required for the acquisition of equipment and their installation • High energy acquisition costs related to the income of the beneficiaries • Constraints on agriculture (i.e., drought, food shortages, tougher working conditions) • Poor financial management • Rejection or reluctance of approval of technology and equipment by beneficiaries • Absence of communication (the beneficiaries and local authorities) around projects before their implementation • Uncertainty related to the request by the target
Socio-Politics	• Change of political regime, with upheavals linked to the vision in the implementation of energy transition policies (the new regime can question forecasts or orientations of the old regime and suspend actions or stop them to initiate new ones) • Corruption • Change in government structure • Internal political instability • Excessive dependence on hydrocarbons, other unsuitable forms of energy, and impacts on other sectors • Instability in ECOWAS countries, amplifying the migratory flow vector of the increase in energy demand
Socio-Demographic and Cultural Risks	• Negative perception linked to the lack of knowledge about technologies or equipment • Insecurity linked to ethnic and religious conflicts
Natural Risks	• Meteorological hazards (i.e., storms, floods, fires) that have direct consequences on certain installations and sources of energy production • Floods that prevent (by degradation or blockage of the road) access to certain beneficiary localities • Dangers of the entire chain of transformation of thermal materials (from mining operations to radioactive waste), leading to the absence of satisfactory answers concerning the storage of waste • Questionable adaptability of the technology to climate change
Legal and Regulatory Risks	• Change in budgetary orientation • Lack of legal provisions that can regulate the renewable energy sector
Financial Risks	• Lack of ambitious financial incentives for the private sector • Difficulties in recovering costs following the introduction of new technologies • Equipment price volatility • Non-profitability and attractiveness of renewable technologies
External Risks	
Partnerships	• Foreign investors may arouse, rightly or wrongly, mistrust (thus, in the event of a change of regime or government, foreign groups become the target of administrative, fiscal, and judicial harassment) • Distrust of local authorities regarding contracts that are too advantageous • Investors who deal with drastic changes in social, tax, or environmental legislation and may question the realization of certain projects • Long processes dependent on budgets or sectoral and geographical priorities • Non-recurring projects • Need to find funding for preliminary studies • Lack of alignment of policy documents, strategies, and actions of the sector with international commitments in favor of the climate
Commercial Agreements	• A change in legislation applicable to exchange controls relating to the repatriation of funds abroad or a new tax regime that is too onerous, calling into question the bankability of a project. • Risk related to legal uncertainty during the execution of a project (with an executor, agent, or company hired to carry out certain activities).
International Situations	• Thirst for energy in developed countries (still 60% of final energy consumed in France in 2019) is not decreasing, while demand in emerging countries (i.e., China, India, or Brazil) explodes • Competition for fossil resources is a source of international tension and potential conflict (consequences could affect Benin given the [energy] partnership relations it maintains with most of countries) • Exposure to political risk constitutes major risk given strategic nature of the energy sector and colossal financial needs necessary for the development of projects in this area • Unfavorable economic conditions negatively affect investment prospects in the hydrocarbons sector

RISK MAPPING

Analysis of Tax Regulations

The risks mentioned direct the reflections toward an objective analysis on the question of whether Decree No. 2018 - 360 of July 31, 2018 (the tax regime applicable to public-private partnership contracts), is an incentive for investors in the energy. To this end, some advantages emerge from the said regime. They can also be seen in the following articles:

- Article 3 stipulates that in the design, construction, or extension phase, investments or works carried out under a public-private partnership contract benefit from total exemption from taxes, duties, and fees collected by the state and its branches, with the exception of road tax, statistical tax, and any community levy. The same applies in the event of renewal.
- Article 4 in the operation or management phase stipulates that the tax regime applicable in the context of a public-private partnership contract is that of common law. However, if due to constraints imposed by the state or operating environment of the investments covered by the contract and situations of imbalance appear in the economics of the contract, the contracting authority may grant the private partner, in the exploitation or management, tax privileges derogating from common law. Apart from these two articles mentioned which can be considered as incentives for investments in the energy sector, those remaining refer either entirely or in large part to the conditions for the application of taxes and levies. For example, articles 5, 8, and 9 are evocative.
- In article 5, it is stated that "the exemptions provided for under this decree do not apply to taxes and duties paid or withheld at source on behalf of others. Except for the public procurement regulation fee, they also do not apply to fees for services provided by public or similar entities."
- Article 8 specifies that "the tax regime applicable to public-private partnership contracts extends, with regard to indirect taxes and duties, to public contracts carried out by means of private financing."
- Article 9 supplements the one mentioned above and provides that "subject to the provisions of this decree, public contracts with private financing and contracts executed under public-private partnership contracts remain subject to the other tax obligations in force in the Republic of Benin." With regard to these articles of the present tax system, it can be concluded that there are incentive measures in general (therefore, also applicable to the energy sector), but this system is not exempt from binding measures and it will be up to each partner, investor, or private sector actor to analyze each article to foresee the consequences that could arise from their commitments. In view of this, the risk of withdrawal, reluctance, or distrust still looms.
- Also, the verifications carried out to ascertain the effectiveness of the operationalization of the content of Chapter XII relating to the financial and tax provisions of Law No. 2020 - 05 of April 1, 2020, on the electricity code in the Republic of Benin in the general tax code have resulted in a negative finding. From 2020 (year of adoption of the code) until 2022, no provision relating to energy taxation appears except the tax on the consumption of electricity and water supplied by the state.

OBSTACLES

The success of the acceleration of access to energy, as well as that of the intensification of the energy transition, are imperative for the actors at various levels in Benin. Still, such a will can be blunted or stopped by obstacles, which is why it is essential that the said obstacles are identified and inherent measures are taken. Benin is now in the process of adopting clean energy in accordance with its adherence to the SDGs. This state is noticeable in off-grid electrification (EHR) in rural areas, especially through the installation of solar power plants and mini-power plants. However, some SDG trends are stagnant in Benin, including most ECOWAS countries per a report dated July 2022.

Thus, efforts should be made to improve them, particularly the SDGs for which major challenges remain related to SDG 1 (no poverty), SDG 3 (good health and well-being), SDG 5 (gender equality), SDG 6 (clean water and sanitation), SDG 7 (clean, affordable energy), SDG 16 (peace, justice, and strong institutions), and SDG 17 (partnership for goals) (Baseline Pilot Report, 2022).

The SDG in this study is that of clean and affordable energy (SDG 7). Thus, the energy transition initiated by Benin must continue. The obstacles presented here, therefore, will take more account of those relating to the energy transition, which constitutes a logical continuation of the acceleration of access to energy because it meets the same energy needs of the country and the framework of the SDGs.

POLICIES

There are major political obstacles related to energy transition procedures and strategies. Thus, certain political decisions prove to be ineffective due to silos in the administrative management of the territory. This includes hostility toward the mobilization of parties at the local level when dealing with collaborative projects. To illustrate this, Jo Spiegel, mayor of Kingersheim, indicated that in an energy transition strategy, "creating an energy transition department, with a separate budget and a dedicated team that will work in isolation" would be ineffective. On the contrary, it is necessary to green all the departments of the territorial administration, so all the projects and initiatives integrate an ecological dimension (wwww.lemonde.fr).

Often, social unrest and security issues are major structural obstacles that come into focus in relation to the development of political actions in the field of energy transition. Table 2 should be used to adopt a synthetic approach in the presentation of other obstacles relating to energy transition issues.

Table 2. Political obstacles and effects related to the energy transition

Political Obstacles	Possible Effects
Political instability, political violence, regime change: Elections in 2018, riots, strikes, terrorism, (civil) war, expropriation, breach of contracts	• Damage to power plants and distribution lines with a consequent loss of revenue and restoration costs • Strikes by employees, neglected maintenance, and loss of revenue • Loss of investment before its amortization in the event of expropriation
Institutional risks: Poor performance of the bodies responsible for regulating the electricity market	• Delay in the process of obtaining the concession and/or authorization

COMMERCIAL

Regarding trade barriers, the fundamental element may be purely economic. To this end, given the cost of the energy transition, wanting to simultaneously decarbonize and denuclearize the economy is suicidal. For example, a major obstacle related to solar energy is the high cost of production and difficulties related to market development. The materials needed to manufacture solar energy are expensive and it is economically unfeasible to implement the infrastructure to support solar electric systems. Thus, until solar system costs can be reduced, this technology will only be used to augment conventional power generation or power remote locations (2022 gamblewiz.com). Renewable energies also make it possible to avoid risks associated with nuclear power.

Still, these energy options pose problems related to economic profitability. In addition to the various obstacles mentioned, trade flows impact contracts and disputes related to energy exchange between countries (Mathieu and Shiells, 2002).

FINANCIAL

Financial obstacle are presented in Table 3.

Table 3. Financial barriers and effects to energy transition

Obstacles	Possible Effects
Difficulties in accessing bank financing: Lack of access to bank financing or unfavorable conditions	• Unavailability of funding • High financing costs
Currency issues: Appreciation or depreciation of currencies	• Increased spending on imported goods (turbines, panels, batteries) • Reimbursing a credit in another currency may be more expensive
Counterbalancing barriers: Mini-grid: • Non-payment of customers • Low purchasing power of customers • Fluctuations in demand **Injection into the network:** • Non-payment and solvency of the main customer (Off-taker risk)	• Loss of revenue • Insufficient/lower than expected liquidity
Lack of liquidity and refinancing	Liquidity risks resulting from revenue shortfalls or mismatches between the timing of receipts and payments. At the same time, borrowers might not be able to refinance an existing loan due to inadequate loan terms or the maturity of the loan not matching the duration of the project.
Lack of appropriate financial incentives for risk reduction for private developers of the energy sector, incentives that can reduce the risks of removal for the sale of energy.	Lack of enthusiasm or interest of actors who can make private investments in energy transition.
Lack of interesting financing mechanisms for both national and international companies.	Lack of financial resources to finance energy projects.

Tax

There are fiscal obstacles that can slow down or block the progress of the energy transition. These obstacles and their possible effects are presented in Table 4.

Table 4. Tax obstacles and effects related to energy transition

Obstacles	Possible Negative Effects
Unavailability of tax and customs advantages	• Increased costs due to unforeseen taxes/customs fees • Loss of investment before its amortization in the event of a takeover/absorption
Energy transition faces taxation issues	• Difficulties of partners or companies to comply with tax-related obligations • Slowdowns or impossibility of carrying out energy transition projects

Legal and Regulatory

From a legal and regulatory point of view, some national laws are unsuited to the structuring of energy projects that comply with international standards and requirements of foreign donors. Examples include state monopolies and the non-existence of a regulated market open to competition. Thus, the following instruments can be identified:

- Law No. 2020-05 of April 1, 2020, on the electricity code in the Republic of Benin
- Article 23 relating to the qualification of companies that operate in the electricity sector, provides that "the procedures for purchase include mechanisms giving preference to domestic firms. In the event of competition, a 15% bonus is granted to the consortium comprising at least one national company."

When analyzing this legal system, which promotes contributions to the development of local companies in the energy sector, it is easy to identify flaws. Several questions, in fact, should have been raised prior to the development of such a provision in this code:

- Are national companies putting their projects or offers to competition less competent than foreign ones?
- Is a competent foreign company that is unable to apply for a consortium not entitled to tax benefits to better support its costs and succeed in its work?

The nationalism put forward in this article can be detrimental to the realization of an energy project if competence is not included the same way as patriotism economics. Thus, the sustainability of a completed project is strongly linked to quality (apart from the other related factors). Also, upon discovering this article, the risk of reluctance, flight, abandonment, and the fear of legal trouble could arise among foreign companies. In a specific context, this would be better equipped than national ones to achieve. Among the legal instruments that may draw attention to related risks, Law No. 2020-02 of March 20, 2020, discusses the Investment Code in the Republic of Benin. In fact, in its article on the common law

regime from which investors in Benin can benefit, this law mentions specificities, some of which are worded as follows:

- The basic privileged regimes offer national and foreign companies under Beninese law customs and tax advantages. These are the diets below.
- "A" applies to companies whose amount, excluding taxes, of investments is greater than or equal to 50 million (50,000,000) and less than or equal to 1 billion (1,000,000,000) CFA francs
- "B" applies to companies whose investment amount, excluding taxes, is greater than 1 billion (1,000,000,000) and less than 50 billion (50,000,000,000) CFA francs

The special diets are:

- The sectoral incentive scheme, which aims to encourage investment in economic activities or sectors considered strategic for companies eligible under schemes A and B in accordance with a decree issued by the council of ministers.
- The specific investment regime, which aims to facilitate the implementation of infrastructure and equipment projects for cultural, sports, health, and educational tourist use. It also aims to facilitate the construction of certain infrastructures for industry and commerce intended, in particular, for the storage of products like gas, hydrocarbons, and chemicals.

The support initiative introduced in this article is commendable and could, indeed, interest foreign investors in the same way as nationals. However, the basis on which this measure relates is the cost of investment. In addition, the other case mentioned is that of the specific regimes. It takes into account the incentive measures that relate specifically to the storage of products (i.e., gas, hydrocarbons, and chemicals), whereas the energy sector is at the heart of development and should be a priority (especially the energy transition aspect). The risks incurred relate to the fact that:

- Foreign companies and investors with an investment cost below those fixed to benefit from special treatment are disturbed by financial difficulties during the implementation of their projects, considering the existing and applicable tax provisions.
- Investors in the energy sector do not feel the terrain is less favorable to their investment because their sector, although important, is not on the list of regimes that can benefit from special support.

The last instrument that can, in the same way as those mentioned above, corroborate the possible problems mentioned is Decree No. 2021-005 of January 6, 2021. This decree discusses approvals for the regimes of the investment code in Benin. It is noted that the possibility of access to approvals only account for national companies. In addition, the energy sector is not eligible for sectoral incentive schemes, as article 5 gives an exhaustive list. The said areas are agro-industry, agriculture, digital, health, technical, and vocational training.

Potential investors and entrepreneurs, especially foreign ones, could assume a restriction of their chances of following certain legal paths to practice in Benin and set up projects in their sector. In reality, the risks related to legal and regulatory provisions are not unique to Benin. In fact, countries like Tunisia have also displayed them. It would, therefore, be good for the case of Tunisia to be briefly mentioned here (with details in the appendix). In this country, there is the law of May 11, 2015, which defines the legal regime relating to the realization of electricity production projects from green energies.

This text legalizes the initiatives of independent producers (i.e., local authorities, public companies, and private companies), liberalizing production and export through self-consumption, the independent production of electricity to meet the needs of national consumption, and export. Other texts include:

- The decree of August 24, 2016, which sets the conditions and procedures for carrying out projects and selling them to the Tunisian Electricity and Gas Company (STEG).
- The decree of July 26, 2017, relating to the operation and organization of the Energy Transition Fund.
- That of February 9, 2017, which establishes the specifications for connection to the STEG network, the contract for self-production, and the purchasing power parity for the authorization system.
- The decree of August 30, 2018, approving the revision of the standard contract for the sale to STEG of electrical energy produced from renewable energies subject to authorization.

These texts, in the absence of harmonization and coordination between the actors concerned (i.e., developers, electricity carriers, and unions), would have, according to experts, blurred the operation and management of renewable energies. A reversal of the case of Benin in the analysis shows a weakness in the legislative framework accompanying the transfer of technology and the creation of industries specialized in renewable energies.

Added to this is the absence of ecological taxation. The consequences of these situations could be manifested by a fear of partners and companies to invest in Benin's renewable energies because they are concerned about being suprised by new laws during the execution of their energy projects. However, it is useful to adopt a prudent posture in the sense that all the resources and facilities offered by the Electricity Code and the packages of fiscal and parafiscal measures of an incentive nature vis-à-vis investments in the electricity sector energy are not yet fully explored and are often ignored by energy players (even the big ones), especially the private sector.

In short, the provisions presented in this section should be compared with the electricity regulatory index which, by definition, is a composite index that measures the level of development of the regulatory frameworks of the sector. Plus, electricity in African countries should be measured against international standards and best practices. It is made up of the following pillars:

- Regulatory Governance Index (RGI)
- Regulatory Substance Index (RSI)
- Regulatory Effect Index (REI)

The RGI assesses the extent to which the laws, procedures, standards, and policies governing the electricity sector provide a transparent, predictable, and credible regulatory framework that meets international standards.

The RGI, therefore, assesses the institutional and legal design of the regulatory framework, within which regulatory decisions are made. It is made up of eight indicators. The RSI, on the other hand, assesses the extent to which electricity sector regulators are fulfilling their mandate and implementing practices and processes that affect regulatory outcomes. The RSI assesses the content of the regulations and the decisions implemented by the regulators. It is made up of seven indicators. The RGI and RSI together assess the effectiveness of the regulatory environment in supporting power sector performance, promoting efficiency, and achieving national goals. The ROI measures, from the point of view of electricity distribution companies and/or consumers, the degree of positive or negative impact of the regulatory authority on the area. ROI assesses the extent to which regulatory actions and decisions achieve the intended results for the industry. ROI is calculated by aggregating the survey responses from utility companies and consumers. Given the limited number of responses from electricity consumers in the 2020 assessment, the 2020 ERI included in its final calculation only the results of the effect index of the electricity companies. The ROI for electricity companies includes three sub-indicators. Table 5 contains the main indicators of each pillar of the ERI.

Table 5. Main indicators of the pillars of the ERI 2020

Regulatory authorities		Electricity Firms
Regulatory Governance Index	Regulatory substance index	Regulatory effect index
1: Legal mandate	9: Economic regulation	16: Financial performance and competitiveness
2: Clarity of roles and objectives	10: Technical regulation	17: Quality of electricity supply (commercial and technical)
3: Independence	11: Licensing framework	18: Facilitation of access to electricity
4: Responsibility	12: Institutional capacity	
5: Transparency of decisions	13: Development of renewable energies	
6: Predictability	14: Mini-grids and off-grid systems	
7: Participation	15: Development of energy efficiency	
8: Free access to information		

Regarding the evaluation of ERI in Africa, the results obtained in 2020 highlighted the case of several African countries, including Benin. Overall, Uganda was identified as the best performing country in the 2020 ISE, with a score of 0.801. The other performers and their respective scores are Namibia (0.759), Tanzania (0.721), Zambia (0.655), and Kenya (0.633). These are the top five performers of the 2020 CRI. These countries have well-developed regulatory frameworks for the electricity sector. In addition, their regulators can exercise the necessary regulatory authority over regulated entities. Regarding the case of Benin, it is presented as one of the countries with regulatory frameworks emerging in 2020. Table 6 presents the results of these countries.

When analyzing the results in Table 6, the nascent regulatory institutions have obtained good results in RGI. However, they present a low score in the RSI and ROI. This finding indicates that countries that have recently established regulatory institutions are able to learn from the experience of those that have established electricity regulatory regimes. This result is based on sector reforms implemented since the end of the 1990s. Regarding the ROI, most of the countries in the sample are in the low performance range. Only Benin, Niger, and Sierra Leone scored above 0.500. These results suggest that nascent regulators, including Benin, could rise to the top of the regulatory ladder by learning from their peers in the different sub-regions of Africa and through a vigorous program of capacity building.

Table 6. Performance of countries with nascent regulatory institutions

Countries	Years of Activity	Regulatory Governance Index (RGI)	Regulatory Substance Index (RSI)	Regulatory effect index (ROI)	Rank ERI 2020
Chad	1	0.556	0.034	0.184	35
Mauritius	4	0.689	0.097	0.135	32
Liberia	3	0.625	0.239	0.184	31
Guinea	1	0.584	0.302	0.393	25
Botswana	2	0.637	0.305	0.228	30
Dem. Rep of Congo	1	0.399	0.357	0.375	26
Mozambique	3	0.619	0.412	0.277	28
Sierra Leone	5	0.749	0.511	0.498	12
Niger	3	0.702	0.581	0.571	8
Benin	5	0.758	0.729	0.404	16

Source: Indice de réglementation de l'électricité en Afrique, 2020_BAD

OPERATIONAL

The biggest mistake players can make is a goal to push through the energy transition without citizen involvement. "Without citizen participation, any energy transition project is doomed to failure," commented Françoise Coutant, vice president of the Nouvelle Aquitaine region. Spiegel noted, "Not only must citizens be involved, but we must also start by implementing solutions that will have an economic interest for them or for the community. We have to show them that the energy transition reduces consumption and, therefore, expenses. This can be done quite simply with smart heating, heating networks, geothermal energy, or even LED public lighting … the return on investment of which is easily demonstrated."

The media regularly reminds us of risks that can turn into major obstacles, including:

- Destruction of infrastructure caused by natural disasters (which are also consequences of climate change)
- Power outages that result from obsolete regulations
- Failure to modernize the network

Another obstacle that can arise and cause energy transition initiatives to fail would be to place all trust in a single company that promises to take ownership of the work. In the opinion of Spiegel and Coutant, it is better to bet on a group of local artisans whose specialties are complementary and skills will have been approved (www.lemonde.fr).

We must also address the lack of technical capacity to manage renewable energy power plants. This includes a lack of technical capacity related to the planning, development, financing, and operation of renewable energy projects in the public and private sectors in Benin. In particular, the capacity of the domestic private sector is very weak. Some renewable energy sources (i.e., wind, solar, and biomass) are perceived as difficult to manage due to the variability of electricity production. Also, for some energy generation sources like renewable biomass, skilled individuals will be needed to manage the system.

RECOMMENDATIONS

To overcome problems related to the intensification of access to energy and, above all, to succeed in energy transition, legislators must be aware of the opportunities and constraints they could face. They must also engage in opportunities to encourage a solid renewable energy agenda post-2030 based on:

- The structuring and strengthening of the sustainable energy solutions production sector (i.e., biofuel, carbonization, and improved cooking stoves) to standardize local quality and add value to territories.
- The mobilization of local actors and public decision makers, strengthening their capacities related to challenges of biomass energy. Regarding energy-climate planning, steps should be taken to promote sustainable, modern, and quality energy solutions.
- Enhancement of forest sites through support for income-generating activities (i.e., beekeeping and mushroom cultivation) and efficient techniques relateed to charcoal production, delimbing, and recovery of wood scraps.
- Sensitization of the population to promote the adoption of dynamic energy simulation on a large scale in rural and urban areas.
- Building the capacity of decision makers and networking with public, private, and civil society actors at the departmental level. This will promote collective decisions around biomass energy issues consistent with national guidelines around training, sharing of experience, exchange visits, and advocacy,
- Capitalization of project lessons with local stakeholders and promotion of actions at regional and national levels.
- The adoption of a favorable legal framework to pool risks related to energy performance guarantee, an obligation to connect to heating networks, rules in co-ownership, and new contractual documents (i.e., green lease and energy performance contract) that guarantee access for all to high-performance buildings.
- Support for innovation that allows the development (in the territories) of an industrial fabric oriented toward products and services with environmental added value (eco-materials, heat recovery system, and innovative buildings). Methods will be supported to renovate the old park while respecting its heritage.
- The establishment of a mechanism that adjusts the prices of products imported at the borders of the European Union (EU). This can prevent unfair competition from countries that do not comply with EU environmental standards. The proceeds will be donated to the taxed countries via a green fund, allowing them to reduce emissions.
- Support for the identification of a nationally tailored approach for rural electrification.
- Support for the establishment of the appropriate institutional and legislative framework.
- Promotion of an environment that enables private sector participation.

- Promotion of a regional policy on rural electrification.

AUTHOR NOTE

The views expressed in this article are my personal views and do not represent those of the Centre d'Etudes Diplomatiques et Stratégiques de Paris (CEDS) or any other organizations.

REFERENCES

Agence Béninoise d'Electrification Rurale et de Maîtrise d'Energie (ABERME). (2009). *Document de Politique Nationale de Maîtrise d'Energie (PONAME) Rapport proviso ire*. PONAME.

Akponikpè, P. B. I., Tovihoudji, P., Lokonon, B. O. K., Kpadonou, E., Amegnaglo, C. J., Segnon, A. C., & Aho, N. (2019). Etude de Vulnérabilité aux changements climatiques du Secteur Agriculture au Bénin. Berlin: Climate Analytics gGmbH.

Amoussou, E., Awoye, H., Vodounon, H. S. T., Obahoundje, S., Camberlin, P., Diedhiou, A., & Boko, M. (2020). Climate and Extreme Rainfall Events in the Mono River Basin (West Africa): Investigating Future Changes with Regional Climate Models.

ARE. (2019). *Révision des conditions tarifaires de la SBEE*. ARE.

Asian Development Bank. (2012). *Climate Risk and Adaptation in the Electric Power Sector*. Asian Development Bank.

Badarou, R., & Kouletio, E. C. H. (2009). *Systèmes énergétiques : Vulnérabilité – Adaptation – Résilience*. VAR.

Banque Africaine de Développement (BAD). (2020). *Indice de réglementation de l'électricité en Afrique*. BAD.

Bazyomo, S. D., Lawin, A. E., Coulibaly, O., Wisser, D., & Ouedraogo, A. (2016).. . *Forecasted Changes in West Africa Photovoltaic Energy Output by, 2045*, 1–15. doi:10.3390/cli4040053

Bekoe, E. O., & Logah, F. Y. (2013). The impact of droughts and climate change on electricity generation in Ghana. *Environmental Sciences, 1*(1), 13–24. doi:10.12988/es.2013.13002

Benin. (2015). *Deficit Energetique Et Competitivite De L'economie Beninoise*. Benin.

Bénin. (2018). *Programme De Croissance Pour Le Developpement Durable (PC2D) 2018-2021*. Benin.

Biao, E. I. (2017). Assessing the impacts of climate change on river discharge dynamics in Oueme River basin (Benin, West Africa). *Hydrology, 4*(4), 47. doi:10.3390/hydrology4040047

Oxford Bibliographies. "Political Economy." Accessed Feb. 25, 2021

Burillo, D. (2018). Effects of climate change in electric power Infrastructures.

Cronin, J., Anandarajah, G., & Dessens, O. (2018). Climate change impacts on the energy system: A review of trends and gaps. *Climatic Change, 151*(2), 79–93. doi:10.100710584-018-2265-4 PMID:30930505

Daron, J. D. (2014). *Regional Climate Messages for West Africa*, 1–30. Cariaa Assar.

Ministère de l'Energie (ME), Direction Générale de l'Energie (DGE). (2017). *Rapport SIE 2017.* ME.

Ministère de l'Energie. (2019). *Assurer une transition énergétique pour le développement économique et social durable.* ME.

Décret N° 2021-005 du 06 janvier 2021 portant agréments aux régimes du code des investissements au Bénin.

Developpment, I. E. (2017). (*IED*). Plan Directeur d'Electrification Hors Réseau.

République du Bénin, ministère de l'Energie. (2020). *Politique Nationale des Energies Renouvelables (PONADER).* ME.

Ebinger, J., & Vergara, W. (2011). *Climate Impacts on Energy Systems.* World Bank. doi:10.1596/978-0-8213-8697-2

Elizbarashvili, M., Chartolani, G., & Khardziani, T. (2018a). Variations and trends of heating and cooling degree-days in Georgia for 1961–1990 year period. *Annals of Agrarian Science, 16*(2), 152–159. doi:10.1016/j.aasci.2018.03.004

Fay, M., Block, R. I., & Ebinger, J. (2009). *Adapting to Climate Change in Eastern Europe and Central Asia.* World Bank. doi:10.1596/978-0-8213-8131-1

General Directorate of Energy (DGE). (2017). *Système d'Information Energétique du Bénin: Rapport annuel 2015 et évolution 2010-2015[Energy Information System of Benin: Annual report of 2015 and trend 2010-2015*]. DGE.

GIEC. (2014). *Changements climatiques 2014 Rapport de synthèse.* GIEC.

Gnanglè, C. P., Kakaï, R. G., Assogbadjo, A. E., Vodounnon, S., Afouda, J., & Sokpon, N. (2011). Tendances Climatiques Passees. *Modelisation, 8*, 27–40.

Hamududu, B., Killingtveit, A., & Engineering, E. (2012). *Assessing Climate Change Impacts on Global Hydropower,* 305–322. World Bank. doi:10.3390/en5020305

Hellmuth, M., Cookson, P., & Potter, J. (2017). *Adressing Climate Vulnerability for Power System Resilience and Energy Security.* ClimateLinks.

IAEA. (2019). *Adapting the energy sector to climate change.* VIENNA.

IEA. (2015). *Energy and climate change.* Routledge Handbook of Global Environmental Politics., doi:10.4324/9780203799055

IEA. (2021b). *Net Zero by 2050 A Roadmap for the Global Energy Sector.* IEA.

International Monetary Fund. (2021) What Is Capitalism? IMF, larepublica.cd.

IRENA. (2021). *La transition vers les énergies renouvelables en Afrique.* IRENA.

Jason Vogel, Abt Associates, Inc. Lorine Giangola, Abt Associates, Inc. Sherry Stout, U.S. National Renewable Energy Laboratory Nathan Lee, U. S. N. R. E. L. (2019). *A Comprehensive Vulnerability Assessment Of The Lao Pdr Power Sector Usaid*. National Renewable Energy Laboratory.

Kalogirou. (2014). *Solar Space Heating and Cooling*. doi:10.1016/B978-0-12-397270-5.00006-6

Kohomlan, G., & Yehouénou, M. (2020). *Transition énergétique au Bénin: Quel apport du solaire*. [Thesis, Université d'Abomey-Calavi].

Kondi, V. G. A., Hingray, B., Diedhiou, A., & Francois, B. (2019). Weather sensitivity of electricity demand in West African megacities [abstract]. *Geophysical Research Abstracts, 21*, EGU2019–EGU18831.

Lawin, A. E., Houngue, R., M'Po, Y. N., Houngue, N. R., Attogouinon, A., & Afouda, A. A. (2019). Mid-Century Climate Change Impacts on Oueme River Discharge at Bonou Outlet (Benin). *Hydrology, 6*(3), 20. doi:10.3390/hydrology6030072

Levesque, A., Pietzcker, R. C., & Luderer, G. (2019). Technological Forecasting & Social Change Halving energy demand from buildings : The impact of low consumption practices. *Technological Forecasting and Social Change, 146*(March), 253–266. doi:10.1016/j.techfore.2019.04.025

Loi N° 2020-02 du 20 mars 2020 portant Code des investissements en République du Bénin

Loi N° 2020-05 du 1er avril 2020 portant code de l'électricité en République du Bénin

Mathieu, P., & Shiells, C.R. (2002). *Les difficultés du secteur de l'énergie dans la Communauté des États indépendants*. ME.

Matthew McCartney. (2012). *Gerald Forkuor, Aditya Sood, Barnabas Amisigo, F. H. and L. M*. The Water Resource Basin Climate in the Volta River Implications of Changing.

MEF (2020): *Évolution récente de l'économie béninoise et Perspectives à moyen terme* MEF.

Ministère du Plan et du Développement (MPD). (2018). *Plan National de Développement 2018-2025*. MPD.

Ministre du Cadre de Vie et du Développement Durable. (2019). *Troisième communication nationale du Benin*. MCVDD.

Omri, A. (2016). *Analyse de la transition vers les énergies renouvelables en Tunisie: Risques, enjeux et stratégies à adopter. Economies et finances*. Université Côte d'Azur; Université de Sfax (Tunisie).

Osse, R., Tokponnon, F., Okê, M., Adjinda, S., Zounmenou, A., & Bokonon-Ganta, E. H. (2019). *Etude de Vulnérabilité aux changements climatiques du Secteur Santé au Bénin*. Cotonou: Climate Analytics gGmbH.

PANA-ENERGIE. (2019). *Rapport final - Evaluation de la vulnérabilité et de l'adaptation dans le secteur énergie au Benin*. PE.

Pöyry Energy Gmb. (2017). GIS Hydropower Resource Mapping – Country Report for Benin, 1–19. EcoWrex. www.ecowrex.org

Ratri, D. N., Whan, K., & Schmeits, M. (2019). A comparative verification of raw and bias-corrected ECMWF seasonal ensemble precipitation reforecasts in Java (Indonesia). *Journal of Applied Meteorology and Climatology*, *58*(8), 1709–1723. doi:10.1175/JAMC-D-18-0210.1

Sarra, A. (2020). *Les obstacles au développement des énergies vertes en Tunisie*. Web Manager Center. https://www.webmanagercenter.com/2020/11/04/458166/les-obstacles-au-developpement-des-energies-vertes-en-tunisie-1-4/ Consulté, le 5 juillet 2023

Sintondji, L. O., Badou, D. F., Ahouansou, M., Hounkpe, J., Assogba Balle, R., Gaba, C., & Vissin, E. (2019). *Etude de Vulnérabilité face aux changements climatiques du Secteur Ressources en Eau au Bénin*. Climate Analytics gGmbH.

UN Sustainable Development Solutions Network. (2022). *Rapport sur le développement durable pour le Bénin Rapport pilote de référence (Juillet 2022)*. UN.

Chapter 11
The Link Between Green Sukuk and Financial Development:
Which Comes First?

Aysegul Aytac Emin
https://orcid.org/0000-0001-8086-0091
Social Sciences University of Ankara, Turkey

Dogus Emin
Social Sciences University of Ankara, Turkey

ABSTRACT

Although financially developed countries play pioneering roles on the innovative financial instruments, whether high level of financial development leads to a wider range of instruments or having a wider range of instruments leads countries to financially develop has not been fully discovered. Especially for the countries that adapt Islamic financial instruments, the relation between financial development and green financial instruments is still not known. In this context, the objective of this chapter is to investigate whether there is a significant lead/lag relationship between financial development and issuance of green sukuk. While initial results show that countries that are already financially developed are more eager to issue green sukuk, a detailed investigation on the nature of the lead/lag relation reveals that green sukuk issuance leads financial institutions to be more accessible and financial markets to have more depth.

1. INTRODUCTION

The increasing sensitivity towards environmental issues and the mobilization of private sector resources have fueled the development of sustainable finance. This has led to the creation of novel financial instruments, including sustainability-linked financial instruments, which play a significant role in attracting new sources of capital for sustainable development.

Green bonds are one of the prominent tools of sustainable finance. These debt securities are issued specifically to raise capital for environment-friendly projects, such as those related to climate change,

DOI: 10.4018/978-1-6684-9272-7.ch011

affordable and clean energy, and sustainable cities. Green sukuk, on the other hand, is a Sharia-compliant financial instrument used to finance environmentally friendly projects, including renewable energy, clean energy, energy efficiency, and green infrastructure. Green sukuk appeals to both Islamic investors and environmentally conscious conventional investors.

Islamic finance, built on the principles of Islamic law, aligns with the SDGs by promoting social, environmental, and economic well-being. Islamic law seeks to ensure inclusive social justice, equal opportunities, and welfare for all. By emphasizing risk-sharing, the Islamic financial system provides a comprehensive framework for improving financial inclusion, which is crucial for achieving several SDGs. Islamic law also encourages environmental protection, the efficient use of resources, and the avoidance of wasteful consumerism.

However, while Islamic finance excels in charitable and poverty elimination activities, its involvement in environmental and social goals has been limited. Nasr (1989, p. 519) clearly states that Islamic financial system's main principles are "freedom of action and collective responsibility". According to that one of the main motivations behind the Islamic financial activities is to contribute to the good of the society while meeting the needs of individuals (Siddiqi, 1968). Chapra (1992, p. 6) explains the main goal of the Islamic financial system as "eradication of all forms of inequity, injustice, exploitation, oppression and wrong doing". On the other hand, even though Islamic financial system is good at charitable and poverty elimination activities, the system and the players do not have solid and significant environment related activities (Maali et al., 2006). Investigating the social reporting of 19 Islamic banks, Kamla and Rammal (2013) conclude that Islamic financial sector's role in environmental and social goals is almost non-existent. Interviewing 18 senior executives of Islamic financial institutions, Aribi and Arun (2015) reach to conclusion that "the focus of their operations is on Shari'ah compliance, and none reported anything on environmental issues" (p. 792).

While the impact of Islamic finance on the SDGs has been extensively studied from various perspectives, there is a lack of research on the relationship between sustainable Islamic financial tools and the financial development of countries. This article aims to fill this gap by investigating the nature of the relationship between the level of financial development and the issuance of green sukuk. The study explores whether financially developed countries play a pioneering role in green sukuk issuance or if green sukuk issuance leads countries to financial development.

Islamic finance has the potential to contribute significantly to the achievement of the SDGs by promoting social, environmental, and economic well-being. However, there is a need for greater focus on environmental and social goals within Islamic financial institutions. The emergence of green sukuk as a sustainable financial instrument presents an opportunity to bridge this gap and attract both Islamic and conventional investors interested in environmentally friendly projects. By exploring the relationship between green sukuk issuance and financial development, this article aims to shed light on the potential impact of green sukuk on the financial development of countries. According to that, using IMF's Financial Development Index and Geweke Feedback Measure, this paper will answer the following question: Does issuance of a green sukuk leads countries to financially develop?

The remainder of this paper structured as follows. In the following section, we review the related literature. In the next section, the details of data and methodology are explained. In section four, the results are revealed and discussed. And lastly, in the final section, the study is concluded.

2. LITERATURE REVIEW

In recent years, there has been a growing interest in the role of Islamic finance in promoting financial development and achieving the Sustainable Development Goals (SDGs). Islamic finance, with its unique principles and practices, has gained recognition as an alternative and ethical form of financial intermediation. This literature review aims to explore the relationship between Islamic finance and financial development, as well as its contribution to the attainment of the SDGs.

A study conducted by Abduh et al. (2012) analyzed the long- and short-term relationships between the development of conventional and Islamic finance, as well as Bahrain's economic growth. By employing the VECM model and the Johanson-Juselius co-integration test, the authors compared the impact of Islamic and traditional finance on economic growth in Bahrain. The findings revealed a positive correlation between both forms of financial development and economic growth in the long run. However, the study highlighted that the relationship between these two developments is bidirectional in the case of Islamic finance.

Another investigation by Abduh and Omar (2012) focused on the relationship between the growth of Islamic banking and economic expansion in Indonesia. Using the cointegration test and the error correction model, the authors found a long-term beneficial correlation between the development of Islamic finance and economic expansion. It was also observed that there is a reciprocal relationship between financial development and economic growth, indicating that the expansion of Islamic banks in Indonesia both encourages and is stimulated by economic growth. The authors emphasized the effective role of Islamic banks in mediating financial transactions in Indonesia.

Farahani and Dastan (2013) conducted a cointegration and Granger-causality analysis using quarterly data from nine countries. Their study demonstrated a positive connection between Islamic banking financing and economic growth, as well as capital accumulation in the nations under study. These findings contribute to the growing body of evidence supporting the positive impact of Islamic finance on financial development.

Chakravarty and Pal (2013) empirically demonstrated that financial inclusion is a significant determinant of economic development in India. Developing a financial inclusion index, their study established a positive relationship between financial inclusion and economic development. Similarly, Rasheed et al. (2016) revealed that financial inclusion has a positive and significant impact on financial development. These findings emphasize the importance of promoting financial inclusion to foster economic development.

Gheeraert (2014) conducted a study to determine whether Islamic banks act as substitutes or complements to traditional banking. The findings indicated that Islamic banks significantly and positively affect the financial development of countries by contributing to the increase in private credits and bank deposits. This analysis further supports the notion that Islamic finance plays a vital role in promoting financial development.

Ho (2014) highlighted the role of Islamic financial instruments in increasing financial inclusion. By enabling investors to participate in alternative investment products, Islamic financial instruments can help countries enhance financial inclusion. A prime example is the oversubscribed Islamic instrument issued in Indonesia in 2014, which attracted various investors from different backgrounds. Studies have shown that financial inclusion is a crucial pillar of financial stability and economic development. According to that, one of the largest-ever Islamic instrument that was issued in Indonesia in 2014 "was oversubscribed and bought by a variety of investors, including self-employed (32%), private sector employees (27%), housewives (17%), civil servants (4%) and army and police personnel (1%)" (Ahmed and Verbeek, 2015, p.21). Studies show that financial inclusion is one of the pillars of financial stability and economic development (Rao, 2012).

Anwar et al. (2020) investigated the bidirectional relationship between economic growth, deposits in Islamic banks, and the number of offices in the Indonesian Islamic banking industry. Utilizing various analytical methods such as ARDL, VECM, and VDCs, the study found a significant and strong bidirectional relationship between the development of Islamic banking, financial intermediation, and economic growth. These findings further support the positive impact of Islamic finance on financial development and economic growth.

The studies reviewed consistently demonstrate a positive correlation between the development of Islamic finance and economic growth, capital accumulation, and financial stability. Islamic financial instruments have also been shown to promote financial inclusion, which is a crucial driver of financial development. The findings highlight the potential of Islamic finance as an alternative and ethical form of financial intermediation that can contribute to the attainment of the SDGs.

3. DATA AND METHODOLOGY

3.1. Data

To be able to investigate the relation between the issuance of green sukuk and the financial development level, there is a need for two groups of data. In the first group, the variables for the model to determine the financial development levels of the countries should be collected. In this step, we use IMF's Broad-based Index of Financial Development that measures the financial development of the countries by constructing nine sub-indices for depth, access, and efficiency of the financial institutions and financial markets. To be able to construct the depth index of financial institutions 4 variables, for accessibility index 2 variables and efficiency index 6 variables are used. To be able to measure the depth of financial markets, 5 variables, for accessibility index, 2 variables and for the efficiency index, 1 variable are used. Therefore, for the investigation of the financial development levels, in total 20 micro-level variables are collected for 5 countries (Indonesia, Malaysia, Saudi Arabia, Turkey and UAE) for the period of 2014-2021. Table 1 presents the variables under the groups they belong to.

Table 1. Variables that are used for the construction of sub-indices

Financial Institutions	
Depth	Private-sector credit to GDP
	Pension fund assets to GDP
	Mutual fund assets to GDP
	Insurance premiums, life and non-life to GDP
Access	Bank branches per 100,000 adults
	ATMs per 100,000 adults
Efficiency	Net interest margin
	Lending-deposits spread
	Non-interest income to total income
	Overhead costs to total assets
	Return on assets
	Return on equity
Financial Markets	
Depth	Stock market capitalization to GDP
	Stocks traded to GDP
	International debt securities of government to GDP
	Total debt securities of financial corporations to GDP
	Total debt securities of nonfinancial corporations to GDP
Access	Percent of market capitalization outside of top 10 largest companies
	Total number of issuers of debt (domestic and external, nonfinancial and financial corporations)
Efficiency	Stock market turnover ratio (stocks traded to capitalization)

Source: Svirydzenka (2016)

After the variables that are needed to construct the Broad-based Financial Development Index are collected, green-sukuk issuance value data is collected according to the countries and the years. For this purpose, a number of data sources are used: World Bank Global Financial Development Databases, IMF Financial Access Survey, Datastream, Islamic Financial Services Board Database and Statista Database.

As Fuess and Millea (2002, p.284) state "in implementing the Geweke method, the forecast equations must be estimated with stationary time series, otherwise the forecasts may be subject to spurious correlation". Therefore, for both financial development levels of the countries and the green sukuk issuance values, both ADF and PP tests are run to investigate the presence of a unit root. As Table 2 clearly presents, the null of non-stationarity is rejected for both groups. On the other hand, as Geweke technique does not impose restriction on heteroscedasticity and autocorrelation due to it is VAR-based construction, we do not need to worry about the robustness of the data in this regard.

Table 2. Unit root test results

	ADF	PP
Financial Development Index	-7.3645*	-11.7898*
Green Sukuk Issuance Value	-5.3432*	-8.2180*

The critical value for the ADF and PP test statistics is 3.4344 at the 1% significance level.
* denotes the rejection of the null hypothesis at 1% level.

3.2. Methodology

The first step in determining the relationship between the issuance of green sukuk and financial development levels of countries is to assess the financial development levels. This can be done using the Broad-based Financial Development Index introduced by the IMF in 2014. The index consists of two main sub-indices: the financial development of financial institutions and the financial development of financial markets. However, the index has certain limitations. It lacks comprehensive time period data for several institutions and activities and does not consider the variety of financial intermediary types or the organizational complexity of institutions and products. Additionally, it focuses only on the depth, access, and efficiency of financial systems, excluding underlying causes and results such as institutional, regulatory, and legal frameworks, as well as financial stability measures (Svirydzenka, 2016).

To examine the lead/lag relationship between green sukuk issuance volumes and financial development levels, the Geweke Feedback Measure Technique can be applied. This technique is straightforward and provides cardinal measures of the degree of co-movements and feedback between the series. By analyzing the relationship between these variables, it can be determined whether the issuance of green sukuk leads countries to financial development.

3.2.1 Broad-Based Financial Development Index

In this study, in total, 9 different indices are constructed to reach the ultimate financial development levels of the countries. For this purpose, we benefit from the Financial Development Index Pyramid of IMF. According to the pyramid, financial development is measured under two main groups as financial development of financial institutions and financial development of financial markets. To measure how deep, accessible and efficient financial institutions and financial markets are, in total 6 lower level sub-indices are constructed in the first step. In the second step, these sub-indices are aggregated into two higher level sub-indices that reveal the financial development levels of financial institutions and financial markets separately. In the final step, financial institutions and financial markets sub-indices are aggregated to get the overall measure of financial development.

While constructing the Broad-based Financial Development Index, three-step standard procedure is followed. To be able to reduce the dimensionality of a data set and to determine the weights of each indicator, the PCA is used. With this technique, a large number of interrelated variables are reduced to a much smaller number of principal components and the variation present in the data is protected as much as possible.

In the second step, following Sviyrdzenka (2016) all indicators are standardized by using the min-max procedures to bring each indicator to an identical range [0,1].

$$I_x = \frac{x - x_{min}}{x_{max} - x_{min}} \tag{1}$$

In the final step, normalized indicators are aggregated into the six sub-indices. In this rather straightforward step, weighted linear average of the indicators are calculated by using the weights that are obtained in the first step using principal component analysis.

$$FI_j = \sum_{i=1}^{n} w_i I_i \tag{2}$$

$$FM_j = \sum_{i=1}^{n} w_i I_i \tag{3}$$

Lastly, to be able to aggregate the sub-indices, each sub-index scores are re-normalized to bring each index score to [0,1] range using Equation 1.

$$FI = \sum_{j=1}^{n} w_j F_j \tag{4}$$

$$FM = \sum_{j=1}^{n} w_j FP_j \tag{5}$$

$$FD = w_{FI} FI + w_{FM} FM \tag{6}$$

3.2.2. Geweke Feedback Measure

To be able to investigate the lead/lag relation between the value of green sukuk issuance and the financial development, the Geweke Feedback Measure technique is used. As Geweke technique provides cardinal measures of the degree of co-movements and feedback (causality) between the series, it is a quite solid method while investigating whether financial development leads to issuance of green sukuk or contrarily green sukuk issuance significantly contributes to the financial development of the countries.

As Granger causality, Geweke (1982) considers linear projections of two time series. While for the restricted form variable depends on only its own past return -Eq. 7 and Eq. 8-, for the unrestricted form where variable depends on both its own past return and past return of the variable other variable –Eq. 9 and Eq. 10-.

$$x_t = \sum_{i=1}^{\infty} a_{1i} x_{t-i} + u_{1t}, E\left(u_{1t}\right) = 0 \ and \ Var\left(u_{1t}\right) = \sigma_{u_1}^2 \tag{7}$$

$$y_t = \sum_{i=1}^{\infty} c_{1i} y_{t-i} + v_{1t}, E\left(v_{1t}\right) = 0 \ and \ Var\left(v_{1t}\right) = \sigma_{v_1}^2 \tag{8}$$

$$x_t = \sum_{i=1}^{\infty} a_{2i} x_{t-i} + \sum_{i=1}^{\infty} b_{2i} y_{t-i} + u_{2t}, E\left(u_{2t}\right) = 0 \ and \ Var\left(u_{2t}\right) = \sigma_{u_2}^2 \tag{9}$$

$$y_t = \sum_{i=1}^{\infty} c_{2i} y_{t-i} + \sum_{i=1}^{\infty} d_{2i} x_{t-i} + v_{2t}, E\left(v_{2t}\right) = 0 \ and \ Var\left(v_{2t}\right) = \sigma_{v_2}^2 \tag{10}$$

"The value of $\sigma_{u_1}^2$ measures the accuracy of the autoregressive prediction of x_t based on its previous values, whereas the value of $\sigma_{u_2}^2$ represents the accuracy of predicting the present value of x_t based on the previous values of both x_t and y_t. Furthermore, the value of $\sigma_{v_1}^2$ measures the accuracy of the autoregressive prediction of y_t based on its previous values, whereas the value of $\sigma_{v_2}^2$ represents the accuracy of predicting the present value of y_t based on the previous values of both x_t and y_t" (Schelter et al., 2006, p.214). Therefore, jointly considering the Equations 7 and 8 and the Equations 9 and 10, Geweke (1982) obtains the systems of Seemingly Unrelated Regressions (SUR) to get the Geweke measures as following:

$$F_{y \to x} = \ln\left[\sigma_{u_1}^2 / \sigma_{u_2}^2\right]$$

$$F_{x \to y} = \ln\left[\sigma_{v_1}^2 / \sigma_{v_2}^2\right] \tag{11}$$

While, the first measure gives the magnitude of the causality from *y* to *x*, the second measure gives the magnitude of the causality from *x* to *y*.

To be able to compute the contemporaneous relationship between the two series first, the contemporaneous covariance matrix (Σ) is constructed:

$$Cov\left(u_2 v_2\right) = \begin{pmatrix} \sigma_{u_2}^2 & \sigma_{u_2 v_2} \\ \sigma_{u_2 v_2} & \sigma_{v_2}^2 \end{pmatrix} \tag{12}$$

Assuming u_2 and v_2 are serially uncorrelated, the contemporaneous Geweke Feedback Measure can be calculated as follows:

$$F_{x \cdot y} = \ln\left(\frac{\sigma_{u_1}^2 * \sigma_{v_1}^2}{|\Sigma|}\right) \quad (13)$$

4. RESULTS

To be able to investigate the relationship between green sukuk issuance value and financial development levels, first, financial development indices for five countries are constructed for the period of 2014-2021. The below table reveals the financial development scores.

Table 3. Financial development index scores for 2014-2021

	2014	2015	2016	2017	2018	2019	2020	2021
Indonesia	0,348	0,361	0,357	0,370	0,357	0,370	0,363	0,372
Malaysia	0,647	0,644	0,644	0,658	0,649	0,652	0,726	0,751
Saudi Arabia	0,503	0,505	0,531	0,439	0,417	0,399	0,441	0,446
Turkey	0,522	0,519	0,502	0,533	0,526	0,540	0,533	0,530
UAE	0,558	0,476	0,449	0,511	0,501	0,498	0,455	0,476

As can been seen from Table 3, for the investigated period although the scores vary between the years, Malaysia obviously has the most developed financial structure. Following Malaysia, Turkey is the second financially most developed country. While UAE and Saudi Arabia have rather closer financial development index scores and are at third and fourth places, respectively, Indonesia has the least developed financial structure in the country set.

After financial development levels are calculated, the next step is investigating the relationship between green sukuk issuance and financial development levels. For this step, by aggregating the countries' financial development scores and green sukuk issuance values, Geweke Feedback Measures are calculated for three types of relationship. The first feedback measure, Geweke Contemporaneous Feedback Measure, is calculated to investigate the same day relationship between green sukuk issuance value and financial development levels. As Table 4 reveals, the results show that there is no significant contemporaneous correlation between those two variables. In the second step, whether there is a significant lead-lag relation between green sukuk issuance value and financial development level is investigated.

Table 4. Geweke feedback measures between green sukuk issuance value and financial development level

Geweke Contemporaneous Feedback ($GCFM_{GS.FD}$)	**Geweke Unidirectional Feedback Measure from Green Sukuk Issuance Value to Financial Development Level** ($GCFM_{GS \rightarrow FD}$)	**Geweke Unidirectional Feedback Measure from Financial Development Level to Green Sukuk Issuance Value** ($GCFM_{FD \rightarrow GS}$)
2,19	1,31	5,58**

The critical value χ^2_1, is 2.71 for 10% level, 3.84 for 5% level, and 6.63 for 1% level.

Rejection of the null hypothesis is represented by: *, for the 10; **, for the 5; and ***, for the 1% level.

Unidirectional feedback measure from green sukuk issuance value to financial development level shows that green sukuk issuance does not lead the financial development. In other words, green sukuk issuance does not significantly contribute countries to have a better financial development levels. Even if the countries issue more green sukuk, this rather new financial instrument does not lead countries to financially develop. On the other hand, unidirectional feedback measure from financial development to green sukuk issuance shows that there is a significant lead/lag relation between financial development and green sukuk issuance at 95% confidence level. According to that, financial development leads to a higher green sukuk issuance value with a 1-3 years lead/lag period. Therefore, the nature of the relationship between green sukuk issuance and financial development levels can be summarized as, countries that are already financially developed are more eager to issue green sukuk.

As financial development index has various sub-indices, to be able to understand the details of the relation between the green sukuk issuance and components of financial development, there is a need of investigation of the Geweke Feedback Measures for those sub-indices. In the below table, Geweke Contemporaneous Feedback Measures and Geweke Unidirectional Feedback Measures for green sukuk issuance and the financial development sub-indices are revealed.

Table 5. Geweke feedback measures between green sukuk issuance value and financial development sub-indices

	Geweke Contemporaneous Feedback *($GCFM_{GS.FD}$)*	**Geweke Unidirectional Feedback Measure from Green Sukuk Issuance Value to Sub-Index** *($GCFM_{GS \rightarrow SI}$)*	**Geweke Unidirectional Feedback Measure from Sub-Index to Green Sukuk Issuance Value** *($GCFM_{SI \rightarrow GS}$)*
Financial Institutions Access Index	2.01	7.43***	1.94
Financial Institutions Depth Index	1.97	1.11	9.33***
Financial Institutions Efficiency Index	1.69	0.66	3.92**
Financial Institutions Development Index	1.84	1.39	5.65**
Financial Markets Access Index	2.13	0,92	11.24***
Financial Markets Depth Index	8.91***	6.21**	2.66
Financial Markets Efficiency Index	0.78	0.79	4.43**
Financial Markets Development Index	1.75	1.14	8.12***

The critical value χ^2_1, is 2.71 for 10% level, 3.84 for 5% level, and 6.63 for 1% level.

Rejection of the null hypothesis is represented by: *, for the 10; **, for the 5; and ***, for the 1% level.

Although the first part of the analysis reveals that financial development leads countries to issue green sukuk, to be able to understand the clear nature of this relationship, the sub-indices are also investigated. The results are rather surprising compared to the investigation of the composite index as some of the investigated sub-indices are also leaded by issuance of green sukuk. According to that, issuance of green sukuk leads countries to have higher financial institutions access and financial markets depth index scores. In other words, the accessibility of the financial institutions and the depth of the financial markets of the countries that issue green sukuk is expected to increase with 1-3 years lead/lag period. Mohieldin et al. (2012) reveal the mechanism behind this relation by statistically showing that Islamic financing improves the financial inclusion and this enlarges the financial deepening on the markets.

With this detailed analysis, it is also possible to see the mechanism of unidirectional relation between financial development levels and green sukuk issuance value. According to that increasing depth of financial institutions and increasing efficiency of financial institutions leads countries to issue more green sukuk. Furthermore, countries that have higher financial market access index score and financial markets efficiency index score tend to issue green sukuk with 1-3 years lead/lag period compared to the countries with lower index scores. Therefore, results show that countries that increase their performance on the depth and efficiency of financial institutions and accessibility and efficiency of the financial markets, issue green sukuk within 3 years.

As a result, the implications of the findings suggest that financial development and green sukuk issuance are closely related. Countries that are already financially developed are more likely to issue green sukuk. This indicates that green sukuk issuance does not significantly contribute to the financial development of countries. However, financial development does lead to a higher green sukuk issuance value with a lead/lag period of 1-3 years. The observed relationships can be attributed to the mechanism of Islamic financing, which improves financial inclusion and leads to financial deepening in the markets. As the depth and efficiency of financial institutions increase, countries are more inclined to issue green sukuk. Additionally, countries with higher scores in financial market access and efficiency indices are more likely to issue green sukuk.

These findings highlight the importance of developing financial institutions and improving accessibility and efficiency in financial markets to promote the issuance of green sukuk. They also imply that green sukuk can serve as a bridge between conventional and Islamic finance, attracting more investment in environmentally sustainable infrastructure projects.

5. CONCLUSION

Although, Islamic finance naturally promotes some of the SDGs thanks to its characteristics such as prohibition of interest, sadaqa and zakat, it is always criticized on the lack of effort about environmental issues. As this rather new financial instrument, green sukuk, is used to finance the green projects, the criticisms on the ignorance of the Islamic financial system on the environmental issues started to abate. However, the issuance of the green sukuk is still quite limited and it is still not clear which countries are more eager on this rather new green financial instrument. In this very specific study, whether financially developed countries issue more green sukuk or the issuance of green sukuk helps countries to financially develop is investigated. For this purpose, after the construction of Broad-based Financial Development Index of IMF for 5 countries that are on the top of the green-sukuk issuance level on the world, using the Geweke Feedback Measure, the nature of the relation between financial development level and green sukuk issuance is investigated.

Results reveal that there is no same day relationship between the financial development and green sukuk issuance. However, examination of the unidirectional relationships has shown that increasing financial development level leads to more green sukuk issuance. On the other hand, the detailed investigation of the relation between green sukuk and the financial development reveals that green sukuk issuance leads financial institutions to be more accessible and financial markets to have more depth. The investigation of the sub-indices that are used to reach the ultimate financial development levels of the countries shows that high scores on the depth and efficiency of the financial institutions and accessibility and efficiency of the markets leads to more green sukuk issuance. Countries that increase the depth and efficiency of the financial institutions and accessibility and efficiency of the markets are expected to issue green sukuk with 1-3 years lead/lag period. In other words, there is a strong connection between financial development and the issuance of green sukuk. It is observed that countries that are already financially developed are more likely to issue green sukuk, indicating that green sukuk issuance does not significantly contribute to the financial development of countries. However, financial development does lead to a higher value of green sukuk issuance with a time lag of 1-3 years. This relationship can be explained by the role of Islamic financing, which improves financial inclusion and leads to deeper and more efficient financial markets. Countries with higher scores in financial market access and efficiency indices are also more likely to issue green sukuk.

At that point, it should be clearly stated that there are some potential limitations and challenges faced during the analysis. According to that, the findings of the study may not be applicable to countries outside the selected sample as each country has its own unique financial system, regulatory environment, and level of development, which can significantly impact the relationship between financial development and green sukuk issuance. Secondly, the study identifies a relationship between financial development and green sukuk issuance, but it does not establish causality. It is possible that other factors may influence both financial development and green sukuk issuance simultaneously. Additionally, the time lag of 1-3 years may not capture the immediate impact of financial development on green sukuk issuance. Lastly, the study does not explicitly analyze the influence of external factors such as political stability, regulatory frameworks, and investor preferences on green sukuk issuance. These factors could potentially impact the relationship between financial development and green sukuk issuance.

Despite the limitations, the findings of the analysis have several policy implications for promoting green sukuk issuance and encouraging financial development while ensuring environmental sustainability. Firstly, it is important for policymakers and regulators to focus on developing financial institutions. The results indicate that countries with higher financial institution access and efficiency scores are more likely to issue green sukuk. Therefore, efforts should be made to improve the accessibility and efficiency of financial institutions to encourage the issuance of green sukuk. Secondly, policymakers should prioritize improving the accessibility and efficiency of financial markets. Countries with higher financial market access and efficiency index scores were found to be more inclined to issue green sukuk. This suggests that creating a favorable environment for efficient and accessible financial markets can attract more issuances of green sukuk. Thirdly, policymakers should consider the role of Islamic financing in promoting financial inclusion and deepening. The analysis reveals that Islamic financing improves financial inclusion, leading to greater financial deepening in the markets. Therefore, policymakers can explore ways to promote Islamic financing and leverage its positive impact on financial development and green sukuk issuance. Additionally, policymakers should explore measures to bridge the gap between conventional and Islamic finance. Green sukuk can serve as a bridge between the two and attract more investment in environmentally sustainable infrastructure projects. Policymakers can introduce supportive regulations and incentives to encourage investors and issuers to participate in the green sukuk market. Finally, policymakers should ensure that green sukuk issuance aligns with environmental sustainability goals. While financial development can lead to increased green sukuk issuance, it is crucial to ensure that the projects funded through green sukuk contribute to environmental sustainability. Policymakers should establish robust monitoring and reporting mechanisms to track the impact of green sukuk-funded projects and ensure their alignment with sustainable development goals.

Finally, the study opens up avenues for future research to explore other factors that may influence green sukuk issuance, such as environmental policies, investor demand, and the role of international collaborations. These areas of investigation could further enhance the understanding of the relationship between financial development and green sukuk issuance.

REFERENCES

Abduh, M., & Omar, A. M. (2012). Islamic Banking and Economic Growth: The Indonesian Experience. *International Journal of Islamic and Middle Eastern Finance and Management*, *5*(1), 35–47. doi:10.1108/17538391211216811

Abduh, M., Shabri, M., & Kassim, H. S. (2015). Assessing the Contribution of Islamic Finance to Economic Growth. *Journal of Islamic Accounting and Business Research*, *6*, 292–310. doi:10.1108/JIABR-07-2012-0050

Ahmed, H., & Verbeek, J. (2015). *On the Sustainable Development Goals and the Role of Islamic Finance.* (Policy Research Working Paper, No. 7266). World Bank, Washington, DC.

Anwar, S. M., Naidi, N., Salju, S., Wicaksono, R., & Mispiyanti, G. (2020). Islamic Bank Contribution to Indonesian Economic Growth. *International Journal of Islamic and Middle Eastern Finance and Management*, *13*, 75–86. doi:10.1108/IMEFM-02-2018-0071

Buiter, W. H., & Rahbari, E. (2015). Why Economists (and Economies) Should Love Islamic Finance. *Islamic Economics*, *28*(1), 139–162.

Chakravarty, S. R., & Pal, R. (2013). Financial Inclusion in India: An Axiomatic Approach. *Journal of Policy Modeling*, *35*(5), 813–837. doi:10.1016/j.jpolmod.2012.12.007

Chapra, M. U. (1992). Islam and the Economic Challenge. Islamic Economics Series, 17. The Islamic Foundation, Herndon.

Farahani, Y. G., & Dastan, M. (2013). Analysis of Islamic Banks' Financing and Economic Growth: A Panel Cointegration Approach. *International Journal of Islamic and Middle Eastern Finance and Management*, *6*(2), 156–172. doi:10.1108/17538391311329842

Fuess, S., & Millea, M. (2002). Do Employers Pay Efficiency Wage? Evidence from Japan. *Journal of Labor Research*, *23*(3), 279–292. doi:10.100712122-002-1007-5

Geweke, J. (1982). Measurement of Linear Dependence and Feedback between Multiple Time Series. *Journal of the American Statistical Association, 77*(378), 304–313. doi:10.1080/01621459.1982.10477803

Gheeraert, L. (2014). Does Islamic Finance Spur Banking Sector Development? *Journal of Economic Behavior & Organization, 103*, 4–20. doi:10.1016/j.jebo.2014.02.013

Ho, J. (2014). *Indonesia Sells a Record $1.7 Billion of Retail Sovereign Sukuk.* The Jakarta Globe.

Kahf, M. (1989). Zakat: Unresolved Issues in the Contemporary Fiqh. *Journal of Islamic Economics, 2*(1), 1–22.

Kahf, M. (1998). The Concept of Ownership in Islam. In M. Kahf (Ed.), *Lessons in Islamic Economics, Part II* (pp. 241–256). Islamic Research and Training Institute, Islamic Development Bank.

Kamla, R., & Rammal, H. G. (2013). Social Reporting by Islamic Banks: Does social justice matter? *Accounting, Auditing & Accountability Journal, 26*(6), 911–945. doi:10.1108/AAAJ-03-2013-1268

Maali, B., Casson, P., & Napier, C. (2006). Social Reporting by Islamic Banks. *Abacus, 42*(2), 266–289. doi:10.1111/j.1467-6281.2006.00200.x

Mian, A., & Amir, S. (2014). *House of Debt: How They (and You) Caused the Great Recession, and How We Can Prevent It from Happening Again.* University of Chicago Press. doi:10.7208/chicago/9780226277509.001.0001

Mohieldin, M., Iqbal, Z., Rostom, A., & Fu, X. (2012). The Role of Islamic Finance in Enhancing Financial Inclusion in Organization of Islamic Cooperation (OIC) Countries. *Islamic Economic Studies, 20*(2), 55–120.

Nasr, S. V. R. (1989). Islamic Economics: Novel Perspectives. *Middle Eastern Studies, 25*(4), 516–530. doi:10.1080/00263208908700797

OECD. (2015). *Green Bonds Mobilising the Debt Capital Markets for a Low-Carbon Transition.* OECD Publishing.

Rao, N., & Bhatnagar, M. H. (2012). Financial Inclusion: Issues and Prospects. *Pacific Business Review International, 5*(3), 84–96.

Rasheed, B., Law, S. H., Chin, L., & Habibullah, M. S. (2016). The Role of Financial Inclusion in Financial Development: International Evidence. *Abasyn University Journal of Social Sciences, 9*(2), 330–348.

Schelter, B., Winterhalder, M., Eichler, M., Peifer, M., Hellwig, B., Guschlbauer, B., Lucking, C., Dahlhaus, R., & Timmer, J. (2006). Testing for Directed Influences among Neural Signals Using Partial Directed Coherence. *Journal of Neuroscience Methods, 152*(2), 210–219. doi:10.1016/j.jneumeth.2005.09.001 PMID:16269188

Siddiqi, M. N. (1968). The Economic Enterprise in Islam. Islamic Publications (Pvt.) Ltd., Lahore.

Svirydzenka, K. (2016). *Introducing a New Broad-based Index of Financial Development.* (IMF Working Paper, No. 16/5). IMF, Washington, DC.

Yoon, A. (2012). Total Global Losses from Financial Crisis: $15 Trillion. *The Wall Street Journal.*

Zakaria, A. A., & Arun, T. (2015). Corporate Social Responsibility and Islamic Financial Institutions (IFIs): Management Perceptions from IFIs in Bahrain. *Journal of Business Ethics*, *129*(4), 785–794. doi:10.100710551-014-2132-9

Chapter 12
Reinvigorating the Path to SDG 7:
Examining the Link Between Institutional Efficiency and Energy Outcomes in MINT Economies

Ibrahim Nandom Yakubu
https://orcid.org/0000-0003-4424-996X
University for Development Studies, Ghana

Abdul-Hamid Abdul-Wahab
https://orcid.org/0000-0001-7219-1027
University for Development Studies, Ghana

Abdul-Latif Mohammed
The University of Newcastle, Australia

ABSTRACT

This study examines the relationship between institutional efficiency and energy outcomes in the MINT economies (Mexico, Indonesia, Nigeria, and Turkey) over the period 1996–2021. Energy outcomes are measured using various indicators, including energy intensity, total energy consumption, renewable energy consumption, and fossil fuel consumption. The dynamic ordinary least squares (DOLS) technique is utilized to analyze the data. The findings reveal a mixed impact of institutional efficiency on energy outcomes. Higher institutional efficiency is associated with a reduction in energy intensity. Likewise, stronger institutions are linked to a decrease in the share of renewable energy, suggesting challenges in promoting renewable energy adoption in the MINT economies. Furthermore, institutional efficiency is positively related to total energy consumption and the use of fossil fuels, indicating a reliance on traditional energy sources. The study finds no significant effect of industrialization on energy outcomes, while trade openness exhibits a positive and significant impact.

DOI: 10.4018/978-1-6684-9272-7.ch012

INTRODUCTION

Energy is universally acknowledged as a fundamental catalyst for enhancing the production of goods and services, thereby contributing to human well-being within any economy (Apergis & Sorros, 2014). Considering the significant impact that energy holds in achieving economic development, it becomes imperative to emphasize global collaboration in addressing the world's energy needs while ensuring equitable access to clean, reliable, and affordable energy sources. This becomes a shared responsibility and a common objective for all nations (Emodi & Boo, 2015). In contrast, it is critical to recognize that energy consumption is inextricably linked to the main cause of CO_2 and greenhouse gas emissions, exerting a considerable effect on climate change and the growing phenomena of global warming (Ritchie & Roser, 2020).

The increasing accumulation of greenhouse gases in the Earth's atmosphere causes a plethora of environmental problems, including rising sea levels, increased occurrences of extreme weather events, and ecological disruptions (Burke et al., 2018). Climate change's negative impacts not only jeopardize nature's fragile equilibrium but also have far-reaching consequences for human society. Vulnerable communities, particularly in poor nations, confront the brunt of these impacts, facing challenges to food security, relocation as a result of natural catastrophes, and increased health risks (Atanga & Tankpa, 2021).

In light of the detrimental impact of climate change, and in pursuant to the United Nations' Sustainable Development Goal 7 (SDG 7), which is aimed at ensuring access to affordable, reliable, sustainable, and modern energy for all by 2030, the global community is increasingly recognizing the pressing need to transition to cleaner and more sustainable energy sources. Renewable energy, which includes solar, wind, hydro, and geothermal power, presents realistic options that not only drastically cut or eliminate greenhouse gas emissions during generation but also contribute to the achievement of SDG 7.

In recent years, there has been a surge in research on strategies for achieving Sustainable Development Goal 7 (SDG 7). Several studies have been conducted to investigate the drivers of renewable energy usage in different contexts, with varying results (see Ergun et al. 2019; Akintande et al., 2020; Li et al., 2020; Chen et al., 2021; Bekun & Alola, 2022; Mehmood et al., 2022; Lawal, 2023; Wang et., 2023; Sachan et al., 2023). However, it is crucial to note that the assessment of SDG 7 achievement goes beyond renewable energy consumption, incorporating other key criteria that are often disregarded.

In the pursuit of accomplishing SDG 7, this study aims to examine the impact of institutional efficiency on energy outcomes in the MINT economies (Mexico, Indonesia, Nigeria, and Turkey). These economies are poised to become major global players in the upcoming decades as they strive toward achieving fully industrialized status (Yakubu et al., 2022). The realization of these ambitious goals necessitates a strong infrastructure foundation and an efficient energy system that minimizes adverse environmental consequences. Given that institutional efficiency can facilitate the effective implementation of policies, regulations, and initiatives pertaining to clean and sustainable energy, strengthening institutional frameworks in the MINT economies can advance their progress towards SDG 7, resulting in sustainable and environmentally friendly energy systems.

This study makes several valuable contributions to the existing literature. Firstly, to the best of the researchers' knowledge, this study is one of the first of its kind to investigate the impact of institutional efficiency on the achievement of Sustainable Development Goals (SDGs), specifically focusing on multiple factors related to the implementation of SDG 7 within the MINT economies. By filling this research gap, the study provides new insights into the role of institutional efficiency in driving progress toward SDG 7 targets.

Furthermore, the study's focus on the MINT economies adds a unique dimension to the research. These economies are recognized as emerging markets with significant growth potential and have specific socio-economic and environmental contexts. By examining the interplay between institutional efficiency and energy outcomes in these countries, policymakers can design targeted interventions and strategies to improve institutional efficiency and accelerate progress en route for SDG 7.

The rest of the chapter is organized as follows: Section 2 provides a comprehensive review of the existing literature on the drivers of energy outcomes. The research methodology employed in this study is presented in Section 3, followed by a discussion of the findings in Section 4. Finally, Section 5 concludes the chapter by summarizing the key findings and presenting relevant policy implications.

LITERATURE REVIEW

Theoretically, the Public Goods theory might be pertinent to examining the influence of institutional efficiency on energy outcomes. The Public Goods theory is a concept in economics that refers to goods that are non-excludable and non-rivalrous in consumption. This means that once the good is produced, it is available for anyone to use and its consumption by one individual does not reduce the availability of the good for others (Samuelson, 1954; Samuelson, 1955).

Since the 1950s, the economic theory of the public sector has been based on the Public Goods theory. The economics profession has adopted a strict definition of the phrase "public good" and has utilized the concept of a public good to establish a role for government production in the economy, both of which were inspired by two groundbreaking works by Paul Samuelson that were published in 1954 and 1955 (Holcombe, 1997). The theory examines how certain products and services are delivered and used in society with emphasis on the role of government.

In the context of this study, this theory argues that some energy resources, such as clean air and water, are public goods. This means that they are non-excludable and non-rivalrous. As a result, it is difficult for markets to provide these goods efficiently. Governments can therefore play a role in ensuring that these goods are provided in an efficient manner. Accordingly, the theory can give insights into how institutional variables affect renewable energy sources, energy efficiency practices, and the general effectiveness of the energy system in the context of energy outcomes.

Empirically, several studies have explored the relationship between institutional quality and various energy-related outcomes, including energy intensity, energy consumption, renewable energy deployment, carbon dioxide (CO_2) emissions, and the utilization of fossil fuels (Islam et al., 2022; Wang et al., 2022; Godil et al., 2021; Azam et al., 2021; Chen and Zhou, 2021; Tenaw, 2021; Sun et al., 2019).

Improved institutional quality decreases energy intensity and dependence (Ijaz and Chughtai, 2022). Chen and Zhou (2021) found that institutional quality has a negative but significant impact on energy intensity. Similarly, a study by Tenaw (2021) revealed that institutional quality appeared to have a significant negative influence on energy intensity in the long run. The above findings are indirectly supported by Sun et al. (2019) who examined the relationship between institutional quality and energy efficiency. Their findings revealed a positive and significant impact of institutional quality on energy efficiency and thereby indicating a negative impact of institutional quality on energy intensity. The above literature, therefore, suggests that institutional quality has a negative impact on energy intensity

Considering the relationship between institutional quality and energy consumption, Shahbaz et al. (2016) emphasized the need for future research to empirically explore the impact of institutional quality on energy consumption. For instance, Azam et al. (2021) investigated the relationship between institutional quality and environmental indicators in 66 developing countries from 1991 to 2017. The analysis considered various indicators such as CO_2 emissions, CH4 emissions, forest area, organic water pollutants, and energy consumption. The study constructed an institutional quality index based on political stability, administrative capacity, and democratic accountability. Using the system Generalized Method of Moments (GMM) method, the results indicated that institutional quality has a positive influence on several environmental indicators, such as CO_2 emissions, CH4 emissions, and forest area. Moreover, institutional quality was found to have a positive impact on energy consumption, particularly in relation to oil and fossil fuel resources. However, a study by Godil et al. (2021) revealed that institutional quality has a significant negative effect on energy utilization in India.

With regard to the link between institutional quality and renewable energy consumption, Wang et al. (2022) examined the influence of institutional quality and political risk on renewable energy consumption in 32 Organisation for Economic Co-operation and Development (OECD) member countries from 1997 to 2019. Their study disclosed that institutional quality has a significant impact on renewable energy consumption. In line with the work of Wang et al. (2022), Islam et al. (2022) documented a significant positive impact of institutional quality on renewable energy consumption. Likewise, a study by Uzar (2020) examined the possible effects of institutional quality on renewable energy consumption, employing data from 1990 to 2015 for selected 38 economies. The research concluded that institutional quality positively impacts renewable energy consumption in the long run, while CO_2 emission was positive and significant in determining renewable energy consumption. Institutional quality was therefore noted as a crucial strategic option in encouraging the use of renewable energy and resolving environmental problems.

In reference to institutional quality and CO_2 emissions, a study by Azam et al. (2021) demonstrated that institutional quality has a positive influence on several environmental indicators including CO_2 emissions. Also, Tufail et al. (2021) found that institutional quality reduces CO_2 emissions. In the same vein, Khan et al. (2022) noted that improving institutional quality as well as renewable energy consumption have a significant influence on CO_2 emissions. Scholarly work by Cao et al. (2022) demonstrated that institutional quality supports in reducing CO_2 emissions in 36 OECD countries. Similarly, Ali et al. (2023) established that institutional quality decreases CO_2 emissions in the OECD countries. Haldar and Sethi (2021) investigated how institutional quality influences the relationship between energy consumption and CO_2 emissions, together with other variables, in 39 developing countries from 1995–2017. The findings suggested that higher institutional quality strengthens the effectiveness of energy consumption in reducing carbon emissions. The collective effect of institutional quality and sector-specific energy consumption has a significant and negative impact on CO_2 emissions. This outcome supports the need to improve institutions and promote renewable energy for sustainable climate goals. In the case of Africa, Zhang et al. (2023) found that institutional frameworks exacerbate CO_2 emissions.

RESEARCH METHODOLOGY

Sources of Data and Description of Variables

This study utilizes annual data from the MINT economies, covering the period from 1996 to 2021. The data for this study is sourced from the World Bank Development Indicators, ensuring reliable and comprehensive data for analysis. In this study, energy outcomes are considered as the dependent variable, reflecting the various aspects of energy performance within the MINT economies.

To capture the multifaceted nature of energy outcomes, the researchers employ different measures, including energy intensity (ENI), total energy consumption (ENC), renewable energy consumption (REN), and fossil fuel consumption (FOS). Energy intensity is measured using the energy intensity level of primary energy, which is calculated as the ratio of primary energy consumption (measured in million joules) to the constant 2017 purchasing power parity (PPP) GDP (measured in US dollars). This measure provides insights into the energy efficiency and intensity of economic output. Total energy consumption is evaluated through the metric of energy use, measured in kilograms of oil equivalent per capita. This indicator provides an overview of the overall energy consumption patterns within the MINT economies. Renewable energy consumption, expressed as a percentage of total final energy consumption, quantifies the proportion of energy derived from renewable sources, such as solar, wind, hydro, and geothermal power. Furthermore, fossil fuel consumption is assessed by considering the total amount of energy derived from fossil fuel sources, expressed as a percentage of the total energy consumption. This measure allows for the examination of the reliance on fossil fuels within the energy mix of the MINT economies.

In addition to examining the impact of institutional efficiency (INSE) on energy outcomes, this study takes into account the influence of other pertinent factors to ensure a comprehensive analysis. Control variables such as industrialization (INDU), trade openness (TRA), and financial development (FID) are considered, recognizing their potential effects on energy outcomes. To measure institutional efficiency, the study employs the principal component analysis (PCA) technique. This statistical method allows for the construction of an institutional efficiency index based on a set of sub-indicators. The sub-measures used in this analysis include "voice and accountability, political stability and absence of violence, government effectiveness, regulatory quality, rule of law, and control of corruption. Each of these indicators is assigned a score ranging approximately from -2.5 to 2.5, with higher values denoting better governance. The institutional efficiency index provides a composite measure of the overall institutional performance within the MINT economies. This index serves as a comprehensive representation of the effectiveness and quality of the institutional frameworks in these economies, considering various dimensions of governance. For the control variables, industrialization is measured by the annual percentage growth of manufacturing value added. To capture the influence of trade on energy outcomes, the value of imports and exports of goods and services as a percentage of GDP is utilized as a proxy for trade openness. Financial development is measured by the domestic credit provided to the private sector by banks, expressed as a percentage of GDP.

Empirical Model Specification

Given that the study employs a panel approach to analyze the relationship between institutional efficiency and energy outcomes in the MINT economies, the basic empirical model is specified as follows:

$$Yit = \alpha + \beta Xit + \mu it \tag{1}$$

In the equation, Y represents the energy outcomes for country *i* at time *t*, which serves as the dependent variable of interest. The explanatory factors (institutional efficiency and the control variables) are denoted by X, where α represents the intercept and β is the respective regression coefficients of the explanatory factors. The error term μ accounts for unobserved factors and random variations that affect energy outcomes but are not included in the model.

Considering the variables included in the analysis, equation 1 can be adjusted as follows:

$$ENIit = \alpha 0 + \beta 1INSE + \beta 2INDUit + \beta 3TRAit + \beta 4FIDit + \mu it \quad (2)$$

$$ENCit = \alpha 0 + \beta 1INSE + \beta 2INDUit + \beta 3TRAit + \beta 4FIDit + \mu it \quad (3)$$

$$RENit = \alpha 0 + \beta 1INSE + \beta 2INDUit + \beta 3TRAit + \beta 4FIDit + \mu it \quad (4)$$

$$FOSit = \alpha 0 + \beta 1INSE + \beta 2INDUit + \beta 3TRAit + \beta 4FIDit + \mu it \quad (5)$$

Analytical Technique

The estimation of the models in this study is conducted using the dynamic ordinary least squares (DOLS) method, which offers several advantages. The DOLS method is particularly well-suited for capturing long-run relationships and addressing endogeneity issues commonly encountered in panel analysis (Balsalobre-Lorente et al., 2019). By employing this approach, the study is able to account for the dynamic nature of the variables and examine their long-term interactions. Furthermore, when compared to alternative methods for panel cointegration, the DOLS technique exhibits superior asymptotic properties, specifically in reducing bias during variable estimation and standard error estimation (Funk, 2001, cited in Yakubu et al., 2022). This indicates that by utilizing the DOLS approach, the estimation results become more accurate and reliable, thereby contributing to the generation of robust findings.

RESULTS AND DISCUSSIONS

Descriptive Statistics

The descriptive statistics in Table 1 provide valuable insights into the characteristics and distribution of the variables under analysis. Energy intensity (ENI) shows a mean value of 4.509, indicating moderate energy efficiency across the MINT economies. Total energy consumption (ENC) has a much larger mean value of 1111.828, reflecting the substantial energy demands within these economies. Renewable energy consumption (REN) has a mean of 36.763, suggesting a moderate level of reliance on renewable sources. Fossil fuel consumption (FOS) has a higher mean of 65.392, indicating a significant dependence on traditional energy sources. Institutional efficiency (INSE) has a mean close to zero, implying a balanced distribution of efficient and inefficient institutions. Industrialization (INDU) shows a positive mean of 3.797, indicating overall growth in the manufacturing sector. Trade openness (TRA) has a mean of 50.516, suggesting a significant level of international trade. Financial development (FID) has a mean of 24.929, suggesting a moderate level of access to credit for the private sector. The standard deviations provide insights into the variability of the variables, with energy consumption (ENC) having the highest standard deviation of 381.633. The skewness values indicate the degree of symmetry in the distribution, with positive skewness observed for energy intensity (ENI) and institutional efficiency (INSE), indicating a tail towards higher values. The kurtosis values suggest that the variables are generally leptokurtic, with higher kurtosis observed for industrialization (INDU) and financial development (FID), indicating heavy-tailed distributions. The Jarque-Bera tests indicate departures from normality for all variables, with low p-values suggesting non-normal distributions.

Table 1. Descriptive statistics

	ENI	*ENC*	*REN*	*FOS*	*INSE*	*INDU*	*TRA*	*FID*
Mean	4.509	1111.828	36.763	65.392	-6.70E-16	3.797	50.516	24.929
Maximum	10.010	1709.286	88.680	91.057	2.795	21.797	96.186	70.901
Minimum	2.590	659.539	8.970	15.854	-4.068	-11.437	16.352	6.151
Std. Dev.	1.851	381.633	29.896	28.380	2.165	6.113	13.830	15.954
Skewness	1.181	0.246	0.768	-0.812	-0.507	0.220	0.354	1.354
Kurtosis	3.511	1.340	1.929	2.026	1.785	4.183	3.815	4.030
Jarque-Bera	19.467	9.737	14.014	11.644	9.603	6.900	5.049	36.366
Probability	0.000	0.008	0.001	0.003	0.008	0.032	0.080	0.000

Panel Unit Root and Cointegration Tests

The panel unit root tests based on the Fisher Augmented Dickey-Fuller (ADF) and Phillips-Perron (PP) techniques in Table 2 provide insights into the stationarity properties of the variables. In the level form, all variables except for ENI and TRA show significant unit roots, indicating non-stationarity. However, when considering the first difference, all variables exhibit stationarity, as indicated by the significantly negative ADF and PP statistics. This suggests that the variables are integrated at order one (I(1)). Moving on to the cointegration test, the Kao test statistic of -1.777 suggests the presence of cointegration among the variables. The associated p-value of 0.038 indicates that the null hypothesis of no cointegration is rejected at the 5% significance level, providing evidence of a long-run relationship among the variables. Overall, these results suggest that the variables are stationary in first differences and exhibit cointegration, supporting the suitability of the panel data for further analysis.

Table 2. Unit root and cointegration tests

Unit Root Test				
	Level		*First Difference*	
Variables	*ADF-Fisher*	*PP-Fisher*	*ADF-Fisher*	*PP-Fisher*
ENI	12.757	18.542**	18.465**	40.621***
ENC	3.925	4.960	29.838***	68.188***
REN	6.233	10.587	32.496***	54.032***
FOS	6.100	9.073	25.026***	59.222***
INSE	5.155	3.579	19.470**	48.433***
INDU	38.572***	47.417***	84.357***	114.752***
TRA	3.720	6.539	87.865***	92.913***
FID	20.421***	7.936	29.436***	43.048***
Kao Cointegration Test				
			t-statistic	Prob.
ADF			-1.777	0.038

Regression Results

The regression results in Table 3 indicate the estimated coefficients and their statistical significance, providing insights into the impact of institutional efficiency and other control variables on energy outcomes.

Table 3. DOLS estimates: The impact of institutional efficiency on energy outcomes

Variables	*ENI*	*ENC*	*REN*	*FOS*
INSE	-0.891***	117.949***	-14.230***	10.098***
	(0.121)	(24.101)	(1.345)	(0.628)
INDU	0.028	10.356	0.753	0.442**
	(0.043)	(7.921)	(0.461)	(0.207)
TRA	0.087***	22.132***	0.564***	1.224***
	(0.010)	(2.220)	(0.114)	(0.058)
FID	-0.010	-3.783	0.059	-0.005
	(0.018)	(4.492)	(0.206)	(0.117)
R^2	0.396	0.460	0.697	0.898
Adj. R^2	0.371	0.434	0.686	0.893
S.E. of regression	1.415	289.220	16.827	9.322
Long-run variance	4.475	168708.7	634.885	114.698

Standard errors are in parentheses *** p<0.01 ** p<0.05

The results show that institutional efficiency has a significant negative impact on energy intensity, which is consistent with prior studies (Chen & Zhou, 2021; Tenaw, 2021). This suggests that as the institutional frameworks become stronger in the MINT economies, they are able to implement energy efficiency measures, resulting in more efficient use of energy resources. For total energy consumption, the coefficient of 117.949 indicates a positive relationship with institutional efficiency. This implies that higher institutional efficiency in the MINT economies is associated with higher levels of total energy consumption. One plausible reason for this could be that countries with stronger institutions have the capacity to support and facilitate industrial growth, leading to increased energy demand. This result is in line with the findings of Azam et al. (2021) and Godil et al. (2021). In terms of renewable energy consumption, the negative coefficient of -14.230 suggests that higher institutional efficiency is associated with a decrease in the proportion of energy derived from renewable sources. This could be due to the fact that developing economies (as in the case of the countries in the MINT) with weaker institutions may face challenges in implementing policies and providing incentives for renewable energy development. Regarding fossil fuel consumption, the findings indicate that higher institutional efficiency is linked to an increase in the share of energy derived from fossil fuels. This could be attributed to the fact that countries with stronger institutions may have more established and efficient fossil fuel industries, leading to a higher reliance on these traditional energy sources.

The coefficients for industrialization show mixed results. It is not statistically significant in the cases of energy intensity, total energy consumption, and renewable energy consumption, indicating that industrialization may not have a significant direct impact on these energy outcomes. However, it is positively and significantly associated with fossil fuel consumption, suggesting that higher industrialization levels are associated with increased reliance on fossil fuels in the MINT countries. This could be attributed to the energy-intensive nature of industrial activities.

Trade openness exhibits positive and significant coefficients for all energy outcomes, implying that countries with higher trade openness tend to have higher energy consumption and reliance on fossil fuels with efforts to adopt renewable energy. This could be due to increased economic activities associated with trade, leading to greater energy demand.

Financial development does not show a significant impact on energy outcomes, indicating that the level of financial development may not directly influence energy consumption patterns in the MINT economies.

Interpreting the R-squared values, it can be observed that the model for energy intensity (ENI) explains approximately 39.6% of the variation in the dependent variable, while the models for total energy consumption (ENC), renewable energy consumption (REN), and fossil fuel consumption (FOS) have higher R-squared values of 46.0%, 69.7%, and 89.8% respectively. These values indicate that the models capture a substantial portion of the variability in the respective energy outcomes.

CONCLUSION AND RECOMMENDATIONS

This study investigates the relationship between institutional efficiency and energy outcomes in the MINT economies from 1996 to 2021. The energy outcomes are measured using various variables such as energy intensity, total energy consumption, renewable energy consumption, and fossil fuel consumption. The dynamic ordinary least squares (DOLS) technique is applied to analyze the data and estimate the models. The findings of the study reveal that institutional efficiency has a mixed impact on the different energy outcomes. On one hand, it is found that higher institutional efficiency leads to a reduction in energy intensity, indicating a more efficient use of energy in the MINT economies. Additionally, institutional efficiency is associated with a decrease in the share of renewable energy, suggesting that stronger institutions may not be effectively promoting renewable energy adoption. On the other hand, the study finds that institutional efficiency is positively correlated with total energy consumption, implying that as institutional efficiency improves, the overall energy consumption in the MINT economies tends to increase. Moreover, the use of fossil fuels also increases with higher institutional efficiency, indicating a reliance on traditional energy sources. The findings further reveal that industrialization does not have a significant effect on energy intensity, total energy consumption, and renewable energy consumption. However, trade openness has a positive and significant impact on all energy outcomes. Financial development, on the other hand, does not show a significant influence on energy outcomes.

Several policy recommendations may be made based on the study's results to align the MINT economies with the attainment of SDG 7. To begin, there is a need to develop energy-related institutional frameworks and governance structures in order to improve energy efficiency. This may be accomplished by legislative initiatives that enhance energy sector openness, accountability, and effective regulation. Also, capacity-building programs should be developed to improve the technical skills of energy sector professionals, empowering them to adopt and implement energy-efficient techniques. Second, notwithstanding the detrimental link between institutional efficiency and renewable energy share, it is critical to emphasize renewable energy development in order to minimize greenhouse gas emissions.

In addition, although there is a negative link between institutional efficiency and renewable energy share, it is critical to prioritize renewable energy development to decrease greenhouse gas emissions and promote sustainability. To stimulate the adoption of renewable energy technology, policymakers should provide supporting regulatory frameworks, financial incentives, and investment structures. Furthermore, while trade openness has a positive influence on energy outcomes, it is critical to ensure that the energy sector is managed by sustainable trade regulations. Governments should create rigorous systems to monitor and enforce environmental standards in energy-related commerce, boosting the use of cleaner technology and minimizing the environmental footprint related to energy imports and exports.

Despite the insightful conclusions garnered from this research, several limitations are noted. The study, for example, presumes a linear link between institutional efficiency and energy results. The relationship might, however, be more complicated, incorporating non-linear dynamics or threshold effects. Exploring nonlinear interactions and possible thresholds might give a more sophisticated understanding of how institutional efficiency affects energy outcomes. Furthermore, the study focuses specifically on the influence of institutional efficiency on energy outcomes. However, factors such as population growth, urbanization, and income levels all have a substantial impact on energy outcomes. To further understand the complexities of achieving sustainable energy outcomes, future research might investigate the interaction between institutional efficiency and these socioeconomic factors.

REFERENCES

Akintande, O. J., Olubusoye, O. E., Adenikinju, A. F., & Olanrewaju, B. T. (2020). Modeling the determinants of renewable energy consumption: Evidence from the five most populous nations in Africa. *Energy*, *206*, 117992. doi:10.1016/j.energy.2020.117992

Ali, K., Jianguo, D., Kirikkaleli, D., Oláh, J., & Altuntaş, M. (2023). Do green technological innovation, financial development, economic policy uncertainty, and institutional quality matter for environmental sustainability? *All Earth, 35*(1), 82–101. doi:10.1080/27669645.2023.2200330

Apergis, N., & Sorros, J. (2014). The role of R&D expenses for profitability: Evidence from US fossil and renewable energy firms. *International Journal of Economics and Finance, 6*(3), 8–15. doi:10.5539/ijef.v6n3p8

Atanga, R. A., & Tankpa, V. (2021). Climate change, flood disaster risk and food security Nexus in Northern Ghana. *Frontiers in Sustainable Food Systems, 5*, 706721. doi:10.3389/fsufs.2021.706721

Azam, M., Liu, L., & Ahmad, N. (2021). Impact of institutional quality on environment and energy consumption: Evidence from developing world. *Environment, Development and Sustainability, 23*(2), 1646–1667. doi:10.100710668-020-00644-x

Balsalobre-Lorente, D., Gokmenoglu, K. K., Taspinar, N., & Cantos-Cantos, J. M. (2019). An approach to the pollution haven and pollution halo hypotheses in MINT countries. *Environmental Science and Pollution Research International, 26*(22), 23010–23026. doi:10.100711356-019-05446-x PMID:31183758

Bekun, F. V., & Alola, A. A. (2022). Determinants of renewable energy consumption in agrarian Sub-Sahara African economies. *Energy, Ecology & Environment, 7*(3), 227–235. doi:10.100740974-022-00243-8

Burke, P. J., & Kurniawati, S. (2018). Electricity subsidy reform in Indonesia: Demand-side effects on electricity use. *Energy Policy, 116*, 410–421. doi:10.1016/j.enpol.2018.02.018

Cao, H., Khan, M. K., Rehman, A., Dagar, V., Oryani, B., & Tanveer, A. (2022). Impact of globalization, institutional quality, economic growth, electricity and renewable energy consumption on Carbon Dioxide Emission in OECD countries. *Environmental Science and Pollution Research International, 29*(16), 24191–24202. doi:10.100711356-021-17076-3 PMID:34822079

Chen, C., Pinar, M., & Stengos, T. (2021). Determinants of renewable energy consumption: Importance of democratic institutions. *Renewable Energy, 179*, 75–83. doi:10.1016/j.renene.2021.07.030

Chen, Z., & Zhou, M. (2021). Urbanization and energy intensity: Evidence from the institutional threshold effect. *Environmental Science and Pollution Research International, 28*(9), 11142–11157. doi:10.100711356-020-11386-8 PMID:33113064

DiMaggio, P. J., & Powell, W. W. (1983). The iron cage revisited: Institutional isomorphism and collective rationality in organizational fields. *American Sociological Review, 48*(2), 147–160. doi:10.2307/2095101

Emodi, N. V., & Boo, K. J. (2015). Sustainable energy development in Nigeria: Overcoming energy poverty. *International Journal of Energy Economics and Policy, 5*(2), 580–597.

Ergun, S. J., Owusu, P. A., & Rivas, M. F. (2019). Determinants of renewable energy consumption in Africa. *Environmental Science and Pollution Research International, 26*(15), 15390–15405. doi:10.100711356-019-04567-7 PMID:30937739

Godil, D. I., Sharif, A., Ali, M. I., Ozturk, I., & Usman, R. (2021). The role of financial development, R&D expenditure, globalization and institutional quality in energy consumption in India: New evidence from the QARDL approach. *Journal of Environmental Management, 285*, 112208. doi:10.1016/j.jenvman.2021.112208 PMID:33618139

Haldar, A., & Sethi, N. (2021). Effect of institutional quality and renewable energy consumption on CO2 emissions– an empirical investigation for developing countries. *Environmental Science and Pollution Research International, 28*(12), 15485–15503. doi:10.100711356-020-11532-2 PMID:33237563

Holcombe, R. G. (1997). A theory of the theory of public goods. *The Review of Austrian Economics, 10*(1), 1–22. doi:10.1007/BF02538141

Ijaz, S. T., & Chughtai, S. (2022). The impact of financial, economic and environmental factors on energy efficiency, intensity, and dependence: The moderating role of governance and institutional quality. *International Journal of Energy Economics and Policy, 12*(4), 15–31. doi:10.32479/ijeep.13157

Islam, M. M., Irfan, M., Shahbaz, M., & Vo, X. V. (2022). Renewable and non-renewable energy consumption in Bangladesh: The relative influencing profiles of economic factors, urbanization, physical infrastructure and institutional quality. *Renewable Energy, 184*, 1130–1149. doi:10.1016/j.renene.2021.12.020

Khan, A. A., Khan, S. U., Ali, M. A. S., Safi, A., Gao, Y., Ali, M., & Luo, J. (2022). Role of institutional quality and renewable energy consumption in achieving carbon neutrality: Case study of G-7 economies. *The Science of the Total Environment, 814*, 152797. doi:10.1016/j.scitotenv.2021.152797 PMID:34990660

Lawal, A. I. (2023). Determinants of Renewable Energy Consumption in Africa: Evidence from System GMM. *Energies, 16*(5), 2136. doi:10.3390/en16052136

Li, J., Zhang, X., Ali, S., & Khan, Z. (2020). Eco-innovation and energy productivity: New determinants of renewable energy consumption. *Journal of Environmental Management, 271*, 111028. doi:10.1016/j.jenvman.2020.111028 PMID:32778308

Mehmood, U., Agyekum, E. B., Tariq, S., Ul Haq, Z., Uhunamure, S. E., Edokpayi, J. N., & Azhar, A. (2022). Socio-economic drivers of renewable energy: Empirical evidence from BRICS. *International Journal of Environmental Research and Public Health, 19*(8), 4614. doi:10.3390/ijerph19084614 PMID:35457479

Sachan, A., Sahu, U. K., Pradhan, A. K., & Thomas, R. (2023). Examining the drivers of renewable energy consumption: Evidence from BRICS nations. *Renewable Energy, 202*, 1402–1411. doi:10.1016/j.renene.2022.11.080

Samuelson, P. A. (1954). The pure theory of public expenditure. *The Review of Economics and Statistics, 36*(4), 387–389. doi:10.2307/1925895

Samuelson, P. A. (1955). Diagrammatic Exposition of a Theory of Public Expenditure. *The Review of Economics and Statistics, 37*(4), 350–356. doi:10.2307/1925849

Shahbaz, M., Mallick, H., Mahalik, M. K., & Sadorsky, P. (2016). The role of globalization on the recent evolution of energy demand in India: Implications for sustainable development. *Energy Economics, 55*, 52–68. doi:10.1016/j.eneco.2016.01.013

Sun, H. (2019) Institutional quality, green innovation and energy efficiency. *Energy Policy 135:111002*. IDEAS. doi:. 2019.111002 doi:10.1016/j.enpol

Tenaw, D. (2021). Decomposition and macroeconomic drivers of energy intensity: The case of Ethiopia. *Energy Strategy Reviews*, *35*, 100641. doi:10.1016/j.esr.2021.100641

Tufail, M., Song, L., Adebayo, T. S., Kirikkaleli, D., & Khan, S. (2021). Do fiscal decentralization and natural resources rent curb carbon emissions? Evidence from developed countries. *Environmental Science and Pollution Research International*, *28*(35), 49179–49190. doi:10.100711356-021-13865-y PMID:33932218

Uzar, U. (2020). Political economy of renewable energy: Does institutional quality make a difference in renewable energy consumption? *Renewable Energy*, *155*, 591–603. doi:10.1016/j.renene.2020.03.172

Wang, E., Gozgor, G., Mahalik, M. K., Patel, G., & Hu, G. (2022). Effects of institutional quality and political risk on the renewable energy consumption in the OECD Countries. *Resources Policy*, *79*, 103041. doi:10.1016/j.resourpol.2022.103041

Wang, L., Huang, Y., Ghafoor, A., Hafeez, M., & Salahodjaev, R. (2023). Asymmetric macroeconomic determinants of renewable energy consumption: Do financial institutions and ICT trade matter? *Environmental Science and Pollution Research International*, *30*(4), 9841–9851. doi:10.100711356-022-22816-0 PMID:36059017

Yakubu, I. N., Kapusuzoglu, A., & Ceylan, N. B. (2022). ICT trade and energy transition in the BRICS economies. In *Sustainability in Energy Business and Finance: Approaches and Developments in the Energy Market* (pp. 13–24). Springer International Publishing. doi:10.1007/978-3-030-94051-5_2

Yakubu, I. N., Kapusuzoglu, A., & Ceylan, N. B. (2022). Investigating the Role of Export Diversification, Remittances, and Environmental Sustainability in Accordance with Clean Energy and Zero Emission. In *Circular Economy and the Energy Market: Achieving Sustainable Economic Development Through Energy Policy* (pp. 51–65). Springer International Publishing. doi:10.1007/978-3-031-13146-2_5

Zhang, P., Li, Z., Ghardallou, W., Yan, X., & Jie, C. (2023). Nexus of institutional quality and technological innovation on renewable energy development: Moderating role of green finance. *Renewable Energy*, *214*, 233–241. doi:10.1016/j.renene.2023.05.089

Compilation of References

Abdallah, N., & Eltahir, N. (2023). *20 billion investment fun in clean energy*. Reuters. https://www.reuters.com/business/sustainable-business/us-uae-say-20-billion-investment-fund-15-gw-new-clean-energy-2023-01-15/

Abduh, M., & Omar, A. M. (2012). Islamic Banking and Economic Growth: The Indonesian Experience. *International Journal of Islamic and Middle Eastern Finance and Management*, *5*(1), 35–47. doi:10.1108/17538391211216811

Abduh, M., Shabri, M., & Kassim, H. S. (2015). Assessing the Contribution of Islamic Finance to Economic Growth. *Journal of Islamic Accounting and Business Research*, *6*, 292–310. doi:10.1108/JIABR-07-2012-0050

Acquatella, J., & Bárcena Ibarra, A. (2005). *Política fiscal y medio ambiente: bases para una agenda común*. Cepal.

ADB. (2016). *Emissions Tradingschemes And Their Linking: Challenges And Opportunities In Asia And The Pacific*. Asian Development Bank.https://www.adb.org/sites/default/files/publication/182501/emissions-trading-schemes.pdf

Adebayo, T. S., Akadiri, S. S., Uhunamure, S. E., Altuntaş, M., & Shale, K. (2022). *Does political stability contribute to environmental sustainability? Evidence from the most politically stable economies*. National Library of Medicine. https://www.ncbi.nlm.nih.gov/pmc/articles/PMC9800197/

Adebayo, T. S., Akinsola, G. D., Odugbesan, J. A., & Olanrewaju, V. O. (2021). Determinants of environmental degradation in Thailand: Empirical evidence from ARDL and wavelet coherence approaches. *Pollution*, *7*(1), 181–196.

Adebayo, T. S., Ghosh, S., Nathaniel, S., & Wada, I. (2023). Technological innovations, renewable energy, globalization, financial development, and carbon emissions: Role of inward remittances for top ten remittances receiving countries. *Environmental Science and Pollution Research International*, *30*(26), 69330–69348. doi:10.100711356-023-27184-x PMID:37133657

Ades, A., & Di Tella, R. (1999). Rents, competition, and corruption. *The American Economic Review*, *89*(4), 982–993. doi:10.1257/aer.89.4.982

Agence Béninoise d'Electrification Rurale et de Maîtrise d'Energie (ABERME). (2009). *Document de Politique Nationale de Maîtrise d'Energie (PONAME) Rapport proviso ire*. PONAME.

Ahmad, M., Ahmed, Z., Yang, X., Hussain, N., & Sinha, A. (2022). Financial development and environmental degradation: Do human capital and institutional quality make a difference? *Gondwana Research*, *105*, 299–310. doi:10.1016/j.gr.2021.09.012

Ahmad, M., Ul Haq, Z., Khan, Z., Khattak, S. I., Ur Rahman, Z., & Khan, S. (2019). Does the inflow of remittances cause environmental degradation? Empirical evidence from China. *Economic research-. Ekonomska Istrazivanja*, *32*(1), 2099–2121. doi:10.1080/1331677X.2019.1642783

Ahmed, H., & Verbeek, J. (2015). *On the Sustainable Development Goals and the Role of Islamic Finance.* (Policy Research Working Paper, No. 7266). World Bank, Washington, DC.

Ahmed, F., Kousar, S., Pervaiz, A., & Shabbir, A. (2022). Do institutional quality and financial development affect sustainable economic growth? Evidence from South Asian countries. *Borsa Istanbul Review, 22*(1), 189–196. doi:10.1016/j.bir.2021.03.005

Akçay, S. (2019). Do industrialization, democracy, and financial openness promote financial development? Evidence from Turkey. *Turkish Studies, 20*(5), 708–727. doi:10.1080/14683849.2018.1537752

Akintande, O. J., Olubusoye, O. E., Adenikinju, A. F., & Olanrewaju, B. T. (2020). Modeling the determinants of renewable energy consumption: Evidence from the five most populous nations in Africa. *Energy, 206*, 117992. doi:10.1016/j.energy.2020.117992

Akponikpè, P. B. I., Tovihoudji, P., Lokonon, B. O. K., Kpadonou, E., Amegnaglo, C. J., Segnon, A. C., & Aho, N. (2019). Etude de Vulnérabilité aux changements climatiques du Secteur Agriculture au Bénin. Berlin: Climate Analytics gGmbH.

Ali, E. B., Shayanmehr, S., Radmehr, R., Amfo, B., Awuni, J. A., Gyamfi, B. A., & Agbozo, E. (2023). Exploring the impact of economic growth on environmental pollution in South American countries: How does renewable energy and globalization matter? *Environmental Science and Pollution Research International, 30*(6), 15505–15522. doi:10.100711356-022-23177-4 PMID:36169822

Ali, K., Jianguo, D., Kirikkaleli, D., Oláh, J., & Altuntaş, M. (2023). Do green technological innovation, financial development, economic policy uncertainty, and institutional quality matter for environmental sustainability? *All Earth, 35*(1), 82–101. doi:10.1080/27669645.2023.2200330

Ali, M., Kirikkaleli, D., Sharma, R., & Altuntaş, M. (2022). The nexus between remittances, natural resources, technological innovation, economic growth, and environmental sustainability in Pakistan. *Environmental Science and Pollution Research International, 29*(50), 75822–75840. doi:10.100711356-022-21228-4 PMID:35661303

Allan, S. (2010). *Perspectivas OCDE: México Políticas Clave para un Desarrollo Sostenible.* OCDE.

Al-Maamary, H. M., Kazem, H. A., & Chaichan, M. T. (2017). Renewable energy and GCC States energy challenges in the 21st century: A review. *International Journal of Computation and Applied Sciences, 02*(01). https://www.researchgate.net/profile/Hussein-A-Kazem/publication/312534224_Renewable_energy_and_GCC_States_energy_challenges_in_the_21st_century_A_review/links/5880ff344585150dde3f3c83/Renewable-energy-and-GCC-States-energy-challenges-in-the-21st-century-. doi:10.24842/1611/0018

Al-Saati, N. H., Omran, I. I., Salman, A. A., Al-Saati, Z., & Hashim, K. S. (2021). Statistical Modeling of Monthly Streamflow Using Time Series and Artificial Neural Network Models: Hindiya Barrage as A Case Study. *Water Practice & Technology, 16*(2), 681–691. doi:10.2166/wpt.2021.012

Al-Sarihi, A., & Cherni, J. A. (2022). *Political economy of renewable energy transition in rentier states: The case of Oman.* Wiley. https://onlinelibrary.wiley.com/doi/full/10.1002/eet.2041

Amjad, M. A., Asghar, N., & Rehman, H. U. (2021). Can financial development help in raising sustainable economic growth and reduce environmental pollution in Pakistan? Evidence from non linear ARDL model. *Review of Economics and Development Studies, 7*(4), 475–491. doi:10.47067/reads.v7i4.406

Amoussou, E., Awoye, H., Vodounon, H. S. T., Obahoundje, S., Camberlin, P., Diedhiou, A., & Boko, M. (2020). Climate and Extreme Rainfall Events in the Mono River Basin (West Africa): Investigating Future Changes with Regional Climate Models.

Anwar, A., Chaudhary, A. R., & Malik, S. (2023). Modeling the macroeconomic determinants of environmental degradation in E-7 countries: The role of technological innovation and institutional quality. *Journal of Public Affairs*, *23*(1), e2834. doi:10.1002/pa.2834

Anwar, S. M., Naidi, N., Salju, S., Wicaksono, R., & Mispiyanti, G. (2020). Islamic Bank Contribution to Indonesian Economic Growth. *International Journal of Islamic and Middle Eastern Finance and Management*, *13*, 75–86. doi:10.1108/IMEFM-02-2018-0071

Apergis, N., & Sorros, J. (2014). The role of R&D expenses for profitability: Evidence from US fossil and renewable energy firms. *International Journal of Economics and Finance*, *6*(3), 8–15. doi:10.5539/ijef.v6n3p8

Appunn, K. (2019, April 04). *Clean Energy Wire.* National climate measures and European emission trading: Assessing the 'waterbed effect': https://www.cleanenergywire.org/factsheets/national-climate-measures-and-european-emission-trading-assessing-waterbed-effect

Appunn, K. (2021, July 20). *Clean Energy Wire.* Understanding the European Union's Emissions Trading System (EU ETS). https://www.cleanenergywire.org/factsheets/understanding-european-unions-emissions-trading-system

ARE. (2019). *Révision des conditions tarifaires de la SBEE.* ARE.

Arellano, M., & Bover, O. (1995). Another look at the instrumental variable estimation of error-components models. *Journal of Econometrics*, *68*(1), 29–51. doi:10.1016/0304-4076(94)01642-D

Arı, İ. (2010). Emıssıon Tradıng For Combatıng Wıth The Clımate Change And Its Implementatıon In Turkey. *Planning Expertise Thesis.* Ankara: State Planning Organization.

Ari, I., Varoglu, A. (2022). Erupean Union'S Carbon Border Adjustement Mechanism And Its Impact On Turkey. In A. Bektaş (Ed.), Global Climate Change and Sosyo-Economic Impacts (p. 217). Tasav.

Arman, H. (2015). Uncertainties, risks and challenges relating to CO2 emissions and its possible impact on climate change in the United Arab Emirates. *International Journal of Global Warming*, *08*(01), 1–17. https://www.inderscienceonline.com/doi/abs/10.1504/IJGW.2015.071575. doi:10.1504/IJGW.2015.071575

Arminen, H., & Menegaki, A. N. (2019). Corruption, climate and the energy-environment-growth nexus. *Energy Economics*, *80*, 621–634. doi:10.1016/j.eneco.2019.02.009

Ash, J., & Campbell, J. (2016). Climate change and migration: The case of the Pacific Islands and Australia. *Pacific Studies*, *36*(1), 36. doi:10.33318/jpacs.2016.36(1)-4

Asian Development Bank. (2012). *Climate Risk and Adaptation in the Electric Power Sector.* Asian Development Bank.

Asongu, S., & Odhiambo, N. M. (2022). Governance and renewable energy consumption in Sub-Saharan Africa. *International Journal of Energy Sector Management*, *16*(2), 209–223. doi:10.1108/IJESM-10-2020-0009

Assad, M. E., AlMallahi, M. N., Abdelsalam, M. A., AlShabi, M., & AlMallahi, W. N. (2022). *Advances in Science and Engineering Technology International Conferences (ASET)* (pp. 1-4). Dubai: IEEE.

Aswad, N. G., Al-Saleh, Y., & HananTaleb. (2013). Clean energy awareness campaigns in the UAE: An awareness promoters perspective. *International Journal of Innovation and Knowledge Management in the Middle East and North Africa*, *02*(02). https://www.researchgate.net/profile/Yasser-Alsaleh/publication/275299871_Clean_Energy_Awareness_Campaigns_in_the_UAE_An_Awareness_Promoters_Perspective/links/553744500cf268fd001892da/Clean-Energy-Awareness-Campaigns-in-the-UAE-An-Awareness-Promoters-Pers

Atalaya, Y., Kalfagianni, A., & Pattberg, P. (2017). Renewable energy support mechanisms in the Gulf Cooperation Council. *Renewable & Sustainable Energy Reviews*, *72*, 723–733. doi:10.1016/j.rser.2017.01.103

Atalay, Y., Biermann, F., & Kalfagianni, A. (2016). Adoption of renewable energy technologies in oil-rich countries. *Renewable Energy*, *85*, 206–214. https://www.sciencedirect.com/science/article/abs/pii/S0960148115300689?via%3Dihub. doi:10.1016/j.renene.2015.06.045

Atanga, R. A., & Tankpa, V. (2021). Climate change, flood disaster risk and food security Nexus in Northern Ghana. *Frontiers in Sustainable Food Systems*, *5*, 706721. doi:10.3389/fsufs.2021.706721

Ayaz, A. (2022). Unsustainable Systems: Externalization as a Nonviable Form of Migration Management in the Face of Climate Change. *Insight Turkey*, *24*(1), 37–54. https://www.jstor.org/stable/48655650

Ayobamiji, A. A., & Kalmaz, D. B. (2020). Reinvestigating the determinants of environmental degradation in Nigeria. *International Journal of Economic Policy in Emerging Economies*, *13*(1), 52–71. doi:10.1504/IJEPEE.2020.106680

Azam, M., Liu, L., & Ahmad, N. (2021). Impact of institutional quality on environment and energy consumption: Evidence from developing world. *Environment, Development and Sustainability*, *23*(2), 1646–1667. doi:10.100710668-020-00644-x

Babu, M. N., Pavan, P., Mohan, K. R., Rao, G. R., Rao, K. S., & Tejaswi, G. (2023). Energy Management for Renewable Hybrid System Based On Artificial Neural Networks (ANN). *International Journal for Research in Applied Science and Engineering Technology*, *2*(4), 1–14. doi:10.22214/ijraset.2021.33423

Bacchi, C. (2009). *Analysing Policy: What's the Problem Represented To Be?* Bacchi, C., & Goodwin, S. (2016). *Post-structural Policy Analysis: A Guide to Practice*. Palgrave Macmillan.

Bacchi, C. L. (2019). Introducing the 'What's the Problem Represented to be?' Approach. In Introducing the 'What's the Problem Represented to be?' Approach (pp. 427–430). Verlag. doi:10.1515/9783839437322-031

Bachellerie, I. J. (2012). *Renewable Energy in the GCC Countries- Resources, Potential and Prospects*. Gulf Research Centre.

Badarou, R., & Kouletio, E. C. H. (2009). *Systèmes énergétiques : Vulnérabilité – Adaptation – Résilience*. VAR.

Balsalobre-Lorente, D., Gokmenoglu, K. K., Taspinar, N., & Cantos-Cantos, J. M. (2019). An approach to the pollution haven and pollution halo hypotheses in MINT countries. *Environmental Science and Pollution Research International*, *26*(22), 23010–23026. doi:10.100711356-019-05446-x PMID:31183758

Balzacq, T. (2011). *Securitization Theory: How Security Problems Emerge and Dissolve*. Routledge.

Banque Africaine de Développement (BAD). (2020). *Indice de réglementation de l'électricité en Afrique*. BAD.

Bashiru, S., Yakubu, I. N., Bunyaminu, A., & Faryan, M. A. (2022). Drivers of Financial Inclusion: Insights from Sub-Saharan Africa. *Journal of Money and Business*. http://www.mdpi.com

Bayer, P., & Aklin, M. (2020). The European Union Emissions Trading System Reduced CO2 Emissions Despite Low Prices. *Proceedings of the National Academy of Sciences of the United States of America*, *117*(16), 8804–8812. doi:10.1073/pnas.1918128117 PMID:32253304

Baysal, B., & Karakaş, U. (2017). Climate Change and Security: Different Perceptions, Different Approaches. *Uluslararası İlişkiler. International Relations*, *14*(54), 21–44. https://www.jstor.org/stable/26406850

Bazyomo, S. D., Lawin, A. E., Coulibaly, O., Wisser, D., & Ouedraogo, A. (2016).. . *Forecasted Changes in West Africa Photovoltaic Energy Output by*, *2045*, 1–15. doi:10.3390/cli4040053

BBC. (2021). *COP26: India PM Narendra Modi Pledges Net Zero By 2070.* BBC. https://www.bbc.com/news/world-asia-india-59125143#:~:text=Detailing%20what%20he%20termed%20were,the%20country's%20electricity%20from%20coal.: BBC.

Bekoe, E. O., & Logah, F. Y. (2013). The impact of droughts and climate change on electricity generation in Ghana. *Environmental Sciences, 1*(1), 13–24. doi:10.12988/es.2013.13002

Bekun, F. V., & Alola, A. A. (2022). Determinants of renewable energy consumption in agrarian Sub-Sahara African economies. *Energy, Ecology & Environment, 7*(3), 227–235. doi:10.100740974-022-00243-8

Benin. (2015). *Deficit Energetique Et Competitivite De L'economie Beninoise*. Benin.

Bénin. (2018). *Programme De Croissance Pour Le Developpement Durable (PC2D) 2018-2021*. Benin.

Benz, E., & Trück, S. (2009). Modeling the Price Dynamics of CO2 Emissions Allowances. *Energy Economics, 31*(1), 4–15. doi:10.1016/j.eneco.2008.07.003

Bercu, A. M., Paraschiv, G., & Lupu, D. (2019). Investigating the energy-economic growth-governance nexus: Evidence from central and eastern European countries. *Sustainability, 11*(12), 3355. doi:10.3390u11123355

Bettini, G. (2013). Climate Barbarians at the Gate? A critique of apocalyptic narratives on 'climate refugees.'. *Geoforum, 45*, 63–72. doi:10.1016/j.geoforum.2012.09.009

Bettini, G., Nash, S. L., & Gioli, G. (2016). One step forward, two steps back? The fading contours of (in)justice in competing discourses on climate migration. *The Geographical Journal, 183*(4), 348–358. doi:10.1111/geoj.12192

Bezerra, L. G., Gomes, G., & Rodrigues, V. (2022). *Brazil's Federal Government Publishes Decree Establishing National Greenhouse Gas Emissions Reduction System.* Mayer Brown. https://www.mayerbrown.com/en/perspectives-events/publications/2022/05/brazils-federal-government-publishes-decree-establishing-national-greenhouse-gas-emissions-reduction-system

Bhattarai, U., Maraseni, T., & Apan, A. (2022). Assay of renewable energy transition: A systematic literature review. Science of The Total Environment. *The Science of the Total Environment, 833*, 155–159. https://www.sciencedirect.com/science/article/abs/pii/S0048969722022525. doi:10.1016/j.scitotenv.2022.155159

Bhujabal, P., Sethi, N., & Padhan, P. C. (2021). ICT, foreign direct investment and environmental pollution in major Asia Pacific countries. *Environmental Science and Pollution Research International, 28*(31), 42649–42669. doi:10.100711356-021-13619-w PMID:33818724

Biao, E. I. (2017). Assessing the impacts of climate change on river discharge dynamics in Oueme River basin (Benin, West Africa). *Hydrology, 4*(4), 47. doi:10.3390/hydrology4040047

Black, R., Bennett, S. R. G., Thomas, S. M., & Beddington, J. R. (2011). Climate change: migration as adaptation. *Nature, 478*(7370), 447–449. doi:10.1038/478477a PMID:22012304

Bremberg, N., Mobjörk, M., & Krampe, F. (2022). Global Responses to Climate Security: Discourses, Institutions and Actions. *Journal of Peacebuilding & Development, 17*(3), 341–356. doi:10.1177/15423166221128180

Brown, O., Hammill, A., & McLeman, R. (2007). Climate Change as the "New" Security Threat: Implications for Africa. *International Affairs (Royal Institute of International Affairs 1944-), 83*(6), 1141–1154. https://www.jstor.org/stable/4541915

Brown, O. (2008). *Migration and Climate Change*. IOM migration Research Series. doi:10.18356/26de4416-en

Buiter, W. H., & Rahbari, E. (2015). Why Economists (and Economies) Should Love Islamic Finance. *Islamic Economics, 28*(1), 139–162.

Bunyaminu, A., & Yakubu, I. N. (2022). Green Energy Demand and Financial Development: Evidence from Africa. In Finance for Sustainability in a Turbulent Economy (pp. 26-48). IGI Global.

Bunyaminu, A., Mohammed, I., Yakubu, I. N., Shani, B., & Abukari, A. L. (2022). The effect of health expenditure on average life expectancy: Does government effectiveness play a moderating role? *International Journal of Health Governance, 27*(4), 365–377. doi:10.1108/IJHG-03-2022-0027

Burillo, D. (2018). Effects of climate change in electric power Infrastructures.

Burke, P. J., & Kurniawati, S. (2018). Electricity subsidy reform in Indonesia: Demand-side effects on electricity use. *Energy Policy, 116*, 410–421. doi:10.1016/j.enpol.2018.02.018

Burki, U., & Tahir, M. (2022). Determinants of environmental degradation: Evidenced-based insights from ASEAN economies. *Journal of Environmental Management, 306*, 114506. doi:10.1016/j.jenvman.2022.114506 PMID:35051821

Butler, C., Parkhill, K. A., & Luzecka, P. (2018). Rethinking energy demand governance: Exploring impact beyond energy policy. *Energy Research & Social Science, 36*, 70–78. doi:10.1016/j.erss.2017.11.011

Buzan, B., Wæver, O., & de Wilde, J. (1998). *Security: A New Framework for Analysis.* Lynne Rienner Publishers.

C2ES (Center for Climate and Energy Solutions). (2019). *Regional Greenhouse Gas Initiative.* C2ES. https://www.c2es.org/content/regional-greenhouse-gas-initiative-rggi/

Caglar, A. E., Zafar, M. W., Bekun, F. V., & Mert, M. (2022). Determinants of CO2 emissions in the BRICS economies: The role of partnerships investment in energy and economic complexity. *Sustainable Energy Technologies and Assessments, 51*, 101907. doi:10.1016/j.seta.2021.101907

Calderón, J. P. (2010). La política ambiental en México: Gestión e instrumentos económicos. *El cotidiano*, (162), 91-97.

Campos, R. C., & Paz, M. Q. (2014). Secondary Markets. In *Research Handbook on Securities Regulation in the United States* (pp. 185–200). Edward Elgar Publishing. doi:10.4337/9781782540076.00011

Cao, H., Khan, M. K., Rehman, A., Dagar, V., Oryani, B., & Tanveer, A. (2022). Impact of globalization, institutional quality, economic growth, electricity and renewable energy consumption on Carbon Dioxide Emission in OECD countries. *Environmental Science and Pollution Research International, 29*(16), 24191–24202. doi:10.100711356-021-17076-3 PMID:34822079

Carabias, J. (2019). Economic policies with environmental sustainability. *Economía UNAM, 16*(46), 118–125.

Caranci, B., & Econ, C. (2021). A Primer on Carbon Pricing and Carbon Border Adjustments. *TD Economics.* https://economics.td.com/domains/economics.td.com/documents/reports/ff/carbon_border_adjustments.pdf

Castles, S. (2014). International migration at a crossroads. *Citizenship Studies, 18*(2), 190–207. doi:10.1080/13621025.2014.886439

Chakravarty, S. R., & Pal, R. (2013). Financial Inclusion in India: An Axiomatic Approach. *Journal of Policy Modeling, 35*(5), 813–837. doi:10.1016/j.jpolmod.2012.12.007

Chapra, M. U. (1992). Islam and the Economic Challenge. Islamic Economics Series, 17. The Islamic Foundation, Herndon.

Chen, C., Pinar, M., & Stengos, T. (2021). Determinants of renewable energy consumption: Importance of democratic institutions. *Renewable Energy, 179*, 75–83. doi:10.1016/j.renene.2021.07.030

Chen, Z., & Zhou, M. (2021). Urbanization and energy intensity: Evidence from the institutional threshold effect. *Environmental Science and Pollution Research International, 28*(9), 11142–11157. doi:10.100711356-020-11386-8 PMID:33113064

Chien, F. S., Kamran, H. W., Albashar, G., & Iqbal, W. (2021). *Dynamic planning, conversion, and management strategy of different renewable energy sources: A sustainable solution for severe energy crises in emerging economies*. Int. J. Hydrog. Energy. doi:10.1016/j.ijhydene.2020.12.004

Chinoda, T., & Kapingura, F. M. (2023). Digital financial inclusion and economic growth in Sub-Saharan Africa: The role of institutions and governance. *African Journal of Economic and Management Studies*. doi:10.1108/AJEMS-09-2022-0372

Chishti, M. Z. (2023). Exploring the dynamic link between FDI, remittances, and ecological footprint in Pakistan: Evidence from partial and multiple wavelet based-analysis. *Research in Globalization, 6*, 100109. doi:10.1016/j.resglo.2022.100109

Choucri, N., Goldsmith, D., & Mezher, T. (2010). Renewable energy policy in an oil exporting country: The case of the United Arab Emirates. *Renewable Energy Law and Policy Review, 1*(1), 77–86.

Christensen, T., & Lægreid, P. (2007). *The Challenge of Coordination in Central Government Organizations.*

Cingano, F. (2014). *Trends in Income Inequality and its Impact on Economic Growth.* France: (OECD Social, Employment and Migration Working Papers). CONGRESO DE LA UNIÓN.

Clement, V., Rigaud, K. K., de Sherbinin, A., Jones, B., Adamo, S., Schewe, J., Sadiq, N., & Shabahat, E. (2021). *Groundswell Part 2: Acting on Internal Climate migration*. World Bank. https://openknowledge.worldbank.org/handle/10986/36248

Comisión Federal de Electricidad. (2023). *Esquema tarifario vigente*. CFE.mx. https://app.cfe.mx/Aplicaciones/CCFE/Tarifas/TarifasCRECasa/Casa.aspx

Conca, K., Thwaites, J., & Lee, G. (2017). Climate Change and the UN Security Council: Bully Pulpit or Bull in a China Shop? *Global Environmental Politics, 17*(2), 1–20. doi:10.1162/GLEP_a_00398

Council of The European Union. (2023, January 12). *Fit for 55*. Council of The European Union.. https://www.consilium.europa.eu/en/policies/green-deal/fit-for-55-the-eu-plan-for-a-green-transition/ ı

Cousins, S. (2013). UN Security Council: Playing a role in the international climate change regime? *Global Change, Peace & Security, 25*(2), 191–210. doi:10.1080/14781158.2013.787058

Cronin, J., Anandarajah, G., & Dessens, O. (2018). Climate change impacts on the energy system: A review of trends and gaps. *Climatic Change, 151*(2), 79–93. doi:10.100710584-018-2265-4 PMID:30930505

CRS. (2020). *The Regional Greenhouse Gas Initiative: Background, Impacts, and Selected Issues*. Every CRS Report. https://www.everycrsreport.com/reports/R41836.html

Damania, R., Fredriksson, P. G., & List, J. A. (2003). Trade liberalization, corruption, and environmental policy formation: Theory and evidence. *Journal of Environmental Economics and Management, 46*(3), 490–512. doi:10.1016/S0095-0696(03)00025-1

Daron, J. D. (2014). *Regional Climate Messages for West Africa*, 1–30. Cariaa Assar.

Das, A., McFarlane, A., & Carels, L. (2021). Empirical exploration of remittances and renewable energy consumption in Bangladesh. *Asia-Pacific Journal of Regional Science, 5*(1), 65–89. doi:10.100741685-020-00180-6

Das, A., & Sethi, N. (2023). Modelling the environmental pollution-institutional quality nexus in low-and middle-income countries: Exploring the role of financial development and educational level. *Environment, Development and Sustainability, 25*(2), 1492–1518. doi:10.100710668-021-02105-5

Décret N° 2021-005 du 06 janvier 2021 portant agréments aux régimes du code des investissements au Bénin.

Deng, Q. S., Alvarado, R., Cuesta, L., Tillaguango, B., Murshed, M., Rehman, A., Işık, C., & López-Sánchez, M. (2022). Asymmetric impacts of foreign direct investment inflows, financial development, and social globalization on environmental pollution. *Economic Analysis and Policy*, *76*, 236–251. doi:10.1016/j.eap.2022.08.008

Developpment, I. E. (2017). (*IED*). Plan Directeur d'Electrification Hors Réseau.

DEWA. (2020, November 01). *DEWA invests 86 billion in energy sector over the next five years.*. Government of Dubai. https://www.dewa.gov.ae/en/about-us/media-publications/latest-news/2020/11/dewa-invests-aed-86-billion-in-energy-sector-over-the-next-5-years

DiMaggio, P. J., & Powell, W. W. (1983). The iron cage revisited: Institutional isomorphism and collective rationality in organizational fields. *American Sociological Review*, *48*(2), 147–160. doi:10.2307/2095101

Dulaimi, M., Alhashemi, M., Ling, F. Y., & Kumaraswamy, M. (2010). The execution of public-private partnership projects in the UAE. *Construction Management and Economics*, *28*(04), 393–402. doi:10.1080/01446191003702492

Dupont, G., & Baltus, P. (2009). *Dimensioning and Grid Integration of Mega Battery Energy Storage System for System Load Leveling. IEEE Bucharest PowerTech*. IEEE., https://www.ieeexplore.ieeeorg

Ebinger, J., & Vergara, W. (2011). *Climate Impacts on Energy Systems*. World Bank. doi:10.1596/978-0-8213-8697-2

Eggoh, J., Bangake, C., & Semedo, G. (2019). Do remittances spur economic growth? Evidence from developing countries. *The Journal of International Trade & Economic Development*, *28*(4), 391–418. doi:10.1080/09638199.2019.1568522

EIA (Energy Information Administration). (2022a, April 20). *Electricity Explained: Factors Affecting Electricity Prices*. EIA. https://www.eia.gov/energyexplained/electricity/prices-and-factors-affecting-prices.php

EIA (Energy Information Administration). (2022b). *Carbon Dioxide Emissions Coefficients*. EIA.https://www.eia.gov/environment/emissions/co2_vol_mass.php

EIA. (2021). *U.S Energy Information Administration*. EIA. https://www.eia.gov/

Elizbarashvili, M., Chartolani, G., & Khardziani, T. (2018a). Variations and trends of heating and cooling degree-days in Georgia for 1961–1990 year period. *Annals of Agrarian Science*, *16*(2), 152–159. doi:10.1016/j.aasci.2018.03.004

Ellerman, A. D., Convery, F. J., & De Perthuis, C. (2010). *Pricing Carbon: The European Union Emissions Trading Scheme*. Cambridge University Press.

Ellerman, A. D., Marcantonini, C., & Zaklan, A. (2016). The European Union Emissions Trading System: Ten Years and Counting. Review of Environmental Economics and Policy. *Review of Environmental Economics and Policy*, *10*(1), 89–107. doi:10.1093/reep/rev014

Elwereflli, A., & Benhin, J. (2018). Oil a blessing or curse: A comparative assessment of Nigeria, Norway and the United Arab Emirates. *Theoretical Economics Letters*, *08*(05), 1136–1160. http://hdl.handle.net/10026.1/11272. doi:10.4236/tel.2018.85076

Emodi, N. V., & Boo, K. J. (2015). Sustainable energy development in Nigeria: Overcoming energy poverty. *International Journal of Energy Economics and Policy*, *5*(2), 580–597.

EnerData. (2022). *Electricity Domestic Consumption*. EnerData. https://yearbook.enerdata.net/electricity/electricity-domestic-consumption-data.html

Energy.Gov. (2023). *About Energy.Gov*. Loan Programs Office. https://www.energy.gov/lpo/about-us-home

Engelbrekt, K. (2016). Climate Change Mitigation. In *High-Table Diplomacy* (pp. 157–196). Georgetown University Press., https://www.jstor.org/stable/j.ctt1c84cd2.11

Engels, A. (2009). The European Emissions Trading Scheme: An Exploratory Study of How Companies Learn to Account for Carbon. *Accounting, Organizations and Society*, *34*(3-4), 488–498. doi:10.1016/j.aos.2008.08.005

Environmental and Energy Study Institute. (2021). *Fossil Fuels*. EESI. https://www.eesi.org/topics/fossil-fuels/description

Ergun, S. J., Owusu, P. A., & Rivas, M. F. (2019). Determinants of renewable energy consumption in Africa. *Environmental Science and Pollution Research International*, *26*(15), 15390–15405. doi:10.100711356-019-04567-7 PMID:30937739

European Commission. (2021, July 14). *Regulation Of The European Parliament And Of The Council establishing a carbon border adjustment mechanism.* European Commission. https://eur-lex.europa.eu/legal-content/EN/TXT/HTML/?uri=CELEX:52021PC0564&rid=9

European Commission. (2022). *Climate Action*. European Commission. https://ec.europa.eu/clima/eu-action/eu-emissions-trading-system-eu-ets/revision-phase-4-2021-2030_en

European Commission. (2022). *Climate Action*. International carbon market. https://ec.europa.eu/clima/eu-action/eu-emissions-trading-system-eu-ets/international-carbon-market_en

European Commission. (2022). *Development of EU ETS (2005-2020)*. European Commission. https://ec.europa.eu/clima/eu-action/eu-emissions-trading-system-eu-ets/development-eu-ets-2005-2020_en

European Commission. (2022). *Free allocation for the modernisation of the energy sector*. European Commission. https://ec.europa.eu/clima/eu-action/eu-emissions-trading-system-eu-ets/free-allocation/free-allocation-modernisation-energy-sector_en

European Commission. (2022a). *Climate Action*. European Commission. https://ec.europa.eu/clima/eu-action/eu-emissions-trading-system-eu-ets/development-eu-ets-2005-2020_en

European Commission. (2023). *International carbon market*. European Commission. https://ec.europa.eu/clima/eu-action/eu-emissions-trading-system-eu-ets/international-carbon-market_en)

European Commission. (2023). *Taxation and Customs Union*. Carbon Border Adjustment Mechanism. https://taxation-customs.ec.europa.eu/carbon-border-adjustment-mechanism_en

European Commission. (2023, May 15). *ETS Market Stability Reserve to reduce auction volume by over 272 million allowances between September 2023 and August 2024.* European Commission. https://climate.ec.europa.eu/news-your-voice/news/ets-market-stability-reserve-reduce-auction-volume-over-272-million-allowances-between-september-2023-05-15_en

Farahani, Y. G., & Dastan, M. (2013). Analysis of Islamic Banks' Financing and Economic Growth: A Panel Cointegration Approach. *International Journal of Islamic and Middle Eastern Finance and Management*, *6*(2), 156–172. doi:10.1108/17538391311329842

Fareed, Z., Rehman, M. A., Adebayo, T. S., Wang, Y., Ahmad, M., & Shahzad, F. (2022). Financial inclusion and the environmental deterioration in Eurozone: The moderating role of innovation activity. *Technology in Society*, *69*, 101961. doi:10.1016/j.techsoc.2022.101961

Farooq, U., Tabash, M. I., Anagreh, S., Al-Rdaydeh, M., & Habib, S. (2023). Economic growth, foreign investment, tourism, and electricity production as determinants of environmental quality: Empirical evidence from GCC region. *Environmental Science and Pollution Research International*, *30*(16), 45768–45780. doi:10.100711356-023-25545-0 PMID:36707478

Favasuli, S., & Sebastian, V. (2021, June 10). *Voluntary carbon markets: how they work, how they're priced and who's involved.* S&P Global. https://www.spglobal.com/commodityinsights/en/market-insights/blogs/energy-transition/061021-voluntary-carbon-markets-pricing-participants-trading-corsia-credits

Fay, M., Block, R. I., & Ebinger, J. (2009). *Adapting to Climate Change in Eastern Europe and Central Asia.* World Bank. doi:10.1596/978-0-8213-8131-1

Felli, R. (2013). Managing Climate Insecurity by Ensuring Continuous Capital Accumulation: 'Climate Refugees' and 'Climate Migrants.'. *New Political Economy, 18*(3), 337–363. doi:10.1080/13563467.2012.687716

Feng, Y. (1997). Leonardo R. Arriola,2009). Democracy, Political Stability and Economic Growth. *British Journal of Political Science, 27*(03), 391–418. https://www.cambridge.org/core/journals/british-journal-of-political-science/article/abs/democracy-political-stability-and-economic-growth/1630FBD0E7690CAF595EE9C612E405AE. doi:10.1017/S0007123497000197

Fletcher, A. L. (2009). Clearing the air: The contribution of frame analysis to understanding climate policy in the United States. *Environmental Politics, 18*(5), 800–816. doi:10.1080/09644010903157123

Fredriksson, P. G., & Svensson, J. (2003). Political instability, corruption and policy formation: The case of environmental policy. *Journal of Public Economics, 87*(7-8), 1383–1405. doi:10.1016/S0047-2727(02)00036-1

Fredriksson, P. G., Vollebergh, H. R., & Dijkgraaf, E. (2004). Corruption and energy efficiency in OECD countries: Theory and evidence. *Journal of Environmental Economics and Management, 47*(2), 207–231. doi:10.1016/j.jeem.2003.08.001

Frieden, J. (2020). *International Monetary Fund.* International Monetary Fund web. https://www.imf.org/en/Publications/fandd/issues/2020/06/political-economy-of-economic-policy-jeff-frieden

Fuess, S., & Millea, M. (2002). Do Employers Pay Efficiency Wage? Evidence from Japan. *Journal of Labor Research, 23*(3), 279–292. doi:10.100712122-002-1007-5

Fu, F. Y., Alharthi, M., Bhatti, Z., Sun, L., Rasul, F., Hanif, I., & Iqbal, W. (2021a). The dynamic role of energy security, energy equity and environmental sustainability in the dilemma of emission reduction and economic growth. *Journal of Environmental Management, 280*, 111828. Advance online publication. doi:10.1016/j.jenvman.2020.111828 PMID:33360740

Garone, L. F., Villalba, P. A. L., Maffioli, A., & Ruzzier, C. A. (2020). Firm-level Productivity in Latin America and the Caribbean. *Research in Economics, 74*(2), 186–192. doi:10.1016/j.rie.2020.04.004

Garrido, S. M., Lalouf, A., & Moreira, A. J. (2020). *Energías renovables y procesos de desarrollo inclusivo y sustentable: de las políticas públicas puntuales a los abordajes sistémicos.*

GATT. (2022). *WTO rules and environmental policies: GATT exceptions.* World Trade Organization. https://www.wto.org/english/tratop_e/envir_e/envt_rules_exceptions_e.htm

General Directorate of Energy (DGE). (2017). *Système d'Information Energétique du Bénin: Rapport annuel 2015 et évolution 2010-2015[Energy Information System of Benin: Annual report of 2015 and trend 2010-2015*]. DGE.

Gera, R., Narwal, R., Jain, M., Taneja, G., & Gupta, S. (2018). Sustainable Development Goals: Leveraging the Global Agenda for Driving Health Policy Reforms and Achieving Universal Health Coverage in India. *Indian Journal of Community Medicine : Official Publication of Indian Association of Preventive & Social Medicine, 43*(4), 255–259. doi:10.4103/ijcm.IJCM_41_18 PMID:30662175

Geweke, J. (1982). Measurement of Linear Dependence and Feedback between Multiple Time Series. *Journal of the American Statistical Association, 77*(378), 304–313. doi:10.1080/01621459.1982.10477803

Gheeraert, L. (2014). Does Islamic Finance Spur Banking Sector Development? *Journal of Economic Behavior & Organization*, *103*, 4–20. doi:10.1016/j.jebo.2014.02.013

GIEC. (2014). *Changements climatiques 2014 Rapport de synthèse*. GIEC.

Gnanglè, C. P., Kakaï, R. G., Assogbadjo, A. E., Vodounnon, S., Afouda, J., & Sokpon, N. (2011). Tendances Climatiques Passees. *Modelisation*, *8*, 27–40.

Godil, D. I., Sharif, A., Ali, M. I., Ozturk, I., & Usman, R. (2021). The role of financial development, R&D expenditure, globalization and institutional quality in energy consumption in India: New evidence from the QARDL approach. *Journal of Environmental Management*, *285*, 112208. doi:10.1016/j.jenvman.2021.112208 PMID:33618139

Government of Canada. (2022). *Carbon Pollution Pricing Systems Across Canada*. Government of Canada. https://www.canada.ca/en/environment-climate-change/services/climate-change/pricing-pollution-how-it-will-work.html

Government of Canada. (2022). *Carbon Pollution Pricing Systems Across Canada*. Government of Canada. https://www.canada.ca/en/environment-climate-change/services/climate-change/pricing-pollution-how-it-will-work/industry.html

Government of Canada. (2022). *The Government of Canada strengthens pollution pricing across the country*. Government of Canada. https://www.canada.ca/en/environment-climate-change/news/2022/11/the-government-of-canada-strengthens-pollution-pricing-across-the-country.html

Governmment of Canada. (2011, July). *Canada's Emissions Trends*. Environment Canada. https://www.ec.gc.ca/doc/publications/cc/COM1374/ec-com1374-en-s3.html

Greene, W. H. (2019). *Econometric Analysis*. Pearson.

Griffiths, S. (2019). Energy diplomacy in a time of energy transition. *Energy Strategy Reviews, 26*, 100-386. https://www.sciencedirect.com/science/article/pii/S2211467X19300793

Griffiths, S., & Sovacool, B. K. (2020). Rethinking the future low-carbon city: Carbon neutrality, green design, and sustainability tensions in the making of Masdar City. *Energy Research & Social Science*, *62*, 101–368. https://www.sciencedirect.com/science/article/pii/S2214629619308904. doi:10.1016/j.erss.2019.101368

Gujarati, D. (2003). Basic Econometrics. Singapura: McGraw-Hill.

Hague, R., & Harrop, M. (2004). *Comparative government and politics* (Vol. 6). Palgrave Macmillan.

Haldar, A., & Sethi, N. (2021). Effect of institutional quality and renewable energy consumption on CO2 emissions– an empirical investigation for developing countries. *Environmental Science and Pollution Research International*, *28*(12), 15485–15503. doi:10.100711356-020-11532-2 PMID:33237563

Hamududu, B., Killingtveit, A., & Engineering, E. (2012). *Assessing Climate Change Impacts on Global Hydropower*, 305–322. World Bank. doi:10.3390/en5020305

Hansen, L. (2019). Post-structuralism. In *The Globalization of World Politics* (pp. 177–191). Oxford University Press. https://www.oxfordpoliticstrove.com/display/10.1093/hepl/9780198825548.001.0001/hepl-9780198825548-chapter-11 doi:10.1093/hepl/9780198825548.003.0011

Harrop, R. H. (2004). *Comparative Government and Politics*. PALGRAVE MACMILLAN.

Hartmann, B. (2010). Rethinking climate refugees and climate conflict: Rhetoric, reality and the politics of policy discourse. *Journal of International Development*, *22*(2), 233–246. doi:10.1002/jid.1676

Hassan Jamil Al Farra, B. A.-H. (2012). The potential role of nuclear energy in mitigating CO2 emissions in the United Arab Emirates. *Energy Policy*, 272–285. http://www.sciencedirect.com

Hay, G. (2021, November 2). *Retrieved from EU-U.S. Green Steel Deal Shows Way For COP26.* Reuters. https://www.reuters.com/breakingviews/eu-us-green-steel-deal-shows-way-cop26-2021-11-02/

Hellmuth, M., Cookson, P., & Potter, J. (2017). *Adressing Climate Vulnerability for Power System Resilience and Energy Security.* ClimateLinks.

Ho, J. (2014). *Indonesia Sells a Record $1.7 Billion of Retail Sovereign Sukuk.* The Jakarta Globe.

Holcombe, R. G. (1997). A theory of the theory of public goods. *The Review of Austrian Economics*, *10*(1), 1–22. doi:10.1007/BF02538141

Holland, A. (2014). *Climate Change and National Security: Briefing Note.* American Security Project. https://www.jstor.org/stable/resrep05973

Holzer, K. (2016). *WTO Law Issues Of Emissions.* https://www.wti.org/media/filer_public/6e/88/6e884b29-f5e2-4a25-85a6-a6edb5c25ed9/working_paper_short_version.pdf: World Trade Institut.

Hommel, D., & Murphy, A. B. (2013). Rethinking geopolitics in an era of climate change. *GeoJournal*, *78*(3), 507–524. https://www.jstor.org/stable/42002526. doi:10.100710708-012-9448-8

Hosein, R. (2021). History of Oil Refining in T&T. In *Oil and Gas in Trinidad and Tobago: Managing the Resource Curse in a Small Petroleum-Exporting Economy* (pp. 49–730). Springer Link. doi:10.1007/978-3-030-77669-5_3

Hotunluoğlu, H., & Tekeli, R. (2007-2). Economic Analysis and Impacts of the Carbon Tax: Does a Carbon Tax Have an Emission Reducing Effect? *Sosyoekonomi*, 107-126.

Hou, Y., Iqbal, W., & Shaikh, G. M. (2019a). Measuring energy efficiency and environmental performance: A case of South Asia. *Processes (Basel, Switzerland)*, *7*(6), 325. Advance online publication. doi:10.3390/pr7060325

Hsu, A., Brandt, J., Widerberg, O., Chan, S., & Weinfurter, A. (2020). Exploring Links Between National Climate Strategies and Non-State and Subnational Climate Action in Nationally Determined Contributions (NDCs). *Climate Policy*, *20*(4), 443–457. doi:10.1080/14693062.2019.1624252

Huber, J., Jara, M., Kim, H., Ter-Minassian, T., & Wagner, R. (2019). *Fixing State-Owned Enterprises: New Policy Solutions to Old Problems.* Inter-American Development Bank.

Huerta, M. M., Guzmán, O. V., & Gonzále, S. F. (2020). *Retos de las políticas públicas para el desarrollo regional sostenible en una sociedad incluyente y solidaria.* Montiel & Soriano.

Hugo, G. (2010). Climate change-induced mobility and the existing migration regime in Asia and the Pacific. In J. McAdam (Ed.), *Climate change and displacement: Multidisciplinary Perspectives.* Hart Publishing. http://hdl.handle.net/2440/63904

Hussain, M., Ye, C., Ye, C., & Wang, Y. (2021). Impact of financial inclusion and infrastructure on ecological footprint in OECD economies. *Environmental Science and Pollution Research International*, 1–8. PMID:34775558

IAEA. (2019). *Adapting the energy sector to climate change.* VIENNA.

ICAP (International Carbon Action Partnership). (2022). *Chile publishes Climate Change Framework Law, Paving The Way for Market-Based Policy.* ICAP. https://icapcarbonaction.com/en/news/chile-publishes-climate-change-framework-law-paving-way-market-based-policy

ICAP (International Carbon Action Partnership). (2023). Mexico ETS Description. ICAP. https://icapcarbonaction.com/en/ets/mexico

ICAP. (2021a, November 17). *ICAP Carbon Action*. Retrieved from Canada-Quebec Cap-and-Trade System: https://icapcarbonaction.com/en/ets-map?etsid=88

ICAP. (2021b, November 17). *ICAP Carbon Action*. Retrieved from Canada-Nova Scotia: https://icapcarbonaction.com/en/ets-map?etsid=88

ICAP. (2021d, November 17). *ICAP Carbon Action*. China National ETS. https://icapcarbonaction.com/en/ets-map

ICAP. (2022). *ICAP*. European Emission Trading System (EU ETS). https://icapcarbonaction.com/en/ets-map?etsid=88

ICAP. (2023). *ICAP Carbon Action*. Beijing Pilot ETS. https://icapcarbonaction.com/en/ets-map

ICAP. (2023). *ICAP Carbon Action*. Chongqinq Pilot ETS. https://icapcarbonaction.com/en/ets-map

ICAP. (2023). *ICAP Carbon Action*. Hubei Pilot ETS. https://icapcarbonaction.com/en/ets-map

ICAP. (2023). *ICAP Carbon Action*. Shangai Pilot ETS. https://icapcarbonaction.com/en/ets-map

ICAP. (2023). *ICAP Carbon Action*. Shenzen Pilot ETS. https://icapcarbonaction.com/en/ets-map

ICAP. (2023). *ICAP Carbon Action*. Tianjin Pilot ETS. https://icapcarbonaction.com/en/ets-map

ICAP. (2023). *ICAP*. About Emissions Trading Systems: https://icapcarbonaction.com/en/about-emissions-trading-systems

ICAP. (2023). *ICAP*. Canada - Québec Cap-and-Trade System: https://icapcarbonaction.com/en/ets/canada-quebec-cap-and-trade-system

ICAP. (2023, May 03). *International Carbon Action Partnership (ICAP)*. EU adopts landmark ETS reforms and new policies to meet 2030 target. https://icapcarbonaction.com/en/news/eu-adopts-landmark-ets-reforms-and-new-policies-meet-2030-target

ICAP. (2023, November 17). *ICAP Carbon Action*. Guamgdong ETS: https://icapcarbonaction.com/en/ets-map

ICAP. (2023, November 2023). *ICAP Carbon Action*. California Cap-and-Trade Program: https://icapcarbonaction.com/en/ets-map

IDDMIB. (2020). *Aluminum Sector Meeting*. Istanbul Ferrous and Non-Ferrous Metals Exporters' Association. https://immib.org.tr/files/metaller/IDDMIB_Aluminium_Sektor_Bulusmas%C4%B1_Rapor_A4%20g%C3%BCncel%202li%20sayfa.pdf

IEA. (2015). *Energy and climate change*. Routledge Handbook of Global Environmental Politics., doi:10.4324/9780203799055

IEA. (2021b). *Net Zero by 2050 A Roadmap for the Global Energy Sector*. IEA.

IEA. (2022, October 26). *Global coal consumption, 2020-2023*. IEA. https://www.iea.org/data-and-statistics/charts/global-coal-consumption-2020-2023

Ijaz, S. T., & Chughtai, S. (2022). The impact of financial, economic and environmental factors on energy efficiency, intensity, and dependence: The moderating role of governance and institutional quality. *International Journal of Energy Economics and Policy*, *12*(4), 15–31. doi:10.32479/ijeep.13157

IMF (International Monetary Fund). (2022). *2022 Article IV Consultation with Member Countries On Common Policies of the Eastern Caribbean Currency Union*. IMF. https://www.imf.org/-/media/Files/Publications/CR/2022/English/1ECCEA2022001.ashx

IMMIB. (2023, March 13). *Istanbul Mineral and Metals Exporters' Associations (IMMIB)*. European Union Carbon Border Adjustment Mechanism. https://immib.org.tr/tr/avrupa-birligi-sinirda-karbon-duzenleme-mekanizmasi

International Monetary Fund. (2021) What Is Capitalism? IMF, larepublica.cd.

Iqbal, S., Bilal, A. R., Nurunnabi, M., Iqbal, W., Alfakhri, Y., & Iqbal, N. (2021a). It is time to control the worst: Testing COVID-19 outbreak, energy consumption and CO < inf > 2 < /inf > emission. *Environmental Science and Pollution Research International*, *28*(15), 19008–19020. doi:10.100711356-020-11462-z PMID:33184786

IRENA. (2021). *La transition vers les énergies renouvelables en Afrique*. IRENA.

IRENA. (2023, July). *World Energy Transitions Outlook 2022 Executive Summary and Introduction*. International Renewable Energy Agency. https://www.irena.org/Digital-Report/World-Energy-Transitions-Outlook-202

Islam, M. M., Irfan, M., Shahbaz, M., & Vo, X. V. (2022). Renewable and non-renewable energy consumption in Bangladesh: The relative influencing profiles of economic factors, urbanization, physical infrastructure and institutional quality. *Renewable Energy*, *184*, 1130–1149. doi:10.1016/j.renene.2021.12.020

Islam, M. S. (2022). Do personal remittances cause environmental pollution? Evidence from the top eight remittance-receiving countries. *Environmental Science and Pollution Research International*, *29*(24), 35768–35779. doi:10.100711356-021-18175-x PMID:35060043

Islam, M. S. (2022). Do personal remittances influence economic growth in South Asia? A panel analysis. *Review of Development Economics*, *26*(1), 242–258. doi:10.1111/rode.12842

Jafri, M. A. H., Abbas, S., Abbas, S. M. Y., & Ullah, S. (2022). Caring for the environment: Measuring the dynamic impact of remittances and FDI on CO2 emissions in China. *Environmental Science and Pollution Research International*, *29*(6), 1–9. doi:10.100711356-021-16180-8 PMID:34495470

Jamil, M., Ahmad, F., & Jeon, Y. (2016). Renewable energy technologies adopted by the UAE: Prospects and challenges – A comprehensive overview. *Renewable & Sustainable Energy Reviews*, *55*, 1181–1194. https://www.sciencedirect.com/science/article/abs/pii/S1364032115006000. doi:10.1016/j.rser.2015.05.087

Jason Vogel, Abt Associates, Inc. Lorine Giangola, Abt Associates, Inc. Sherry Stout, U.S. National Renewable Energy Laboratory Nathan Lee, U. S. N. R. E. L. (2019). *A Comprehensive Vulnerability Assessment Of The Lao Pdr Power Sector Usaid*. National Renewable Energy Laboratory.

Jegou, I., & Rubini, L. (2011). *The Allocation of Emission Allowances Free of Charge: Legal and Economic Considerations*. ICTSD Programme on Competitiveness and Sustainable Development. doi:10.7215/CO_IP_20110826

Jeong, H. W. (2020). Between Economic Diversification and Nation-Branding: The UAE's Pivot to Asia and Innovation Strategies in the Post-Zayed Era. *Journal of Global South Studies*, 181-208. doi:10.1353/gss.2020.0025

Jia, X., Klemeš, J. J., Varbanov, P. S., & Alwi, S. R. (2019). Analyzing the Energy Consumption, GHG Emission,and Cost of Seawater Desalination in China. *Energies*. doi:10.3390/en12030463

Jiang, T., Song, J., & Yu, Y. (2022). The Influencing Factors of Carbon Trading Companies Applying Blockchain Technology: Evidence from Eight Carbon Trading Pilots in China. *Environmental Science and Pollution Research International*, *29*(19), 1–13. doi:10.100711356-021-18425-y PMID:34988820

Jordan, C., & Cunningham, L. (2023). *Renewable Energy and Energy Efficiency Incentives: A Summary of Federal Programs*. Congressional Research Service.

Kahf, M. (1989). Zakat: Unresolved Issues in the Contemporary Fiqh. *Journal of Islamic Economics, 2*(1), 1–22.

Kahf, M. (1998). The Concept of Ownership in Islam. In M. Kahf (Ed.), *Lessons in Islamic Economics, Part II* (pp. 241–256). Islamic Research and Training Institute, Islamic Development Bank.

Kalogirou. (2014). *Solar Space Heating and Cooling*. doi:10.1016/B978-0-12-397270-5.00006-6

Kamla, R., & Rammal, H. G. (2013). Social Reporting by Islamic Banks: Does social justice matter? *Accounting, Auditing & Accountability Journal, 26*(6), 911–945. doi:10.1108/AAAJ-03-2013-1268

Kaufman, N., Krause, E., & Desousa, K. (2018). *Achıevıng U.S. Emıssıons Targets Wıth A Carbon Tax*. World Resources Institute. https://files.wri.org/d8/s3fs-public/us-emission-targets-with-carbon-tax.pdf

Kaufmann, D., Kraay, A., & Mastruzzi, M. (2011). The worldwide governance indicators: Methodology and analytical issues1. *Hague Journal on the Rule of Law, 3*(2), 220–246. doi:10.1017/S1876404511200046

Kazim, A. (2010). Strategy for a sustainable development in the UAE through hydrogen energy. *Renewable Energy, 35*(10), 2257–2269. https://www.sciencedirect.com/science/article/abs/pii/S0960148110001308. doi:10.1016/j.renene.2010.03.013

Kelly, C. (2021). Leveraging renewable energy technologies for climate change mitigation and adaptation in the Middle East:The role of public-private partnerships. In C. Kelly (Ed.), *The Climate Change Policy and Law in the Middle East and Noth Africa Region*. Roudledge.

Kelman, I. (2015). Difficult decisions: migration from Small Island Developing States under climate change. *Earth's Future, 3*(4), 133–142. doi:10.1002/2014EF000278

Khalid, K., Usman, M., & Mehdi, M. A. (2021). The determinants of environmental quality in the SAARC region: A spatial heterogeneous panel data approach. *Environmental Science and Pollution Research International, 28*(6), 6422–6436. doi:10.100711356-020-10896-9 PMID:32997249

Khan, A. A., Khan, S. U., Ali, M. A. S., Safi, A., Gao, Y., Ali, M., & Luo, J. (2022). Role of institutional quality and renewable energy consumption in achieving carbon neutrality: Case study of G-7 economies. *The Science of the Total Environment, 814*, 152797. doi:10.1016/j.scitotenv.2021.152797 PMID:34990660

Khan, N., Zafar, M., Okunlola, A. F., Zoltan, Z., & Robert, M. (2022). Effects of Financial Inclusion on Economic Growth, Poverty, Sustainability, and Financial Efficiency: Evidence from the G20 Countries. *Sustainability, 14*(19), 12688. doi:10.3390u141912688

Khan, Z. U., Ahmad, M., & Khan, A. (2020). On the remittances-environment led hypothesis: Empirical evidence from BRICS economies. *Environmental Science and Pollution Research International, 27*(14), 16460–16471. doi:10.100711356-020-07999-8 PMID:32124280

Klepp, S. (2017). *Climate Change and migration—An overview, Oxford Research Encyclopedia of Climate Science*. Oxford Research Encyclopedia of Climate Science.

Klepp, S., & Herbeck, J. (2016). The politics of environmental migration and climate justice in the Pacific region. *Journal of Human Rights and the Environment, 7*(1), 54–73. doi:10.4337/jhre.2016.01.03

Kohomlan, G., & Yehouénou, M. (2020). *Transition énergétique au Bénin: Quel apport du solaire*. [Thesis, Université d'Abomey-Calavi].

Kondi, V. G. A., Hingray, B., Diedhiou, A., & Francois, B. (2019). Weather sensitivity of electricity demand in West African megacities [abstract]. *Geophysical Research Abstracts*, *21*, EGU2019–EGU18831.

KPMG. (2023). *KPMG*. ETS, CBAM nad Social Climate Fund. https://home.kpmg/xx/en/home/insights/2022/05/ets-cbam-and-social-climate-fund.html

Langbein, L., & Knack, S. (2010). The Worldwide Governance Indicators: Six, One, or None. *The Journal of Development Studies*, *46*(02), 350–370. https://www.tandfonline.com/doi/abs/10.1080/00220380902952399?role=button&needAccess=true&journalCode=fjds20. doi:10.1080/00220380902952399

Lara, B. M. (2021). Calentamiento global y desarrollo sostenible, avances y retos actuales en la política pública de México. *Ciencia económica, 15*, 25-41.

Lashof, D. (2019, February 04). *World Resources Institut*. 5 Things To Look For In The Green New Deal. https://www.wri.org/insights/5-things-look-green-new-deal

Lawal, A. I. (2023). Determinants of Renewable Energy Consumption in Africa: Evidence from System GMM. *Energies*, *16*(5), 2136. doi:10.3390/en16052136

Lawin, A. E., Houngue, R., M'Po, Y. N., Houngue, N. R., Attogouinon, A., & Afouda, A. A. (2019). Mid-Century Climate Change Impacts on Oueme River Discharge at Bonou Outlet (Benin). *Hydrology*, *6*(3), 20. doi:10.3390/hydrology6030072

Le, H. P., & Ozturk, I. (2020). The impacts of globalization, financial development, government expenditures, and institutional quality on CO 2 emissions in the presence of environmental Kuznets curve. *Environmental Science and Pollution Research International*, *27*(18), 22680–22697. doi:10.100711356-020-08812-2 PMID:32323231

Le, T. H., Le, H. C., & Taghizadeh-Hesary, F. (2020). Does financial inclusion impact CO2 emissions? Evidence from Asia. *Finance Research Letters*, *34*, 101451. doi:10.1016/j.frl.2020.101451

Levesque, A., Pietzcker, R. C., & Luderer, G. (2019). Technological Forecasting & Social Change Halving energy demand from buildings : The impact of low consumption practices. *Technological Forecasting and Social Change*, *146*(March), 253–266. doi:10.1016/j.techfore.2019.04.025

Lewsey, C., Cid, G., & Kruse, E. (2004). Assessing Climate Change Impacts On Coastal Infrastructure in the Eastern Caribbean. *Marine Policy*, *28*(5), 393–409. doi:10.1016/j.marpol.2003.10.016

Li, J., Zhang, X., Ali, S., & Khan, Z. (2020). Eco-innovation and energy productivity: New determinants of renewable energy consumption. *Journal of Environmental Management*, *271*, 111028. doi:10.1016/j.jenvman.2020.111028 PMID:32778308

Lockwood, M., Kuzemko, C., Mitchell, C., & Hoggett, R. (2016). Historical institutionalism and the politics of sustainable energy transitions: A research agenda. *Environment and Planning C: Government and Policy.*

Loi N° 2020-02 du 20 mars 2020 portant Code des investissements en République du Bénin

Loi N° 2020-05 du 1er avril 2020 portant code de l'électricité en République du Bénin

Lowndes, V., & Roberts, M. (2013). *Why Institutions Matter: The new institutionalism in political science*. Palgrave Macmillan. doi:10.1007/978-1-137-32913-4

Lucas, H., Ferroukhi, R., & Hawila, D. (2013). Renewable Energy Auctions in Developing. ⟨https://www.irena.org/DocumentDownloads/Publications/IRENA_Renewable_energy_auctions_in_developing_countries.pdf

Lundqvist, L. J. (2001). A Green Fist in a Velvet Glove: The Ecological State and Sustainable Development. *JSTOR Collection*, 472-475.

Maali, B., Casson, P., & Napier, C. (2006). Social Reporting by Islamic Banks. *Abacus, 42*(2), 266–289. doi:10.1111/j.1467-6281.2006.00200.x

Malone, E. L. (2013). Climate Change and National Security. *Weather, Climate, and Society, 5*(1), 93–95. https://www.jstor.org/stable/24907507. doi:10.1175/WCAS-D-12-00016.1

Maruta, A. A., Banerjee, R., & Cavoli, T. (2020). Foreign aid, institutional quality and economic growth: Evidence from the developing world. *Economic Modelling, 89*, 444–463. doi:10.1016/j.econmod.2019.11.008

Mathieu, P., & Shiells, C.R. (2002). *Les difficultés du secteur de l'énergie dans la Communauté des États indépendants*. ME.

Matthew McCartney. (2012). *Gerald Forkuor, Aditya Sood, Barnabas Amisigo, F. H. and L. M.* The Water Resource Basin Climate in the Volta River Implications of Changing.

Mauro, P. (1995). Corruption and growth. *The Quarterly Journal of Economics, 110*(3), 681–712. doi:10.2307/2946696

McDonald, M. (2023). Immovable objects? Impediments to a UN Security Council resolution on climate change. *International Affairs, 99*(4), 1635–1651. doi:10.1093/ia/iiad064

MEF (2020): *Évolution récente de l'économie béninoise et Perspectives à moyen terme* MEF.

Mehmood, U., Agyekum, E. B., Tariq, S., Ul Haq, Z., Uhunamure, S. E., Edokpayi, J. N., & Azhar, A. (2022). Socio-economic drivers of renewable energy: Empirical evidence from BRICS. *International Journal of Environmental Research and Public Health, 19*(8), 4614. doi:10.3390/ijerph19084614 PMID:35457479

Mendivil, A., & Niño, G. (2016). *Una política energética sustentable: Un pendiente en México.* México, F. D. L. O.

Mengi-Dinçer, H., Ediger, V., & Yesevi, Ç. (2021). Evaluating the International Renewable Energy Agency through the lens of social constructivism. *Renewable & Sustainable Energy Reviews, 152*, 111–705. https://www.sciencedirect.com/science/article/abs/pii/S1364032121009795. doi:10.1016/j.rser.2021.111705

Metcalf, G. E., & Weisbach, D. (2009). The Design of a Carbon Tax. *The Harvard Environmental Law Review, 33*, 499.

Methmann, C., & Oels, A. (2015). From 'fearing' to 'empowering' climate refugees: Governing climate-induced migration in the name of resilience. *Security Dialogue, 46*(1), 51–68. https://www.jstor.org/stable/26292938. doi:10.1177/0967010614552548

Mezher, T., Dawelbait, G., & Abbas, Z. (2012). Renewable energy policy options for Abu Dhabi: Drivers and barriers. *Energy Policy, 42*, 315–328. https://www.sciencedirect.com/science/article/abs/pii/S0301421511009876. doi:10.1016/j.enpol.2011.11.089

Mian, A., & Amir, S. (2014). *House of Debt: How They (and You) Caused the Great Recession, and How We Can Prevent It from Happening Again.* University of Chicago Press. doi:10.7208/chicago/9780226277509.001.0001

Micheli, J. (2002). Política ambiental en México y su dimensión regional. *Región y Sociedad, 14*(23), 129–170.

Ministère de l'Energie (ME), Direction Générale de l'Energie (DGE). (2017). *Rapport SIE 2017.* ME.

Ministère de l'Energie. (2019). *Assurer une transition énergétique pour le développement économique et social durable.* ME.

Ministère du Plan et du Développement (MPD). (2018). *Plan National de Développement 2018-2025.* MPD.

Ministre du Cadre de Vie et du Développement Durable. (2019). *Troisième communication nationale du Benin.* MCVDD.

Mohamed Aslam, A. L., & Alibuhtto, M. C. (2023). Workers' remittances and economic growth: new evidence from an ARDL bounds cointegration approach for Sri Lanka. *Journal of Economic and Administrative Sciences.*

Mohan, P. S. (2022). Implementing Nationally Determined Contributions Under the Paris Agreement: An Assessment of Climate Finance in Caribbean Small Island Developing States. *Climate Policy*, *22*(9-10), 1281–1289. doi:10.1080/14693062.2022.2101978

Mohieldin, M., Iqbal, Z., Rostom, A., & Fu, X. (2012). The Role of Islamic Finance in Enhancing Financial Inclusion in Organization of Islamic Cooperation (OIC) Countries. *Islamic Economic Studies*, *20*(2), 55–120.

Molefe, K., & Choga, I. (2017). Government expenditure and economic growth in South Africa: A vector error correction modelling and Granger causality test. *Journal of Economics and Behavioral Studies*, *9*(4 (J)), 164–172. doi:10.22610/jebs.v9i4(J).1831

Moskalenko, B., Lyulyov, O., Pimonenko, T., & Kobushko, I. (2022). Institutions' Effect on a Country's Investment Attractiveness within Sustainable Development. *Virtual Economics*, *5*(4), 50–64. doi:10.34021/ve.2022.05.04(3)

Mosteanu, N. R. (2019). Intelligent foreign direct investments to boost economic development – UAE case study. *Conference proceedings of the Academy of Business and Retail Management (ABRM). 10*, (pp. 1-9). The Business and Management Review.

Mountford, H., & McGregor, M. (2018, November 15). *World Resources İnstitut.* A Carbon Price Can Benefit the Poor While Reducing Emissions. https://www.wri.org/insights/carbon-price-can-benefit-poor-while-reducing-emissions

Murooshid, H. (2018). The Adoption of Renewable Energy Policies in a Rentier State: A Case Study of the United Arab Emirates. *Arab World Geographer*, *21*(1), 43–57. doi:10.5555/1480-6800.21.1.43

Murphy, A. (2019). The United Nations Security Council and Climate Change: Mapping a Pragmatic Pathway to Intervention. *Carbon & Climate Law Review, 13*(1), 50–62. https://www.jstor.org/stable/26739643

Musah, A., & Yakubu, I. N. (2022). Exploring industrialization and environmental sustainability dynamics in Ghana: A fully modified least squares approach. *Technological Sustainability*, *2*(2), 142–155. doi:10.1108/TECHS-06-2022-0028

Myers, N. (1993). Environmental Refugees in a Globally Warmed World. *Bioscience*, *43*(11), 752–761. doi:10.2307/1312319

Naqbi, S. A., Tsai, I., & Mezher, T. (2019). Market design for successful implementation of UAE 2050 energy strategy. *Renewable and Sustainable Energy Reviews*. Elsevier. https://sci-hub.se/10.1016/j.rser.2019.109429

Nasr, S. V. R. (1989). Islamic Economics: Novel Perspectives. *Middle Eastern Studies*, *25*(4), 516–530. doi:10.1080/00263208908700797

Nathaniel, S., Adeleye, N., & Adedoyin, F. F. (2021). Natural resource abundance, renewable energy, and ecological footprint linkage in MENA countries. *Estudios de Economía Aplicada*, *39*(02). doi:10.25115/eea.v39i2.3927

Navarrete Ávila, H., & Sun, L. X. (2023). *Pobreza de la energía eléctrica en México y sus perspectivas ante la eliminación de subsidios. Hatso-Hnini.* Revista De Investigación De Paisajes Y Espacio Construido, 1-15. revistahatsohnini.com.mx/index.php/inicio/article/view/16

Ndombi Avouba, F. G., Akougbe, A. I. S., & Ndombi Ondze, C. L. I. L. (2023). Non-linearity between financial inclusion and economic growth in sub-saharan Africa: What implications for the West African Economic and Monetary Union (WAEMU)? *Cogent Economics & Finance*, *11*(1), 2158630. doi:10.1080/23322039.2022.2158630

Neves, S. A., Marques, A. C., & Patrício, M. (2020). Determinants of CO2 emissions in European Union countries: Does environmental regulation reduce environmental pollution? *Economic Analysis and Policy*, *68*, 114–125. doi:10.1016/j.eap.2020.09.005

Nguyen, C. P., Su, T. D., & Nguyen, T. V. H. (2018). Institutional quality and economic growth: The case of emerging economies. *Theoretical Economics Letters*, *8*(11), 1943–1956. doi:10.4236/tel.2018.811127

Nicolli, F., & Vona, F. (2015). The evolution of renewable energy policy in OECD countries: Aggregate indicators and determinants. In F. Schneider, A. Kollmann, & J. Reichl (Eds.), *Political Economy and Instruments of Environmental Politic* (pp. 117–148). The MIT Press. doi:10.7551/mitpress/10274.003.0009

Nurmi, H. (2017). *Models of Political Economy*. Routledge.

O'Riordan, T., & Voisey, H. (1997). The political economy of sustainable development. *Environmental Politics*, *6*(1), 1–23. doi:10.1080/09644019708414309

Oakes, R., Milan, A., & Campbell, J. (2016). *Kiribati: Climate Change And Migration Relationships Between Household Vulnerability, Human Mobility And Climate Change Report*. Research Gate. doi doi:10.13140/RG.2.2.11824.05122

OCDE. (2006). *Políticas Públicas para un Mejor Desempeño Económico*. Centro de la OCDE en México para América Latina.

OECD. (2013). *Expanding access to clean energy for green growth and development*. OECD. https://www.oecd.org/daf/inv/investment-policy/CleanEnergyInfrastructure.pdf

OECD. (2015). *Green Bonds Mobilising the Debt Capital Markets for a Low-Carbon Transition*. OECD Publishing.

OECD. (2021). *Green Growth and Developing- A Summary for Policy Makers*. 2012: Green Growth and Development.

OECD. (2023, 05 15). *Green Growth Indicators*. OECD.Stat. https://stats.oecd.org/Index.aspx?DataSetCode=GREEN_GROWTH

Olawuyi, D. S. (2021). *Climate Change Law and Policy in the Middle East and North Africa Region*. Routledge. doi:10.4324/9781003044109

Omri, A. (2016). *Analyse de la transition vers les énergies renouvelables en Tunisie: Risques, enjeux et stratégies à adopter. Economies et finances*. Université Côte d'Azur; Université de Sfax (Tunisie).

Osse, R., Tokponnon, F., Okê, M., Adjinda, S., Zounmenou, A., & Bokonon-Ganta, E. H. (2019). *Etude de Vulnérabilité aux changements climatiques du Secteur Santé au Bénin*. Cotonou: Climate Analytics gGmbH.

Ossola, A. (2017, May 22). How HIV became a matter of international security. *The Independent*. https://www.independent.co.uk/news/long_reads/how-hiv-became-a-matter-of-international-security-a7732701.html

Oxford Bibliographies. "Political Economy." Accessed Feb. 25, 2021

Özcan, M., Ergün Yüksel, B., & Ocaklı, E. (2022). Evaluation of voluntary carbon markets in Turkey. *Duzce University Journal of Science & Technology*, 10-25.

Ozturk, I., & Ullah, S. (2022). Does digital financial inclusion matter for economic growth and environmental sustainability in OBRI economies? An empirical analysis. *Resources, Conservation and Recycling*, *185*, 106489. doi:10.1016/j.resconrec.2022.106489

Pal, S., & Bandyopadhyay, I. (2022). Impact of financial inclusion on economic growth, financial development, financial efficiency, financial stability, and profitability: An international evidence. *SN Business & Economics*, *2*(9), 139. doi:10.100743546-022-00313-3

PANA-ENERGIE. (2019). *Rapport final - Evaluation de la vulnérabilité et de l'adaptation dans le secteur énergie au Benin*. PE.

Pata, U. K., & Yilanci, V. (2020). Financial development, globalization and ecological footprint in G7: Further evidence from threshold cointegration and fractional frequency causality tests. *Environmental and Ecological Statistics*, *27*(4), 803–825. doi:10.100710651-020-00467-z

Patil, P. G., Virdin, J., Diez, S. M., Roberts, J., & Singh, A. (2016). *Toward a Blue Economy: A Promise for Sustainable Growth in the Caribbean.* World Bank., Retrieved from https://openknowledge.worldbank.org/handle/10986/25061 doi:10.1596/25061

Pedro, F., Subosa, M., Rivas, A., & Valverde, P. (2019). *Artificial intelligence in education: Challenges and opportunities for sustainable development.* UNESCO.

Phillips, P., & Hansen, B. (1990). Statistical Inference in Instrumental Variables Regression with I(1) Processes. *The Review of Economic Studies*, *57*(1), 99–125. doi:10.2307/2297545

Piguet, E., Pécoud, A., & de Guchteneire, P. (2011). migration and Climate Change: An Overview. *Refugee Survey Quarterly*, *30*(3), 1–23. https://www.jstor.org/stable/45054544. doi:10.1093/rsq/hdr006

Pleuger, G. (2014). Climate Change as a Threat to International Peace – The Role of the UN Security Council. In S. von Schorlemer & S. Maus (Eds.), *Climate Change as a Threat to Peace* (pp. 33–36). Peter Lang AG. https://www.jstor.org/stable/j.ctv2t4cvp.6

Poudineh, R., Sen, A., & Fattouh, B. (2018). Advancing renewable energy in resource-rich economies of the MENA. *Renewable Energy*, *123*, 135–149. https://www.sciencedirect.com/science/article/abs/pii/S0960148118301587. doi:10.1016/j.renene.2018.02.015

Pöyry Energy Gmb. (2017). GIS Hydropower Resource Mapping – Country Report for Benin, 1–19. EcoWrex. www.ecowrex.org

Project, A. S. (2012). *Part Two: Climate Change & Global Security.* American Security Project. https://www.jstor.org/stable/resrep05971

Rahman, M. M., & Sultana, N. (2022). Impacts of institutional quality, economic growth, and exports on renewable energy: Emerging countries perspective. *Renewable Energy*, *189*, 938–951. doi:10.1016/j.renene.2022.03.034

Ranson-Cooper, H., Farbotko, C., & McNamara, K. (2015). Being(s) framed: The means and ends of framing environmental migrants. *Global Environmental Change*, *35*, 106–115. doi:10.1016/j.gloenvcha.2015.07.013

Rao, N., & Bhatnagar, M. H. (2012). Financial Inclusion: Issues and Prospects. *Pacific Business Review International*, *5*(3), 84–96.

Rasheed, B., Law, S. H., Chin, L., & Habibullah, M. S. (2016). The Role of Financial Inclusion in Financial Development: International Evidence. *Abasyn University Journal of Social Sciences*, *9*(2), 330–348.

Ratri, D. N., Whan, K., & Schmeits, M. (2019). A comparative verification of raw and bias-corrected ECMWF seasonal ensemble precipitation reforecasts in Java (Indonesia). *Journal of Applied Meteorology and Climatology*, *58*(8), 1709–1723. doi:10.1175/JAMC-D-18-0210.1

Raza, M. A. A., Yan, C., Abbas, H. S. M., & Ilahi, S. (2023). Do Remittance Inflows, Investment Attributes, and Regional Integration Accelerate Sustainable Economic Growth in Asia? *Journal of the Knowledge Economy*, 1–16. doi:10.100713132-023-01126-x

Rehman, A. U., Malik, A. H., Md Isa, A. H. B., & Jais, M. B. (2023). Dynamic impact of financial inclusion and industrialization on environmental sustainability. *Social Responsibility Journal*, *19*(5), 906–929. doi:10.1108/SRJ-07-2021-0275

Remling, E. (2020). migration as climate adaptation? Exploring discourses amongst development actors in the Pacific Island region. *Regional Environmental Change*, *20*(1), 3. doi:10.100710113-020-01583-z

République du Bénin, ministère de l'Energie. (2020). *Politique Nationale des Energies Renouvelables (PONADER)*. ME.

RGGI (Regional Greenhouse Gas Initiative). (2023). *Regional Greenhouse Gas Initiative (RGGI): An Initiative of Eastern States of the US.* RGGI. https://www.rggi.org/program-overview-and-design/elements

RGGI. (2023). *Elements of RGGI.* The Regional Greenhouse Gas Initiative (RGGI) an initiative of Eastern States of the EUS. https://www.rggi.org/program-overview-and-design/elements

Ritchie, H., Roser, M., & Rosado, P. (2020). CO_2 and Greenhouse Gas Emissions. Our World in Data. *Our World in Data.* https://ourworldindata.org/co2-emissions?utm_source=tri-city%20news&utm_campaign=tricity%20news%3A%20outbound&utm_medium=referral

Riva, F. R., Paes-De-Souza, M., & Talamini, E. (2022). REDD+: Analysis of Its Components Through a Systematic Review of Scientific Literature from Brazil and Indonesia. *International Forestry Review*, *24*(1), 72–84. doi:10.1505/146554822835224829

Rodríguez Padilla, V. (2016). Industria eléctrica en México: Tensión entre el Estado y el mercado. *Problemas del Desarrollo*, 33–55.

Rogelj, J., Den Elzen, M., Höhne, N., Fransen, T., Fekete, H., Winkler, H., Schaeffer, R., Sha, F., Riahi, K., & Meinshausen, M. (2016). Paris Agreement Climate Proposals Need a Boost to Keep Warming Well Below 2 C. *Nature*, *534*(7609), 631–639. doi:10.1038/nature18307 PMID:27357792

Roodman, D. (2009). How to do xtabond2: An introduction to difference and system GMM in Stata. *The Stata Journal*, *9*(1), 86–136. doi:10.1177/1536867X0900900106

Rychnovská, D. (2014). Securitization and the Power of Threat Framing. *Perspectives*, *22*(2), 9–31. https://www.jstor.org/stable/24625251

Saadaoui, H., & Chtourou, N. (2022). Do institutional quality, financial development, and economic growth improve renewable energy transition? Some evidence from Tunisia. *Journal of the Knowledge Economy*, 1–32. doi:10.100713132-022-00999-8

Sabaratnam, M. (2020). Post-colonial and decolonial approaches. In *The Globalization of World Politics* (pp. 160–176). Oxford University Press., https://www.oxfordpoliticstrove.com/display/10.1093/hepl/9780198825548.001.0001/hepl-9780198825548-chapter-10

Sachan, A., Sahu, U. K., Pradhan, A. K., & Thomas, R. (2023). Examining the drivers of renewable energy consumption: Evidence from BRICS nations. *Renewable Energy*, *202*, 1402–1411. doi:10.1016/j.renene.2022.11.080

Said, E. W. (2014). *Orientalism.* Knopf Doubleday Publishing Group.

Saidi, K., & Mbarek, M. B. (2016). Nuclear energy, renewable energy, CO2 emissions, and economic growth for nine developed countries: Evidence from panel Granger causality tests. *Progress in Nuclear Energy*, *88*, 364–374. doi:10.1016/j.pnucene.2016.01.018

Saint-Germain, P. M. (2007, 08 02). *Faculty Integrating Technology.* CSULB. home.csulb.edu: https://home.csulb.edu/~msaintg/ppa590/intro.htm

Salazar-Xirinachs, J. M. (2023). *Fiscal Panorama of Latin America and the Caribbean.* Santiago: United Nations PUblication.

SalemS. B.JagadeesanP. (2022;Stewart M. Godwin,2017). Food supply chain in pandemic, geopolitical, and climate change era - efforts of United Arab Emirates (UAE). AgriRxiv. https://www.cabidigitallibrary.org/doi/abs/10.31220/agriRxiv.2022.00142

Salimi, M., Husseinpour, M., & Borhani, T. N. (2022). Analysis of Solar Energy Development Strategies for a Successful Energy Transition in the UAE. *Processes*. https://www.mdpi.com/2227-9717/10/7/1338

Samour, A., Shahzad, U., & Mentel, G. (2022). Moving toward sustainable development: Assessing the impacts of taxation and banking development on renewable energy in the UAE. *Renewable Energy*, *200*, 706–713. doi:10.1016/j.renene.2022.10.020

Samuelson, P. A. (1954). The pure theory of public expenditure. *The Review of Economics and Statistics*, *36*(4), 387–389. doi:10.2307/1925895

Samuelson, P. A. (1955). Diagrammatic Exposition of a Theory of Public Expenditure. *The Review of Economics and Statistics*, *37*(4), 350–356. doi:10.2307/1925849

Sancı, S. (2022). *2022 Fertilizer Report*. Istanbul Chemicals and Chemical Products Exporters' Association.

Sankaran, V., & Chopra, A. (2020; Petch, Neil,2016, October 12). Creating Global Sustainable Smart Cities (A Case Study of Masdar City). *First International Conference on Advances in Physical Sciences. 1706.* IOP Publishing Ltd. Entrepreneur Middle East. https://iopscience.iop.org/article/10.1088/1742-6596/1706/1/012141/meta

Sarra, A. (2020). *Les obstacles au développement des énergies vertes en Tunisie*. Web Manager Center. https://www.webmanagercenter.com/2020/11/04/458166/les-obstacles-au-developpement-des-energies-vertes-en-tunisie-1-4/ Consulté, le 5 juillet 2023

Sarwar, S., Farooq, M. U., Shahzad, U., & Zaijun, L. (2019). The impact of carbon emission and forest activities on health outcomes: Empirical evidence from China. *Environmental Science and Pollution Research International*, *26*(13), 12894–12906. doi:10.100711356-019-04779-x PMID:30888615

Savvanidou, E., Zervas, E., & Tsagarakis, K. P. (2010). Public acceptance of biofuels. *Energy Policy*, *38*(07), 3482–3488. https://www.sciencedirect.com/science/article/abs/pii/S0301421510001023. doi:10.1016/j.enpol.2010.02.021

Schelter, B., Winterhalder, M., Eichler, M., Peifer, M., Hellwig, B., Guschlbauer, B., Lucking, C., Dahlhaus, R., & Timmer, J. (2006). Testing for Directed Influences among Neural Signals Using Partial Directed Coherence. *Journal of Neuroscience Methods*, *152*(2), 210–219. doi:10.1016/j.jneumeth.2005.09.001 PMID:16269188

Scott, S. (2022). Great Power Responsibility for Climate Security in the United Nations Security Council. In R. Falkner & B. Buzan (Eds.), Great Powers, Climate Change, and Global Environmental Responsibilities (p. 0). Oxford University Press. doi:10.1093/oso/9780198866022.003.0009

Scott, S. V. (2015). Implications of climate change for the UN Security Council: Mapping the range of potential policy responses. *International Affairs (Royal Institute of International Affairs 1944-), 91*(6), 1317–1333. https://www.jstor.org/stable/24539058

Scott, S. V., & Nguyen, N. (2023). The UN Security Council and Climate Security: Responding to a Multifaceted Threat. In A. Warren (Ed.), *Global Security in an Age of Crisis* (pp. 374–394). Edinburgh University Press. https://www.jstor.org/stable/10.3366/j.ctv32vqn3h.22

Scott, S. V., & Andrade, R. C. D. (2012). The Global Response to Climate Change: Can the Security Council Assume a Lead Role? *The Brown Journal of World Affairs*, *18*(2), 215–226. https://www.jstor.org/stable/24590874

Scott, W. R. (2013). *Institutions and organizations: Ideas, interests, and identities*. Sage publications.

Secretaría General. (2015). *Ley general del equilibrio ecológico y la protección al ambiente.* Mexico: Secretaría de Servicios Parlamentarios.

Sefia. (2022). *Turkey Steel Sector Report: Production, Trade and Decarbonization Process.* Sustainable Economy and Finance (Sefia).

Sekantsi, L. P., & Timuno, S. (2017). Electricity consumption in Botswana: The role of financial development, industrialisation, and urbanization. *Review of Economic and Business Studies, 10*(1), 75–102. doi:10.1515/rebs-2017-0049

Sekrafi, H., & Sghaier, A. (2018). Examining the relationship between corruption, economic growth, environmental degradation, and energy consumption: A panel analysis in MENA region. *Journal of the Knowledge Economy, 9*(3), 963–979. doi:10.100713132-016-0384-6

SENER. (2016). *Prospectiva de Energías Renovables 2016-2030.* Gobierno de México.

SENER. (2023, July). *GOBIERNO DE MEXICO.* Sener. https://www.gob.mx/sener/articulos/politicas-publicas-del-sector-energetico

Shahbaz, M., Mallick, H., Mahalik, M. K., & Sadorsky, P. (2016). The role of globalization on the recent evolution of energy demand in India: Implications for sustainable development. *Energy Economics, 55*, 52–68. doi:10.1016/j.eneco.2016.01.013

Shaheen, A., Sheng, J., Arshad, S., Muhammad, H., & Salam, S. (2020). Forecasting the determinants of environmental degradation: A gray modeling approach. *Energy Sources. Part A, Recovery, Utilization, and Environmental Effects*, 1–21. doi:10.1080/15567036.2020.1827090

Shahzadi, H. N., Sheikh, S. M., Sadiq, A., & Rahman, S. U. (2023). Effect of Financial Development, Economic Growth on Environment Pollution: Evidence from G-7 based ARDL Cointegration Approach. *Pakistan Journal of Humanities and Social Sciences, 11*(1), 68–79. doi:10.52131/pjhss.2023.1101.0330

Sharma, R., Shahbaz, M., Kautish, P., & Vo, X. V. (2021). Does energy consumption reinforce environmental pollution? Evidence from emerging Asian economies. *Journal of Environmental Management, 297*, 113272. doi:10.1016/j.jenvman.2021.113272 PMID:34280860

Sharmin, F., & Khan, M. R. (2016). A causal relationship between energy consumption, energy prices and economic growth in Africa. *International Journal of Energy Economics and Policy, 6*(3), 477–494.

Shukla, P. R., Skea, J., & Reisinger, A. (2022). [*Mitigation of Climate Change: Working Group III Contribution to the Sixth Assessment Report of the Intergovernmental Panel on Climate Change.* Intergovernmental Panel on Climate Change.

Siddiqi, M. N. (1968). The Economic Enterprise in Islam. Islamic Publications (Pvt.) Ltd., Lahore.

Sindico, F. (2007). Climate Change: A Security (Council) Issue? *Carbon & Climate Law Review, 1*(1), 29–34. https://www.jstor.org/stable/24323646

Singh, D., & Stakic, N. (2021). Financial inclusion and economic growth nexus: Evidence from SAARC countries. *South Asia Research, 41*(2), 238–258. doi:10.1177/0262728020964605

Sintondji, L. O., Badou, D. F., Ahouansou, M., Hounkpe, J., Assogba Balle, R., Gaba, C., & Vissin, E. (2019). *Etude de Vulnérabilité face aux changements climatiques du Secteur Ressources en Eau au Bénin.* Climate Analytics gGmbH.

Sisodia, G. S., Awad, E., Alkhoja, H., & Sergi, B. S. (2020). Strategic business risk evaluation for sustainable energy investment and stakeholder engagement: A proposal for energy policy development in the Middle East through Khalifa funding and land subsidies. *Business Strategy and Environment.* https://onlinelibrary.wiley.com/doi/abs/10.1002/bse.2543

Skjærseth, J. B., & Wettestad, J. (2010). Making the EU Emissions Trading System: The European Commission as an Entrepreneurial Epistemic Leader. *Global Environmental Change*, *20*(2), 314–321. doi:10.1016/j.gloenvcha.2009.12.005

Smith, E. S. (2020). *Climate Change in Women, Peace and Security National Action Plans*. Stockholm International Peace Research Institute. https://www.jstor.org/stable/resrep25311

Smith, R., & McNamara, K. (2015). Future migrations from Tuvalu and Kiribati: Exploring Government, civil society and donor perceptions. *Climate and Development*, *7*(1), 47–59. Advance online publication. doi:10.1080/17565529.2014.900603

Snow, D., & Benford, R. (1988). Ideology, Frame Resonance and Participant Mobilization. *International Social Movement Research*, *1*, 197–217.

Sołoducho-Pelc, L., & Sulich, A. (2020). Between sustainable and temporary competitive advantages in the unstable business environment. *Sustain*, *12*(21), 32–88. doi:10.3390u12218832

Sovacool, B. (2016). *The History and Politics of Energy Transitions: Comparing Contested Views and Finding Common Ground*. Oxford University Press. doi:10.35188/UNU-WIDER/2016/124-6

Staempfli, F. (2017). *Framing Environmental migration—An Analysis of Indian Government Policies*. Semantic Scholar. https://www.semanticscholar.org/paper/Framing-Environmental-migration-An-Analysis-of-Staempfli/feae85c24f8897610171e5389b545c9296f196b6

Staff Writer. (2022). UAE strengthens ties with South Kora across energy value chains. *Arabian Business*. https://www.arabianbusiness.com/industries/energy/uae-strengthens-ties-with-south-korea-across-energy-value-chains

Steel Exporters Association. (2022). *Steel Exporters Association*. Statistics. https://www.cib.org.tr/en/statistics.html

Steel Exporters' Association. (2021). *2022 Shape The World With Turkish Steel*. Steel Exporters' Association.

Steinmo, S. K, T., & F, L. (1992). Historical institutionalism in comparative politics. Cambridge: Cambridge University Press.

Stenqvist, C., & Åhman, M. (2016). Free Allocation in the 3rd EU ETS period: Assessing Two Manufacturing Sectors. *Climate Policy*, *16*(2), 125–144. doi:10.1080/14693062.2014.979130

Stern, D. I. (2012). Modeling international trends in energy efficiency. *Energy Economics*, *34*(6), 2200–2208. doi:10.1016/j.eneco.2012.03.009

Subramaniam, Y., Masron, T. A., & Loganathan, N. (2022). Remittances and renewable energy: an empirical analysis. *International Journal of Energy Sector Management*.

Sulich, A., & Sołoducho-Pelc, L. (2021). Renewable energy producers' strategies in the Visegrád group countries. *Energies*, *14*(11), 30–48. doi:10.3390/en14113048

Sun, H. (2019) Institutional quality, green innovation and energy efficiency. *Energy Policy 135:111002*. IDEAS. doi:.2019.111002 doi:10.1016/j.enpol

Svirydzenka, K. (2016). *Introducing a New Broad-based Index of Financial Development*. (IMF Working Paper, No. 16/5). IMF, Washington, DC.

Tamargo, J. L. (2002). *La gestión ambiental en México*. Semarnat.

Tao, C., & Wang, Y. (2020). The spatial spillover effect of China's government health expenses on the regional economy: Empirical analysis based on the spatial panel model. *Journal of Coastal Research*, *103*(sp1), 95–100. doi:10.2112/SI103-020.1

TCFD. (2022). *The challenge we're addressing*. Task Force on Climate-related Financial Disclosures. https://www.fsb-tcfd.org/about/#task-force-members

TCMB. (2023). *Central Bank of the Republic of Turkey*. Central Bank of the Republic of Turkey. https://www.tcmb.gov.tr/wps/wcm/connect/EN/TCMB+EN/Main+Menu/About+the+Bank/Organization/Head+Office/

Tenaw, D. (2021). Decomposition and macroeconomic drivers of energy intensity: The case of Ethiopia. *Energy Strategy Reviews*, *35*, 100641. doi:10.1016/j.esr.2021.100641

TFCD. (2022). *Task Force on Climate-Related Financial Disclosures*. Climate Change Presents Financial Risk To The Global Economy. https://www.fsb-tcfd.org/

The National. (2023). Shikh Mohammed approces master plan for palm jebel ali. *The National*. https://www.thenationalnews.com/uae/2023/05/31/sheikh-mohammed-approves-master-plan-for-palm-jebel-ali/

The White House. (2021, October 28). *President Biden Announces the Build Back Better Framework*. The White House. https://www.whitehouse.gov/briefing-room/statements-releases/2021/10/28/president-biden-announces-the-build-back-better-framework/

The White House. (2022, August 16). *The White House*. Bill Signed: H.R. 5376. https://www.whitehouse.gov/briefing-room/legislation/2022/08/16/bill-signed-h-r-5376/

The World Bank. (2020). Environmental Sustainability and Urban Resilience (P174000). United Mexicans States: International Bank.

The World Bank. (2022a). *What Is Carbon Pricing?* Pricing Carbon. https://www.worldbank.org/en/programs/pricing-carbon

The World Bank. (2022b). *Carbon Pricing Dashboard*. What is Carbon Pricing? https://carbonpricingdashboard.worldbank.org/what-carbon-pricing

The World Bank. (2023). *State and Trends of Carbon Pricing 2023*. The World Bank.

Thornton, F., James, S., Dun, O., Farbotko, C., McNamara, K. E., McMichael, C., Coelho, S., Kim, R. M., Ngo, L., & Westbury, T. (2021). *Policy developments and options to address human mobility in the context of climate risk in the Pacific Islands region*. eSpace Library. https://espace.library.uq.edu.au/view/UQ:f9872cf

Toke, D. (2010). Wind Power in UK and Denmark: Can Rational Choice Help Explain Different Outcomes? *Environmental Politics*, *11*(04), 83–100. doi:10.1080/714000647

Torne, C. (2019). *ENERGY TRANSITION IN MEXICO: THE SOCIAL DIMENSION OF ENERGY AND THE POLITICS OF CLIMATE CHANGE*. Federal Ministry for the Environment, Nature Conservation, and Nuclear Safety.

Trade Map. (2023). *TradeMap*. Trade Map. https://www.trademap.org/Product_SelCountry_TS.aspx?nvpm=1%7c792%7c%7c%7c%7c2523%7c%7c%7c4%7c1%7c1%7c1%7c2%7c1%7c1%7c1%7c1%7c1

Tufail, M., Song, L., Adebayo, T. S., Kirikkaleli, D., & Khan, S. (2021). Do fiscal decentralization and natural resources rent curb carbon emissions? Evidence from developed countries. *Environmental Science and Pollution Research International*, *28*(35), 49179–49190. doi:10.100711356-021-13865-y PMID:33932218

Turcotte, I., Gorski, J., & Riehl, B. (2019). The Pan-Canadian Price On Pollution. In *A New Era Of Climate Policy In*. Pembina Institute.

Turkish Cement Manufacturers' Association. (2022). *Statistics*. Turkish Cemenr Manufacturers' Association. https://www.turkcimento.org.tr/en/statistics/exports

Turkish Steel Steel Exporters' Association. (2021). *Turkish Steel Steel Exporters' Association 2021 Working Report*. Turkish Steel Steel Exporters' Association.

UAE Ministry of Climate Change and Environment. (2023). *About*. UAE Ministry of Climate Change and Environment. https://www.moccae.gov.ae/en/about-ministry/about-the-ministry.aspx

UK Government. (2023, Apr 17). *Department for Business, Energy and Industrial Strategy*. Guidance Participating in the UK ETS. https://www.gov.uk/government/publications/participating-in-the-uk-ets/participating-in-the-uk-ets

Umair, M., Yousuf, M. U., Ul-Haq, J., Hussain, Z., & Visas, H. (2023). Revisiting the environmental impact of renewable energy, non-renewable energy, remittances, and economic growth: CO2 emissions versus ecological footprint for top remittance-receiving countries. *Environmental Science and Pollution Research International*, *30*(23), 1–15. doi:10.100711356-023-26812-w PMID:37055685

UN Environmental Programme. (2022, October). *Environmental Governance*. UNEP. https://www.unep.org/regions/west-asia/regional-initiatives/environmental-governance

UN Sustainable Development Solutions Network. (2022). *Rapport sur le développement durable pour le Bénin Rapport pilote de référence (Juillet 2022)*. UN.

UNDP. (2017). *INSTITUTIONAL AND COORDINATION MECHANISMS*. United Nations Development Programme.

UNFCCC (United Nations Framework Convention on Climate Change). (2018). INDCs as Communicated by Parties. UNFCCC. https://www4.unfccc.int/sites/submissions/indc/Submission%20Pages/submissions.aspx

United Arab Emirates Embassy. (2023). *Climate and Energy*. United Arab Emirates Embassy Wadhington DC: https://www.uae-embassy.org/discover-uae/climate-and-energy/uae-energy-diversification

United Nations. (1992). *United Nations Framework Convention*. UNFCCC. https://unfccc.int/resource/docs/convkp/conveng.pdf

United Nations. (2015). *Paris Agreement*. UN. https://unfccc.int/process-and-meetings/the-paris-agreement/the-paris-agreement

United Nations. (2018). *7.d Paris Agreement*. United Nations.

UNSC. (2007). *5663rd meeting* (S/PV.5663). United Nations Security Council.

UNSC. (2011). *6587th meeting* (S/PV.6587). United Nations Security Council.

UNSC. (2017a). *7857th meeting* (S/PV.7857). United Nations Security Council.

UNSC. (2017b). *7861st meeting* (S/PV.7861). United Nations Security Council.

UNSC. (2017c). *7894th meeting* (S/PV.7894). United Nations Security Council.

UNSC. (2017d). *7906th meeting* (S/PV.7906). United Nations Security Council.

UNSC. (2017e). *7911th meeting* (S/PV.7911). United Nations Security Council.

UNSC. (2017f). *8047th meeting* (S/PV.8047). United Nations Security Council.

UNSC. (2017g). *8069th meeting* (S/PV.8069). United Nations Security Council.

UNSC. (2017h). *8080th meeting* (S/PV.8080). United Nations Security Council.

UNSC. (2017i). *8106th meeting* (S/PV.8106). United Nations Security Council.

UNSC. (2017j). *8144th meeting* (S/PV.8144). United Nations Security Council.

UNSC. (2017k). Resolution 2349 (Vol. S). United Nations Security Council., RES/2349.

UNSC. (2018a). *8156th meeting* (S/PV.8156). United Nations Security Council.

UNSC. (2018b). *8162nd meeting* (S/PV.8162). United Nations Security Council.

UNSC. (2018c). *8185th meeting* (S/PV.8185). United Nations Security Council.

UNSC. (2018d). *8212th meeting* (S/PV.8212). United Nations Security Council.

UNSC. (2018e). Resolution 2408 (Vol. S). United Nations Security Council., RES/2408.

Ünvan, Y. A., & Yakubu, I. N. (2020). Do bank-specific factors drive bank deposits in Ghana? *Journal of Computational and Applied Mathematics*, *376*, 112827. doi:10.1016/j.cam.2020.112827

Urgewald. (2021). Groundbreaking Research Reveals the Financiers of the Coal Industry. *Urgewald.* https://coalexit.org/sites/default/files/download_public/Financing%20GCEL%202020_Press%20Release_urgewald.pdf

Utile, T. I., Ijirshar, V. U., & Adoo, S. E. M. (2021). Impact of institutional quality on economic growth in Nigeria. *Gusau International Journal of Management and Social Sciences*, *4*(3), 21–21.

Uzar, U. (2020). Political economy of renewable energy: Does institutional quality make a difference in renewable energy consumption? *Renewable Energy*, *155*, 591–603. doi:10.1016/j.renene.2020.03.172

Uzun, A., & Doğan, A. (2014). The Effects of FreeTrade Agreements on Turkey's Foreign Trade. *Cumhuriyet University Journal of Economics and Administrative Sciences*, 325-344.

Vakulchuk, R., Overland, I., & Suryadi, B. (2023). ASEAN's energy transition: How to attract more investment in renewable energy. *Energy, Ecology & Environment*, *8*(1), 1–16. doi:10.100740974-022-00261-6

van Munster, R. (2018). Securitization. *The Concise Oxford Dictionary of Politics and International Relations.* Oxford Press. https://www.oxfordbibliographies.com/display/document/obo-9780199743292/obo-9780199743292-0091.xml

Van, L. T. H., Vo, A. T., Nguyen, N. T., & Vo, D. H. (2021). Financial inclusion and economic growth: An international evidence. *Emerging Markets Finance & Trade*, *57*(1), 239–263. doi:10.1080/1540496X.2019.1697672

Vatamanu, A. F., & Zugravu, B. G. (2023). Financial development, institutional quality and renewable energy consumption. A panel data approach. *Economic Analysis and Policy*, *78*, 765–775. doi:10.1016/j.eap.2023.04.015

Velho, A., & Thomas Olalde, O. (2016). *Othering and its effects: Exploring the concept.*

Vinay, S., Parikh, K., Parikh, J., Ghosh, P., Tot, M., & Das, A. (2023). *Pathways to net zero emissions for the Indian power sector.* Elseiver.

Vogler, J. (n.d.). Environmental issues. In J. Baylis, S. Smith, & P. Owens (Eds.), *The Globalization of World Politics* (pp. 387–403). Oxford University Press. https://www.oxfordpoliticstrove.com/display/10.1093/hepl/9780198825548.001.0001/hepl-9780198825548-chapter-24

Wang, E., Gozgor, G., Mahalik, M. K., Patel, G., & Hu, G. (2022). Effects of institutional quality and political risk on the renewable energy consumption in the OECD Countries. *Resources Policy*, *79*, 103041. doi:10.1016/j.resourpol.2022.103041

Wang, L., Huang, Y., Ghafoor, A., Hafeez, M., & Salahodjaev, R. (2023). Asymmetric macroeconomic determinants of renewable energy consumption: Do financial institutions and ICT trade matter? *Environmental Science and Pollution Research International*, *30*(4), 9841–9851. doi:10.100711356-022-22816-0 PMID:36059017

Wang, W., Luo, Y., Xie, P., Luo, Z., & Zhao, D. (2016). The Key Elements Analysis of Guangdong & Shenzhen ETS & Tips for China National ETS Construction. *Zhongguo Renkou Ziyuan Yu Huanjing*, *14*(4), 282–291. doi:10.1080/10042857.2016.1258801

Wang, Y., Yao, G., Zuo, Y., & Wu, Q. (2023). Implications of Global Carbon Governance for Corporate Carbon Emissions Reduction. *Frontiers in Environmental Science*, *11*, 3. doi:10.3389/fenvs.2023.1071658

Wang, Z., Zaman, S., Zaman, Q. U., & Rasool, S. F. (2021). Impact of remittances on carbon emission: Fresh evidence from a panel of five remittance-receiving countries. *Environmental Science and Pollution Research International*, *28*(37), 52418–52430. doi:10.100711356-021-14412-5 PMID:34008066

Wei, S. J. (2001). *Corruption in Economic Transition and Development: Grease or Sand?* United Nations.

Wenham, C. (2019). The oversecuritization of global health: Changing the terms of debate. *International Affairs*, *95*(5), 1093–1110. doi:10.1093/ia/iiz170

Wildgrube, T. (2022). *Fit for 55? An Assessment of the Effectiveness of the EU COM's Reform Proposal for the EU ETS (No. 22/04)*. (EWI Working Paper).

Wolfers, A. (1952). "National Security" as an Ambiguous Symbol. *Political Science Quarterly*, *67*(4), 481–502. doi:10.2307/2145138

World Bank Group and International Carbon Action Partnership. (2022). *A Handbook on Design and Implementation*. World Bank Group. https://documents1.worldbank.org/curated/en/541731484292546048/pdf/108879-TURKISH-PUBLIC-ETSHandbookTurkishFullReport.pdf

World Bank. (2020). *Climate Change*. World Bank. https://www.worldbank.org/en/topic/climatechange

World Bank. (2022). *AskWBCaribbean: Talking Energy, Finding Solutions*. World Bank. https://www.worldbank.org/en/events/2022/10/11/caribbean-talking-energy-finding-solutions

Wu, L., & Broadstock, D. C. (2015). Does economic, financial and institutional development matter for renewable energy consumption? Evidence from emerging economies. *International Journal of Economic Policy in Emerging Economies*, *8*(1), 20–39. doi:10.1504/IJEPEE.2015.068246

Wyett, K. (2014). Escaping a Rising Tide: Sea Level Rise and migration in Kiribati. *Asia & the Pacific Policy Studies*, *1*(1), 171–185. doi:10.1002/app5.7

Yakubu, I. N., & Musah, A. (2022). The nexus between financial inclusion and bank profitability: a dynamic panel approach. *Journal of Sustainable Finance & Investment*, 1-14.

Yakubu, I. N., & Musah, A. (2022). The Nexus between financial Inclusion and bank profitability: a dynamic panel approach. *Journal of Sustainable Finance and Investment*. doi:10.1080/20430795.2022.2105792

Yakubu, I. N., Kapusuzoglu, A., & Ceylan, N. B. (2020). Determinants of Working Capital Management of Manufacturing Firms in Ghana Under Innovative Work Behaviour Perspective. *Strategic Outlook for Innovative Work Behaviours: Interdisciplinary and Multidimensional Perspectives*, 235-252.

Yakubu, I. N., Kapusuzoglu, A., & Ceylan, N. B. (2021). Environmental impact of economic globalization and renewable energy consumption in the OPEC countries. *Strategic Approaches to Energy Management: Current Trends in Energy Economics and Green Investment*, 155-171.

Yakubu, I. N., Kapusuzoglu, A., & Ceylan, N. B. (2021). Urbanization, fossil fuel consumption and carbon dioxide emission in Ghana: the STIRPAT model approach. *Strategic Approaches to Energy Management: Current Trends in Energy Economics and Green Investment*, 201-216.

Yakubu, I. N. (2019). Does corruption grease or sand the wheels of bank profitability in Ghana? *Cogent Economics & Finance*, *7*(1), 1701909. doi:10.1080/23322039.2019.1701909

Yakubu, I. N., & Bunyaminu, A. (2021). Financial Inclusion and Economic Growth in West Africa: The Moderating Effect of Financial Openness. *Empirical Economics Letters*, *20*(2), 155–164.

Yakubu, I. N., Kapusuzoglu, A., & Ceylan, N. B. (2022). ICT trade and energy transition in the BRICS economies. In *Sustainability in Energy Business and Finance: Approaches and Developments in the Energy Market* (pp. 13–24). Springer International Publishing. doi:10.1007/978-3-030-94051-5_2

Yakubu, I. N., Kapusuzoglu, A., & Ceylan, N. B. (2022). Investigating the Role of Export Diversification, Remittances, and Environmental Sustainability in Accordance with Clean Energy and Zero Emission. In *Circular Economy and the Energy Market: Achieving Sustainable Economic Development Through Energy Policy* (pp. 51–65). Springer International Publishing. doi:10.1007/978-3-031-13146-2_5

Yılmaz, O., & Çakaloğlu, M. (2021). The Transformation of Central Banks In Response To Climate Change: Green Central Banking. *Business, Economics and Management Research Journal*, 135-156.

Yılmazcan, H., & Çakmak, H. (2018). As A Financial/Effective Vehicle In The Prevention Of Climate Change "Carbon Emission Tax Or Carbon Emission Trading? ". *Proceeding of the İnternational Congress on Business and Marketing*, Maltepe University.

Yoon, A. (2012). Total Global Losses from Financial Crisis: $15 Trillion. *The Wall Street Journal*.

Yoro, K. O., & Daramola, M. O. (2020). CO2 Emission Sources, Greenhouse Gases, and the Global Warming Effect. In *Advances in Carbon Capture* (pp. 3–28). Woodhead Publishing. doi:10.1016/B978-0-12-819657-1.00001-3

Yuliani, D. (2017). *Is Feed-In-Tariff Policy Efffective for Increasing Deployment of Renewable Energy in Indonesia*. Oxford University Press.

Zakaria, A. A., & Arun, T. (2015). Corporate Social Responsibility and Islamic Financial Institutions (IFIs): Management Perceptions from IFIs in Bahrain. *Journal of Business Ethics*, *129*(4), 785–794. doi:10.100710551-014-2132-9

Zhang, D., Karplus, V. J., Cassisa, C., & Zhang, X. (2014). Emissions Trading in China: Progress and Prospects. *Energy Policy*, *75*, 9–16. doi:10.1016/j.enpol.2014.01.022

Zhang, K., Xu, D., Li, S., Zhou, N., & Xiong, J. (2019b). Has China's Pilot Emissions Trading Scheme Influenced the Carbon Intensity of Output? *International Journal of Environmental Research and Public Health*, *16*(10), 1854. doi:10.3390/ijerph16101854 PMID:31130641

Zhang, L., Zeng, Y., & Li, D. (2019a). China's Emissions Trading Scheme: First Evidence on Pilot Stage. *Polish Journal of Environmental Studies*, *28*(2), 543–551. doi:10.15244/pjoes/84871

Zhang, P., Li, Z., Ghardallou, W., Yan, X., & Jie, C. (2023). Nexus of institutional quality and technological innovation on renewable energy development: Moderating role of green finance. *Renewable Energy*, *214*, 233–241. doi:10.1016/j.renene.2023.05.089

Zhao, J., Zhang, T., Arshad, A., Chen, J., Ji, H., & Wang, T. (2023). An empirical investigation of the impact of renewable and non-renewable energy consumption and economic growth on climate change, evidence from emerging Asian countries. *Frontiers in Environmental Science*, *10*, 1–16. doi:10.3389/fenvs.2022.1085372

Zhao, L., & Qamruzzaman, M. (2022). Do urbanization, remittances, and globalization matter for energy consumption in belt and road countries: Evidence from renewable and non-renewable energy consumption. *Frontiers in Environmental Science*, *10*, 723. doi:10.3389/fenvs.2022.930728

Zhongming, Z., Linong, L., Xiaona, Y., Wangqiang, Z., & Wei, L. (2021). *The Role of China's ETS in Power Sector Decarbonisation*. International Energy Agency.

About the Contributors

Ibrahim Nandom Yakubu holds a Ph.D. in Banking and Finance. He is a highly motivated and accomplished researcher with expertise in inclusive finance, financial markets, corporate governance, and sustainability. As an Adjunct Lecturer at the University for Development Studies, Ghana, he brings extensive knowledge and experience to his role, mentoring students and conducting independent research in the field of finance. Ibrahim Nandom's dedication and expertise have garnered recognition within the academic community. As a Commonwealth Scholar, he exemplifies his commitment to excellence in research and scholarship. Actively engaged in his field, he is a member of the African Accounting and Finance Association (AAFA) and holds the role of associate editor for the prestigious Review of Business Management (RBGN) Journal. His exceptional research contributions have been acknowledged with the esteemed Emerald Literati Awards for Research Excellence (Outstanding Paper category) in 2022. With a strong quantitative background, Ibrahim has published several book chapters and research articles addressing critical issues in finance and sustainability.

* * *

Mubarik Abdul Mumin is a dedicated lecturer at the University for Development Studies School of Business, renowned for his expertise in procurement and supply chain management. Born into a family of twelve children, he emerged as a determined scholar, driven by a thirst for knowledge and a passion for business. His academic journey began with distinction in his basic education, followed by a pursuit of business accounting during his senior high school years. Alongside his studies, he embraced leadership roles, serving as School Prefect, SRC president, GMSA president, and GMSA vice president at the zonal level, demonstrating his natural ability to inspire and influence others. Fuelled by his ambition, he embarked on his undergraduate studies in integrated business studies, with a specialization in management, at the esteemed University for Development Studies. There, he thrived academically and graduated with honours, earning a second class upper degree. Upon completing his national service at the Tamale Metro Assembly, he joined the Netherlands initiative for capacity development in higher education, where he immersed himself in the world of logistics and supply chain management. Eager to advance his knowledge, he enrolled in an MPhil program in logistics and supply chain management at the prestigious Kwame Nkrumah University of Science and Technology from 2018 to 2020. In December 2020, Mr. Mubarik embarked on an exciting new chapter as an assistant lecturer at the University for Development Studies. His exceptional teaching skills, coupled with his extensive research experience, quickly propelled him to the position of lecturer. Throughout his nearly three years in academia, he has collaborated with esteemed colleagues on several ground-breaking research projects, which await publication in renowned journals. Driven by his unwavering commitment to professional growth, Mr. Mubarik has secured an esteemed supervisor from Sheffield University for his upcoming PhD project, set to commence in September 2023. This Endeavor promises to further enhance his expertise and contribute to the ever-evolving field of procurement and supply chain management. As a visionary educator, researcher, and aspiring PhD candidate, Mr. Mubarik continues to inspire and shape the minds of future business leaders. With his dedication to academic excellence, passion for his subject matter, and unwavering pursuit of knowledge, he is undoubtedly poised to make a lasting impact in the world of procurement and supply chain management.

İzzet Ari received his BSc degree in Environmental Engineering from METU in 2005, MSc degree in Environmental Engineering from METU in 2010, and Sussex University (UK) in 2013. In 2015, he received his Ph.D. He has worked in public institutions for almost 15 years. He worked as Assistant Deputy Expert, Planning Expert and Head of Department at the State Planning Organization. In addition to these duties, he has participated in the international climate change negotiations under the United Nations Framework Convention on Climate Change on behalf of Turkey on a regular basis since 2007. Between the years 2011-2018, he contributed to the of the United Nations on Agenda 2030, Sustainable Development Goals and Objectives, Development Finance and Green Economy. He taught Energy Policy and Finance at METU and Global Climate Change at Hacettepe University as a part-time lecturer. He has been working on climate change and development, sustainable energy policies, energy and finance, green growth and sustainable development goals. He published articles, books and book chapters in international publishers.

Ayşegül Aytaç Emin, PhD, is a Lecturer at Social Sciences University of Ankara. Her main research interests include macroeconomic analyses and financial economics with a special focus on Islamic finance, banking and financial crises. She holds a BS degree in Economics and an MA degree in Economics from Bilkent University. From 2014 to 2017 she worked in Turkey Economic Policy Research Foundation of Turkey (TEPAV, Turkey) as a research associate. During the Turkey's G20 Presidency in 2015, she worked in TOBB (The Union of Chambers and Commodity Exchanges of Turkey) as a General Content Coordinator for Business 20 and she was also a Research Associate in the Think 20 process. She holds a PhD degree in Economics in Hacettepe University. She has several published articles, sectoral projects and policy notes within the scope of her research interest.

Alhassan Bunyaminu is currently a Senior lecturer at the University of Professional Studies, Accra and he was the Head of Research for the Faculty of Accounting and Finance. He previously thought at the West End University College, Kasoa, Ghana, University of Applied Management (A German University, Ghana Campus) and City of Bristol College, Bristol, UK. He has over 15 publications in Star rated Journals. Bunyaminu holds a PhD in Finance from the University of Central Nicaragua, European Programmes, Austria and he is a Chartered Global Investment Analyst (CGIA). He has Masters in Statistics and Management Science from University of the West of England, UK; Bachelors of Science Degree (Hons) in Statistics from the Open University, UK and Higher National Diploma in Agricultural Engineering from Tamale Technical University (formally Tamale Polytechnic), Tamale, Ghana. Bunyaminu is an experienced and goal-oriented Lecturer, Consultant and Financial Analyst with experience in the analysis and interpretation of complex data for forecasting and optimization using modern software/ programming languages; underpinned by solid academic background and proven people management skills. Bunyaminu is also a local governance expert and offer consultancy and research services to Metropolitan, Municipal and District Assemblies (MMDAs) across Ghana and Sierra Leone. Bunyaminu is also a capacity building and training provider for public and private organizations in management and finance. He is also a motivational speaker and inspires the youth in secular and religious matters. Bunyaminu has published extensively in star rated journals and serves as a reviewer of journals published by Emerald, Taylor & Francis, SAGE and Springer and continues to mentor up and coming lecturers to attain greater heights in teaching and research.

Don Charles has a BSc in Economics (2006), MSc in Economics (2009) and a PhD in Economics (2017) from the University of the West Indies St Augustine Campus. He presently has 20 years of experience, which covers economic research, lecturing, project management, procurement, event management, industrial relations, and administration. He has also worked in the public sector, academia, and in UN organizations. Presently in 2022 he has 51 peer reviewed publications. His research interests are mainly in energy economic, econometrics, international trade and value chains, climate change policy, and portfolio finance.

E. Ivette Cota-Rivera received a M.Eng. from the Autonomous University of Baja California (UABC, Universidad Autonoma de Baja California). In 2016, she received her Ph.D. in Energy Engineering and is currently working as a pro fessor in the Energy Engineering program at the Polytechnic University of Baja California (UPBC, Universidad Politecnica de Baja California). Her research interests include energy efficiency and sustainability, artificial intelligence, energy science and technology, as well as programming

Doğuş Emin is an associate professor in the Department of Business Administration at Social Sciences University of Ankara (SSUA). He graduated from Bilkent University, Department of Management in 2008. After completed his Master's degree at University of Bath in 2009, he received his Ph.D. from University of Leicester in 2014. His recent research interests have been focused on financial crises, integration of stock markets, financial modelling and asset pricing models.

Abelardo Mercado Herrera is Doctor of Science and Master of Science from the National Institute of Astrophysics, Optics and Electronics, specializing in Astrophysics, Postdoctorate in Astrophysics from the Institute of Astronomy of the National Autonomous University of Mexico, Electronics Engineer from the Autonomous University of Baja California . He is a specialist in the mathematical-statistical description of stochastic and/or deterministic processes, nonlinear systems, complex systems, chaos theory, among others, as well as their application to physical phenomena such as astronomy, economics, finance, telecommunications, science social etc., in order to determine the underlying dynamics in such processes, and if necessary, their connection with real physical variables and possible prediction. He has worked on the development of various electronic circuits, interfaces and programs to carry out electrical tests in the industry, as well as in scientific instrumentation, applied to telemetry, infrared polarimetry, optics and spectroscopy. He has also specialized in image analysis, measurement techniques and noise reduction.

Abdul-Latif Mohammed is currently pursuing his PhD at the Newcastle Business School, University of Newcastle, Australia. His research focuses on managing hybrid identities in social enterprises. He received his international master's in business administration from Zhejiang Normal University, China. His areas of interest are performance measurements systems, HR, institutional and paradox theories, conflict resolutions in organisations, SDGs, and renewable energy.

Ibrahim Mohammed is an Associate Professor with over a decade and a half of teaching, researching and consulting experience.

Fabian N. Murrieta-Rico received B.Eng. and M.Eng. degrees from Instituto Tecnológico de Mexicali (ITM) in 2004 and 2013 respectively. In 2017, he received his PhD in Materials Physics at Centro de Investigación Científica y Educación Superior de Ensenada (CICESE). He has worked as an automation engineer, systems designer, as university professor, and as postdoctoral researcher at Facultad de Ingeniería, Arquitectura y Diseño from Universidad Autónoma de Baja California (UABC) and at the Centro de Nanociencias y Nanotecnología from Universidad Nacional Autónoma de México (CNyN-UNAM), currently he works as professor at the Universidad Politécnica de Baja California. His research has been published in different journals and presented at international conferences since 2009. He has served as reviewer for different journals, some of them include IEEE Transactions on Industrial Electronics, IEEE Transactions on Instrumentation, Measurement and Sensor Review. His research interests are focused on the field of time and frequency metrology, synthesis and characterization of zeolites, and highly sensitive chemical detectors.

Alhassan Musah is an interdisciplinary professional, and a senior lecturer in the Department of Sustainable Development Studies of the University for Development Studies. Alhassan holds a Bachelors Degree in Commerce from the University of Cape Coast, a Masters degree in Microfinance from the Universita Degli Studi Di Bergamo, Italy, a PhD in Endogenous Development from the University for Development Studies, and a Certificate in Project Management from the Maastricht School of Management, the Netherlands. Alhassan is also a Chartered Accountant. He is a Fellow of the Association of Chartered Certified Accountants (ACCA, UK) and a member of the Institute of Chartered Accountants, Ghana. His current research interests include inclusive finance, sustainable development, corporate sustainability and greening of business.

Jesús Heriberto Orduño-Osuna has obtained a Bachelor's degree in Mechatronics Engineering from Universidad Politécnica de Baja California. Currently, he is concurrently pursuing Master's degrees in Computer Science and Applied Mathematics at Universidad Internacional de La Rioja in Mexico. Professionally, he holds the esteemed position of a professor at his alma mater. In this role, he has the privilege of imparting his knowledge and experience to enthusiastic engineering and technology students.

Seydou Oumarou is currently an assistant professor at Abdou Moumouni University of Niamey,Niger Republic. He holds a PhD degree in Banking and Finance from Ankara Yıldırım Beyazıt University since 2020,

Maria E. Raygoza-L, Ph. D. in Chemistry and Energy, from Engineering Institute of Universidad Autónoma de Baja California, and a Bachelor of Industrial Engineering with a specialization in Manufacturing, currently works as a full-time professor and researcher at Universidad Politécnica de Baja California and as a Subject Professor at Universidad Autónoma de Baja California, in areas of Energy

Engineering and Renewable Energies. Extensive experience in industry, her research interests include renewable energy, energy efficiency, environmental, energy management systems, and integration of public policies for sustainable development.

Aysel Varoglu holds a BS degree in Economics from Gazi University (2013) and an MA degree in Energy Economics and Management from Social Sciences University of Ankara (2022). She works on energy economics and analysis at the Ministry of Trade. She has published research articles and book chapters on the strategic and economic importance of energy and climate change. Her research interests are mainly in the macroeconomic impacts of energy and climate change

Index

I

K

L

M

N

O

P

R

S

T

U

Recommended Reference Books

IGI Global's reference books are available in three unique pricing formats:
Print Only, E-Book Only, or Print + E-Book.

Order direct through IGI Global's Online Bookstore at **www.igi-global.com** or through your preferred provider.

ISBN: 9781668445488
EISBN: 9781668445501
© 2022; 334 pp.
List Price: US$ **240**

ISBN: 9781668467503
EISBN: 9781668467527
© 2022; 296 pp.
List Price: US$ **240**

ISBN: 9781799889007
EISBN: 9781799889021
© 2022; 340 pp.
List Price: US$ **215**

ISBN: 9781799898511
EISBN: 9781799898535
© 2022; 276 pp.
List Price: US$ **250**

ISBN: 9781799896913
EISBN: 9781799896937
© 2022; 219 pp.
List Price: US$ **215**

ISBN: 9781668436868
EISBN: 9781668436875
© 2022; 2,064 pp.
List Price: US$ **2,085**

Do you want to stay current on the latest research trends, product announcements, news, and special offers?
Join IGI Global's mailing list to receive customized recommendations, exclusive discounts, and more.
Sign up at: **www.igi-global.com/newsletters.**

Publisher of Timely, Peer-Reviewed Inclusive Research Since 1988

IGI Global
PUBLISHER of TIMELY KNOWLEDGE

www.igi-global.com Sign up at www.igi-global.com/newsletters facebook.com/igiglobal twitter.com/igiglobal linkedin.com/igiglobal

Ensure Quality Research is Introduced to the Academic Community

Become an Evaluator for IGI Global Authored Book Projects

The overall success of an authored book project is dependent on quality and timely manuscript evaluations.

Applications and Inquiries may be sent to:
development@igi-global.com

Applicants must have a doctorate (or equivalent degree) as well as publishing, research, and reviewing experience. Authored Book Evaluators are appointed for one-year terms and are expected to complete at least three evaluations per term. Upon successful completion of this term, evaluators can be considered for an additional term.

If you have a colleague that may be interested in this opportunity, we encourage you to share this information with them.

www.ingramcontent.com/pod-product-compliance
Lightning Source LLC
LaVergne TN
LVHW080526300926
849162LV00007B/1545
9781668492727